ENDURING CITY
Belfast in the Twentieth Century

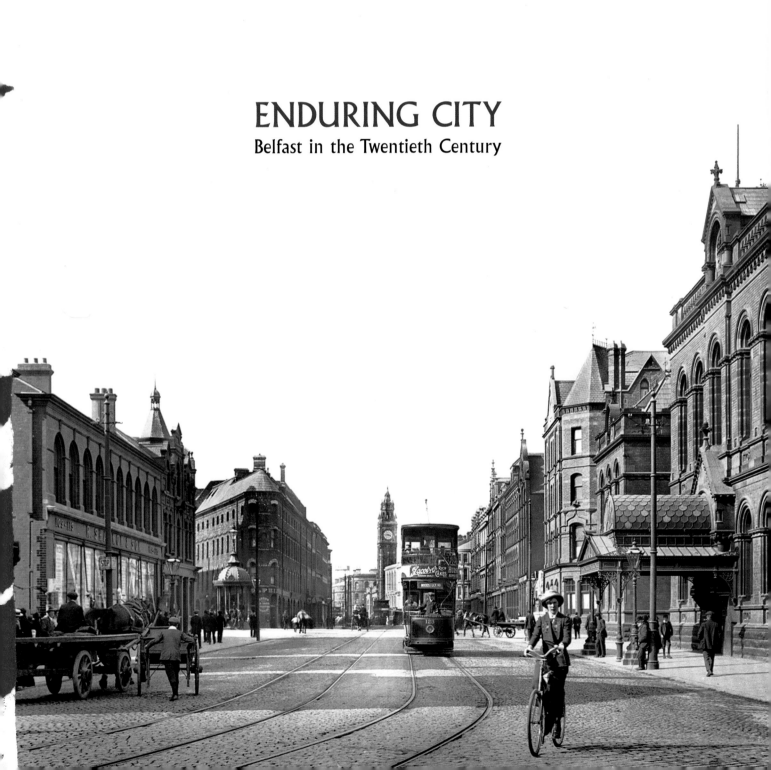

ENDURING CITY

Belfast in the Twentieth Century

Edited by Frederick W. Boal and Stephen A. Royle

with the cartographical assistance of Maura E. Pringle

BLACKSTAFF PRESS

IN ASSOCIATION WITH BELFAST CITY COUNCIL
AND IRISH HISTORIC TOWNS ATLAS, ROYAL IRISH ACADEMY

Page i: A cyclist on Victoria Street, *c.* 1915
ULSTER FOLK & TRANSPORT MUSEUM

Frontispiece: Laganside at dusk
CHRIS HILL

Page v: Samson and Goliath, and the Albert Bridge
ROBERT SCOTT

Page vi: Edward VII at the unveiling of the statue of his mother, Queen Victoria, at Belfast City Hall, 27 July 1903. After saluting the statue, he was heard to remark, 'Beautiful, isn't it? The best I have seen.'
ALUN EVANS

First published in 2006 by
Blackstaff Press Limited
4c Heron Wharf, Sydenham Business Park
Belfast BT3 9LE

© Foreword, Emrys Jones, 2006
© Introduction, Frederick W. Boal and Stephen A. Royle, 2006
© The contributors, 2006
© Photographs as indicated in captions, 2006

Design by Dunbar Design and Graphic Base

Printed by W. & G. Baird Ltd, County Antrim

A CIP catalogue record for this book is available from the British Library

ISBN 0-85640-790-9

This publication is grant-aided by Belfast City Council.
The views expressed are not necessarily shared or endorsed by the Council. The Council does not accept any responsibility or liability for same.

www.blackstaffpress.com
www.belfastcity.gov.uk

To my mother, Mabel Boal, whose life began with the Belfast
of 1900, who experienced the story of the city in the twentieth century
and who lives on into the twenty-first (FWB), and to our grandchildren,
Jake Searle (SAR), Jason Apsley, Lauren, Liam and Gemma Boal (FWB),
born near the turn of the twenty-first century, who will see how
the Belfast story turns out.

VICTORIA RI

FROM MY HEART
I THANK MY
BELOVED PEO
PLE MAY GOD
BLESS THEM

1837—18

Contents

Lord Mayor's Letter

As Lord Mayor of Belfast, I warmly welcome the publication of *Enduring City: Belfast in the Twentieth Century*. Published during Belfast City Hall's Centenary Year, this book forms a key element of 'Celebrate Belfast 2006', a year-long programme of events designed to showcase the cultural wealth of our city.

Enduring City is the result of a partnership between Belfast City Council, Blackstaff Press and the Royal Irish Academy. The book supports and supplements parts I and II of the Irish Historic Towns Atlas for Belfast which are being produced by the Royal Irish Academy and partially funded by Belfast City Council.

Enduring City is breathtaking in scope in that it provides a fascinating social commentary, discussing in detail the life and times of Belfast, its people, buildings and culture. The book also displays the rich history of the city by gathering together a wonderful array of photographs to illustrate the momentous events of the last century.

I trust you will enjoy delving into Belfast's past and learning more about its people, its historical and physical background, infrastructure, education, health and the many other subject areas covered in this book. As *Enduring City* amply illustrates, we have much to be proud of and to look forward to in this great city which has so much to offer us all.

Pat Mc Carthy

LORD MAYOR
COUNCILLOR PAT McCARTHY
JULY, 2006

Foreword

Emrys Jones

Every city is unique – geographically because it has a location shared by no other, and historically because it is an expression of a rich pageant of life over the years peculiar to that city. It is these characteristics that give it its personality and demand that it has a unique name. Moreover, the lives of its people – and what is a city but its people? – are etched in the landscape they have created; its streets, houses, mills, churches, monuments all bear an ineradicable social imprint. Belfast is not only the succession of buildings that has accumulated over time, but also an expression of the ideas, endeavours, aspirations – and conflicts – that have given life and meaning to the city for over four centuries.

I knew nothing of Belfast when I arrived in the city – courtesy of the Liverpool boat – in 1950 (Figure F.1). By the time I left, nine years later, I had walked every street, scoured its history, analysed its population in detail and mapped almost everything that was mappable, including its religious sects and the segregation that these engendered. As a stranger, it was difficult to get near the soul of the city, but I had the benefit of objectivity as well as a Celtic empathy with some of the problems of identity, which were so basic a part of its ethos. Looking back, I now realise that I was set midway in the period under review in this book. Behind me was half a century of changes, which I did my best to understand; before me a momentous period, the elements of which were only half-hidden in the 'present' of the 1950s. The academic outcome of my work (Figure F.2) forbade a subjective appraisal and the view of a 'foreigner' might, rightly, be dismissed by the natives as not attuned to the feelings of Belfast people; but I do recall clearly my own impressions of what made Belfast what it was, of its social divides, neighbourhood cohesions and the inherent instability of its political structure.

Looking back at the first half of the century, it seemed to me that continuity prevailed over change. In spite of two world wars, the Troubles of the early twenties, depression and boom, the Belfast of mid-century was not that different from the city which had ushered it in. Many Victorian values still survived. There was continuing confidence in the Protestant ascendancy and faith in industrial supremacy, the assurance of continuing growth in people and in prosperity. Some underlying and well-established social beliefs and behaviour were very tangible. There was little to shake the acceptance of the relative roles of men and women, or the superiority of men. Bars, for example, were the domain of men; in spite of women's contribution to mill life in west Belfast, a woman's life was regarded as being in the home, at least outside of working hours. I remember taking the baby in the pram to Botanic Gardens and being tapped on the shoulder by a stranger, with the comment, 'You must be English.' No

Opposite
FIGURE F.1
A couple strolling through Smithfield market in the 1950s

ULSTER MUSEUM

FIGURE F.2
Dust jacket for Emrys Jones's seminal work, *A Social Geography of Belfast*, published in 1960

OXFORD UNIVERSITY PRESS

self-respecting Ulsterman would stoop to such domesticity; nor, if I believed what I saw, did he deign to help his wife carry the shopping home on Saturday. The sexes kept to themselves. When the coffee break came in the long practical sessions I taught at the Queen's University, the women would first disappear *en bloc*, and when they returned in fifteen minutes the men would leave the class – to a man. I wondered, too, why everyone seemed to go home for lunch, unless it were for the joy of riding on those magnificent trams. And Sabbatarianism here long outlived its decline in Britain: children's swings in public parks were still chained on Saturday evening, and sectarianism saw to it that Sunday congregations were as strong as they had ever been. There was a general acceptance of the rigidity of social structure and of social behaviour. Adherence to an acknowledged social etiquette avoided conflict.

Belfast in mid-century was a very friendly city. Even with a population of half a million it would have been difficult to lose oneself in it; it was not made for anonymity. It felt like a very large market town in which personal contact was still important. A purchase in even so large a store as Anderson and McAuley brought an offer of a discount if you opened an account. Surely discount comes with cash? Not so. In the days before commercialism took over completely, paying cash was a sign of terminating the contract; much better to maintain and extend the relationship, so that the commercial contract becomes a social one – as every small shopkeeper in the countryside knows. In Belfast, shopping was not merely the acquisition of goods but the making of new friends. Where else would an assistant in a department store like Robinson and Cleaver have taken me down to the entrance to point out the shop that sold the item they did not have! It was not that Belfast lacked sophistication, but rather that a strong residue of traditional values centring on personal relationships kept breaking through.

During the first half-century Belfast acquired a magnificent city hall and a parliament building, signs of a coming of age, though they also presaged the dangers of one city dominating the northern state. Queen's University thrived – at that time it had no rival. It was a busy, bustling town, fast outgrowing its Victorian framework but indelibly stamped with the legacy of a Victorian heyday; rows of mechanically built bye-law houses flanking 'dark satanic mills', with outliers of opulent villas and considerable wealth. The forces that had produced it had also created great disparities between rich and poor and between those with power and those without. And a newcomer to the city was warned not to question this 'natural order' of things or enquire too deeply into inequalities that were best tolerated.

From mid-century to the new millennium the Belfast story is a turbulent one, both economically and socially. A city that had thrived on an industrial base found itself wallowing in a post-industrial era. Its difficulties were summed up in the figures of unemployed, which grew rapidly from the 1960s to 21 per cent by 1981. This coincided with the increasing segregation that followed the social conflicts of the late 1960s and 1970s. Deprivation and conflict are never evenly spread; they focus on pockets of despair, like vicious sores on the social body – but poisoning the entire system as well. Oddly the blight on the city's fortunes came soon after the first comprehensive plan for its future was published in 1964. Although Belfast had shared in many of the housing characteristics and changes in the United Kingdom as a whole, this was an opportunity to take a grip on the future. Long before steps could be taken in this direction, the city was in turmoil. The keyword in post-war planning in Britain was 'choice', and in Belfast choice, paradoxically, did no more than aggravate the underlying tendency to segregation, often under the most tragic circumstances. Communities took on a defensive role for people seeking any kind of security in a very uncertain environment.

The unrest was against a background of trends affecting all the cities of the United Kingdom. The main economic change was the rapid decline of manufacturing industries and their replacement by service industries. Textiles and shipbuilding became things of the past. The growth of offices in Belfast since the 1980s has been quite remarkable, and is adding a new dimension to the centre, in this way emphasising the centripetal forces that have shaped the city in the past. But its population has followed centrifugal forces, with a sharp decline in the numbers in the inner city since 1971. As in the United Kingdom as a whole, home ownership has bid fair to take over from renting as the dominant tenure. In the last thirty years, fortuitously with its greatest social challenge, there is a feeling that the physical dimensions of the city are beginning to be purposively shaped. The vision of a more controlled future environment was part of the Matthew regional plan of 1964, but urgency was given to some of these ideas by the turmoil of the following three decades.

The outcomes, which are dealt with in the following chapters, now have a framework against which progress can be measured. A phoenix can arise. It will be different from the Belfast I first saw in the 1950s, but I hope that its personality will survive. Its setting is constant; the beauties of the lough, the brooding presence of Cave Hill, the soft Castlereagh Hills; and straddling the Lagan, the constant bustle of an industrious and friendly people. It may well be that an increasing prosperity will allow political and social differences to be seen in a more generous perspective and allow Belfast to look upon its diversity as an asset rather than as an impediment to progress.

ACKNOWLEDGEMENTS

The gestation of this volume stems from the links established between Belfast City Council and the Royal Irish Academy with regard to the publication of the two fascicles on Belfast in the Irish Historic Towns Atlas series, dealing with the period up to 1840 (Raymond Gillespie and Stephen A. Royle [2003], Irish Historic Towns Atlas, no. 12, *Belfast, part I, to 1840)* and from 1841 to 1900 (Stephen A. Royle [forthcoming], Irish Historic Towns Atlas, no. 18, *Belfast, part II, 1840–1900). Enduring City* was always going to be to a very different format to the other publications, hence the involvement of Blackstaff Press in its publication, but in the temporal sense, it is Belfast part III, and one of the co-editors, Stephen Royle, is proud to have played a part in all three publications.

The year 1960 saw the publication of Emrys Jones's *A Social Geography of Belfast.* This volume, which has become a classic, examined Belfast up to the middle of the twentieth century. In consequence, we considered it highly appropriate to invite Professor Jones to write a foreword to *Enduring City.* We were very pleased when he accepted our invitation.

We would like to thank Belfast City Council for their financial support of this book. Briony Crozier, formerly of the city's Development Department, was very helpful in the early stages in setting up the work. All new maps and diagrams were drawn by Maura E. Pringle in the School of Geography, Queen's University Belfast, from data supplied by the authors, and all figures without a specific attribution were drawn by her. The British Academy aided the project by awarding Stephen Royle a small research grant, which led to the employment for a few months of Edel McClean, then of the School of Geography, Queen's University Belfast, as a research assistant. We are also deeply grateful to all those who have contributed to the writing of this volume. Moreover, we are very grateful for the support provided by Blackstaff Press, and in particular we wish to thank Hilary Bell for an extremely thorough copy-edit of what was a complex, multi-authored manuscript.

John D. Brewer, Margaret C. Keane, David N. Livingstone (chapter 10) would like to record their thanks to Kathy Apsley for her work with the Belfast street directories, to Maura E. Pringle for much cartographic assistance, and to Edel McClean for providing various pieces of information.

Alun Evans (chapter 14) wishes to thank Roger Blaney, Ruth Barrington, Robert Beatty, Joseph Clint, Anna Day, Larry Geary, Henry Halliday, John Robb and William Rutherford.

Jonathan Bardon (with respect to chapter 16) would particularly like to thank Raymond O'Regan for detailed material on the showband era; also Paddy McGinley, Zoë Mageean, Dermot Neary, George Parker, Jackie Smyth and the late Annie Johnston for their invaluable reminiscences.

LIST OF ABBREVIATIONS

ARP	adult resident population
AUTT	Alternative Urban Transport Technologies
BBC	British Broadcasting Corporation
BCDR	Belfast and County Down Railway
BMA	Belfast Metropolitan Area
BMAP	Belfast Metropolitan Area Plan
BMTP	Belfast Metropolitan Transport Plan
BST	Belfast Street Tramways Company
BUA	Belfast Urban Area
BUAP	Belfast Urban Area Plan
CBD	Central Business District
DCA	District Council Area
DTI	Department of Trade and Industry
GEM	Global Entrepreneurship Monitor
GNR	Great Northern Railway
GVA	Gross Value Added
ID	industrial development
IRA	Irish Republican Army
MONICA	Multinational MONItoring of trends and determinants in CArdiovascular disease
NIHE	Northern Ireland Housing Executive
NISRA	Northern Ireland Statistics and Research Agency
OECD	Organisation for Economic Co-operation and Development
OPEC	Organization of Petroleum-Exporting Countries
PACE	Protestant and Catholic Encounter
PR	proportional representation
PRIME	Prospective Epidemiological Study of Myocardial Infarction
PRONI	Public Record Office of Northern Ireland
RDS	Regional Development Strategy
RIBA	Royal Institute of British Architects
RSPB	Royal Society for the Protection of Birds
RTS	Regional Transportation Strategy
RUC	Royal Ulster Constabulary
SBRC	Small Business Research Centre
TEA	Total Entrepreneurial Activity
TTWA	Travel To Work Area
UDR	Ulster Defence Regiment
UTA	Ulster Transport Authority
UVF	Ulster Volunteer Force
VAT	Value Added Tax
YMCA	Young Men's Christian Association

LIST OF CONTRIBUTORS

JONATHAN BARDON was born in Dublin in 1941 and has lived and taught history in Belfast since 1963. His publications include: *Belfast: An Illustrated History* (Blackstaff Press, 1982); *A History of Ulster* (Blackstaff Press, 1992); *Belfast: A Century* (Blackstaff Press, 1999); and *Beyond the Studio: A History of BBC Northern Ireland* (Blackstaff Press, 2000). He has scripted many radio and television programmes, was Chairman of the Community Relations Council (1996–2002) and was appointed OBE in 2002.

FREDERICK W. BOAL is Professor Emeritus of Human Geography at Queen's University Belfast. He has also taught at three Canadian universities: Alberta, Carleton and Toronto. His research has focused on ethnic conflict in cities. He was appointed OBE in 1999 'for services to regional planning and urban development in Northern Ireland'.

JOHN D. BREWER is Professor of Sociology at the University of Aberdeen. He has held visiting appointments at Yale, Oxford, Cambridge and the Australian National University, and was Professor of Sociology at Queen's University Belfast before his move to Aberdeen. He is a Fellow of the Royal Society of Arts, an Academician in the Academy of Social Sciences and a Member of the Royal Irish Academy.

PATRICIA CRAIG is a critic and author. She was born in Belfast, lived in London for many years, and now lives in County Antrim. A regular contributor to the *TLS* (among other publications), she has edited a number of anthologies for Oxford University Press (including *The Oxford Book of Ireland* [1998]), Penguin (including *The Penguin Book of British Comic Writing* [1992]), and Blackstaff Press (including *The Belfast Anthology* [1999]). Her biography of Brian Moore was published by Bloomsbury in 2002, and her *Ulster Anthology* (Blackstaff Press) is forthcoming in November 2006.

E.J. CREIGHTON was a Nurse Tutor in Belfast when she completed a BSc with the Open University. After taking early retirement, she studied for a BA honours degree in geography at Queen's University Belfast and then researched education in the city.

ALUN EVANS holds a Personal Chair in the Department of Epidemiology and Public Health at Queen's University Belfast. His main interests lie in the genetic epidemiology of cardiovascular disease; he co-ordinates MORGAM, a large European project, which is amalgamating studies of the genetics of coronary heart disease in twenty centres in twelve member states. He has published extensively and is an author of the third edition of the monograph *Cardiovascular Survey Methods* (WHO: Geneva, 2004). His other main interest lies in the social history of medicine.

MARK HART is Professor of Small Business in the Small Business Research Centre (SBRC), Kingston Business School, Kingston University. Over the last twenty-five years he has worked and published extensively in the general area of enterprise, small business and regional and local economic development in Ireland, the United Kingdom and the European Union.

NUALA C. JOHNSON is a cultural-historical geographer at the School of Geography, Queen's University Belfast. She has published a range of journal articles and book chapters on national identity, the heritage industry, monuments and memorials, and social memory. She is author of *Ireland, the Great War and the Geography of Remembrance* (Cambridge University Press, 2003) and co-editor of *A Companion to Cultural Geography* (Blackwell, 2004). She is currently working on a major project on botanical gardens.

EMRYS JONES was born in Aberdare, South Wales, was educated at the University of Wales, Aberystwyth – and remains a Welsh-speaking Welshman. Short stints at University College London and in the United States, were followed by seven very happy years at Queen's University Belfast, resulting in *A Social Geography of Belfast* (Oxford University Press, 1960). The next quarter century was spent as Professor of Geography at the London School of Economics, producing works on urban and social geography. He was awarded the Victoria Medal of the Royal Geographical Society and was elected a Fellow of the British Academy.

MARGARET C. KEANE is Head of Geography at St Mary's University College, Belfast. Her research has centred on community division, especially in Belfast, and she is co-author of *Them and Us? Attitudinal Variation among Churchgoers in Belfast* (Institute of Irish Studies, Queen's University Belfast, 1997, with F.W. Boal. and D.N. Livingstone).

PAUL LARMOUR is an architectural historian and building heritage consultant, and an Honorary Member of the Royal Institute of the Architects of Ireland and of the Royal Society of Ulster Architects. Since 1979 he has lectured at the School of Architecture, Queen's University Belfast, where he has been a Reader since 1996. He is author of many articles and books on historic architecture and design in Ireland.

DAVID N. LIVINGSTONE is Professor of Geography at Queen's University Belfast and has held visiting positions in both the USA and Canada. He is a Fellow of the British Academy and a Member of the Royal Irish Academy. His most recent book is *Putting Science in Its Place* (University of Chicago Press, 2003).

MARIE-THÉRÈSE M^cGIVERN is Director of Development for Belfast City Council. She began her career as a teacher in further education and then moved to the field of employability and enterprise. Before joining the council she worked in Making Belfast Work, the urban regeneration programme of the Department of Social Development, first as a team leader in west Belfast and then heading up the Policy, Planning and Research Unit for the initiative. She is a visiting Professor in the Faculty of Engineering and the Built Environment at the University of Ulster and an Honorary Member of the Royal Society of Ulster Architects.

BILL MORRISON is a planning consultant. He is an architect-planner, and a former Divisional Planning Manager for Belfast. He is a Fellow of the Irish Academy of Engineering and a visiting Professor in Urban Planning and Design at the University of Ulster.

RUSSELL C. MURRAY was a student at the universities of St Andrews and Dundee. After obtaining a PhD at the latter, he joined the Geography Department of Queen's University Belfast, where he remained from 1971 to 1979. He subsequently held research or teaching posts at the universities of Exeter, Edinburgh and Bradford. He is now very happily retired.

WILLIAM J.V. NEILL teaches urban planning at Queen's University Belfast. He qualified as an urban planner from the University of Michigan and worked for many years for the State of Michigan, specialising in planning for metro Detroit. He obtained his doctorate in urban planning from the University of Nottingham. Formerly with the Department of Planning and Landscape at the University of Manchester, his latest books include *Urban Planning and Cultural Identity* (Routledge, 2004) and *Cultural Inclusion in the European City* (edited with Hanns-Uve Schwedler, Macmillan, 2006). He is Belfast born and bred.

STEPHEN A. ROYLE read geography at St John's College, Cambridge, and took a PhD at Leicester University. He has taught at Queen's University Belfast since 1976 and is now Reader in Geography. He is joint author and author of parts I and II respectively of the Royal Irish Academy's Irish Historic Towns Atlas on Belfast, which form a precursor to this book.

AUSTIN SMYTH, awarded a PhD (Queen's University Belfast) in 1982 for his study on the effects of the Troubles on transport, was appointed to the first Chair of Transport in Ireland in 1989. He prepared/advocated the ecomomic cases for the Belfast cross-harbour rail bridge and Great Victoria Street station. Appointed Chair of Transport Economics at the Transport Research Institute in Edinburgh in 1999 and, in 2002, Director General at the National Institute for Transport and Logistics, Dublin, he became Head of the new transport department at the University of Westminster in 2006. He lives in Belfast.

FIGURE S.1
The Town Hall in Victoria Street, completed in 1871,
was soon felt to be too modest for the needs of the city,
and the first stone of the City Hall was laid in 1898.

Foundations

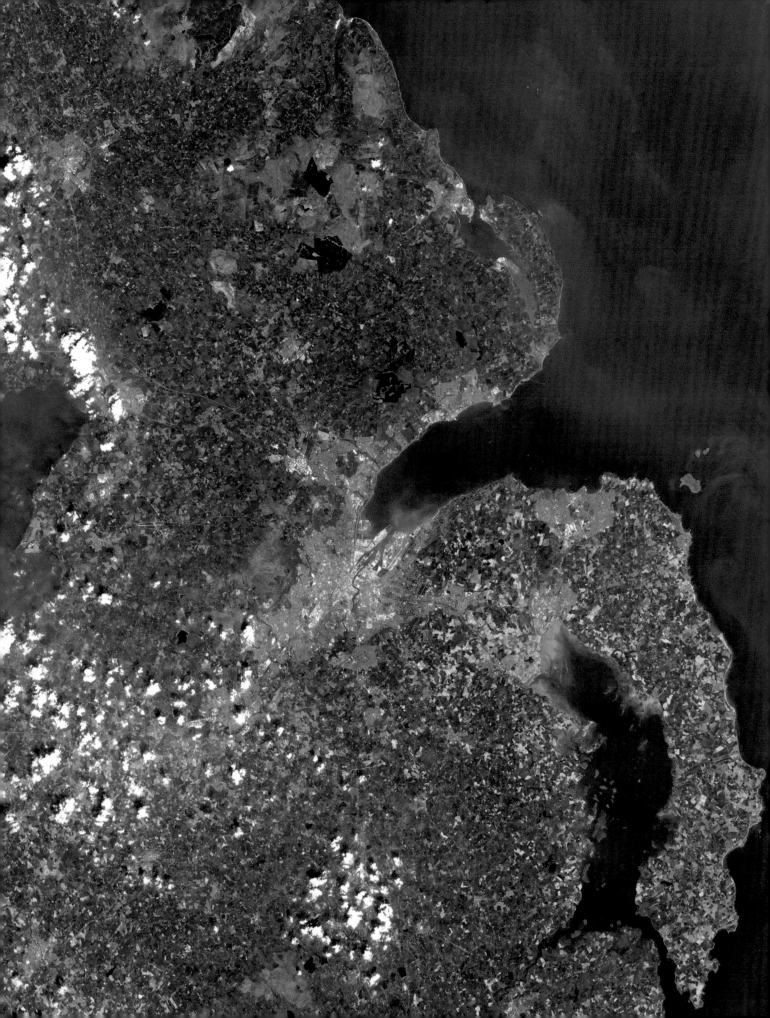

1
Enduring City

Frederick W. Boal and

Stephen A. Royle

Cities are large concentrations of people in relatively small areas. But they are much more than that. Historically cities are locations that had their origin and subsequent development through providing the basis for a wide range of functions – exerting control (ecclesiastical, governmental, military), producing commodities (goods, knowledge), distributing those commodities and consuming them. Cities usually serve all these functions, but they vary in the degree to which they do so. They also evolve functionally, in that the emphasis of one period (say, control) may shift to something different (say, distribution).

FIGURE 1.1
At century's end: Belfast and its extensions gathered round the head of Belfast Lough, May 2001 (Landsat 7 satellite image from a height of 705km/437 miles)

ERA MAPTEC

The sociologist Claude Fischer has suggested that urban-ness (cities) can be contrasted with rural-ness.[1] He puts this idea forward as a series of polarities: art versus nature; strangeness versus familiarity; individualism versus community; change versus tradition. These generalisations are overdrawn but they nonetheless may help point us towards some of the distinguishing characteristics of city life. However, it can equally be argued that cities themselves contain these polarities. There is familiarity in many city neighbourhoods, while most of the city's population are strangers to each other; cities provide community whilst also offering a more unfettered environment where individualism can flourish; cities certainly display change, but they also hold on tenaciously to elements from their past.

As we have already noted, many cities act as centres of control at regional, national or even global levels. To survive and be functionally effective, however, a basis for urban order must be established within the city itself. This urban order must encompass many matters – flows of water, waste and energy; flows of people, goods and information; the built form of streets, buildings and open spaces; health; education; production of goods and services; safety; and more. As the Canadian urban geographer Larry Bourne reminds us, cities have to work, noting, however, that some cities work better than others.[2]

We started by saying that cities are concentrations. Another word frequently used in this context is 'agglomeration' (Figure 1.2). Urban economists refer to the advantages of agglomeration as 'agglomeration economies'. By locating close to each other, many activities can gain from sharing common facilities, expertise and information. Large concentrations of people and economic activities can provide the basis for many specialised services in areas such as health care and education, financial services, and so

FIGURE 1.2
Immigrants, commuters
and urban agglomerators:
starlings, February dusk
and the Albert Bridge

FREDERICK W. BOAL

on. Words like 'proximity', 'interaction' and 'co-operation' spring to mind. But urban agglomeration is not all positive in its consequences. We have crowding, competition for scarce resources, congestion, pollution. If these become too severe, the very existence of the city is threatened.

In the twentieth century developments in transportation and telecommunications have provided the technological basis for urban dispersal, with frequent references being made to suburbanisation and sprawl. But urban concentration is still a dominant (indeed an ever more dominant) feature of human occupancy of planet earth. Thus cities have not dispersed to form some kind of amorphous soup. Instead, they continue to maintain their agglomerative coherence, albeit at much lower densities than was the case before the twentieth century.

Cities function as nodes and are centres of exchange – people, commodities and information flow in and out. Cities are gathering places and, in consequence, are heterogeneous locations. This is true for many aspects of city life, but never more so than with the citizens themselves. By drawing in populations from distant places, variety is inevitably installed. This can be highly enriching but there is a fine line regarding the resultant mixing of different peoples between something very positive and something with negative potential, generating conflict, segregation and tendencies towards disintegration. Here, as John Short puts it,[3] we have the juxtaposition of strangers in what nonetheless has to be a shared city.

Cities are places of change and stability. Within the fabric of the city, change occurs at different speeds in different parts. The street patterns and the main sewer networks are perhaps the components most resistant to change; legally defined property boundaries may also behave this way. Individual buildings do change, but mostly only quite slowly, while their internal partitioning may be subject to more rapid modification. Finally, within building interiors, the contents (furniture, equipment) may change most rapidly of all. Change and stability are also manifest in the dynamism with which people and functions enter, occupy and leave buildings. They flow through them, adapting to the spaces therein or adapting the spaces themselves to better match needs, desires and aspirations. Meanwhile, to quote one of Winston Churchill's well-known aphorisms, 'we shape our buildings and afterwards our buildings shape us'.[4] Indeed, he might have gone on to say that we then proceed to reshape our buildings. We might go further still and apply these ideas not just to individual buildings but to whole cities as well.

Belfast, then, is one city amongst many worldwide. Though we can recognise a multitude of common characteristics shared by the phenomenon we call 'city', we also recognise that each urban place is unique. We will not rehearse here the uniqueness of Belfast, but will leave the chapters that follow to do that for us. However, there is one aspect of Belfast that we must stress, particularly since we have built it into the very title of this book – *Enduring City*. We apply the term 'enduring' to Belfast in the sense that the city and its peoples have experienced pain and hardship without giving up. Anyone aware of Belfast's twentieth-century history, either as a resident or an outside observer, will be forcefully struck by the very considerable pounding the place has taken economically, politically, socially, militarily and indeed psychologically. Some of these traumas have been shared by many other cities; some have been particularly sharply manifest in Belfast itself. We are thinking here about the sinking of the *Titanic*; the slaughter at the Somme in 1916; the Troubles of the early 1920s; the economic depression of the 1930s; the devastation of the blitz in 1941; the deindustrialisation of the later part of the twentieth century; the Troubles of the last three decades of the century. Yet Belfast has endured, probably because of the sheer gritty cussedness of her citizens. But she has also endured as a city because cities themselves are hardy creations with many positive attributes that, on balance, outweigh their all too evident disadvantages.

THE STRUCTURE OF THE BOOK

This book is divided into seven sections, followed by a list of Key Readings for those who wish to follow up on any of the topics. The first section, 'Foundations', sets the scene with this introductory chapter followed by Stephen Royle's chapter 2, which deals with how Belfast arrived at the twentieth century and shows that many of the issues the city faced in that turbulent century had their foundations in earlier eras.

Belfast had a population of hundreds of thousands throughout the twentieth century and these people, their buildings, their workplaces and the transport systems that moved them about are considered in the next section, 'Nuts and Bolts'. Paul Larmour in chapter 3 details the changes in the built fabric of Belfast, from the Victorian industrial city to the postindustrial, service-oriented city of 100 years later. Some buildings constructed at the height of Belfast's prosperity at the start of the period were particularly fine – and Larmour is among a number of authors to identify the 1906 City Hall as an important symbol in the Belfast story. There remain good buildings from throughout the twentieth century, but Larmour is critical of the way some have been lost in the name of redevelopment, after the blitz and the Troubles had caused their own share of damage. There is now some protection. Thirteen Conservation Areas in Belfast guard a range of building types, from the grandeur of the city centre and Queen's University district to rows of Victorian Belfast terraces in McMaster Street. However, Larmour criticises the way in which the early twenty-first-century redevelopment of the Victoria Square area has impacted on the City Centre Conservation Area.

Severe population loss in the inner reaches of the urban area and its redistribution beyond the city boundary are recorded in detail in Fred Boal's chapter 4. This also deals with that significant theme of Belfast's population story, the segregation between Protestants and Catholics, resulting in and, perhaps, also partly causing Belfast's sectarian rivalries.

Belfast's roller-coaster and radically transforming economy is examined by Mark Hart in chapter 5. Notable periods include the 1930s with its severe unemployment and, fifty years later, the elimination of many of the core traditional industries of the city – linen, shipbuilding and engineering – and a radical shift to a service-dominated economy.

Austin Smyth's focus on transport in chapter 6 moves the city from the tram and trolley-bus era through to an overdependence on the private car, with, perhaps, signs now that public transport might again become more important. However, Smyth fears that the decentralisation pressures that affected Belfast for the last decades of the twentieth century might preclude a full restoration of the city's heart.

The third section, 'Shaping the City', deals with how Belfast was governed and planned throughout the twentieth century. Government of a severely divided city is inevitably a difficult enterprise, as is revealed by Jonathan Bardon in chapter 7. The problems and the changing issues that had to be faced may be summarised by Bardon's assertion that there was 'something strained about the prevailing atmosphere of self-congratulation of the Edwardian period', whilst later periods are characterised by telling subheadings such as the 'housing scandal' of the 1920s and the 'bogs, bins and bodies' era of the 1970s and 1980s. However, by the late century a 'new era of compromise and acceptance of change' had emerged with the ending of Unionist domination and a city leadership that takes more control of its affairs and its future.

Bill Morrison's chapter 8 details the changing issues the city's planners faced throughout the century. And change they did. The city of Belfast ended the century as the only area of Northern Ireland still losing population. Compare that to the problems of the early 1960s when there had to be a 'Stop Line' imposed around the city's suburban fringe to prevent further growth.

The section ends with a focus on Belfast's river, the Lagan, by Fred Boal in chapter 9. He takes us on journeys upstream at the century's start and at its end, the different views showing how Belfast has altered and how the shaping of the city has affected the river itself, and how changes to the river have, in turn, impacted on the city.

As we noted earlier, Belfast is a city like any other, but it has its own particularities. Sometimes these are just extreme manifestations of commonplace themes. Thus all cities house people of different religions, but Belfast is one of few where a consideration of this topic can be put within a section labelled 'Together and Apart', which also deals with major civil strife. Though with justification some would claim that religion has provided societal glue, acting as a brake to some of the excesses of ethno-national conflict in the city, it cannot be ignored that Belfast has had to endure the consequences of what John Brewer, Margaret Keane and David Livingstone in chapter 10 refer to as 'an environment of politicised faith'.

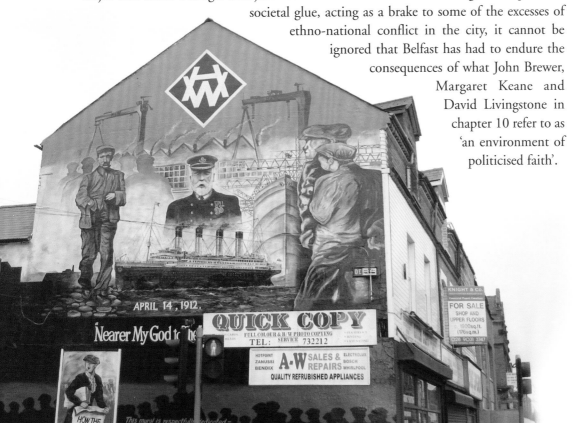

FIGURE 1.3
Titanic mural, Dee Street
STEPHEN A. ROYLE

FIGURE 1.4
The Cathedral Quarter,
part of the Belfast mosaic

STEPHEN A. ROYLE

Bill Neill in chapter 11 considers how the city has been viewed by its varied inhabitants, including council members – 'imaging and visioning' are the contemporary phrases. He makes a serious charge, backed by a poem by John Hewitt, that the city was allowed to drift after the Second World War. 'You coasted too long' is the poem's last line – for 1969 was on the horizon. Neill, like some of the other contributors, sees more hope at the century's end than for much of its earlier periods. The urban regeneration plans of the 1980s and 1990s bring a new look to the old place – his 're-imaged city'. Look for confirmation of that in Fred Boal's chapter 9, especially the three illustrations of the area south of Queen's Bridge (see Figures 9.9a, 9.9b and 9.9c). However, like Larmour, Neill is critical of some regenera-tion; his depiction of it as putting 'lipstick on the gorilla' is challenging.

One of the 'visioning' problems Belfast had to face was the severe blow administered by the sinking of Harland and Wolff's pride and joy, the *Titanic*, in 1912 (the sinking of this ill-starred ship is depicted on the Belfast mural shown in Figure 1.3). Moreover, in the same pre-First World War era, the increasingly fierce arguments over Home Rule began to throw a political and economic shadow across the city. This was to be followed by the traumas of the war itself, manifested for Belfast in its sharpest form in the horrific loss of life in the trenches and shell-pocked terrain of the Somme in 1916. The memo-rialisation of this episode is analysed in Nuala Johnson's chapter 12, where she vividly lays out the imprinting of the Somme on both the city's space and on the memory of its citizens.

The two world wars affected Belfast, as they did most European cities, in various ways; in the Second World War the blitz had a particularly marked impact on the city, as detailed in Fred Boal's addendum to chapter 13. The core of that chapter, by Russell Murray, deals with Belfast's most notorious particularity – the violent manifestations of ethno-national conflict that have been a fundamental part of this city's endurance in the twentieth centu-ry. Murray presents a statistical and cartographic dissection of the deaths that were a product of this conflict, both in the early 1920s and in the post-1969 period.

The fifth section, 'Mind and Body', returns to more general matters: the way in which the city provided health care and education and also a consideration of what every city has but what some would consider rather well developed in Belfast – its pop-ular culture. Alun Evans in chapter 14 takes a city where many young men were not deemed healthy enough to be enlisted as cannon fodder for the Boer War, and shows health status and health-care provision improving enormously, if sometimes only at a slow pace. The beneficial effects of legislation such as the Maternity and Child Welfare Act of 1918 are discussed, but as late as 1941 the appearance of the undersized, under-fed citizens of Belfast, flushed from their homes during the blitz, surprised the presumably better-fed moderator of the Presbyterian Church. Evans details improve-ments in sanitation (enjoy the turf spittoon), but considers also diseases prevalent in Belfast, including those of industrial origin. He worries still at Belfast residents' morbidity rates, associated with lifestyle issues, and his conclusion that health inequalities have persisted is another matter for concern.

E.J. Creighton's story of education in chapter 15 resonates with Evans's chapter. The century started with conditions that were a 'disgrace to civilisation', followed by reform under the 1923 Education Act and the creditable performance of the interwar Belfast Education Committee, which left a legacy of fine school buildings, many still in use. Belfast ended the century with largely decent school buildings, education for all to sixteen, with most staying on for further study. Such progress would be commonplace in Western cities. However, education highlights, again, Belfast's particularities, and Creighton outlines how the segregated system ensures that the vast majority of the city's Catholic and Protestant children attend different schools, as they do throughout Northern Ireland. Schools with a religious basis are not unknown elsewhere, of course, but the high level of segregation in Belfast points to the city's individual, not universal, attributes. Only nearing the century's end does a movement towards integrated schooling become evident.

Belfast's divisions show up once more in Jonathan Bardon's chapter 16, which examines the city's vibrant popular culture – without ever using the word *craic*. Their impact was felt, especially, during the Troubles, with the severe curtailment of public entertainment for much of the 1970s, most markedly in the city centre.

The divisions in some senses lead to Belfast being not one city but a series of villages, with the different groups leading largely separate lives outside (and for most during the twentieth century, inside) the workplace, only occasionally bumping into each other in shared spaces such as the city centre. More than most urban places, Belfast is a city made up of smaller districts, a mosaic with the tiles themselves having sharp boundaries (Figure 1.4 shows even a district mapped out in tiles). Hence the title of the sixth section, 'The Belfast Mosaic', for Patricia Craig's chapters 17 and 18 on Belfast's twentieth-century literature. Her first chapter shows how Belfast changed from the era the young John Hewitt had 'heard about but truly never knew'. Local writers have not shied from Belfast's intercommunal rivalry, encapsul- ated in Craig's first heading: 'Is them 'uns bate?' She deals with the notion of 'Belfast's bigotries' and the existence of opposed interpretations of events – 'And one read black where the other read white' – all starkly emphasising aspects of the fractured nature of the city's social fabric. She notes Brian Moore writing of the negativity of Belfast 'from its Catholic/Protestant divide to its backwardness and bad weather', a reference to 'the self-destructing city'.

Craig's second piece, chapter 18, considers literature about the districts of Belfast. Taking a cue from Hugh Shearman's statement that he was 'born in a village in the city of Belfast', her title is 'Village Voices'. Craig writes: 'it's true to say that the sad catalogue of atrocities has left no part of the city unscathed, and virtually no stretch of pavement without its bloody associations', but a perusal of this chapter also shows that the quality of Belfast writers is to be celebrated, even if some of their themes are bleak. Indeed, the

FIGURE 1.5
C.S. Lewis enters the wardrobe in his 1998 centenary statue at Holywood Arches, Newtownards Road.

STEPHEN A. ROYLE

early twenty-first century has seen new international recognition of one of our authors – C.S. Lewis (Figure 1.5) – whose *Chronicles of Narnia: The Lion, the Witch and the Wardrobe* has been dramatised in a Hollywood movie.

Chapter 2 looked back at the foundations for twentieth-century Belfast. The book ends by looking forward, with Marie-Thérèse McGivern's chapter 19, 'Belfast: the Way Ahead', the sole chapter in the final section, 'Into the Twenty-First Century'. She does not duck the ugly issues that blighted aspects of our city's experience in the twentieth century, nor the fact that there remain 'serious underlying social, economic and structural problems'. However, McGivern is able to note that Belfast 'has made significant gains' in the relatively short period since the ceasefires of 1994 and she feels that given favourable circumstances and good leadership Belfast has at least the 'possibility of becoming a successful modern European city'.

MAKING BRIDGES

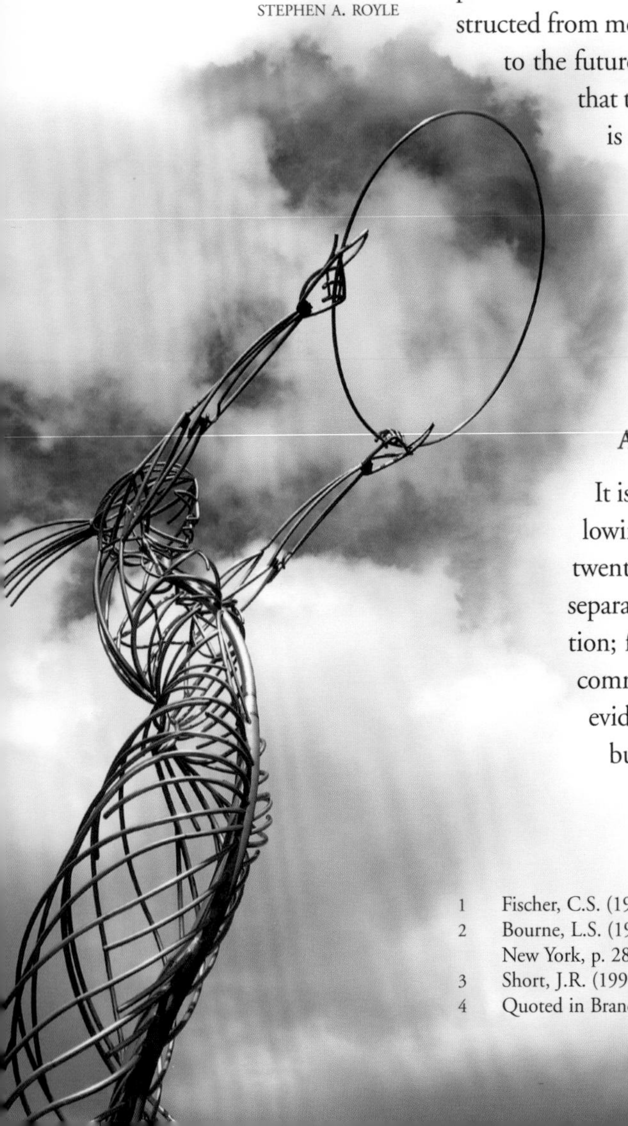

FIGURE 1.6
The Angel of Thanksgiving
in Thanksgiving Square

STEPHEN A. ROYLE

At the start of the new millennium, by Queen's Bridge, in what had been a neglected corner of the central city (see Figure 9.9b), stands a new symbol for Belfast and a new place-name. In Thanksgiving Square a large sculpture – the Angel of Thanksgiving – constructed from metal tubing represents a female figure standing on the globe, her arms raised to the future and holding the ring of thanksgiving (Figure 1.6). A sign nearby tells us that this allegorical figure is derived from Classical and Celtic mythology. Graffiti is one of Belfast's enduring traditions and on this sign, in very twenty-first-century text-speak, urgent capitals recently protested 'MONEY 4 THIS BUT CANT FEED THE POOR' – a legitimate grievance, perhaps. It is encouraging to see, however, that the sculptor's aim, also printed on the sign, has not been attacked or defaced, and this beacon of hope and reconciliation has been left unmolested to preside over the square in her quest 'to make bridges across the divides in our community'.

AN INVITATION

It is now time to invite our readers to explore the chapters presented in the following pages. The contributors to *Enduring City* seek to examine across the twentieth century the complex web of interactions, interrelations, conflicts and separations that makes up Belfast's recent history. From construction to destruction; from urban order to urban disorder; from expansion to contraction; from community to separation; from pleasure to pain – all these polarities have been evident to varying degrees. Much of the time Belfast has been no playground, but playground imagery still comes to mind: roller-coaster rides, swings and roundabouts, climbing frames and slides – all are suggestive of the experience of Belfast in the twentieth century.

1   Fischer, C.S. (1976) *The urban experience*, Harcourt, Brace, Jovanovich: New York.
2   Bourne, L.S. (1982) *Urban spatial structure: an introductory essay on concepts and criteria*, Oxford University Press: New York, p. 28.
3   Short, J.R. (1996) *The urban order*, Blackwell: Malden, MS, p. 226.
4   Quoted in Brand, S. (1994) *How buildings learn*, Phoenix Illustrated: London, p. 3.

W hen Belfast arrived at the first year of the twentieth century, it brought with it baggage – both physical and social – from previous eras. In order, then, to understand how the city would continue its journey through the century, it is necessary to study its voyage to the year 1900 (Figure 2.1).

2
Belfast
Foundations of the Twentieth Century

Stephen A. Royle

FIGURE 2.1
The Long Bridge, Belfast, by A. Nicholl
ULSTER MUSEUM

THE SEVENTEENTH CENTURY

Modern Belfast began in 1603. There was an earlier Belfast; its Irish name, Béal Feirste, meaning 'approach to the sandbar', is associated with its function as a fording point of the River Lagan.[1] Situated on the west, County Antrim, bank of the river, Belfast had a castle from the late twelfth century, but as it was at least three times destroyed and rebuilt, its success in guarding the ford was not unbroken. The Chapel of the Ford (built before 1306) occupied the site of the present St George's Church of Ireland church on High Street. At first Belfast was overshadowed by Carrickfergus with its great Norman castle on the sea lough, which then bore the name of Carrickfergus Lough after its principal coastal settlement.

Belfast had been considered 'a place meet for a corporate town' in 1573.[2] The earl of Essex started building before the O'Neills took the area in the 1580s, the garrison remaining at Belfast being slaughtered in 1597. Sir John Chichester regained Belfast but was killed shortly afterwards; his brother, Sir Arthur, finally subdued the O'Neills and in reward was granted Belfast and fifty-two surrounding townlands by James I in 1603. He made the 1573 prediction a reality,[3] creating a planned market town and port where the Farset, running from the Antrim Plateau, joins the larger Lagan. Within Belfast lived settlers mainly from England and Scotland, the former mainly adherents of the Anglican (Episcopalian) Church of Ireland. A charter in 1613 created a corporate borough with a sovereign (mayor), twelve burgesses (the modern equivalent would be councillors), and freemen, but power rested with the Chichesters (Figure 2.2). Also governor of Carrickfergus Castle and lord deputy of Ireland, Sir Arthur built Joymount, a splendid Jacobean residence, in Carrickfergus.[4] After his death in 1625, however, his brother and heir, Sir Edward, moved to Belfast as the new town began to eclipse the old.[5] By 1630 Belfast brought Chichester £400 per year – more than Carrickfergus[6] – and by the 1660s Belfast's population had grown to over 1,000.[7]

Early Belfast's lineaments are revealed by the familiar 1685 maps of Thomas Phillips, reproduced in many histories,[8] and also by a map discovered in 2002, dated ''96' (clearly 1696), which depicts the town and its 'banke'[9] – earthen ramparts erected in 1642 for protection in troubled times (Figure 2.3). The 1641 rebellion, when Catholic elements rose up in an attempt to overthrow the Protestant regime in Ireland, and which affected Lisburn directly but not its neighbour Belfast, was followed by the English Civil War, which spread into Ireland. Belfast changed hands without bloodshed more than once during this conflict. Under royalist control, it was besieged for days before surrendering to Commonwealth forces in 1649.[10]

The 1696 map shows that substantial areas of the town remained open space, those to the south (at the top of Figure 2.3) being garden plots belonging to the castle. Belfast was focused on the Farset, the 'Belfast River' (culverted in 1770). On High Street was Corporation Church, a 1657 rebuilding of the Chapel of the Ford, which had been

FIGURE 2.2
A scene from the Luke mural at Belfast City Hall, showing Sir Arthur Chichester reading the town charter, awarded by James I in 1613

BELFAST CITY COUNCIL

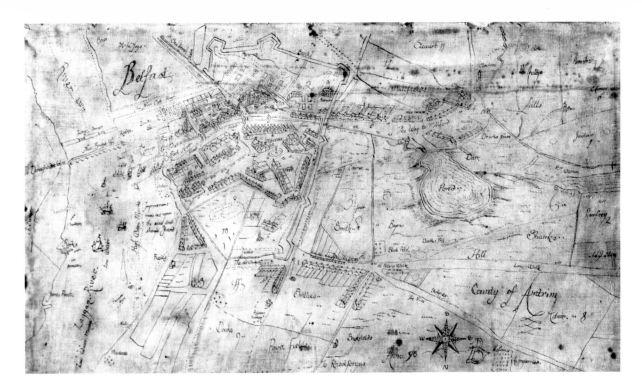

FIGURE 2.3
Map of Belfast, 1696
NATIONAL LIBRARY OF IRELAND

damaged by Cromwell's forces when it was used as the Grand Fort and Citadel. This church was demolished in 1774 and the site reused in 1813 for St George's. Also on High Street was the 1639 Market House (extended in 1663, and later demolished in 1812) and opposite was the 'beauty and glory of the town',[11] the last (1611) castle on the original site, the Chichesters' brick residence, which, with forty fireplaces, was more palace than castle. Belfast had a school and a Presbyterian church dated 1672 (rebuilt 1717 and from 1781–83 replaced by the present First Non-Subscribing Presbyterian Church in Rosemary Street). By the ramparts were the barracks, the town being garrisoned.

Although there would have been warehouses and places of business inside the ramparts, most structures were residential. The majority of these were thatched terraced cottages – some with gardens – but others were more substantial houses. Outside the ramparts, the Falls, 'The Way to Millford', had the fortified dwelling of merchant George McCartney, the mills on the Farset and the houses of the local Irish. This became the 'apex' of Catholic settlement in west Belfast.[12] Beyond the millpond, the Shankill, around St Peter's Walk, had houses with gardens, a cemetery, a death pit and brickfields.

The 'Laggan' had extensive bog lands along its banks, which were being improved in 1696. There was a new cut along the Blackstaff (diverted further south in the early eighteenth century) helping drainage and providing quays (this became May's Dock). Long Bridge (1682), marked as 'New Bridge', is depicted with eleven arches, though it actually boasted twenty-one. It was demolished in 1840 and two years later was replaced by Queen's Bridge. 'Long Cross' marks the ford and this newly found map is the first to depict its precise location.[13]

By 1700 Belfast had mills, brewhouses, sugar refineries, malt-kilns, a pottery, tanneries and, nearby, iron works; and wooden ships were built there.[14] Its principal role, however, was as a trading place. The Lagan was not deep enough for large ships, which stayed downstream in the Pool of Garmoyle, off-loading into smaller vessels. The 1696 map displays such vessels entering the Farset to berth at the 'Key of Belfast'.[15] About fifty merchant families, some shipowners,[16] controlled the port business, based largely on exporting corn and barrelled beef and butter. They had increased the proportion of the lough's trade passing through Belfast rather than Carrickfergus and had been responsible for much of Belfast's recent growth and prosperity. Many merchants, often Scottish Presbyterians, arrived after prospects improved following the 1640s.[17] Merchant families, such as the Warings (an established English family) and the Macartney (sometimes spelt McCartney) family, who were Scots, came also to dominate civic affairs. 'Black George' Macartney, involved in a piped water scheme in the 1670s, was a burgess for forty years and sovereign several times.[18] In 1613 the twelve burgesses were mainly Anglican gentry.

Some versions of the 1685 Phillips map depict planned extensions to the fortifications. These were never built and, unlike Londonderry, which was sheltered behind substantial walls, Belfast surrendered to James II's army in 1689. This force then withdrew before the Williamite army under the command of the duke of Schomberg, 'as the crumbling ramparts were in no condition to withstand a siege'.[19] King William III visited the town in 1690, and was greeted by loyal addresses and celebratory bonfires. Then, as Dennis Kennedy observed, 'Belfast soon exchanged a secondary consequence in the wars for a more durable and more valuable precedence in the arts of peace … While its history is really destitute of memorable incidents … Belfast … commenced a rapid progress to the rank of one of the chief commercial towns in the British dominions',[20] ending the century as the fourth largest Irish port and being mistakenly, if plausibly, called the 'second town in Ireland' in 1702.[21]

THE EIGHTEENTH CENTURY

From 1647 Belfast belonged to the heads of the Chichester family – the earls of Donegall (the title changed to marquis in 1791) – names commemorated in many Belfast streets. In 1708 the Chichesters' home, Belfast Castle, burnt down, killing three of the fourth earl's sisters, a further blow to the family, which had lost the third earl in 1706 at the siege of Monjuich in Spain. The dowager countess and her three surviving children, including the fourth earl, aged thirteen, then abandoned Belfast, whose landlords remained absentees until 1802. Their absence deprived Belfast of leadership and matters were worsened by the youthful inexperience of the fourth earl and by his lifelong mental incapacity. Leases issued by his trustees were short-term arrangements (41 years), without obligation to improve. So leaseholders did not invest, the housing stock fell from 2,100 in 1725 to 1,800 by 1757,[22] and Belfast became impoverished and its industry diminished, the pottery closing in 1720.

In 1757 the fifth earl (later first marquis) of Donegall succeeded his uncle. Although always an absentee, he guided Belfast's development. He chaired the Ballast Board and founded the Exchange (1769) and Assembly Rooms (built in Waring Street above the Exchange in 1777; the building still exists), which became the centre of commercial and social life. He built St Anne's parish church in 1776 (replaced by the cathedral in 1898) and provided land for the Belfast Charitable Society's poorhouse, Clifton House, which still stands in Clifton Street, although funds for its building (1771–74) were raised by public subscription and lottery.[23] He provided land for the White Linen Hall (Figure 2.4), built in1784 (demolished in 1898, the site reused for Belfast City Hall) and encouraged Belfast's trade in bleached linen from rural Ulster. Brown Linen Halls in Donegall

Street (1754, replaced on another site in 1773) traded unbleached linen. Trade was facilitated by the Lagan Navigation, commenced in 1756, and controlled by Donegall from 1779, which eased transport between Belfast, the Lagan Valley and the Lough Neagh basin. In 1787 Donegall bought Ballymacarrett, the County Down townland across the Lagan, to ensure its development complemented rather than competed with Belfast.

In 1799 a newspaper obituary estimated that the first marquis of Donegall had 'laid out above £60,000 in the Lagan Navigation; and the public buildings in this town … remain as monuments of his generosity and public spirit'.[24] The obituary inevitably added that his memory would 'long be respected by a grateful tenantry',[25] but he was not always philanthropic, nor was he the only actor. The Belfast Charitable Society, in addition to helping the poor, became involved in water supply and medical provision. Further, when Donegall released land from 1765 for three named lives or 99 years, it was at the old rents but with the addition of a heavy 'fine' (charge), payments which helped 'defray the family debt and pay for his extravagant lifestyle' in England.[26] Tenants unable to pay fines were evicted, presumably joining the poor in west Belfast and the back alleys. Belfast's middle classes often leased the holdings made available. Long leases encouraged investment, and building

FIGURE 2.4
The White Linen Hall, *c.* 1890
ULSTER MUSEUM

leases required minimum standards of construction, which varied in different streets but generally saw the erection of elegant Georgian houses (Figure 2.5).[27] Some survive near Donegall Place, which was planned, as was Donegall Street and the Smithfield market area,[28] 'before the blight of speculative building … and … the heavy hand of the industrial expansionist smashed [Belfast's eighteenth-century grace] to smithereens'.[29]

Belfast's Georgian rebuilding changed its social geography with the construction of fashionable residences near the White Linen Hall.[30] It also helped recast Belfast's image, as in this 1793 recitation:

> And have not here our souls with freedom glow'd;
> Has she not here long fix'd her lov'd abode?
> Yes – and old time shall yet, with glad surprize,
> View in Belfast a second Athens rise.[31]

An Athens needs culture and debate. Printing businesses had been established in Belfast since the seventeenth century and theatres since 1751. The *Belfast News Letter* was published from 1737, the middle classes frequented the Assembly Rooms, and the Belfast Reading Society of 1787 became the Belfast Society for Promoting Knowledge in 1792, founding the Linen Hall Library – society and library still exist and can be found in

FIGURE 2.5
High Street by J. Nixon, 1786

ULSTER MUSEUM

Donegall Square North. There were many schools; there was music.[32] Debate among the religious denominations was commonplace at this time – not always Protestant versus Catholic: sometimes Presbyterian, or Dissenter, versus Anglican.[33] Catholics occasionally joined with Presbyterians in protest against the unfair electoral system. Presbyterians objected to Belfast's members of parliament being elected by the city's sovereign and burgesses – in effect, chosen by the Anglican Lord Donegall. Catholics had no voting rights.

Presbyterians in the Belfast Volunteers donated £84 of the £170 needed for the first Catholic chapel in the town, St Mary's, Mass having hitherto been celebrated in the open near Friar's Bush and in private houses. At the opening of the chapel in 1784 'the Volunteers, Protestant to a man, paraded in strength and in full uniform, and attended mass in the historic little church which they had already helped to build'.[34] Presbyterians became involved in the United Irishmen movement in the 1790s.[35] These Belfast radicals supported the French Revolution and the Americans in the War of Independence, many Americans being of Ulster birth or parentage, often Presbyterians who themselves had left Ireland to be free of religious persecution. 'That damned sink, Belfast'[36] became a problem to the authorities, martial law being imposed in 1797 when troops damaged radicals' property, including the presses of the *Northern Star*.[37] Such repression had the desired result, for Henry Joy McCracken was the only prominent Belfastman to join the 1798 insurrection. He was captured and publicly hanged in Belfast's Cornmarket, one of seven executions held there.[38] Other prisoners were transported to the USA,[39] until the American authorities no longer permitted transportation to their shores.[40]

Under the stewardship of the first marquis of Donegall population grew (see Table 2.1) and the housing stock almost doubled between 1782 and 1806 to accommodate new residents, many of them industrial workers.[41] Commercial growth (overseen from 1783 by the Chamber of Commerce) was associated with the linen trade and port development. Under the marquis's predecessor, the fourth earl, the authorities had not kept quaysides serviceable nor channels clear, nor did they make improvements – George Quay and Hanover Quay, built in the 1710s, were private ventures of Isaac Macartney. The Ballast Office of 1729, tasked to keep the harbour serviceable and supply ballast, was replaced by the Corporation for Preserving and Improving the Port and Harbour of Belfast (the Ballast Board) in 1785,[42] which commissioned shipbuilder William Ritchie to build Number 1 Clarendon Graving Dock in 1796 (this, with Number 2 Dock of 1826, still exists). Trade, principally with Europe and North America, included shipping emigrants to the latter.[43] Sugar and tobacco were frequent imports; in addition to agricultural produce, linen was an increasingly significant export. Thus the *Iphigenia* from Belfast, bound for Virginia and boarded by a French privateer in 1800, lost linens worth 10,000 US dollars.[44]

TABLE 2.1
Belfast Population, 1757–1901

Year	Population
1757	8,549
1782	13,105
1791	18,320
1806	22,095
1811	27,382
1821	37,277
1831	53,287
1841	63,750*
1851	87,062
1861	121,602
1871	174,412
1881	208,094
1891	255,924
1901	349,180

SOURCE: R. Gillespie and S.A. Royle (2003) Irish Historic Towns Atlas, no. 12, *Belfast part I, to 1840*; census reports

*Belfast population figure for 1841 does not include Ballymacarrett (6,697); including this part of County Down, which was incorporated within the new city boundary in 1837, would give a total figure of 70,447 for Belfast in 1841.

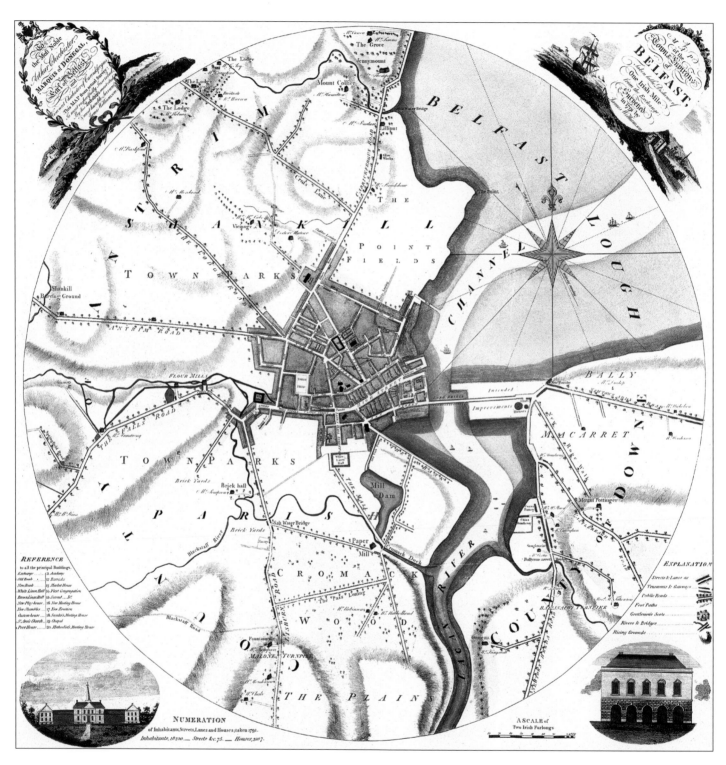

FIGURE 2.6
James Williamson's *Map of the Town and Environs of Belfast*, 1791

James Williamson's 1791 map (Figure 2.6) identifies the new trading facilities at the docks (Belfast was now the third port in Ireland) and inside the town. Foundries, breweries, rope walks, glassworks, and flour and paper mills evidence Belfast's growing industrialisation, although textile factories are not shown. Linen manufacture remained largely a product of rural Ulster, but there were 300 looms in Belfast by 1771.[45] Cotton spinning commenced as a makework scheme in the poorhouse in 1777, but by 1800 there were eleven water-powered cotton spinning mills.[46] Shipbuilding is also not depicted, but this industry revived that year when William Ritchie launched the 300-ton *Hibernia*, the only vessel 'of any burthen' to be built in Belfast for many years.[47] The Belfast Academy (1785) in Academy Street is marked, as is a playhouse. The churches demonstrate the religious diversity of the population. There had been much improvement to the Lagan's banks since 1696, with further schemes at Ballymacarrett identified.

THE NINETEENTH CENTURY

Belfast's industrial development during the nineteenth century was remarkable, given its remoteness and lack of energy supplies and raw materials. By 1825, 3,611 people were employed in cotton manufacture. Initially powered by streams from the Antrim Plateau, by the 1820s steam power had largely taken over. Ulster has little coal, but supplies were readily available from Britain. Perhaps a steam engine caused the six-storey cotton factory of Thomas and Andrew Mulholland to burn down in 1828: 'so rapid was the devouring element that in less than an hour the large and stately fabric was reduced to ruins'.[48] This was one of the chance events that shaped Belfast, for the Mulhollands rebuilt their premises in York Street in 1830 as a linen factory, utilising new flax-spinning technology. By 1860 there were thirty-two linen mills in Belfast and only two spinning cotton.[49]

Industrial Belfast benefited from ample supplies of cheap labour. Even by 1841, before the Great Famine, over half Belfast's workers were in manufacturing and the only counties in Ireland to increase in population during the 1840s were Dublin, Antrim and Down; the Ulster growth was associated with migration because of industrial opportunities in Belfast and smaller towns. Belfast, a city from 1888, became 'Linenopolis' as the mills multiplied.[50] By 1896 there were 69,000 linen workers in Ireland, many in Belfast,[51] and mostly women. The culture of the mills has been celebrated, whilst the health risks from noise, dust and damp have also been charted.[52]

Belfast port had always been handicapped by the shallowness of the Lagan. The Ballast Board dredged sand (subsequently sold as ballast) from the navigation channels, thus maintaining them, but in 1839 a larger channel was dredged, finally permitting substantial vessels to reach Belfast's quaysides. This dredged material was tipped to the County Down side of the channel and thus Dargan's Island (named after William Dargan, the engineer responsible for this work) arose from the shallow sloblands. It was renamed Queen's Island after Victoria's 1849 visit, when she sailed up a new second cut, the Victoria Channel. (In 1899 the familiar trident shape of the waterways at Belfast was completed with the digging of the Musgrave Channel.) Access for larger ships helped

TABLE 2.2
Belfast Port Statistics, 1763–1867

Year	Customs Revenue (GBP)	Vessels	Total tonnage
1763	32,900*	n/a	n/a
1786	n/a	772	34,287
1795	101,376	n/a	n/a
1813	393,512	1,190	97,670
1837	n/a	2,724	288,143
1847	n/a	4,213	538,825
1867	n/a	7,817	1,372,326

SOURCE: D.J. Owen (1917) *A Short History of the Port of Belfast*, Mayne, Boyd and Son: Belfast

*1763 figures include excise, the others do not; n/a = not available

The four partners in Harland and Wolff (*left to right*): G.W. Wolff, W.H. Wilson, W.J. Pirrie and Edward J. Harland

ULSTER FOLK & TRANSPORT MUSEUM

Belfast to become the largest port in Ireland by 1852 (Table 2.2 shows details of the development of Belfast as a port),[53] but required changes to the harbour. Old docks were filled in and the replanned quayside on the Antrim shore became Donegall Quay in the 1850s. Queen's Quay on the Down shore was the coal handling area, fronting Queen's Island, which had become a peninsula. Part of the island was used as a pleasure park, but the Crystal Palace built there was burned down in 1868, and Queen's Island subsequently became devoted to shipbuilding. The leisure activies were moved elsewhere,[54] before Belfast's millennium project, the Odyssey, restored this lost function to the area.

At the start of the nineteenth century shipyards belonging to the Ritchie family and others on the Antrim shore made wooden sailing vessels, a technology whose time was about to expire. The first steam-powered Irish-built vessel was launched by the Ritchies in 1820: 'a handsome vessel of the largest class',[55] but modern shipbuilding in Belfast is principally associated with Edward Harland. Harland, from north-east England and aged only twenty-three, arrived in 1854 to manage Robert Hickson's shipyard on Queen's Island, where flat land with access to the sheltered waters of Belfast Lough provided good sites for shipbuilding, albeit in a crowded environment shared with the port. Harland was ambitious, wanting his own yard. He tried to establish one in Liverpool but, instead, acquired Hickson's yard in 1858 for £5,000, making Gustav Wolff his assistant in 1857, and partner in 1861. Others joined later – notably William Pirrie in 1874 (Figure 2.7).

Once an apprentice of the railway engineer Robert Stephenson, Harland was the company engineer; Wolff, despite claiming that he simply smoked cigars for the firm, ran the drawing office and had important contacts. His uncle, Gustav Schwabe, was a partner in the Liverpool-based shipping concern John Bibby and Sons and twelve of the first fifteen Harland and Wolff ships were built for Bibby. Further, 'according to popular legend, it was during an after-dinner game of billiards at Schwabe's Liverpool home in 1869 that Edward Harland met Thomas Ismay … That evening, Harland was supposed to have agreed to build the ships Ismay needed to allow his newly acquired White Star Line to compete in the North Atlantic emigrant trade.'[56] The 3,808-ton *Oceanic*, the first modern liner, was the initial White Star order in 1870. Personal networks and rapid adoption of new technology, including steel ships from 1880 and innovative engine designs, were of great importance as Belfast lacked a local supply of coal and iron. Even its cheap unskilled labour was of limited utility, for much shipyard work required skilled labour, which had to be recruited from elsewhere in the British Isles. The nineteenth century saw huge increases in world trade, including emigration, and Harland's strong, narrow and long 'coffin' steamers (so-called because of their box-like appearance) were popular.

Harland and Wolff employed 2,400 in 1870 and 14,000 in 1914, mainly men, a counterpart to the female labour in the mills.[57] This, with Belfast's relatively good housing and cheap living costs, helps to explain how the shipyards could attract skilled workers to Belfast.[58] McIlwaine and Lewis (later McIlwaine and McColl) built ships in the Abercorn Basin from the 1870s, and in 1879 former Harland and Wolff employees Frank Workman and George Clark set up 'the wee yard', Workman Clark, initially on the Antrim shore before buying McIlwaine and McColl's premises on the opposite side of the lough (Figure 2.8).[59]

Associated with textiles and shipbuilding were ancillary industries such as engineering. For example, from 1881 the Sirocco works made industrial fans. Belfast Ropeworks, established in 1873 under Gustav Wolff, made ropes for the shipyards, and the factory in east Belfast became the world's largest ropeworks (now the site of the Connswater shopping centre). There were several foundries and the largest, owned by Victor Coates, was also in Ballymacarrett. East Belfast's industrial growth led its landowner, Baron Templemore, nephew of the second marquis of Donegall, to consider in 1853 an ambitious planned development. This proved too expensive to implement fully, but long, straight Templemore Avenue, out of character for east Belfast, was built under the scheme.[60]

FIGURE 2.8
Interior of Engine and
Boiler Works, Workman
Clark, 1902 or 1903
ULSTER MUSEUM

FIGURE 2.9
George Augustus, second
marquis of Donegall
(1769–1844), painted in
1800 by J.J. Masquerier

BELFAST CITY COUNCIL

Templemore's plan exemplified landlord power. From 1799 Belfast itself was the property of the second marquis of Donegall (Figure 2.9). A notorious debtor,[61] the marquis moved to Belfast in 1802, hoping to distance himself from creditors. In need of capital but unable to sell land under the terms of his inheritance, like his father he renewed leases on favourable terms in return for substantial entry fines. From 1822 he made 600 new perpetuity leases in Belfast, relinquishing control of this land. He did not use the fines, totalling £330,000, to repay all debts, preferring to spend them on an extravagant lifestyle, including the building of Ormeau House (1823–30) in Ormeau Park, to where he had moved from Donegall Place in 1807, living first in Ormeau Cottage. Again like his father, the second marquis provided land for public buildings, such as Belfast Academical Institution (1814), the Fever Hospital (1817), Commercial Buildings (1820) and the Gas Works (1823), but his greater impact was due to omission rather than commission, for his new leases allowed entrepreneurs free rein to develop holdings at a period of considerable industrial and commercial opportunity. A similar process happened in Ballymacarrett (part of Belfast after 1837; and more of County Down was taken into the city in the 1852 boundary extension) after Templemore abandoned his scheme.

The second marquis was nevertheless popular in Belfast, being at least a resident landlord. His name usually topped subscription lists, but he did not always pay and at his death in 1844 his debts were an astonishing £400,000. To repay them, his son, the third marquis, was obliged to relinquish the freehold of Belfast and sell holdings in County Antrim through the Encumbered Estates Court,[62] and the Donegalls' influence on Belfast was over. Their estate at Ormeau was used largely as a public park from 1871, with parts being used for a golf course and for housing. The house was demolished in 1870, the bricks reused for Robb's department store, which opened in 1876.[63] The final Donegall Belfast home was another Belfast Castle, constructed on the slopes of Cave Hill in 1870.

Land released by the Donegalls aided Belfast's industrial expansion and was also used for the housing needed for Belfast's mushrooming population. Some housing provided by employers was poor,[64] but most was speculatively provided by small builders for the rental market and was of reasonable standard, constructed of locally made bricks and with slate roofs. Belfast's greatest rate of growth was from 1870 to 1900 when the housing stock quadrupled as engineering and shipbuilding prospered. Bye-laws of 1864, 1865, 1878 and 1889 imposed minimum building standards and Belfast was spared the evils of the industrial housing of earlier expanding towns like Leeds and Nottingham. Rather than their back-to-back housing developments, most Belfast workers occupied terraces that were certainly small, either 'kitchen' or the roomier 'parlour' houses, but had rear access, if only via an alley (Figure 2.10). However, subletting was common and densities high, especially amongst poorly paid textile workers.[65] These houses tended to be close to mills and shipyards in the inner city.

The middle classes occupied larger semidetached or detached houses, still usually of brick and slate. The transport systems of the late nineteenth century, trams especially, enabled them to live towards the edge of the city, as in Bloomfield (Figure 2.11) and Ballyhackamore in east Belfast and the Crumlin and Antrim roads in north Belfast. The wealthy in the early century were accommodated in the Donegall Square area.[66] They or their successors suburbanised to escape the growing clamour of city life; many to the Malone Road in south Belfast, others to outer east Belfast where small estates were created.[67]

Belfast's growth saw immigration, especially from elsewhere in Ulster, increase the Catholic proportion of its population to a third by 1861. Pressures for Catholic emancipation in the early century had alarmed some Protestants, whilst after the election following the 1832 Reform Act, there was fighting in Catholic Hercules Street between Tories and the radicals whose cause had attracted Catholic support. Four died. Other sectarian disputes followed in 1833, 1835, 1841 (during Daniel O'Connell's visit), 1857, 1864 (after which Belfast's police were replaced by the Royal Irish Constabulary), 1872 (during which evictions of Catholics living in Protestant areas and vice versa intensified religious divisions), and 1886 (over the campaign for Home Rule).

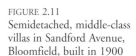

FIGURE 2.10
Late nineteenth-century Belfast terraces, McMaster Street, east Belfast

STEPHEN A. ROYLE

Belfast Corporation was a Protestant, conservative body; the property qualifications for voting tended to favour electors of this ilk. Despite such conservatism, Belfast was quick to make improvements expressing civic pride, including paving, streetlighting, more and better regulated markets, and encouraged developments that reduced overcrowding (such as the replacement of Hercules Street by Royal Avenue in 1880–81). Such developments were aided by substantial funds, especially from the Gas Works, Corporation-owned from 1874, from whose profits Belfast City Hall was erected, opening in 1906. This self-confident building replaced the White Linen Hall in what had become the centre of the city, no longer its southern edge. Contemporary newspaper reportage expressed no regret at the loss of this elegant Georgian building, nor at the equivalent replacement of St Anne's parish church (also demolished in 1898; Figure 2.12) with the new, largely Romanesque cathedral being built in its place. At a public meeting just one person 'thought it would be a pity to do away with the handsome front of the

FIGURE 2.11
Semidetached, middle-class villas in Sandford Avenue, Bloomfield, built in 1900

STEPHEN A. ROYLE

church',[68] and one correspondent to the *Belfast News Letter* wrote: 'ere this some powerful and influential voice would have been raised against the contemplated demolition of St Anne's', it being a 'good and valuable building' which 'forms a most important link between the past history of the church and its present' in a city 'bare enough of monuments and relics of the past'.[69] But these were lonely voices; an architect thought 'the removal of this church of 100 years standing [might] … be to some minds in Belfast a sad loss to architecture. I have met with a little natural sentiment about seeing the last of an old familiar institution, but no distress among people in Belfast for its removal to make way for a more noble church.'[70] There was controversy, as press letters evidence,[71] but it was largely about dogma (in cathedrals there was 'bowing down before idols and altars'[72]) class and cost[73] ('what they wanted was not a cathedral at the present time, but mission halls and mission churches and godly men').[74] As the century ended Belfast people looked forward: 'very proud of ourselves … a cathedral … will be in keeping with our commercial greatness, and being so will of necessity be the finest church of its class in Ireland, even as Belfast is by far the first and foremost of Irish cities'.[75]

The new city was graced also by high Victorian splendours such as the Grand Opera House (1894–95), the Crown bar (1839–40; the famed interior is 1885[76]) and the more mannered buildings of Charles Lanyon, whose Queen's College (1849) helped to make south Belfast the city's premier high status area. An Ordnance Survey map (Figure 2.13) depicts a crowded, intensely built-up industrial city in 1902 whose appearance and functions could hardly have been anticipated from its humble seventeenth-century origins, although the original street pattern can still be recognised.

CONCLUSION

Belfast at the start of the twentieth century was a port and industrial city of a type common in Britain, if rare in Ireland; perhaps only Londonderry on a smaller scale was similar. Belfast's economy was dominated by shipbuilding, textile manufacture and engineering, its townscape by the terraced houses of industrial workers. Semidetached and detached houses were further out. Trams rattling their way into the new century, together with the network of railway lines, knitted city and region

FIGURE 2.12
St Anne's parish church, Belfast, *c.* 1865, demolished in 1898 to make way for the new cathedral

ULSTER MUSEUM

together. The transport hub was the city centre, providing access to the cathedrals of the new age found therein – not just St Anne's and St Peter's (the latter was completed in 1866), but cathedrals of commerce, such as department stores Anderson and McAuley, founded in 1861 in a five-storey building in Donegall Place of 1895–99, and Robinson and Cleaver's (Figure 2.14), founded in 1870, in a six-storey building on the corner of Donegall Place and Donegall Square North built in 1886–88. Opposite, to be unveiled in 1906, was that cathedral of civic power, Belfast City Hall.

FIGURE 2.13
Ordnance Survey map
of central Belfast, 1902

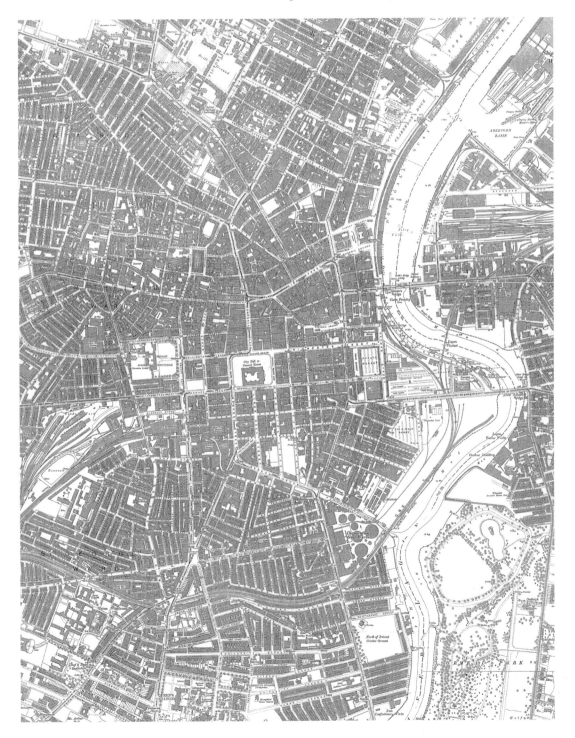

Belfast was reasonably prosperous and quiescent, Home Rule stresses had eased after the defeat of the 1893 Bill, the building boom was under way, and Harland and Wolff had just launched the world's biggest ship, the 17,204-ton *Oceanic II*.[77] The city looked to a bright future but, with hindsight, one can recognise all the signs of trouble ahead. 'See Belfast, devout and profane and hard,' wrote Belfastman Louis MacNeice in 1935.[78] The three adjectives applied equally to the turn of the century. 'Hard' certainly, this was an industrial city. 'Devout', expressed in the number and variety of religious buildings. 'Profane', regarding the unseemly contestation between the adherents of the Christian faiths who worshipped the same God. This sectarianism had already been expressed violently, though never so acutely as it was during the Troubles the twentieth century was to unleash on the people of Belfast, who were destined to inherit these long-established divisions.

FIGURE 2.14
The staircase at
Robinson and Cleaver's
ULSTER MUSEUM

NOTES

1 Gillespie, R., and Royle, S.A. (2003) Irish Historic Towns Atlas, no. 12, *Belfast, part I, to 1840*, Royal Irish Academy: Dublin; in association with Belfast City Council.

2 Benn, G. (1877) *A history of the town of Belfast from the earliest times to the close of the eighteenth century*, Marcus Ward: London, pp. 39–40; Wilson, B. (1967) 'The birth of Belfast', in J.C. Beckett and R.E. Glasscock (eds) *Belfast: origin and growth of an industrial city*, BBC: London, pp. 14–25.

3 Bardon, J. (1982) *Belfast: an illustrated history*, Blackstaff Press: Belfast.

4 Robinson, P. (1996) 'Carrickfergus', in A. Simms, H.B. Clarke and R. Gillespie (eds), *Irish Historic Towns Atlas*, vol. I, Royal Irish Academy: Dublin.

5 Gillespie, R. (1995) 'Landlords and merchants: Belfast 1600–1750', in H.B. Clarke (ed.) *Irish cities*, Mercier Press: Cork, pp. 14–27.

6 Roebuck, P. (1979) 'The making of an Ulster great estate: the Chichesters, barons of Belfast and viscounts of Carrickfergus, 1559–1648', *Proceedings of the Royal Irish Academy*, 79 C, pp. 1– 26; Gillespie and Royle (2003) *Belfast*.

7 Beckett, J.C. (1983) 'Belfast to the end of the eighteenth century', in J.C. Beckett, et al., *Belfast: the making of the city*, Appletree Press: Belfast, pp. 13–26; Bardon, J., and Burnett,

D. (1996) *Belfast: a pocket history*, Blackstaff Press: Belfast. Agnew, by contrast calculated the population at 3,200 in 1669: Agnew, J. (1996) *Belfast merchant families in the seventeenth century*, Four Courts Press: Dublin.

8   As in Bardon (1982) *Belfast*, p. 27.

9   See the discussion of the four Phillips maps and the 1696 map in Gillespie and Royle (2003) *Belfast*, Appendix A.

10   Bardon, J. (1992) *A history of Ulster*, Blackstaff Press: Belfast.

11   Benn, G. (1823) *The history of the town of Belfast*, A. Mackay: Belfast (reprinted Davidson Books: Ballynahinch, 1979), p. 72; see also Patton, M. (1993) *Central Belfast: an historical gazetteer*, Ulster Architectural Heritage Society: Belfast, pp. 47–48.

12   Jones, E. (1952) 'Belfast: a survey of the city', in E. Jones (ed.) *Belfast in its regional setting: a scientific survey*, British Association for the Advancement of Science: Belfast, p. 203.

13   Gillespie and Royle (2003) *Belfast*.

14   Beckett, J. C. (1967) 'The seventeenth century', in Beckett and Glasscock (1967) *Belfast*, pp. 26–38.

15   Owen, D.J. (1917) *A short history of the Port of Belfast*, Mayne, Boyd and Son: Belfast, p. 5.

16   Beckett (1967) 'The seventeenth century', identified sixty-seven Belfast-owned ships in 1682.

17   Beckett (1983) 'Belfast to the end of the eighteenth century'.

18   Agnew (1996) *Belfast*.

19   Kennedy, D. (1967) 'The early eighteenth century', in Beckett and Glasscock (1967) *Belfast*, p. 40.

20   Kennedy (1967) 'The early eighteenth century', pp. 44–45.

21   Sacheverell, W. (1702) *An account of the Isle of Man … with a voyage to I-Columb-Kill*, J. Hartley, R. Gibson and T. Hobson: London, p. 125.

22   Gillespie (1995) 'Landlords'.

23   Larmour, P. (1987) *Belfast: an illustrated architectural guide*, Friar's Bush Press: Belfast.

24   *Belfast News Letter* (1799) 15 January.

25   *Belfast News Letter* (1799) 15 January.

26   Bardon and Burnett (1996) *Belfast*, p. 15; see also Maguire, W.A. (1984) *Living like a lord: the second marquis of Donegall, 1769–1844*, Appletree Press: Belfast, p. 12.

27   Gillespie and Royle (2003) *Belfast*.

28   Brett, C.E.B. (1985) *Buildings of Belfast 1700–1914*, Friar's Bush Press: Belfast.

29   Hayward, R. (1952) *Belfast through the ages*, Dundalgan Press: Dundalk.

30   Royle, S.A. (1991) 'The socio-spatial structure of Belfast in 1837: evidence from the First Valuation', *Irish Geography*, 24, pp. 1–9.

31   Cited in Beckett (1983) 'Belfast to the end of the eighteenth century', p. 26; see also Hewitt, J. (1983) '"The Northern Athens" and after', in Beckett and Glasscock (1967) *Belfast*, pp. 71–82.

32   See the sections of the 'Topographical Information' in Gillespie and Royle (2003) *Belfast*, Education is Section 20, Entertainment is Section 21.

33   Kennedy (1967) 'The early eighteenth century'.

34   Hayward (1952) *Belfast*, p. 32. See also Colgan, B. (1984) *St Mary's, Chapel Lane 1784–1984*, Ronan Press: Lurgan.

35   Curtain, N. (1994) *The United Irishmen*, Clarendon Press: Oxford; Gray, J. (1998) *The sans culottes of Belfast: the United Irishmen and the men of no property*, Belfast Trades Union Council and the United Irishmen Commemoration Society: Belfast.

36   Attributed to Lord Downshire, cited in Gray, J. (1996) 'A tale of two newspapers: the contest between the *Belfast News Letter* and the *Northern Star* in the 1790s', in J. Gray and W. McCann (eds) *An uncommon bookman: essays in memory of J.R.R. Adams*, Linen Hall Library: Belfast, p. 9.

37   Gray (1996) 'A tale of two newspapers'.

38   Benn (1823) *History*, p. 64.

39   *Belfast News Letter* (1798) 7 August; 7 September.

40   *Belfast News Letter* (1798) 9 November.

41   Gillespie and Royle (2003) *Belfast*.

42   Owen (1917) *A short history*.

43   Dickson, R.J. (1966) *Ulster migration to colonial America*, Routledge and Kegan Paul: London; Royle, S.A., and Ní Laoire, C. (2006) '"Dare the boist'rous main": the process of Scots-Irish emigration to North America, 1760–1800', *Canadian Geographer*, 50.1, pp. 55–72.

44   *Belfast News Letter* (1800) 1 August.

45   Young, R.M. (ed.) (1892) *The townbook of the corporation of Belfast*, M. Ward: Belfast.

46   McDowell, R.B. (1967) 'The late eighteenth century', in Beckett and Glasscock (1967) *Belfast*, pp. 55–66.

47   *Belfast News Letter* (1791) 10 July.

48   *Belfast News Letter* (1828) 1 July.

49   Royle, S.A. (1995) 'The growth and decline of an industrial city: Belfast from 1750', in Clarke (1995) *Irish cities*, pp. 28–40.

50   See, for example, O'Connor, E., and Parkhill, T. (eds) (1992) *A life in Linenopolis: the memoirs of William Topping, Belfast Damask weaver, 1903–56*, Ulster Historical Foundation: Belfast.

51   Bardon (1982) *Belfast*.

52   Messenger, B. *Picking up the linen threads: a study in industrial folklore*, Blackstaff Press: Belfast; Bardon (1982) *Belfast*.

53   Bardon (1982) *Belfast*.

54   Black, E. (1988) *The people's park: the Queen's Island, Belfast, 1849–1879*, Linen Hall Library: Belfast; Scott, R. (2000) *A breath of fresh air: the story of Belfast's parks*, Blackstaff Press: Belfast.

55   *Belfast News Letter* (1820) 14 March.

56   Lynch, J.P. (2001) *An unlikely success story: the Belfast shipbuilding industry, 1880–1935*, The Belfast Society: Belfast, p. 9.

57   Lynch (2001) *Belfast shipbuilding*, notes that of 100,809 manufacturing workers in Belfast in 1905 43.7 per cent were female, an unusually high proportion for a shipbuilding city.

58   Lynch (2001) *Belfast shipbuilding*; Moss, M.S., and Hume, J.R. (1986) *Shipbuilders to the world: 125 years of Harland and Wolff*, Blackstaff Press: Belfast.

59   Lynch, J. (2004) *Forgotten shipbuilders of Belfast: Workman, Clark, 1880–1935*, Friar's Bush Press: Belfast.

60   Royle, S.A., Boal, F.W., and Pringle, M.E. (1983) 'New information on the development of Ballymacarrett: Lord Templemore's plan of 1853', *Ulster Journal of Archaeology*, 46, pp. 137–41.

61   Maguire, W.A. (1976) 'Lord Donegall and the sale of Belfast: a case history from the Encumbered Estates Court', *Economic History Review*, 29.4, pp. 570–84.

62   Maguire, W.A. (1993) *Belfast*, Ryburn: Keele.

63   Scott (2000) *Belfast's parks*.

64   Bardon (1982) *Belfast*, p. 125.

65   Froggatt, P. (1981) 'Industrialisation and health in Belfast in the early nineteenth century', in D. Harkness and M. O'Dowd (eds) *The town in Ireland*, Appletree Press: Belfast, pp. 155–85.

66   Royle (1991) 'Belfast in 1837'.

67   Campbell, R.T., and Royle, S.A. (1997) 'East Belfast and the suburbanization of north-west County Down in the nineteenth century', in L.J. Proudfoot (ed.) *Down: history and society, interdisciplinary essays on the history of an Irish county*, Geography Publications: Dublin, pp. 629–62.

68   *Belfast News Letter* (1895) 11 April.

69   *Belfast Telegraph* (1895) 25 April.

70   *Irish Builder* (1899) 1 October.

71   *Belfast Telegraph* (1895) 25 April; *Belfast Weekly Telegraph* (1895) 25 May; *Belfast News Letter* (1895) 15 June, and 8, 9, 11, 12, 14, 16, 17, 18, 19 and 21 October.

72   *Belfast News Letter* (1895) 7 June.

73   *Belfast News Letter* (1895) 11 October.

74   *Belfast Weekly Telegraph* (1895) 15 June.

75   *Irish Ecclesiastical Gazette* (1895) 21 June.

76   Patton (1993) *Central Belfast*.

77   Bardon (1982) *Belfast*.

78   MacNeice, L. (1935) 'Valediction', in L. MacNeice (1966) *Collected poems*, Faber and Faber: London.

FIGURE S.2
The *Titanic* in the final stages of construction

Nuts and Bolts

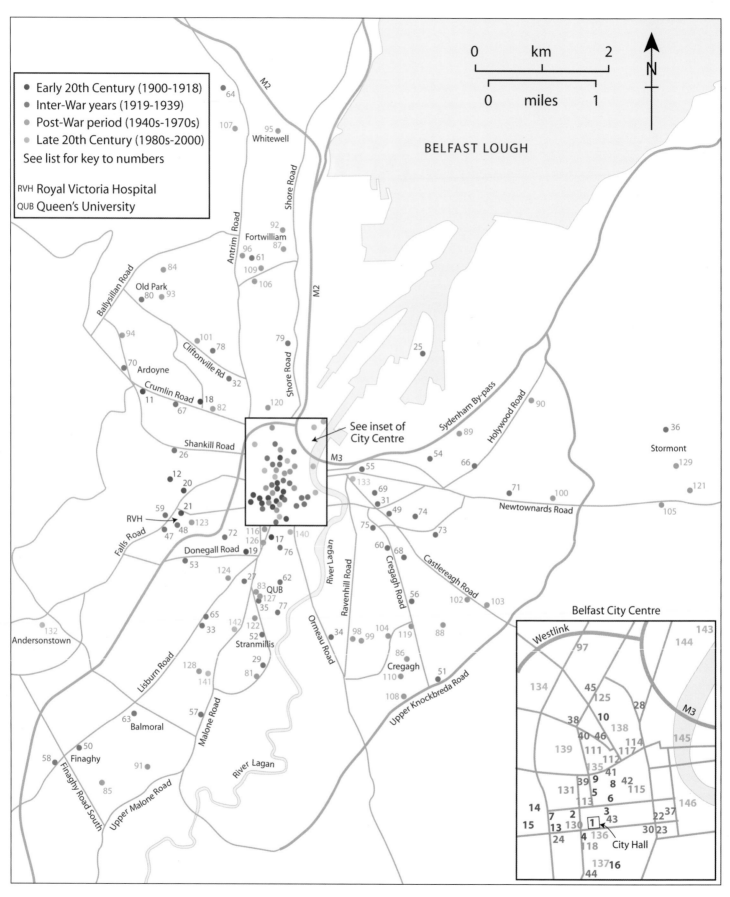

FIGURE 3.1
Notable twentieth-century buildings in Belfast (see corresponding numbered list of buildings at end of chapter, pp. 52–53)

PAUL LARMOUR

The essential shape and form of central Belfast was established well before the twentieth century, with an organic layout from at least as early as the seventeenth century at its core, fringed by an eighteenth-century grid, while its overall 'historic' architectural character was determined largely in the nineteenth century when Belfast became the most important commercial manufacturing centre in Ireland. Many of the city's most significant public buildings were erected in the Victorian era. It was in such a context that the architects of Belfast were to build in the twentieth century, from its opening phase, the Edwardian era, whose architecture was to some extent a late extension of the Victorian in terms of character, through later phases, displaying various shades of 'modernity' in design, until the end of the century.

3

Bricks, Stone, Concrete and Steel

The Built Fabric of Twentieth-Century Belfast

Paul Larmour

FIGURE 3.2
Clarence Gallery, Clarence Street, by
Robinson Patterson Partnership, 1988

SCENIC IRELAND

While buildings of earlier stages in the history of Belfast still form an important part of the fabric of the twentieth-century city and provide the foil to much of its later development, this is not the place to recount them in detail. They have been identified and described elsewhere.[1] Some of the city's twentieth-century architecture has also been identified and published elsewhere, but in surveys of limited scope.[2] Thematic surveys of types and styles can highlight the period in detail, but for the general story of buildings in Belfast over the whole of the century a broadly chronological approach is useful. A glossary of architectural terms is to be found at the end of this chapter.

THE EDWARDIAN ERA: PROVINCIAL POMP

The twentieth century in Belfast opened with a number of important works in progress, most notably the City Hall (Figure 3.3; the location of this and other buildings mentioned in the text is found in Figure 3.1). It had been started at the end of the previous century with a competition in 1896 which was won by a then relatively unknown English architect, Alfred Brumwell Thomas,[3] to whom the building brought fame, wealth, and a knighthood when it opened in 1906. A magnificent building, one of the most important examples of the Baroque Revival anywhere in the British Isles, it is built of Portland stone with features derived from prominent classical buildings in

FIGURE 3.3
Belfast City Hall, Donegall Square, by Alfred Brumwell Thomas, 1896–1906

SCENIC IRELAND

London, particularly St Paul's Cathedral, which inspired the form of its central dome and its corner cupolas, with plentiful use internally of Italian and Greek marbles, oak panelling, rich plasterwork and heraldic glass. A perfect expression of the prosperity and civic pride of the city at the turn of the century, it is the complete embodiment of Edwardian splendour and still dominates the city centre a century after its opening.

The City Hall was built on the site of the old White Linen Hall, a modest late eighteenth-century building that was demolished in the early 1890s to make way for the new municipal centrepiece. Following this lead, much of the remaining small scale eighteenth- to early nineteenth-century development around Donegall Square was replaced at the turn of the century by more grandiose commercial buildings. In the stylistic free-for-all that marked this period in architecture everywhere in the British Isles, their treatments varied. The Scottish Provident Institution, occupying much of Donegall Square West, completed in 1902 to the designs of Young and Mackenzie,[4] responded to the City Hall in its Baroque Revivalism executed in pale Giffnock sandstone, whereas the Ocean Buildings on the opposite side, on Donegall Square East, also completed in 1902 and designed by the same architects, is an embattled and towering gabled pile in red sandstone overlaid with oriels and Late Gothic detail. The inconsistency in styling between these two buildings of similar function was hardly due to carelessness but more likely the result of the clients' desire to look different from their rivals. Shortly afterwards, a third large commercial office block was added to the surroundings of the City Hall – the Scottish Temperance Buildings on Donegall Square South, built in 1904 to the designs of Henry Seaver,[5] also in red Scottish sandstone but in a turreted and gabled style reminiscent of French châteaux and Scottish castles.

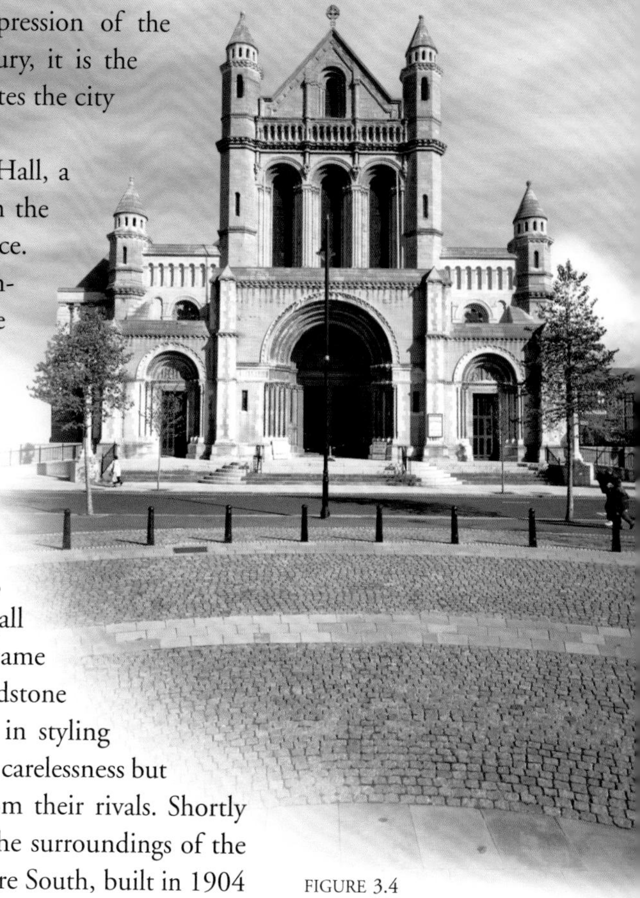

Elsewhere in the city centre some other new buildings at the start of the century showed the influence of Art Nouveau, that most vital new style that swept much of Europe at the time but which had only a slight impact on Irish architecture. Its wavy lines can be seen at 36 Donegall Place, designed for the jeweller and clockmaker Sharman D. Neill by Vincent Craig in 1903, and in the ground floor of Chichester Buildings, Chichester Street, by Thomas Houston in 1906, while some of its decorative details embellish the former Crymble's Music Depot, 58 Wellington Place (1903), by W.J.W. Roome,[6] the Mayfair Building, Arthur Square, by Blackwood and Jury (1906), and most notably the same architects' Castle Buildings, Castle Place (1904–07), a steel-framed building with a ceramic facing of Doulton's 'Carraraware'. With its well-modelled frieze and spandrel panels of swirling pomegranates and foliage, it has the most striking Art Nouveau façade in Ireland.[7]

Just as the City Hall had been conceived and started in the late Victorian era but not opened until the early years of the new century, so too was another large public monument, St Anne's Church of Ireland Cathedral in Donegall Street (Figure 3.4),

FIGURE 3.4
St Anne's Cathedral, by Thomas Drew, consecrated in 1904

SCENIC IRELAND

33

FIGURE 3.5
Presbyterian Assembly
Buildings, Fisherwick Place,
by Young and Mackenzie,
1900–05

PAUL LARMOUR

FIGURE 3.6
Side view of Municipal Technical
Institute, College Square East, by
Samuel Stevenson, 1900–07

PAUL LARMOUR

designed in 1898 by Thomas Drew[8] in French Romanesque style and consecrated in 1904 (although far from being complete at that time). Like the City Hall, it, too, was built at the expense of a prominent landmark of the Georgian town, the old parish church of St Anne (see chapter 2).

The mid to late nineteenth century had seen a vast number of churches being built for all denominations in Belfast, the nineteenth century being the great church-building period in Ireland generally, and so there were comparatively few new churches needed in the Edwardian era. Those that were built perpetuated the conservative and conventional historic-style Revivalism that had characterised the Victorian era. The most prominent examples were Holy Cross Roman Catholic Church, Crumlin Road (1900–02), in Lombardic Romanesque style, by Doolin, Butler and Donnelly of Dublin, and the Roman Catholic Church of the Most Holy Redeemer, Clonard Gardens (1908–11), in French Gothic style, by J.J. McDonnell, both built, like most of the new churches, well beyond the city centre. The Presbyterian Assembly Buildings (1900–05), built as the headquarters of the Presbyterian Church in Ireland rather than as a congregational church, were, however, located in the city centre, in Fisherwick Place, and formed one of its most prominent and enduring landmarks (Figure 3.5). Designed by Young and Mackenzie, they were built of sandstone in a Tudor style with a welter of Late Gothic detail and distinctly Scottish features, such as corbelled turrets and a crown spire reminiscent of St Giles' Cathedral in Edinburgh.

At the same time, not far to the north, in College Square East, and still forming a splendid focus along Great Victoria Street, was built the Municipal Technical Institute (1900–07), a massive Baroque Revival building in Portland stone designed by Samuel Stevenson, echoing to some extent the style of the City Hall but not so distinguished in design (Figure 3.6). It is very similar in overall form and mass to such contemporaries in England as the War Office in Whitehall, London (1898–1906), and the Mersey Docks and Harbour Board Building in Liverpool (1903–07). The Technical Institute masked part of the early nineteenth-century Academical Institution's façade behind it, and at the same time diminished the effect of one of the rare spaces of Georgian planned formality in Belfast, but its grandiose bulk did add greatly to the image of imperial splendour in the city centre.

The memory of the generally small scale development and residential character of the Georgian town receded further in the Edwardian era, when the terraced houses along the south side of College Square were replaced by the County Down Weaving Company's factory in Murray Street (1908–10), designed by James Hanna, its looming mass originally relieved by copper cupolas. Hanna's warehouses and factories were visually the most interesting industrial buildings of the Edwardian era in Belfast, being enlivened by freely treated Classical touches and zoomorphic carvings, as at the former Walpole Brothers' warehouse at 19 and 21 Alfred Street (1911–12). Of more plain appearance but more constructionally advanced were Somerset's Linen Factory, Hardcastle Street, by W.J.W. Roome (1904), the first reinforced concrete framed building in Ireland, and the Albion Works, Wenwood Street, by Watt and Tulloch (1909), built using the same French-originated Hennebique system of reinforced concrete floors and internal pillars, with exterior wall fillings of red brick. When first built, these warehouses stood in the midst of densely packed streets of workers' terraced houses on the fringe of the city's commercial centre, but that type of housing layout was largely swept away in the 1980s.

Standing in a similar relationship to the same type of residential development, although further out from the city centre, were the public libraries of the Edwardian years. These were the Ballymacarrett Branch Public Library of 1902–03 (now demolished), by Blackwood and Jury, and the Carnegie Libraries designed by Watt and Tulloch at Oldpark Road (1905–06), Donegall Road (1907–09; Figure 3.7), and Falls Road (1905–08), all in a free Tudor style in red brick with sandstone details, except for the Falls Road branch, which is in that Edwardian form of English Classical style popularly and flippantly known as 'Wrenaissance', in reference to the influence of Sir Christopher Wren.

FIGURE 3.7
Carnegie Library, Donega
Road, by Watt and
Tulloch, 1907–09

FIGURE 3.8
Telephone House, Cromac
Street, by the Northern Ireland
Office of Works, 1932–34

SCENIC IRELAND

A similar affection for the English Renaissance determined the architectural style of the original Royal Victoria Hospital of 1900–03 on Grosvenor Road (now demolished), designed by the English architects Henman and Cooper of Birmingham, but such a conventional dressing belied the special importance of its internal planning and mechanical services, which were the most up to date of their time.[10] Its innovative design represented a revolution in hospital layout, while it also appears to have been the first major building in the world to have been fully air-conditioned for human comfort (see chapter 14). For a general hospital its location was not a central one, but after much discussion at the time it had been concluded that the healthy and elevated site on what was then open ground was sufficient compensation for the long distance from the docks and the shipbuilding yards.

Even further out from the city centre, the Edwardian era saw an increasing number of attractive and picturesque suburban villas being built in 'old English' style, particularly in Malone and Stranmillis to the south of the city,[11] and Knock to the east, but also in smaller enclaves such as Cliftonville to the north. The style was characterised by half-timbered gables and roughcast walls, often with red tiled roofs, leaded windows, and Art Nouveau or Arts and Crafts details, while the settings were deliberately leafy in a conscious attempt by the middle classes to escape from the rigours of the industrial city and adopt the guise of the countryside. Most new housing in the early years of the century was, however, built of plain red brick, whether in seemingly endless terraces for the working classes located close to the factories and foundries, or rather roomier detached villas for their wealthier fellow citizens.

THE INTERWAR YEARS: CAPITAL STATUS

It was only slowly after the First World War that there were any further important additions to the architecture of Belfast or noticeable changes to the appearance of the city. There were a few new buildings designed in a conventional Classical taste – including the Northern Bank of 1919 by Godfrey Ferguson, and the Ulster Bank of 1919–22 by James Hanna, opposite each other in Victoria Street and Cromac Street respectively, and, on a larger scale, the red sandstone Presbyterian War Memorial Hostel in Howard Street (1922–25), designed by John Young of Young and Mackenzie in a 'stripped Classical' style, also in the city centre – as well as the Harbour Power Station of 1919–23 (now demolished), at Wolff Road, an impressive red brick building designed by James Gamble, built far from the city centre. Otherwise, nothing of special significance was built by the early 1920s. In the mid to late 1920s other buildings in restrained Classical style were the public library, Shankill Road (1926–28) by T.W. Henry, the Agriculture Building (now the School of Geography, Archaeology and Palaeoecology) for Queen's University in Elmwood Avenue (1924–28) and the Central Labour Exchange in Corporation Street (1926), both by the Northern Ireland Office of Works under the direction of its chief architect, Roland Ingleby Smith.

The most outstanding example of the work produced in the new government architect's office in the interwar years was Stranmillis College, Stranmillis Road (1928–30), a teachers' training college built in the southern suburbs and designed in the office's usual neo-Georgian style in rustic brick with stone details, while their most prominent building in the city centre was the towering Telephone House (Figure 3.8), containing the central telephone exchange for the city, in Cromac Street (1932–34). It was a massive steel-framed building, block-clad in granite, grey brickwork and Portland stone; more modernistic in style than neo-Georgian, as befitted its modern function and largely engineering purpose. The silver-grey bricks were apparently chosen over Belfast's more usual red bricks so as to avoid any suggestion of overweight and to achieve as much of a sense of lightness as possible in such a massive building. There were also nine small satellite exchanges built at different points in the city well beyond the centre in the early 1930s, in such places as Paulett Avenue, Clifton Park Avenue, Lisburn Road and Ormeau Road, providing visible evidence of the spread of this new method of communication. Those that were not later remodelled are easily identifiable by their conventional treatment in rustic brick with flat parapet roofs and small-paned windows.

The period between the two world wars saw Belfast enriched by three large and important new public buildings by outside architects, all of Portland stone in full-blooded Classical style. The earliest of the trio was the Municipal Museum and Art Gallery in the Botanic Gardens on Stranmillis Road, originally designed in 1913–14 by James Cumming Wynnes of Edinburgh but delayed in construction by the First World War until 1924–29, when only one wing of the original scheme was actually completed; it was to stand unfinished until the modern extension of 1963–71. Much less exuberant than the City Hall, the museum was conceived in a rather academic neo-Classical mood, its choice of Ionic order influenced, no doubt, by the recent extension to the British Museum.

The other two important public buildings were built as a consequence of the city's newly gained capital status following the establishment of the state of Northern Ireland.

FIGURE 3.9
Parliament Buildings, Stormont, Upper Newtownards Road, by Arthur Thornley, 1927–32
SCENIC IRELAND

The first of these was Parliament Buildings (1927–32) at Stormont, magnificently sited in a commanding situation in a large park to the east of the city and 4 miles (6.4 km) from its centre (Figure 3.9). It was designed by Arnold Thornley of Liverpool in a rather severe neo-Classical style of Greek character, with a formally planned interior containing an abundance of carved, modelled and coloured ornament. The building was placed at the top of a broad processional avenue that rises gradually for three-quarters of a mile (1.2 km) from the main road and culminates in a flight of approach steps 90 feet (27.4 m) wide. Fine entrance gateways to Upper Newtownards Road and to Massey Avenue, together with porters' lodges of Portland stone in appropriate style, completed the well-organised setting. Like A.B. Thomas at the City Hall, Thornley was knighted following completion of the whole project.

The other big government-sponsored monument of the new state was the Royal Courts of Justice (1928–33), built in the city centre (Figure 3.10). Designed by James G. West of the Imperial Office of Works in London, this steel-framed building, with giant Corinthian-columned recessed porticoes leading to a large marble-lined central hall, is one of the grandest buildings in Belfast, with frontages to three streets – Chichester Street, May Street and Oxford Street. The provision of foundations for the Law Courts, incidentally, gave some trouble, as it stood in one of the most water-logged parts of the city and it was found necessary to drive over 1,000 reinforced concrete piles, averaging 54 feet (16.5 m) long, into the stiff red clay which lay about 40 feet (12.2 m) below the surface.

With the completion of the Law Courts, followed shortly afterwards by Telephone House, the old 'markets area' of the city had undergone an architectural transformation in line with the new Northern Ireland government's aim to improve the city's architecture so far as it lay in its power to do so. Indeed, it had been originally intended at the outset to have the Law Courts built in Portland stone, but just before construction began, the British government, committed to build them in pursuance of

FIGURE 3.10
The Royal Courts of Justice,
Chichester Street, by
James G. West, 1928–33

SCENIC IRELAND

the Government of Ireland Act, 1920, decided to reduce the cost by substituting stone with brick. The Northern Ireland government took exception, their view being that so important and large a building should be of stone, and despite the adamant stance of the authorities in London, undertook to defray the difference in cost between brick and stone. By the early 1930s, with the Law Courts, Parliament Buildings, Telephone House and the museum, the city could boast of architecture to match its new capital status.

The interwar years were not all neo-Classical or neo-Georgian. The Bank of Ireland in Royal Avenue (1928–30), designed by McDonnell, Dixon and Downes of Dublin, introduced the 'modern' style to Belfast (Figure 3.11). Steel-framed, clad in Portland stone, with Art Deco details, it made the most of a narrow site in one of the finest positions in the city centre, at the corner of Royal Avenue and Upper North Street. The way its modern design made it stand out in distinctive fashion was noted by a few other commercial enterprises and its example was followed with varying degrees of success by the likes of Donegall Chambers in Donegall Place, designed by Kendrick Edwards in 1932, and the former Sinclair's Department Store, Royal Avenue, designed by James Scott in 1935, on a site directly opposite the new Bank of Ireland. The jazzy 'step-form' gabled façade of Sinclair's was faced with cream-coloured faience, a ceramic material that became much in vogue throughout the British Isles in the interwar era, particularly for buildings of modernistic design.

FIGURE 3.11
Bank of Ireland, Royal Avenue

SCENIC IRELAND

A conspicuous addition was made to the commercial heart of the city in 1929–30 with the building of the Woolworth's 'super-store' on a historic site at the corner of High Street and Cornmarket, previously occupied by an unremarkable Victorian warehouse but originally the site of the old seventeenth-century market house, in its time the town's most important public building. Steel-framed with a facing of artificial stone bearing Art Deco details, the Woolworth's block, which was partly built for the gentlemen's outfitters Montague Burton, was designed by W. Priddle of London and built by the Woolworth's Construction Department of Liverpool. Shortly afterwards, in 1931–32, a shop of similar stylistic treatment but very much smaller, decorated with elephant heads, was built for Burton's at 25–27 Ann Street to the designs of Harry Wilson of Leeds.

New buildings elsewhere in the city centre included the white-tiled Imperial House, Donegall Square East (1935) by Kendrick Edwards, the ponderously dull BBC Headquarters of 1936–38 in Ormeau Avenue by James Miller of Glasgow, torn between neo-Georgian and 'modern' styling, and the equally imposing Belfast Co-operative Society's large extension of 1930–32, designed by Samuel Stevenson in a rather old-fashioned Classical style, but one which brought some architectural dignity and importance to York Street. Of a number of new shopping arcades established in the interwar years North Street Arcade of 1936, with a front also on Donegall Street, was the most substantial and enduring, designed in overtly modern style by Cowser and Smyth.

Well beyond the city centre the Royal Victoria Hospital site was consolidated by the addition of the new Belfast Hospital for Sick Children on Falls Road (1928–32) by Tulloch and Fitzsimons, and the Royal Maternity Hospital (1932–33) by Young and Mackenzie, both offering improved and enlarged facilities over outmoded nineteenth-century predecessors in the inner city. Both new hospitals were in versions of neo-Georgian style. A similarly conservative architectural taste governed church building at the time, in a field where traditional values were paramount. Accomplished examples of interwar churches, all in fairly conventionally treated Romanesque or Gothic Revival styles, included, for the Church of Ireland: St Clement's, Templemore Avenue (1928–30), and St Polycarp's, Upper Lisburn Road (1929–32), by Blackwood and Jury; St Finian's, Cregagh Park (1930), and St Bartholomew's, Stranmillis Road (1930), by W.D.R. Taggart; St Simon's, Donegall Road (1930), by R.M. Close; St Christopher's, Mersey Street (1931), by R.H. Gibson and H. Seaver, and St Martin's, Kenilworth Street (1933), by Seaver alone. For the Presbyterians there was Cregagh Road (1927) by J.C. Stevenson, McCracken Memorial, Malone Road (1932), by Hobart and Heron, and Lowe Memorial, Upper Lisburn Road (1933–34), by Tulloch and Fitzsimons; and for the Roman Catholics there was the Dominican College Chapel, Falls Road (1926–30), St Anthony's, Woodstock Road (1936–38), and St Therese's, Somerton Road (1936–39), all by Padraic Gregory.[12] One of the more unusual and most attractive new churches was the First Church of Christ Scientist, University Avenue (1936–37), by Clough Williams-Ellis of London, in a form of neo-Georgian.

Two buildings in strikingly modern style were the King's Hall of 1933–34 (Figure 3.12), a very large exhibition hall by Leitch and Partners of London for the Royal Ulster Agricultural Society, forming a prominent landmark on the Lisburn Road, which was the main approach to the city from the south, and the Floral Hall of 1935–36, a place of recreation and entertainment in Hazelwood Gardens (now in the grounds of Belfast Zoo), Antrim Road, designed by David Boyd. Modern styling was also the hallmark of an extensive series of cinemas built during the boom period of cinema popularity in the 1930s, usually in the form of Art Deco façades, sometimes sporting futuristic motifs, but occasionally adopting the more muted language of the emerging International Style in architecture.[13] The largest of the thirties cinemas in Belfast, the Ritz in Fisherwick Place of 1935–36, was designed by outside architects Kemp and Tasker of London, and located in the city centre, but the rest were the work of local men, among whom a few specialists emerged, and were dispersed around the suburban residential areas. The most characteristic examples were by John McBride Neill,[14] and included the Apollo, Ormeau Road (1933), the Picturedrome, Mountpottinger Road (1934), the Majestic, Lisburn Road (1935–36), the Strand, Holywood Road (1935), the Curzon, Ormeau Road (1935–36), the Troxy, Shore Road (1935–6), and the Forum, Crumlin Road (1937). Another series was designed by Thomas McLean and included the Savoy, Crumlin Road (1934), the Regal, Lisburn Road (1935), the Capitol, Antrim Road (1935), and the Broadway, Falls Road (1936), while the Stadium, Shankill Road (1935), was the work of Robert Sharpe Hill. The Stadium was, incidentally, at the centre of a controversy in 1935 surrounding the building of cinemas near churches in Belfast: permission to build it had at first been refused following protests from various church committees, the city Corporation having passed a general resolution under the Planning Act that prevented the erection of cinemas within 360 feet (110 m) of a place of worship, but following an appeal to the Ministry of Home Affairs, the resolution was later rescinded. Most of these cinema buildings have since been either closed or demolished (see chapter 16).

A more enduring series of buildings, and the most architecturally important of the interwar years in Belfast, were the schools built by the city's Education Committee. Its programme of well-laid out and -equipped new schools began with some designed by W.G. Davies, such as Euston Street and Templemore Avenue (later Rupert Stanley College), both dating from 1924–26, and Park Parade and Everton both of 1925–27, but it was those designed by Davies's successor, Reginald S. Wilshere, that achieved special notice. Largely owing to Wilshere's efforts, school design in Belfast was completely transformed: air and light were provided in abundance while spaciousness and cheerfulness were the dominant characteristics. In architectural styles his schools ranged from neo-Georgian of English origin to a more modernistic idiom derived from contemporary German, Scandinavian and Dutch design. Most were built in rustic brick with dressings of artificial or reconstituted stone with both flat roofs and roofs of Roman tiles. Ironically, considering their architectural merits, which were widely acknowledged, most of his schools were situated in sites well beyond the city centre, which did not allow them to make any great change in the general appearance of the city. Nevertheless, each in its own locality provided what was more often than not the only positive architectural note in surroundings that were characterised by the

FIGURE 3.12
King's Hall, Lisburn Road, by Leitch and Partners, London, 1933–34

SCENIC IRELAND

dull monotony of row upon row of plain red brick housing. Good examples include: Strandtown Primary School, North Road (1928–30), which was awarded the first Royal Institute of British Architects (RIBA) Ulster Architecture Medal in 1930; Linfield Primary School, Blythe Street (1929); Elmgrove Primary School, Beersbridge Road (1930–33); Avoniel Primary School, Avoniel Road (1933–35); Nettlefield Primary School, Radnor Street (1934-36); McQuiston Memorial (now School of Music), Donegall Pass (1934); Botanic Primary School,[15] Agincourt Avenue (1936–39); The Model Primary School, Cliftonville Road (1936); Grove Primary School, North Queen Street (1937); and Carrs Glen Primary School, Oldpark Road (1938). Wilshere's schools were widely admired, not only hailed as the first really modern schools in the whole of Ireland, but also considered to be amongst the best in the British Isles (see chapter 15).

In the house-building field in the interwar years the special features that had set some Edwardian villas apart from the normal red brick monotony of the city were adopted on a more widespread scale, but at a debased level, as street upon street of roughcast houses and terraces were built with a minimal amount of half-timbering in their gables, whether for public authority housing, or for private developments. This dilution and commercialisation of earlier Edwardian Arts and Crafts ideals brought its own monotony to the suburban housing scene in the 1920s and 1930s.

THE POSTWAR PERIOD: RECONSTRUCTION AND EXPANSION

In Belfast, as everywhere else in the United Kingdom, construction work was severely curtailed for the six years' duration of the Second World War. There were a few isolated buildings in Belfast dating from the war years, such as the Henry Garrett Building at Stranmillis College (1944), designed by T.F.O. Rippingham, and the Masonic Hall, Crumlin Road (1938–40), designed by John MacGeagh;[16] they demonstrated a continuity with the 1930s in their restrainedly modern style, in rustic brick with flat roofs. Indeed, one important building in a comparable style completed just after the war, the Sir William Whitla Hall at Queen's University, built in 1945–49, had been originally designed in 1936 and started in 1939 before construction was interrupted.

When the war ended in 1945, normal building was slow to resume in the city centre, even though there was a need for reconstruction following the German air raids of 1941 when much damage was done. Almost all the area of Bridge Street in the city centre was destroyed outright with further damage along the north side of High Street which necessitated the eventual demolition of some formerly exuberant late Victorian commercial and office buildings, while further out from the centre much of York Street was badly damaged and Charles Lanyon's majestic mid-nineteenth-century Classical-style railway station destroyed. Most of the cleared sites, some of them quite extensive, remained vacant throughout the immediate postwar era and thereby created an unfortunate image of partial dereliction that pervaded parts of the city until comparatively recent years.

The main preoccupations in the immediate postwar era were public housing and factories: places to live and places to work. A number of new housing estates were built mainly on the fringes of the city, some of them designed by the architects in the newly formed Northern Ireland Housing Trust, but others by private architects on behalf of the Trust. Most were in a straightforward and plain traditional domestic idiom, of two storeys with rectangular plans and tiled or slated pitched roofs, whether with roughcast brick walls, such as those at Sunningdale in north Belfast, designed by T.T. Houston, or with *in situ* concrete walls as at Finaghy, designed by Gibson and Taylor. One of the earliest and the most admired for its layout was Cregagh Estate (1945–50; Figure 3.13) in east Belfast, designed by T.F.O. Rippingham. It was notable in having continuous frontages with no views of back gardens. Owing to the scarcity of materials at the time, a strictly utilitarian type of design and structure was necessary, the lack of roofing tiles or slates and a shortage of bricklayers leading to the adoption of flat concrete roofs and restricting brickwork to the outer walls only. A primary school was built in the central open space in 1949, also to the designs of Rippingham, and later, shops and community buildings were built flanking the main approach to the estate.

FIGURE 3.13
Cregagh Housing Estate, Cregagh Road and Mount Merrion Avenue, by T.F.O. Rippingham, for the Northern Ireland Housing Trust, 1945–50

PAUL LARMOUR

At another flat-roofed estate, the Whitewell Estate (1947–49), Whitewell Road, in north Belfast, not only traditional forms but also traditional materials were eschewed. It was the first of a number of Trust estates in Northern Ireland built in the Orlit system of precast concrete frames, floor and roof beams, and precast concrete block walls, which had the advantages of speedy, simple erection requiring little skilled labour and little need for timber, but subsequent problems with these new materials eventually led to drastic remodelling of the buildings.

During the war, and immediately after it, the Corporation was also involved in dealing with the housing shortage. Under the direction of Wilshere, it built the Mount Vernon Estate of 1948 in north Belfast, as well as a great number of temporary prefabricated Arcon bungalows and converted Nissen huts (now replaced). Whether public or private, most housing of the postwar era bore an impoverished look in its dull red brick or plain white roughcast conformity to the exigencies of postwar economic restrictions.

As part of the effort initiated by the Ministry of Commerce to create new industry and to attract outside firms to Northern Ireland, a number of factories were built in Belfast in the late 1940s to early 1950s, the concentration being in the Castlereagh district well to the east of the city. They were generally of rustic brick with artificial stone or concrete dressings and steel-framed windows, in a fairly sober modern style, typical examples being the Lord Roberts Memorial Workshop (1946), built for the training and employment of severely disabled ex-servicemen, and the British Tabulating Machine Company factory (1948–49), one of the largest buildings of its kind in the United Kingdom. The most publicised was the 'Festival of Britain factory', designed for the Ministry of Commerce by Ferguson and McIlveen as an 'advance' factory but which formed the centrepiece of the Ulster Farm and Factory Exhibition in 1951 as part of the festival celebrations, before being taken over by the Short Brothers and Harland aircraft company.

FIGURE 3.14
The Synagogue, Somerton
Road, by Yorke, Rosenberg
and Mardall, 1961–64

SCENIC IRELAND

The 1950s saw a number of new schools being built in suburban areas. The first to be opened after the war was Sydenham Primary School, Strandburn Street (1949–51), designed by Wilshere and built largely of aluminium due to the shortage of traditional materials. Wilshere also used the Bristol system of prefabricated aluminium units, manufactured by the Shorts aircraft firm, at Ashfield Girls' High School, Holywood Road (1949–51), Annadale Grammar School, Annadale Embankment (1953), Harberton Special School, Harberton Park and Taughmonagh Primary School, Findon Gardens (1954), and Lowood Junior (now Primary) School, Sherringhurst Park (1954). For the Girls' Model Secondary School, Dunkeld Gardens (1951–56), however, Wilshere employed the Orlit system of precast concrete elements, while his Wheatfield Primary School, Alliance Road (1949–52), and Ballygolan Primary School, Serpentine Road (1955), were in rustic brick. Meanwhile, a series of schools for the Roman Catholic authorities was built to the designs of McLean and Forte, namely St Patrick's Secondary, Antrim Road (1952–55), where they used the Orlit system, St Patrick's Girls' Primary, Lancaster Street (1953–55), St Monica's Girls' Intermediate, Ravenhill Road (1954), and St Augustine's Boys' Secondary, Ravenhill Road (1958), all in a rather ponderous modern style. Two of the more interesting schools of the period were Carolan Girls' Grammar School (1958), designed by Wilshere's successor, Donald Shanks, in which a two-storeyed version of the Bristol system was combined with a natural stone 'feature' wall, and Greenwood Primary School, Upper Newtownards Road (1954–57), by Henry Lynch-Robinson, in which curtain wall glazing, with coloured panels, a hallmark of postwar modern architecture internationally, was introduced.

Church building in the 1950s was characterised by its conservative nature, some architects favouring a rather historicist neo-Gothic, with simplified detailing, as in St Barnabas' Church of Ireland, Duncairn Gardens (1955–56), and St Silas' Church of Ireland, Cliftonville Road (1956–58), both by John MacGeagh, and St John Evangelist Church of Ireland, Castlereagh Road (1955–57), by Gibson and Taylor. Others strove to achieve a more modern look while retaining a traditional layout, as at Orangefield Presbyterian Church, Castlereagh Road (1955–57), designed by Gordon McKnight. The early 1960s saw some striking blends of old and new in churches by Denis O'D. Hanna, such as the Church of the Pentecost, Mount Merrion Avenue (1961–63), and St Molua's Church, Upper Newtownards Road (1961–62), both for the Church of Ireland. The first really modern ecclesiastical building in Belfast was the Synagogue of 1961–64 on Somerton Road (Figure 3.14), designed by the internationally famous firm of Yorke,

Rosenberg and Mardall of London, of circular plan with a folded timber roof. Not long afterwards, this departure into unusual plan form was followed at St Clement's Roman Catholic Retreat Chapel, Antrim Road (1966–67), designed by Corr and McCormick of Londonderry in an oval shape with a copper-sheathed timber shell dome. Other notable modern churches in a variety of unfamiliar new forms included: St Bernadette's Roman Catholic Church, Knockbreda Road (1966), by P. and B. Gregory; the Dominican Convent Chapel in Fortwilliam Park (1964), by W.D. Bready; and St Andrew's Church, Rosetta Road, originally built as a combined Presbyterian and Methodist church (1971–73), by Gordon McKnight, an unusual case of two denominations sharing the same building.

There were few new buildings erected in the city centre in the early 1950s. An exception was the Masonic Hall of 1950 in Rosemary Street, by Young and Mackenzie, in a retrograde neo-Georgian style. A few years later the same architects were responsible for the blocks lining each side of Bridge Street, now newly widened following the widespread destruction in the blitz, the east side being rebuilt in neo-Georgian style in 1955 and the west in a more modern style in 1957. Most new building from the mid-1950s on was in uncompromisingly modern style usually characterised by the use of curtain wall glazing. Prominent examples were the Belfast (later Northern) Bank, Donegall Square North (1957–60), by Cowser and Smyth, and Transport House, High Street (1956–59), by J.J. Brennan (Figure 3.15). Built for the Amalgamated Transport and General Workers' Union, Transport House was a dramatic working of International Style architectural themes, with its upper storeys sailing out on 'pilotis' or pillars, its towered form offering a twentieth-century challenge to one of the landmarks of the old Victorian city, the Albert Memorial clock tower standing on the other side of Victoria Street.

Taller blocks followed in the city centre area at the College of Technology, Millfield, of 1956–60 (now demolished), by Gibson and Taylor, Churchill House, Victoria Square, of 1963–66 (also now demolished), a very dominant 'tower and podium' arrangement of government offices, designed by Harry Wightman of the Ministry of Finance, and Fanum House, Great Victoria Street (1967–68), by Ian Campbell, impressive in its austerity. Shortly afterwards came River House, High Street (1970), another 'tower and podium' office block, designed by James Munce Partnership, and the rather overpoweringly tall Windsor House in Bedford Street. Similarly conspicuous tall blocks appeared on the skyline beyond the city centre, including multistorey flats at Cregagh Estate (1958–61), the first of their type in Northern Ireland, built by the Northern Ireland Housing Trust, and Artillery Flats, North Queen Street (1961), designed by the City Architect's Department under J.H. Swann. Displaying somewhat more panache were Dundonald House, Upper Newtownards Road (1961–63), built as government offices

FIGURE 3.15
Transport House, High Street, by J.J. Brennan, 1956–59
SCENIC IRELAND

by Gibson and Taylor, and the Ashby Institute, Stranmillis Road (1960–65), designed for Queen's University by Cruickshank and Seward of Manchester. Such multistorey blocks were fairly few and far between, peppering the city's skyline at intervals rather than clustered together, in most cases built perhaps more as a result of a compulsive desire to demonstrate the city's modern aspirations, in conformity with a prevailing international urban fashion elsewhere, than as a strict necessity caused by any lack of local building space.

FIGURE 3.16
Ulster Museum, Botanic Gardens, extension by Francis Pym, 1963–71

PAUL LARMOUR

Other notable buildings of the 1960s, whose bold forms in concrete or steel with extensive areas of glazing underlined the supremacy of the 'modern movement' in architecture by this time, included the Microbiology Building at the Royal Victoria Hospital (1961), mainly in precast concrete, by Casson and Condor of London, the Medical Biology Centre, Lisburn Road (1963–68), by Samuel Stevenson and Sons for Queen's University, where the original balance of building masses with open space in front was all important, but has now been altered, and the Ulster College of Art and Design, York Street (1960–70), designed by Donald Shanks for the Belfast Education Department, another prominent building whose original appearance is being progressively altered. The Ulster Bank, Great Victoria Street (1961), by Houston and Beaumont, was an unexceptional work of the period but became something of a landmark due to the twin bronze figures on its gable in 'contemporary' taste by the sculptress Elizabeth Frink. The most outstanding building of the 1960s, however, was the Ulster Museum extension (1963–71), designed by Francis Pym of London, a boldly expressive conception in poured concrete added on to the existing prewar neo-Classical wing and presenting a good, though rather 'brutal', example of a more sculptural phase of modern architecture than Belfast had hitherto experienced (Figure 3.16).

Even before the Ulster Museum extension was finished, civil unrest had broken out in Northern Ireland in 1969, and the following years, particularly the 1970s, were characterised by frequent terrorist bombing and arson attacks on buildings, while the normal pattern of civilised living was severely disrupted. Fortunately, in the midst of all the useless and wanton destruction of what was popularly referred to as the 'Troubles' most that was worthy of preservation in the city's architectural heritage escaped serious damage, John Lanyon's late Victorian gas offices in Ormeau Avenue being one of the few complete losses of any special architectural note. Despite such a generally unpromising background and unsatisfactory state of affairs, some new buildings of considerable architectural interest or merit, mostly all locally designed, were constructed in Belfast in the 1970s. They included extensions to Victoria College girls' school, Cranmore Park (1972), by Shanks Leighton Kennedy and Fitzgerald, a vigorous and confident handling of concrete; Castle Buildings, at the Stormont Estate (1973–77), by the Chief Architect's Branch of the Department of Finance, a strongly sculptural complex of government offices; and the Northern Bank Head Office, Donegall Square West (1970–76), by Building Design Partnership, a stylish but restrained addition in Portland stone of rectilinear design to the city centre's main square, although now slightly spoiled by alterations to its entrance. All three were reflections of mainstream modern movement architectural development of the time, while the Fountain Centre of 1977–78 in College Street, by Lindsay Johnston of Dublin, with its open-air upper level walkway reached from the street by an escalator, was an interesting and novel concept for Belfast, but one which ultimately suffered due to its isolation. It was a rare instance of a new shopping development in a decade when retail growth in the city had been virtually brought to a halt by the Troubles.

THE LATE TWENTIETH CENTURY: BUILDING ON THE PAST

New buildings in Belfast in the 1980s and 1990s were to mirror the economic revival and new prosperity of the city, as the stagnation that had gone along with political disruption gave way to a period of urban regeneration. In architectural terms the new buildings of Belfast were to echo the changing forms of new architecture worldwide, as mainstream modern movement design was gradually displaced to some extent by a more eclectic approach. Respect for the past became a consideration in some new designs as architects

FIGURE 3.17
Interior of the Grand Opera House, following its refurbishment in 1980
SCENIC IRELAND

FIGURE 3.18
Grand Opera House, Great Victoria Street, a late Victorian building, restored in 1980

SCENIC IRELAND

confronted questions of context and urban identity. The rise of a heritage consciousness, reinforced by the statutory listing of buildings of special architectural or historic interest, a process introduced to Northern Ireland in 1972, led to a resurgence of public pride in the achievements and relics of the past and a growing understanding of the concept of local distinctiveness. Such local pride was to be crystallised in the repeated repair and conservation of the Grand Opera House (a fine building of 1894–95 designed by Frank Matcham; Figures 3.17 and 3.18), which had been damaged in successive terrorist bomb attacks, mostly aimed at the Europa Hotel (built 1970–71) across the road. Its refurbishment and reopening in 1980 heralded a revival of entertainment and cultural life in the city.

A concern for more appropriate forms in architecture led to the newly established Northern Ireland Housing Executive (NIHE) consistently producing good public housing in a demonstrably domestic idiom dispersed all over the city. Typical of the remarkable change in approach from the impersonal system-built large scale concrete slab blocks of the 1960s and 1970s, to small scale brick-built terraces or neighbourhood clusters of traditional-looking houses of the 1980s and 1990s, often with polychromatic detailing of pseudo-Victorian type, are such NIHE schemes as Bearnagh Glen Sheltered Housing, Glen Road (1982), well to the west of the city, and Loughlea Housing, Short Strand (1984), by McAdam Design, and Carrick Hill housing (1991–95), both of which fringe the city centre. Carrick Hill was built in Upper Library Street to replace the unpopular Unity Flats of the 1960s, but in most areas these new developments were built to replace repetitive rows of nineteenth-century terraced housing.

Private house builders in the 1980s and 1990s, meanwhile, sought sanctuary in the suburbs, developing earlier open areas, many of them previously the garden settings of large Victorian mansions, or retreated to open fields beyond the city, adding to the metropolitan sprawl and merging with earlier outlying village settlements. Once again the relentless repetitiveness of most of this type of development was the predominant characteristic, overshadowing any claims to local uniqueness.

Notable new buildings of the 1980s in the city centre were Calvert House, Castle Place (1983–85), by Kennedy Fitzgerald and Associates, a highly glazed steel-framed 'infill' office block with arched openings recalling the Victorian era, and 5 Donegall Square South (1984–87) by Robinson and McIlwaine, facing the back of the City Hall, from which it took the cue for both its Classical allusions and the use of Portland stone. The 1980s also saw some notable cases of extensive modernisation of existing buildings, most dramatically at the former Clarence Gallery, Clarence Street (1988), by the Robinson Patterson Partnership, where the entire gable end of a nineteenth-century warehouse, facing onto Linenhall Street, was replaced by glass, but also very successfully at 41–43 Hill Street (1988–89), converted by Barrie Todd Architects for their own offices from another old warehouse which they refronted in modern brick and glass. Such enthusiastic and earnest retention of existing buildings of no special historic interest was in marked contrast to the comprehensive redevelopment of a section of Royal Avenue, where several historic landmarks of the Victorian era, including the General Post Office and the Grand Central Hotel, both of which seemed eminently listable as structures to be protected, were ruthlessly demolished to make way for the CastleCourt shopping complex of 1985–90. Designed by Building Design Partnership, CastleCourt comprises a vast internal galleried atrium with an extensive façade constructed largely of glass and tubular steel framing, punctuated by circular towers. This was the largest private investment in Northern Ireland since the Second World War. Notwithstanding the regrettable demolitions, which included the eradication of most of Smithfield Square, whose formal layout dated from the late eighteenth century even if most of its buildings were from the mid to late nineteenth century, CastleCourt's commercial success marked a significant milestone in the regeneration of Belfast, while its bold 'Hi-Tech' architectural treatment has dramatically enlivened the city centre streetscape, bringing new commercial life to what had become a rather 'dead' area.

Elsewhere in the early nineties new buildings of acknowledged high quality in a thoroughly modernist idiom included the new Central Fire Station, Bankmore Street (1991), markedly angular in form, and Glenveagh Special School, Harberton Park (1993), a display of 'Hi-Tech' complexity of almost industrial character, both designed by Kennedy Fitzgerald and Associates. The same architects were also responsible for the carefully crafted St Brigid's Roman Catholic Church, Windsor Avenue (1996–97), laid out on a traditional basilican plan. It was a rare case in the late twentieth century of a large scale new ecclesiastical building in Belfast.

An upsurge in provision of new office accommodation in the 1990s saw many new individual blocks in the city centre, whose large and sometimes crudely derivative forms fitted into their surroundings with varying degrees of success, and, all too often, imposed an oppressive increase in scale. There was also an office precinct created around the old Clarendon Docks (Figure 3.19) on the northern fringe of the city centre. Such buildings there as the Hamilton Building, a shipping office of 1995–96 by Christopher Campbell Architects, in a thoroughly modern Hi-Tech style of symbolic intent (being partly designed to look like a ship), and Clarendon House of 1998 by Knox and Markwell, with segmental brick arches that allude to the city's industrial past, indicate the variety of architectural expression at the end of the century.

The Clarendon Dock development was only part of a wider focus on the riverside areas of Belfast. The Laganside Development Corporation, established in 1989, was set up to develop the land on both banks of the River Lagan as well as improve the environmental

FIGURE 3.19
Office precinct of the 1990s at the rejuvenated Clarendon Docks

SCENIC IRELAND

quality of the river itself. Accordingly, the Lagan Weir of 1994, designed along with its adjoining interpretative centre by Ferguson and McIlveen, was built to enable boating and other water sports to take place upriver, independent of tidal changes. New residential schemes of private apartments were built on the east side of the river from 1993 onwards, most if not all of them disappointing in their slavish adherence to brickwork conformity and unredeemed by some wilful constructional gestures, while the west side, along Oxford Street, became a cultural and commercial heartland with a hotel and offices grouped around a combined concert hall and conference centre (see chapter 9). This centrepiece, the Waterfront Hall (1992–96) by Robinson and McIlwaine, was the first major civic building in Belfast in the twentieth century to be designed by local architects (Figure 3.20). With a circular exterior constructed of Portland stone, red brick and granite, and with a vast expanse of glazing and a low copper-covered domical roof, the hall was endowed with generously scaled interior spaces, and successfully conveyed an impression of civic importance. Indeed, its success was such that it became a symbol for the new image of the city, akin to the role of the City Hall a century earlier.

The civic inspiration that had seen the City Hall built in what had been an era of supreme confidence at the start of the century, but which had been lost in the mire of the Troubles in the 1960s and 1970s, had clearly been regained to be given emphatic built form in this flagship for the 'new Belfast'. Notwithstanding some sense of a lost opportunity in terms of the relationship between the Waterfront Hall and its later neighbours, and a more vital connection with the river, this building has proved a fitting monument with which to mark the end of the twentieth century in Belfast.

CONCLUSION
THE BUILT FABRIC OF TWENTIETH-CENTURY BELFAST

Over the course of a century Belfast had seen some fundamental changes to its physical form and appearance. In 1901 it had a skyline of Victorian factory chimneys and church spires. By 2001 the church spires still remained but the factory chimneys, as well as most of the factories themselves, had gone. In the last few decades many of the other largely utilitarian buildings of the nineteenth century – the ropeworks, foundries, gas works and shipbuilding yards, as well as most of the linen mills – also disappeared as the long-established traditional manufacturing base of the burgeoning Victorian city rapidly dwindled. Listed building legislation introduced in the early 1970s enforced the retention of some buildings of the past, but not all that was important, while officially declared conservation areas were established too late or their guidelines applied too inconsistently to prevent the destruction of much that gave the city its special character and illustrated its social and industrial history.

Many buildings were lost over the century, in some cases simply due to the natural process of piecemeal demolition and replacement, under the influence of architectural trends and the opportunities provided by new materials and technological advances, and arising from the local social and economic circumstances. Too often, however, change has been more sweeping, and the rapid growth of the nineteenth-century city has been matched at times by an equally rapid dismantling. Aside from the unavoidable damage caused by the blitz of 1941 and the self-inflicted destruction by terrorist bombings and sectarian burnings a few decades later, there was an overzealous approach to large scale clearance on the fringes of the city centre by comprehensive redevelopment from the 1960s on. Eagerness then to clear away older housing was unfortunately not matched in the early years by an ability to replace it at both a commensurate rate and in a form that would prove endearing. As familiar streets and places in largely residential districts were thereby wiped out, so too were others of more mixed building type nearer the city centre, the victims of road developments that cut across the city grain.

Such official heavy-handedness, with a consequent loss of familiar townscape and historic landmarks, is unfortunately still apparent in the recent large scale devastation of an entire precinct within the City Centre Conservation Area, which has involved not only the eradication of an existing historic street pattern including the obliteration of Victoria Square, one of the few long-standing public open spaces in the area, but also, sensationally, the deliberate and calculated blowing up of Churchill House, the most accomplished tall building in the city centre and one which itself had been fitted into the existing area with at least some degree of sensitivity. Thus not only has the ethos of conservation area legislation been ignored, but also the less clearly defined but nevertheless easily perceptible existing 'sense of place' of an organically developed part of the city has been disregarded. Unlike the case of CastleCourt over a decade before, desperation for large scale investment cannot be offered as an excuse for such crude intervention in what should have been a more patient and piecemeal process of replacing the existing tissue of the city.

The recent transformation of Belfast's appearance has been rapid, and seemingly irresistible commercial pressures are clearly already a problem for the early twenty-first century. The eventual outcome of such pressures in terms of the continued validity of Belfast's claims to have any special or 'unique' local character is uncertain, but the lure of the city as a place to build is obviously still as strong as ever.

FIGURE 3.20
Waterfront Hall, Lanyon Place, Oxford Street, by Robinson and McIlwaine, 1992–96
SCENIC IRELAND

NOTABLE TWENTIETH-CENTURY BUILDINGS IN BELFAST

A selection of buildings cited in the text, set out in four main periods. While this list is almost entirely confined to buildings that still stand, the sites of a few of the more important demolished buildings are also included. In most cases the buildings are identified here either by their original name or by a long-standing name as referred to in the text, and their locations are shown in Figure 3.1.

EARLY TWENTIETH CENTURY
1900–1918

1 Belfast City Hall, Donegall Square
2 Scottish Provident Institution, Donegall Square West
3 Ocean Buildings, Donegall Square East
4 Scottish Temperance Buildings, Donegall Square South
5 36 Donegall Place
6 Chichester Buildings, Chichester Street
7 58 Wellington Place
8 Mayfair Building, Arthur Square
9 Castle Buildings, Castle Place
10 St Anne's Church of Ireland Cathedral, Donegall Street
11 Holy Cross Roman Catholic Church, Crumlin Road
12 Church of the Most Holy Redeemer, Clonard Gardens
13 Presbyterian Assembly Buildings, Fisherwick Place
14 Municipal Technical Institute, College Square East
15 County Down Weaving Company factory, Murray Street
16 Walpole Brothers' warehouse, 19 and 21 Alfred Street
17 Somerset's Linen Factory, Hardcastle Street
18 Carnegie Library, Oldpark Road
19 Carnegie Library, Donegall Road
20 Carnegie Library, Falls Road
21 Royal Victoria Hospital, Grosvenor Road (original ward block demolished)

INTERWAR YEARS
1919–1939

22 Northern Bank, Victoria Street
23 Ulster Bank, Cromac Street
24 Presbyterian War Memorial Hostel, Howard Street
25 Harbour Power Station, Wolff Road (demolished)
26 Public Library, Shankill Road
27 former Agriculture Building (later School of Geography, Archaeology and Palaeoecology), Elmwood Avenue
28 Central Labour Exchange, Corporation Street
29 Stranmillis College, Stranmillis Road
30 Telephone House, Cromac Street
31 Telephone Exchange, Paulett Avenue
32 Telephone Exchange, Clifton Park Avenue
33 Telephone Exchange, Lisburn Road
34 Telephone Exchange, Ormeau Road
35 Municipal Museum and Art Gallery, Stranmillis Road
36 Parliament Buildings, Upper Newtownards Road
37 Royal Courts of Justice, Chichester Street
38 Bank of Ireland, Royal Avenue
39 Donegall Chambers, Donegall Place
40 former Sinclair's Department Store, Royal Avenue
41 former Woolworth's building, High Street
42 former Burton's shop, 25–27 Ann Street
43 Imperial House, Donegall Square East
44 BBC Headquarters, Ormeau Avenue
45 former Belfast Co-operative Society, York Street
46 North Street Arcade, North Street and Donegall Street
47 Belfast Hospital for Sick Children, Falls Road
48 Royal Maternity Hospital, Grosvenor Road
49 St Clement's Church of Ireland Church, Templemore Avenue
50 St Polycarp's Church of Ireland Church, Upper Lisburn Road
51 St Finian's Church of Ireland Church, Cregagh Park
52 St Bartholmew's Church of Ireland Church, Stranmillis Road
53 St Simon's Church of Ireland Church, Donegall Road
54 St Christopher's Church of Ireland Church, Mersey Street
55 St Martin's Church of Ireland Church, Kenilworth Street
56 Cregagh Presbyterian Church, Cregagh Road
57 McCracken Memorial Presbyterian Church, Malone Road
58 Lowe Memorial Presbyterian Church, Upper Lisburn Road
59 Dominican College Chapel, Falls Road
60 St Anthony's Roman Catholic Church, Woodstock Road
61 St Therese's Roman Catholic Church, Somerton Road
62 First Church of Christ Scientist, University Avenue
63 King's Hall, Lisburn Road
64 Floral Hall, Belfast Zoo, Antrim Road
65 former Majestic Cinema, Lisburn Road
66 Strand Cinema, Holywood Road
67 former Savoy Cinema, Crumlin Road
68 Euston Street Primary School
69 former primary school, Templemore Avenue (later Rupert Stanley College)
70 former Everton School, Crumlin Road

71 Strandtown Primary School, North Road
72 Linfield Primary School, Blythe Street
73 Elmgrove Primary School, Beersbridge Road
74 Avoniel Primary School, Avoniel Road
75 Nettlefield Primary School, Radnor Street
76 School of Music, Donegall Pass
77 Botanic Primary School, Agincourt Avenue
78 The Model School, Cliftonville Road
79 Grove Primary School, North Queen Street
80 Carr's Glen Primary School, Oldpark Road

POSTWAR PERIOD
1940s–1970s

81 Henry Garrett Building, Stranmillis College,
    Stranmillis Road
82 Masonic Hall, Crumlin Road
83 Sir William Whitla Hall, Queen's University Belfast,
    University Road
84 Sunninghill Estate, Sunningdale Gardens
85 Finaghy Estate, Benmore Drive
86 Cregagh Estate, Cregagh Road
87 Mount Vernon Estate, Shore Road
88 former 'Festival of Britain' factory, Montgomery Road
89 Sydenham Primary School, Strandburn Street
90 Ashfield Girls' High School, Holywood Road
91 Harberton Special School, Harberton Park;
    Taughmonagh Primary School, Findon Gardens
92 Lowood Primary School, Sherringhurst Park
93 Girls' Model Secondary School, Dunkeld Gardens
94 Wheatfield Primary School, Alliance Road
    (partially demolished)
95 Ballygolan Primary School, Serpentine Road
96 St Patrick's Secondary School, Antrim Road
97 St Patrick's Primary School, Lancaster Street
98 former St Monica's Intermediate School for Girls,
    Ravenhill Road
99 former St Augustine's Boys' Secondary School,
    Ravenhill Road
100 Greenwood Primary School, Upper Newtownards Road
101 St Silas' Church of Ireland Church, Cliftonville Road
102 St John Evangelist Church of Ireland Church,
    Castlereagh Road
103 Orangefield Presbyterian Church, Castlereagh Road
104 Church of the Pentecost, Mount Merrion Avenue
105 St Molua's Church of Ireland Church,
    Upper Newtownards Road
106 The Synagogue, Somerton Road

107 St Clement's Roman Catholic Retreat Chapel,
    Antrim Road
108 St Bernadette's Roman Catholic Church, Knockbreda Road
109 Dominican Convent Chapel, Fortwilliam Park
110 St Andrew's Presbyterian Church, Rosetta Road
111 Masonic Hall, Rosemary Street
112 Shop premises, Bridge Street
113 Northern Bank, Donegall Square North
114 Transport House, High Street
115 Churchill House, Victoria Square (demolished)
116 Fanum House, Great Victoria Street
117 River House, High Street
118 Windsor House, Bedford Street
119 multistorey flats, Cregagh Estate, Cregagh Road
120 Artillery Flats, North Queen Street
121 Dundonald House, Upper Newtownards Road
122 Ashby Institute, Stranmillis Road
123 Microbiology Building, Royal Victoria Hospital,
    Grosvenor Road
124 Medical Biology Centre, Lisburn Road
125 Ulster College of Art and Design, York Street
126 Ulster Bank, Great Victoria Street
127 Ulster Museum extension, Stranmillis Road
128 Victoria College, Cranmore Avenue
129 Castle Buildings, Stormont Estate,
    Upper Newtownards Road
130 Northern Bank Head Office, Donegall Square West
131 Fountain Centre, College Street

LATE TWENTIETH CENTURY
1980s–2000

132 Bearnagh Glen Sheltered Housing, Bearnagh Drive,
    Glen Road
133 Loughlea Housing, Short Strand
134 Carrick Hill Housing, Upper Library Street
135 Calvert House, Castle Place
136 5 Donegall Square South
137 Clarence Gallery, Clarence Street
138 architects' studios, 41–43 Hill Street
139 CastleCourt shopping complex, Royal Avenue
140 Central Fire Station, Bankmore Street
141 Glenveagh Special School, Harberton Park
142 St Brigid's Roman Catholic Church, Windsor Avenue
143 Hamilton Building, Clarendon Dock, Corporation Street
144 Clarendon House, Clarendon Dock, Corporation Street
145 Lagan Weir, Donegall Quay
146 Waterfront Hall, Oxford Street

GLOSSARY OF ARCHITECTURAL TERMS

Art Deco	a modernistic style of the 1920s and 1930s, its name coined from the Exposition des Arts Décoratifs in Paris in 1925, characterised by step-form shapes and geometrically stylised ornamentation.
Art Nouveau	a curvilinear style in architecture of the 1890s to early 1900s characterised by the use of undulating wavy forms and decorative details derived from plant motifs.
Arts and Crafts	an architectural idiom that relates to the English-originated Arts and Crafts movement of the late nineteenth to early twentieth century in which a romantic nostalgia for an idealised medieval world was expressed in re-created vernacular forms.
Baroque Revival	a phase of architecture in the late nineteenth to early twentieth century in which the exuberant and curvaceous forms, florid ornamentation and often complex spatial relationships of seventeenth- and early eighteenth-century Baroque Classicism were re-created.
Brutalism (sometimes called 'New Brutalism')	a type of modern architecture, from the 1950s onwards, emphasising stark forms particularly in raw concrete.
Classicism	the revival of, or return to, the principles and stylistic features of Greek or Roman architecture, often inspired at second hand by the classical trends of the Renaissance; see also neo-Classicism and stripped Classicism.
curtain wall	in modern architecture, a non-load-bearing skin or cladding of glass or panels suspended on the outside in front of the main structural supports.
Gothic	the phase of medieval architecture that dominated Western Europe from the twelfth to the sixteenth century characterised by the use of pointed arches. Details varied from one country to another, as well as showing development from 'early' to 'late'.
Hi-Tech (sometimes spelt High-Tech)	a particularly mechanistic idiom in modern architecture of the late twentieth century involving steel and glass, often with extravagant use of tubular supports
International Style	a style of modern architecture characterised worldwide by cubic shapes in asymmetrical arrangements, with large windows, flat roofs, walls in smooth planes usually white rendered but also in brickwork and other materials, and generally lacking ornamentation or decorative mouldings or details.
modern movement	the consciously 'modern' development in architecture worldwide in the twentieth century intended to supersede all historical Revivalist styles; it embraced both Art Deco and the International Style.
neo-Classicism	a strand of Classical Revivalism in architecture that derived inspiration directly from antique Greek or Roman sources rather than indirectly from the Renaissance.
neo-Georgian	a style derived from eighteenth-century Georgian architecture, in both stone and brick, popular from the 1910s to 1930s.
Revivalism	in architecture, the later reuse or re-creation of earlier styles.
Romanesque	the phase of medieval architecture that dominated Western Europe from the tenth to the twelfth centuries characterised by the use of round arches; details varied from one country to another.
stripped Classicism	a form of Classical Revivalism in which the elements are not fully developed but represented only in an abstract manner.
Tudor	a phase of English architecture from the late fifteenth to the sixteenth century characterised mainly by the use of flat, four-centred arches.

NOTES

1   Brett, C.E.B. (1967 and 1985) *Buildings of Belfast 1700–1914*, Weidenfeld and Nicolson: London; revised, Friar's Bush Press: Belfast; Walker, B.M., and Dixon, H. (1983) *No mean city: Belfast 1880–1914*, Friar's Bush Press: Belfast, and (1984) *In Belfast town 1864–1880*, Belfast: Friar's Bush Press; Larmour, P. (1987) *Belfast, an illustrated architectural guide*, Friar's Bush Press: Belfast.

2   Nesbit, N. (1969) *The changing face of Belfast*, Ulster Museum: Belfast; McKinstry, R.J. (1971) 'Contemporary architecture', in M. Longley (ed.) *Causeway: the Arts in Ulster*, Arts Council of Northern Ireland: Belfast, pp. 27–42; Larmour, P. (1973) 'The inter-war years in Belfast', in *Big A3: the Magazine of the Department of Architecture, QUB*, Department of Architecture, Queen's University Belfast: Belfast; Evans, D. (1977) *An introduction to modern Ulster architecture*, Ulster Architectural Heritage Society: Belfast; Patton, M. (1997) *Central Belfast: an historical gazetteer*, Ulster Architectural Heritage Society: Belfast; Evans, D., and Larmour, P. (1995) *Queen's, an architectural legacy*, Institute of Irish Studies, Queen's University Belfast: Belfast; and Larmour, P. (1996) 'Belfast', in J.S. Turner (ed.) *The dictionary of art*, Macmillan: London, vol. 3, pp. 536–37.

3   Larmour, P. (2004) 'Sir Brumwell Thomas', *Oxford dictionary of national biography*, Oxford University Press: London, vol. 54, pp. 295–96.

4   Larmour, P. (1996) 'Young and Mackenzie', in Turner (1996) *Dictionary of art*, vol. 33, p. 566.

5   Larmour, P. (1995) 'The Squire of Malone' [Henry Seaver 1860–1941], *Perspective* (Journal of the Royal Society of Ulster Architects), 3.3, January/February, pp. 59–60.

6   Larmour, P. (1997) 'From building site to mission field' [W.J.W. Roome 1865–1937], *Perspective* (Journal of the Royal Society of Ulster Architects), 5.5, May/June, pp. 45–49.

7   Larmour, P. (1985) 'Castle Buildings: an Edwardian emporium in Belfast', *Ulster Architect*, January, pp. 3–4.

8   Larmour, P. (1996) 'The first president of the RSUA' [Sir Thomas Drew 1838–1910], *Perspective* (Journal of the Royal Society of Ulster Architects), 4.5, May/June, pp. 61–63; and Larmour, P. (2004) 'Sir Thomas Drew', *Oxford dictionary of national biography*, Oxford University Press: London, vol. 16, pp. 914–15.

9   Larmour, P. (1984) 'A pioneering reinforced building in Belfast: Somerset's factory in Hardcastle Street', *Ulster Architect*, October, pp. 12–16.

10 Larmour, P. (1996) 'A revolution in hospital design', *Perspective* (Journal of the Royal Society of Ulster Architects), 4.3, January/February, pp. 38–40; and Larmour, P. (1997) 'Royal Victoria Hospital, Belfast', in A. Becker, J. Olley and W. Wang (eds) *20th century architecture: Ireland*, Prestel: Munich and New York, pp. 90–91.

11 Larmour, P. (1991) *The architectural heritage of Malone and Stranmillis*, Ulster Architectural Heritage Society: Belfast.

12 Larmour, P. (1995) 'A gifted poet and architect' [Padraic Gregory 1886–1962], *Perspective* (Journal of the Royal Society of Ulster Architects), 4.1, September/October, pp. 47–49.

13 Larmour, P. (1996) 'Cinema Paradiso' [cinema architecture in Belfast], *Perspective* (Journal of the Royal Society of Ulster Architects), 4.4, March/April, pp. 23–27.

14 Larmour, P. (1997) 'The big feature' [John McBride Neill 1916–1996], *Perspective* (Journal of the Royal Society of Ulster Architects), 5.4, March/April, pp. 45–49.

15 Larmour, P. (1997) 'Botanic Primary School, Belfast', in Becker, Olley and Wang (1997) *20th century architecture: Ireland*, p. 116.

16 Larmour, P. (1985) 'The work of the late John MacGeagh ARIBA', *Ulster Architect*, June, pp. 9–12; Larmour, P. (1985) 'A perfectionist in brickwork' [John MacGeagh 1901–1985], *Perspective* (Journal of the Royal Society of Ulster Architects), 3.4, March/April, pp. 53–55.

To paint a picture of the population of Belfast that covers the whole of the twentieth century is not an easy task. While the eleven censuses provide a wealth of data, there are two quite severe limitations: there have been major changes from one census to another both in terms of the kind of social information collected and of the geographical areas covered. To have population data that maintain continuity for comparative purposes across the twentieth century, both in terms of *kind* and of *area,* means that the range of data that can be used is quite limited. This chapter concentrates on six aspects of Belfast's population – the numbers of people; the dwelling units and their occupancy; the numerical balance between females and males; the age of the population; religious affiliation and segregation; and migration. The chapter then concludes with a short overview of the dynamics of population change in Metropolitan Belfast (Figure 4.1) across the twentieth century.

4
Big Processes and Little People

The Population of Metropolitan Belfast 1901–2001

Frederick W. Boal

FIGURE 4.1
Belfast from the Royal Victoria Hospital, looking towards North Down, 1994

ESLER CRAWFORD

COUNTING HEADS

In 1901 the population of the City[1] of Belfast was recorded as 349,180. One hundred years later, in 2001, the same geographical area[2] recorded a population of 232,319. From a demographic perspective three numbers have contributed to this change – the number of births, the number of deaths and the number of people migrating in and out.

When we count the population of an area named 'Belfast' what do we mean? From a limited perspective 'Belfast' is the area marked out by the city boundary (and governed from the City Hall). However, the spread of buildings stretches well beyond this limit to form a continuously built-up area that embraces locations such as Lisburn, Castlereagh, Holywood and Newtownabbey. Going one step further, and viewing Belfast at the end of the twentieth century, we can consider places such as Carrickfergus, Antrim, Comber, Newtownards and Bangor as falling within a broadly defined 'Metropolitan Belfast' (Metro) (see Figure 4.2). In this chapter we will call these three zones 'Belfast City' (City), 'Outer Suburbs'[3] and 'Outer Metro'. All three together constitute Metropolitan Belfast, while Belfast City and Outer Suburbs form the Belfast Urban Area (BUA).

If we return to our comparison of the 'Belfast' of 1901 with that of 2001, we can provide a more detailed picture (Table 4.1). Comparing 2001 with 1901, we see that Metro Belfast is half as big again in population terms. On the other hand, City is a third smaller in 2001 than it was a century earlier. The biggest change of all is seen in the Outer Suburbs area, which has almost four and a half times the number of people at the end of the twentieth century as it had at the beginning. So overall, the Metro population has grown by almost 250,000 people, but the core City has shrunk by well over 100,000. The picture over the century seems to be one of very considerable population growth in the Outer Suburbs and Outer Metro, partly counterbalanced by a contracting City at Metro's heart.

FIGURE 4.2
The component parts of Metropolitan Belfast used in the analysis of population, 1901–2001

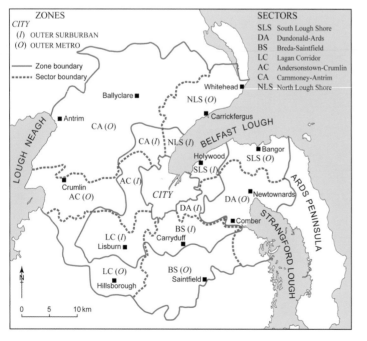

TABLE 4.1

Population of the Component Parts of Belfast, 1901 and 2001

	1901	2001	Change 1901–2001	% Change 1901–2001
City	349,180	232,319	-116,831	-34
Outer Suburbs	48,329	265,541	+217,212	+449
Outer Metro	80,860	225,587	+144,727	+179
BUA*	397,509	497,860	+100,351	+25
Metropolitan Belfast**	478,369	723,447	+245,078	+51

SOURCE: Derived from Census of Ireland 1901 and Census of Northern Ireland 2001

*Belfast Urban Area (City plus Outer Suburbs)
**City plus Outer Suburbs plus Outer Metro

But what of the 100 years between 1901 and 2001? When we look across the whole century we see that a comparison that jumps from 1901 to 2001 hides a great deal. What were the changes in the components of Metro Belfast over the twentieth century? Figure 4.3 provides the answers. First the City itself. Here we see growth occurring up to the time of the Second World War; then up to 1951 the population was almost static. This halt to growth presaged a quite remarkable decline first evident in the 1950s, with an even more dramatic population 'crash' from 1961 right through to 1991. It was only in the last decade of the century that population numbers more or less stabilised. The inset graph on Figure 4.3 shows that the growth up to the Second World War was just the final fling of a trend that can be seen to have extended from at least 1851. If we attach numbers to these trends, we can record a growth in the City's population between 1901 and 1937 of some 61,000. The City's population peaked in 1951 at 444,000, this peak marking the start of a dramatic plunge to 236,000 in 1991, a massive loss of 208,000 (47 per cent) in forty years. The social, economic and political implications of this population loss were enormous.

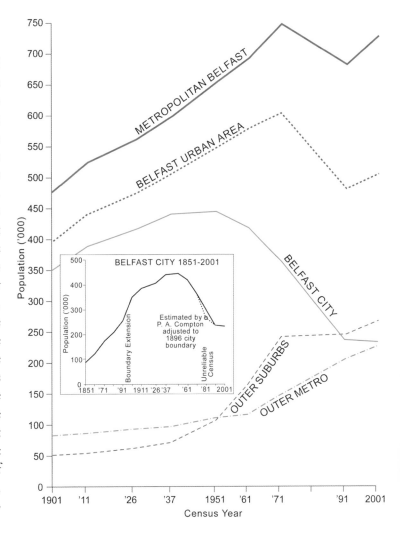

FIGURE 4.3
Population change, 1901–2001: Metropolitan Belfast and component parts

The growth in the first three decades of the twentieth century was mainly achieved by the City spreading itself into the open lands that existed within its boundary, which had been put in place in 1896. Thus this growth was 'suburban', since the City could achieve its edge growth within its own boundaries. But what was happening in the zone beyond the City boundary, the area we have labelled the Outer Suburbs? Here growth is present throughout the century – slow until after the Second World War, very rapid from this period until 1971, then a static spell until 1991. Renewed growth in this zone is evident in the last decade of the century, triggered partly by relaxations in the planning limit (the Matthew Stop Line, see chapter 8) most evident at Cairnshill in the south and Poleglass in the south-west.

If we combine the City with the Outer Suburbs to form the BUA, we see continued growth right through from 1901 to 1971. In the early decades of the century it was the City that contributed most to this growth (between 1901 and 1937 the City contributed 86 per cent of the growth), but between 1937 and 1951 the City contributed only 13 per cent. From 1951 onwards there is a dramatic change. While the BUA continued to grow during the two decades 1951–71, this was entirely due to massive suburban expansion. Indeed, during this period the City was actually serving as a drag on BUA growth (the City losing almost 82,000 people, while the Outer Suburbs gained 136,000). From

1971 to 1991 the City continued to lose population (a loss of almost 126,000), but in this period suburban growth completely failed to compensate for this decline (the Outer Suburbs grew by a mere 4,000 people). In consequence, during the two decades 1971–91 the BUA as a whole lost population. Thus, while the City acted as a counterweight to BUA overall growth in the 1951–71 period, it massively contributed to its population decline in the subsequent two decades (1971–91). Since 1991 the BUA has resumed growth in the Outer Suburbs, in part dependent on the limited relaxation of the physical growth limit (the so-called Stop Line; again see chapter 8).

If we look beyond the BUA to the outer reaches of the Metropolitan area (Outer Metro), we can observe a pattern of population change quite unlike that of the City and even showing differences from the Outer Suburbs. Outer Metro has been anchored throughout the twentieth century by the presence of a number of long-established towns – Carrickfergus, Antrim, Comber, Newtownards and Bangor. Most of the growth in Outer Metro has accreted onto these centres. The population curve for Outer Metro falls simply into two parts, both of which are characterised by growth. Up to 1961 there was a gradual expansion of population (81,000 in 1901 to 115,000 in 1961), but this was then followed by a sustained, dramatic growth to century end (from 115,000 in 1961 to 226,000 in 2001). The Outer Suburbs and Outer Metro as a whole grew significantly in the last few decades of the twentieth century. However, growth stalled in the Outer Suburbs between 1971 and 1991, while it was represented by a 40 per cent spurt in Outer Metro.

The radical reordering of the population distribution of Metro Belfast over the span of the twentieth century can be stressed by comparing the relative contributions of the three major components of Metro to the total. In 1901 the City contributed 73 per cent to the total, the Outer Suburbs just over 10 per cent and Outer Metro almost 17 per cent. At century end the City contributed less than one-third (32.1 per cent), the Outer Suburbs had overtaken the City with almost 37 per cent, while Outer Metro's contribution had grown to over 31 per cent. As the population curves in Figure 4.3 show, the three component parts of Metro were far apart in their population sizes in 1901, but were very similar 100 years later.

Sectors

A characteristic of the growth of many cities is the emergence of distinctive sectors. This is particularly marked in Belfast, first because of the way urban growth has been topographically channelled by the hills and Belfast Lough, and second, by the formation and prolonged existence of several world-renowned ethno-religious 'wedges' (most notably 'The Falls' and 'The Shankill'). We can briefly explore these sectors to see the ways each contributes to more general population

FIGURE 4.4
The six Super Sectors used in the analysis of the population of Belfast City, 1901–2001

TABLE 4.2
Belfast City: Inner Arc Wards, 1901 and 1971

Ward	1901	1971	1971 as % of 1901
Dock	21,427	9,650	45
Court	18,917	4,769	25
St George's	19,231	8,860	46
Smithfield	13,652	4,646	34
Inner Arc total	73,227	27,925	38

SOURCE: Census of Ireland 1901and Census of Northern Ireland 1971

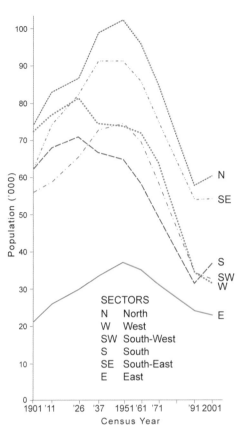

FIGURE 4.5
Population change, Belfast City Super Sectors, 1901–2001

dynamics of the three components of Metro Belfast (City, Outer Suburbs and Outer Metro).

First within the City itself. For the purpose of this analysis the City has been divided into six large segments called Super Sectors: North, West, South-West, South, South-East and East (Figure 4.4; see also Appendix A.1). Up to 1926 all these sectors contributed to growth (Figure 4.5). However, between 1926 and 1937 population decline set in for two of the six sectors – the South (Malone–Lisburn Road area) and the West (Shankill). It was only from 1951 onwards that the other four sectors joined in this decline. Both of these patterns emphasise once again that City population decline long predates the outbreak of the so-called Troubles. Overall, the most dramatic decline has been in the West sector, where the 2001 population was only 39 per cent of that in the peak year (1926). A decline only slightly less in magnitude is recorded for the South-West (Falls) sector, with the 2001 population being only 43 per cent of that in the peak year (1951). But it must be reiterated that all the sectors are now much reduced in population numbers from their respective peaks.

The large size of the sectors we have had to use for this analysis inevitably hides much detail. Fortunately it is possible to get a more refined indication of population change for parts of the inner City for the censuses between 1901 and 1971. Four relatively small wards were designated in 1896 and continued to be part of the census record until 1971. Table 4.2 shows the shifting population numbers for these wards between 1901 and 1971. The wards form an arc (the Inner Arc) to the north, west and south-west of the city centre. Thus, while the City in 1971 still had almost 14,000 more people than it had in 1901 (despite the population decline that had set in by the 1950s), the Inner Arc wards had over 45,000 fewer. This means that for many of the first seventy years of the century the inner City was declining, while the areas out to the boundary continued to grow. It is evident, therefore, that the population data for the Super Sectors as wholes hide a great deal of internal variation.

The inner City population decline, partly measured by the Inner Arc data, continued beyond 1971. As already noted, it is not possible to track this beyond 1971 using Inner Arc census numbers, but we can still gain some insight into inner City population reduction beyond 1971 by setting up a substitute 'Inner Arc' using data for the Crumlin, Falls, New Lodge and Shaftesbury wards. In 1971 this area had a population of 52,000, declining to just over 20,000 by 2001 (a reduction of 61 per cent). We can also get some further insight into late twentieth-century inner City population decline by looking at an area focused round the Shankill Road. In 1971 this area had a population of over 28,000; by 2001 only slightly over 8,000 people remained (a decline of 71 per cent). Overall, then, we can see that the population 'thinning' of the inner City in the second half of the twentieth century has been enormous, as the densely packed terraced streets of the late Victorian city were demolished and then replaced at a much lower density, or, in some cases, not replaced at all.

What of sectoral change in the Outer Suburbs and Outer Metro? As we have already seen, the Outer Suburbs have been a growth zone throughout the twentieth century, but this growth has not been evenly distributed (Figure 4.6). If we rank the Outer Suburban sectors according to their growth over the 100-year period, we get the result as shown in Table 4.3. The greatest proportionate change has occurred in those sectors where expansion has been into virtually greenfield locations, and less so where significant towns already existed (Lisburn, Holywood, Glengormley and Whiteabbey). When we view change in the intervening years between 1901 and 2001 we see a slow growth in all sectors until after the Second World War, followed by a massive expansion up to 1971 in all sectors bar one (South Lough Shore Inner). At this point and from then until 1991 there is a dramatic change – slow growth in the Lagan Corridor, in the Andersonstown–Crumlin Inner sector and in the Breda–Saintfield corridor, combined with actual population loss in the Dundonald–Ards Inner sector and in the North Lough Shore Inner. Only in the sector out through Glengormley (Carnmoney–Antrim Inner) is rapid growth maintained. Finally, the South Lough Shore Inner segment (Holywood), squeezed as it is between the lough and the hills, stayed almost the same. Subsequently, however, in the 1991–2001 period signs of a new wave of growth emerge, most dramatically in Andersonstown–Crumlin Inner.

What of the outer reaches of Metro? Here four sectors are characterised by the pre-existence of major population nodes (Bangor, Newtownards, Comber, Antrim and Carrickfergus). The most striking area of all here is South Lough Shore Outer (Bangor), where over the century the population has expanded by over 500 per cent. However, in addition to the sectors dominated by large town nodes there are a further three sectors that have shown little change in population numbers over the 100 years – being as yet mostly open countryside beyond the grasp of Metro expansion. The only indicator of some growth is in the Andersonstown–Crumlin Outer sector, where Crumlin itself appears to be emerging as a modest growth pole.

FIGURE 4.6
Population change, Outer Suburbs Sectors, 1901–2001

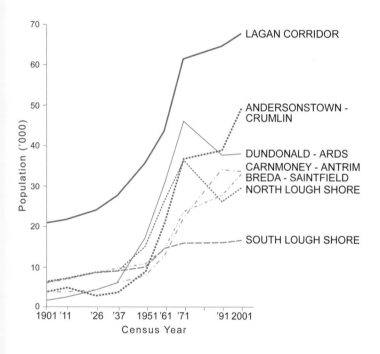

TABLE 4.3
Percentage Change in Population, Outer Suburbs Sectors, 1901–2001

Sector	% Growth 1901–2001
Dundonald–Ards Inner	2,275
Andersonstown–Crumlin Inner	925
Carnmoney–Antrim Inner	764
Breda–Saintfield Inner	503
North Lough Shore Inner	415
Lagan Corridor Inner	227
South Lough Shore Inner	152

SOURCE: Derived from Census of Ireland 1901 and Census of Northern Ireland 2001

DWELLINGS AND PEOPLE

Dwellings are the residential containers for people. The census definition of 'dwelling' has varied over the twentieth century, so that the data are not strictly comparable from one census to another.[4] However, definitional variation is likely to have only a small impact on the numbers recorded.

We can look at 'dwellings' in two ways – their physical presence on the ground and the number of people they contain. First let us look at the actual number of dwellings. In 1901 there were just over 100,000 dwellings in the area we have defined as Metro Belfast, 72 per cent of these being within the City itself. By 2001 the number of dwellings had increased to almost 300,000, with the City's proportion dropping to 35 per cent. Four maps (Figures 4.7a, 4.7b, 4.7c and 4.7d) show the spread of Metro from 1900 through 1960 to 2000. In 1900 (Figure 4.7a) Metro Belfast was characterised by a high density core with three low density extensions – north along the Antrim Road, south along the Malone Road and east along the Upper Newtownards Road. Beyond this was found a number of small but identifiable outlying nodes – Carrickfergus, Antrim, Lisburn, Newtownards, Comber, Bangor and Holywood. By 1937–38 (Figure 4.7b) there is evidence of some suburban spread to the east, to the north and to the south-west. By 1961 (Figure 4.7c) much of the previously open land within the City boundary had been built on, with development starting to push into the Dundonald gap in the east, beginning to extend south-westwards through Finaghy, through Andersonstown in the south and south-west, growing northwards in the relatively narrow lowland between Cave Hill and the sea, and extending round the foot of Carnmoney Hill

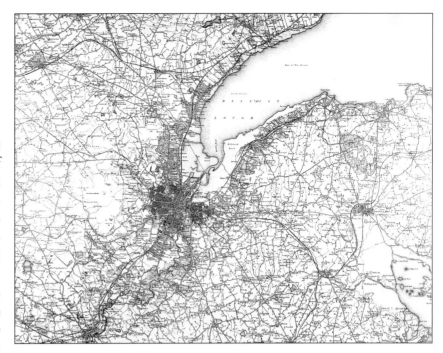

FIGURE 4.7a
Belfast area, 1900 (section of the one-inch Ordnance Survey map)

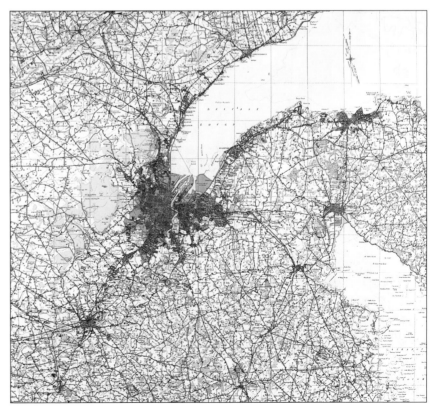

FIGURE 4.7b
Belfast area, 1937–38. This land-use map was produced by the Land Use Survey of Northern Ireland. The survey was carried out by members of the Geographical Association (Northern Ireland). The results were published as a series of maps at the scale of one inch to one mile. Red represents land occupied by urban development at a high density (together with bog land in rural areas). Purple represents land occupied by suburban houses with gardens.

(Figure 4.8). The outer nodes (Bangor, Newtownards, Antrim, Carrickfergus) have also become more evident, while there are signs of clusters emerging at Glengormley and Whiteabbey and at Dunmurry.

However, the great era of Metro expansion still lay ahead. While just over 60,000 dwellings were added to Metro in the first half of the twentieth century, there was a net[5] increase of 128,000 between 1951 and 2001. Of course not all of this entailed expansion at the urban edge. The growth in apartment living, including the subdivision of larger existing units, and the tendency to build houses and apartments in the garden spaces of low density dwellings in some of the older suburbs are all part of a general process now referred to as 'densification'. The use of so-called brownfield sites in the inner City also should be noted. Nonetheless a comparison of Figure 4.7c with Figure 4.7d dramatically underlines the urban spread in the last forty years of the twentieth century, whether it be in the shape of further aggregations in the south-west (Andersonstown–Poleglass), in the Newtownbreda–Carryduff area to the south-east, or in the flood that has engulfed Carnmoney Hill in the north. In the same period the outer nodes have greatly extended and now form striking nucleations on the edge of our Metro map.

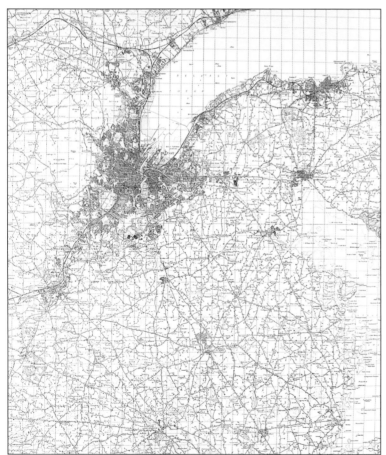

FIGURE 4.7c
Belfast area, 1961 (section of the one-inch Ordnance Survey map)

ORDNANCE SURVEY OF NORTHERN IRELAND

FIGURE 4.7d
Belfast area, 2000 (section of the 1:50,000 Ordnance Survey map)

ORDNANCE SURVEY OF NORTHERN IRELAND

FIGURE 4.8
The view from Carnmoney,
over the cemetery and down
to the sea

SCENIC IRELAND

While the number of dwellings in Metro has tripled over the twentieth century, this has not been a consistent feature and, as indicated by the analysis of urban spread provided above, has impacted quite differently on the various components of the Metro area. Up to the 1930s there was a modest growth rate in the City, in the Outer Suburbs and in Outer Metro. After that, and continuing until the 1970s, growth in the number of dwellings sharply accelerated in both the Outer Suburbs and in Outer Metro, but this was accompanied by a marked slow-down in the City itself. Another turning point was 1971, with a slowing of growth in the Outer Suburbs and, most dramatically of all, a significant *decline* in the number of dwellings in the City – in fact, a net loss of 17,000 housing units. Finally, in the last decade of the twentieth century growth in the number of dwellings continued unabated in the Outer Suburbs and in Outer Metro, while the decline in the size of the City's housing stock had almost ceased. The decline in the size of the City's housing stock between 1971 and 1991 can be largely attributed to the massive redevelopment programme undertaken by the Northern Ireland Housing Executive (NIHE), with many more dwellings being removed than were replaced. For instance, the so-called 'put back rate' in Belfast in the 1990s was only 42 per cent. Some loss of housing stock can also be attributed to the ethno-national conflict that was a feature of the two decades from 1971. Also contributing to the 'thinning' of the population have been declining family sizes and a growth in the proportion of households containing only one person.

Just as with population numbers, so with dwellings. While the City contributed 73 per cent of Metro's population in 1901, it contained almost 72 per cent of the dwellings. One hundred years later the City contributed only 33 per cent of Metro's population and only 35 per cent of the dwellings.

Not surprisingly, as the population fluctuates so does the number of dwellings, though dwellings change less rapidly than population. However, while this applies as a general rule, some quite revolutionary transformations have also taken place. This can be seen vividly in Figure 4.9, which shows the number of persons per dwelling at each census throughout the twentieth century. Taking Metro as a whole,

FIGURE 4.9
Persons per dwelling,
Metropolitan Belfast
components, 1901–2001

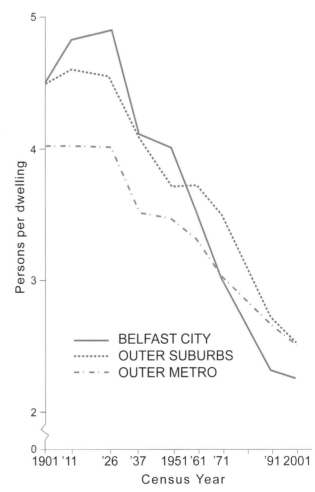

there were 4.4 persons per dwelling in 1901 and just over 2.4 at century end – a decline of almost 50 per cent. This massive thinning out of population at the level of individual dwellings has contributed greatly to population loss in the City, while it has ensured that population gain in the Outer Suburbs and in Outer Metro has been much more space-consuming than it would otherwise have been. To look at this in another way, we can calculate that if we were to house the 2001 population of Metro (723,447) at the persons-per-dwelling density that existed 100 years earlier, then there would be a requirement for 164,410 dwellings, rather than the 297,699 on the ground at century end. Putting it yet another way, if we were to place people in the 297,699 dwellings of 2001 at the 1901 density of 4.4, then Metro's population in 2001 would have been over 1.3 million.

Figure 4.6 also shows the way the persons-per-dwelling transformation took place between 1901 and 2001. What we basically see is a tendency towards increasing 'crowd-ing' in the City in the first quarter of the century. From the census of 1926 onwards, however, the number of people in each dwelling begins to decline, not only in the City, but right across the Metro area. This decline has continued to the present, with a rever-sal of the relative position of the City, on the one hand, and the Outer Suburbs and Outer Metro, on the other. Thus, while the highest per-dwelling densities were found in the City in the early decades of the century, now the City has the lowest density.

FIGURE 4.10
Females per hundred males, Belfast City Super Sectors, 1901, 1951 and 2001

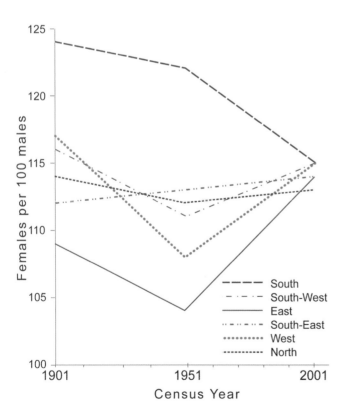

FEMALE METRO?

Throughout the twentieth century the Metro area has had a female majority, varying from just under 54 per cent in 1901 to just over 53 per cent in 2001. During this time the City was somewhat more 'female' in numerical terms than the Outer Suburbs and Outer Metro. However, much more striking vari-ations in female/male proportions can be seen when the geography is looked at in finer detail.

When the detailed counts were being extracted from the var-ious censuses it was immediately evident that the least urbanised sections of Metro were also those with a male numer-ical predominance. It was also evident that as the City and the surrounding towns grew out across the countryside, so male majorities switched to female. For instance, if we take the areas used as the basic building blocks for our analysis of population (district electoral divisions, and later wards), we find that in the parts of Metro beyond the City 41 per cent had male majori-ties in 1901, 33 per cent in 1951 and only 9 per cent in 2001.

Within the City, all the Super Sectors had female majorities throughout the twentieth century (Figure 4.10). However, we also see that in 1901 and again in 1951 there were considerable variations between the sectors – for instance, from a 124:100 female:male ratio in the South sector in 1901 to 109:100 in the East, and from 122:100 in the South in 1951 to 104:100 in the

East. Strikingly, however, this intersectoral vari-ability almost disappears by 2001.

We can offer a number of pointers to process-es that have generated these shifting sex ratios in the City's population. First, the pattern sug-gests that the balance of in-migration into Belfast before 1900 was in favour of females, demonstrated indirectly by the fact that at the 1871 and 1881 censuses the female:male ratio was 119:100. Second, with reference to 1901, we have noted some quite large scale variations in the sex ratios between different parts of the City. It is possible that the marked female pre-dominance in the South sector was due, in the main, to the large scale presence of female

FIGURE 4.11
A young girl at work in a linen factory, *c.* 1915

ULSTER FOLK & TRANSPORT MUSEUM

domestic servants. The female predominance in the West and South-West sectors (Shankill and Falls) could be a consequence of the demand for female labour in the linen industry (Figure 4.11), while the relatively small female predominance in the East could similarly be labour related – in this case, the overwhelmingly male-heavy industry employment provided by the shipyard and related activities.

By 1951 the female predominance in the City had declined, as in-migration declined, though there was still considerable intersectoral variation in the sex ratios. The South continued to have the largest female predominance, the East the smallest.

At the end of the twentieth century we can observe a new pattern of sex ratios. Most notably the intersectoral variation has almost disappeared (115:100 at the largest to 113:100 at the smallest), this contrasting markedly with 1901 (124:100 to 109:100) and 1951 (122:100 to 104:100). The most likely explanation for this is the almost complete disappearance of the manufacturing industries that previously had highly selective labour demands in specific parts of the City. The second change to note between 1951 and 2001 is the increase in female predominance. The main contributor to this is likely to be the overall ageing of the City's population, combined with a heavy female predominance in the older age groups (see Figure 4.12c in the following section).

AGE

The population of the vast majority of cities or metropolitan areas will be made up of people of a wide range of ages. However, the proportion in each age group can vary over time and from one area to another. For instance, the proportion of the population in the youngest age category can vary over the years – likewise with the most elderly age groups. Or some parts of a city may be significantly different from others in their age structure; one neighbourhood may have a relatively elderly population, another may be quite youth-ful. In light of this let us examine Metro Belfast over the span of the twentieth century.

First let us look at three population pyramids for the City: for 1901, 1951 and 2001 (Figure 4.12 a, b and c). The pyramids show the numbers of people in each five-year age group, distinguishing between females and males. The 1901 pyramid demonstrates a youthful age structure – large numbers in the young age groups, small in the old. However, there is one striking irregularity in this pyramid – the large number of females in the 21–25 age group. This reinforces our earlier finding that previous to 1900 there had been a disproportionate flow of young female migrants into the city, drawn by work opportunities in textiles and domestic service.

By 1951 the pyramid has matured. There are now proportionately fewer children, while the 'elderly' top of the pyramid has begun to widen out. Fifty years later, in 2001,

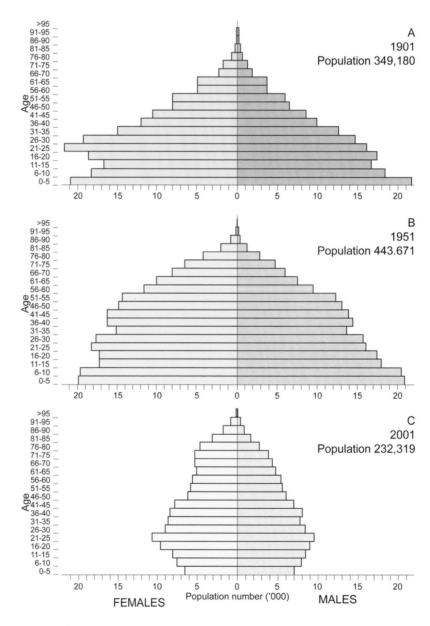

FIGURE 4.12
Population pyramids, Belfast City: (A) 1901; (B) 1951; and (C) 2001

the population pyramid has been fundamentally reshaped. Now the proportion of the population that is composed of children (under fifteen years of age) has greatly shrunk, while the older age categories have greatly expanded.

We can observe the century-long dynamic evolution of the age structure of the City in another way by examining Table 4.4. First, we can see that the proportion of the population under fifteen years of age declined over the century from just about one-third to one-fifth. The proportion of the under fifteens that is female remains rock steady, however, expressing the fundamental tendency for slightly more boys than girls to be born. The decline in the proportionate size of the younger section of the population is more than counterbalanced by a growth in the proportion over sixty years of age from 8 per cent in 1901 to almost 25 per cent in 2001. Underlying this is not just a tendency for younger people to migrate from the City to the suburbs but a century-long process where life expectancies have risen markedly. We do not have life expectancy data for the City, but in the wider context of Northern Ireland female life expectancy rose from 46.7 years in 1900–02 to 79.6 in 1998–2000; for males the equivalent ages are 47.1 and 75.2 (see chapter 14). Within the older age groups there is a marked female predominance, this being particularly the case with the over eighties – and this predominance strengthens over the century, reflecting a more rapidly growing longevity amongst females. In this context, and bearing in mind that *Enduring City* is a book about the whole of the twentieth century, it is interesting to note that the number of people over the age of 100 in the City[6] of Belfast increased from 4 in 1901 to 32 in 2001. Of the 4 centenarians in 1901, 3 were female; in 2001 of the 32, 29 were female.

Data providing detailed breakdowns in age structure for the different sectors in the City are not available for century-long comparative purposes. We can, however, give some indication of the internal variations in age structure by examining the presence of those under the age of fifteen in our six Super Sectors. Table 4.5 ranks the sectors according to the proportion of their population in the under fifteen category. These rankings are provided for four census years – 1901, 1937, 1971 and 2001. Some radical transformations can be seen here. In 1901 it was the East and South-East of the City that had the younger population; in 2001 it was the South-West and the North. Evidence from

TABLE 4.4

Percentage of City Population under 15 years, over 60 years and over 80 years (Total and Female), 1901, 1951 and 2001

Census Year	Under 15 Years (%)	Under 15 Years (% female)	Over 60 Years (%)	Over 60 Years (% female)	Over 80 Years (%)	Over 80 Years (% female)
1901	32.6	49.7	8.0	57.5	0.69	59.5
1951	26.4	49.1	17.4	57.8	2.74	61.6
2001	19.8	49.1	24.7	58.5	7.21	67.2

SOURCE: Census of Ireland 1901 and Census of Northern Ireland 1951 and 2001

TABLE 4.5

City Super Sectors Ranked According to the Percentage of
Their Population under 15 years, 1901, 1937, 1971 and 2001

Rank	1901	1937	1971	2001
1	E	SW	SW	SW
2	SE	W	W	N
3	W	N	N	W
4	N	E	E	E
5	SW	SE	SE	SE
6	S	S	S	S

SOURCE: Derived from Census of Ireland 1901 and Census of Northern Ireland
1937, 1971 and 2001

TABLE 4.6

Age Comparisons, City and the Rest of Metro
(Outer Suburbs plus Outer Metro), 1901, 1937, 1971 and 2001

Census Year	Under 15 Years (%)		Over 60 Years (%)	
	City	Rest of Metro	City	Rest of Metro
1901	32.6	31.7	5.4	10.5
1937	27.3	25.2	10.6	13.7
1971	26.2	29.8	18.6	13.6
2001	19.8	20.9	19.8	18.5

SOURCE: Census of Ireland 1901 and Census of Northern Ireland 1937, 1971 and
2001

other sources suggests that the 'religious' geography of the City is a key to explaining this. In 1901, at least in working-class Belfast, Protestant families were on average bigger than Roman Catholic ones, but as the century wore on Catholics increasingly had the larger families. Differential out-migration of younger Protestants to the suburbs may also have contributed to this change in the age composition of the sectors. Thus the South-West of the City (Falls) takes over as the youngest Super Sector from 1937 onwards, and by century end it is followed in second place by the North. One Super Sector stands out for century-long consistency – the South (Malone, Stranmillis, Lisburn Road). The relatively low proportion in the under fifteen group here is partly a product of the distinctive 'overrepresentation' of those in their late teens and early twenties, clustered in accommodation in proximity to Queen's University (particularly in the second half of the century). This overrepresentation is statistically reinforced in 2001 by changes made in the way the census enumerated students.

If it is difficult to obtain age composition data for the City that are comparable across the twentieth century, it is even more so for those parts of Metro beyond the 1896 City limits. However, we can get a few broad indications (Table 4.6). There is a clear tendency for the City to be younger in both 1901 and 1937, due, perhaps, to differential migration of young people of family forming age from rural areas to the urban. The age differentials between the City and the rest of Metro become slight by the end of the century. The greatest contrast between the City and the Outer Suburbs and Outer Metro is recorded in 1971, where the area beyond the City boundary emerges as significantly more youthful than that within. The suggestion here is that the 1971 data 'capture' the effects of the large scale out-migration of younger households to the burgeoning public sector estates in the Outer Suburbs and beyond.

RELIGIOUS AFFILIATION

Religious affiliation is an important dimension of population everywhere in the world. However, in Belfast 'religion' has a significance beyond matters of faith – religious affiliation is taken not only as a marker of belief systems but also of ethno-national (political) orientation.[7] With the former, differences can range over a whole series of Christian denominations and other faith communities; with the latter, the simple bipolar distinction is between 'Catholics' and 'Protestants'. Here we will concentrate on the latter dimension (see chapter 10 for discussion of denominations).

Historically Belfast has always been a city with a Protestant majority. If we examine trends from the 1830s to 2001 (Figure 4.13) we can see that Catholics as a proportion of the City's population reached a peak in the 1860s (34.1 per cent), this followed by a steady proportionate decline all the way to 1926 (23 per cent). This decline did not mean that the *number* of Catholics decreased. Rather, it means that the number of Protestants grew at a faster rate than that of Catholics. The Catholic proportionate decline ceased in the 1920s, and this was followed by a steadily increasing proportion right up to the end of the twentieth century. Thus by 2001, the Catholic[8] proportion of the City's population (at 42.1 per cent) was higher than it had been at any time in the past.

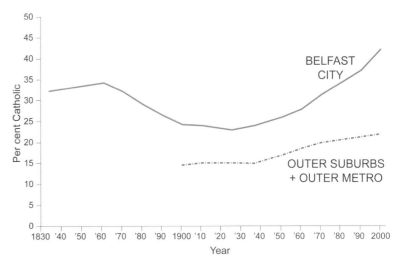

FIGURE 4.13
Percentage of Catholic population, Belfast City, 1835–2001, and Outer Suburbs and Outer Metro, 1901–2001

While the Catholic proportion within the City has ranged from 23 per cent to 42 per cent, this is set within the framework of the wider Metro area, which has been consistently more Protestant than the City (14.6 per cent Catholic in 1901 rising to 21.6 per cent in 2001). Of course, within this very broad-brush picture there have been, and continue to be, major contrasts in the religious geography at a more local level.

Let us first compare the beginning and the end of the twentieth century. The data for this comparison are found in Table 4.7. A number of observations can be made. First, we see that the City has been proportionately more Catholic than the Outer Suburbs, which in turn have been more Catholic than Outer Metro. Second, across the century the Catholic proportion has increased significantly in all three of the major segments of Metro. Third, we can note that the rising Catholic proportion in the City has taken place in a context of population decrease, while such proportionate increases in the Outer Suburbs and in Outer Metro have taken place in a context of overall population growth. The changes in the City provide a particularly striking situation. Here the number of Catholics in 2001 is somewhat greater than the number in 1901, but for Protestants there has been a large numerical decline over the same period. Thus the proportionate increase in Catholics in the City is not, in the main, due to growth in the numbers of Catholics, but to decline in the numbers of Protestants.

TABLE 4.7
Religious Affiliation, Metropolitan Belfast, 1901 and 2001

Area	1901			2001		
	Catholics	Others	% Catholic	Catholics	Others	% Catholic
City	84,888	264,138	24.3	98,020	123,158	42.1
Outer Suburbs	7,856	40,368	16.3	93,004	160,951	35.0
Outer Metro	6,881	73,985	8.5	29,631	181,203	13.3
Metro*	99,625	378,491	20.8	220,655	465,312	32.2

SOURCE: Derived from Census of Ireland 1901 and Census of Northern Ireland 2001

*Metropolitan Belfast (City plus Outer Suburbs plus Outer Metro)

If we look more closely at the geographical patterns of the religious distribution at the beginning and at the end of the twentieth century, we can see that the proportionate growth in Catholics has impacted most markedly on a relatively small number of areas. Within the City itself, and looking at the Super Sectors (Table 4.8), we see that the sharpest increases in the Catholic proportion have taken place in the North and in the South of the City. The significance of the South-West Super Sector (Falls) as the dominant Catholic concentration has been reinforced over the century. On the other hand, much of the East of the City has seen proportionate decline or only a small increase on an initially small base.

The dynamics of the religious geography are, if anything, even more striking in the Outer Suburbs and Outer Metro. The South-West of the Outer Suburbs has seen the most dramatic change. Here the area from Andersonstown to Poleglass has changed from 29 per cent Catholic in 1901 to 92 per cent Catholic in 2001, through a process whereby a predominantly Protestant rural area became overwhelmingly Catholic and suburban.

The impact of this urban spread process is also seen in the outer reaches of the South-West sector, with a particular focus on the growing settlement of Crumlin. Other segments of Metro beyond the City boundary showing significant Catholic numerical and proportionate growth lie along the Breda–Saintfield axis, BS (*I*), and in the north through Glengormley, CA (*I*), and in Antrim town, CA (*O*). Finally there has been a lesser zone of Catholic growth in the segment between Finaghy and Lisburn, LC (*I*) (for locations see Figure 4.2).

A second category of segments shows only small proportionate growth in the Catholic community. All these segments lie to the east of the City, from Holywood to Bangor – SLS (*I*) and SLS (*O*) – and from Castlereagh to Newtownards – DA (*I*) and DA (*O*). Finally, there is an area of Catholic decline along the north shore of Belfast Lough, most marked in the Rathcoole area of Newtownabbey, NLS (*I*). We can also note that 2 segments of the 14 comprising Metro beyond the City are still strongly rural and Protestant in character. The segregation suggested by these patterns requires further examination. We now turn to this task.

Segregation

The fundamental underlying feature of the geography of Catholics and Protestants in Belfast in the twentieth century is one of segregation. This being so, it is important to examine this segregation and its dynamics in some detail.

There may well have been little or no Catholic–Protestant residential segregation in Belfast's early days, as the town was inhabited only by English and Scots settlers. However, there was an appendage outside the walls (earthen banks) of Belfast that was probably occupied by native Irish. So if there was segregation in the early days, it was at a macro scale, not at the level of streets and neighbourhoods.

Belfast grew slowly in the eighteenth century and the scant evidence suggests that, at most, Catholics formed 5 per cent of the population, with some degree of segregation. The nineteenth century was very different – this was Belfast's boom time (see chapter 2: Table 2.1). The labour-force needs of the industrial city were met mainly from the rural

TABLE 4.8
Belfast City, Percentage of Catholic Population in Each Super Sector, 1901 and 2001

Super Sector	1901 % Catholic	2001 % Catholic
E	9.5	4.7
SE	15.9	22.4
S	15.9	50.7
SW	64.7	85.2
W	11.5	19.9
N	24.7	58.9
City	24.3	42.1

SOURCE: Derived from Census of Ireland 1901 and Census of Northern Ireland 2001

hinterland. A fundamental consequence of this was that the proportion of Catholics in Belfast rose rapidly, so that by 1840 one-third of the inhabitants were recorded as being of that persuasion. Catholics (that is, native Irish) were no longer outside the walls but resided in large numbers within the greatly expanded town. There were also many Protestants of rural origin in the stream of in-migrants and it has been suggested that the passions of the Ulster countryside were imported into Belfast with far-reaching consequences.

There are no statistics available to permit any reliable quantification of Catholic–Protestant segregation levels in nineteenth-century Belfast, but there are clear indicators that segregation was a feature of the city, and that such segregation increased significantly in the second half of the century.[9]

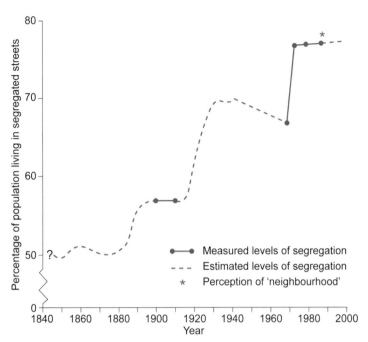

FIGURE 4.14
The segregation ratchet

FREDERICK W. BOAL

By the beginning of the twentieth century it becomes possible to measure segregation in a precise manner.[10] Data from the 1901 census show that almost 60 per cent of the city's inhabitants were residing in streets that could be described as highly segregated (more than 90 per cent of the residents being either Catholic or Protestant). This percentage had risen to 67 by the late 1960s and over the last three decades of the twentieth century was recorded at around 77 per cent.

Segregation between Catholics and Protestants, then, has been a major feature of the city for the past two centuries, and appears to have increased markedly during that time. This pattern of change has been labelled the 'segregation ratchet' by David Smith and Gerald Chambers (Figure 4.14).[11] Residential segregation levels escalate in a series of sharp jumps, with only gradual and modest decline in the intervening periods. Let us briefly explore what underlies this pattern.

Segregation: the underlying factors

Segregation between Protestants and Catholics in Belfast can be interpreted by describing the period 1600–2000 in terms of four phases.[12] The first three phases set the scene for the twentieth century. In the first phase we can refer to the *colonial city*, when, as noted above, Belfast slowly grew as a settler town, inhabited by Protestant people of English and Scottish origins.

The second phase we describe as the *immigrant-industrial city*. The industrial expansion of Belfast in the nineteenth century created a huge demand for labour, particularly in the burgeoning textile and engineering factories. Most of the immigrants thus drawn into Belfast's labour pool originated in the rural north of Ireland. Though Protestants also contributed greatly to this flow, it is useful, as Tony Hepburn has shown, to consider early nineteenth-century Belfast as Protestant territory where Catholic migrants were the incomers. Hepburn suggests that the Catholic community could be considered 'the Irish in Belfast', comparable to the Irish immigrants in Glasgow, Liverpool and Boston.[13] In all these situations a significant degree of ethnic segregation was the norm, with residential clustering providing a supportive community environment for the newcomers. In addition, such clustering can be seen as a response to hostile surroundings where the Irish immigrants were not welcomed with open arms by many members of the respective 'host' populations.

The immigrant model is a helpful interpretative device in any analysis of segregation in Belfast. However, two qualifications must be entered. First, unlike other urban immigrant environments, segregation in Belfast did not decline with time – the 'immigrants' (the Catholics) did not become assimilated into the receiving population matrix. Second, the 'host' population of nineteenth-century Belfast (the Protestants) were much less certain of their own position than equivalent populations in cities such as Glasgow or Liverpool. Though a substantial majority in the city, they would have been conscious of their minority demographic status in the island of Ireland as a whole. The 'Irish' immigrants were not incomers from distant lands – they were part of the much larger 'native' population just outside the 'gates'.

In the third phase we refer to the *ethno-national city emergent*. Overlapping with industrialisation, and intensifying as the nineteenth century progressed, we can note the emergence of an imperative amongst some Irish Catholics founded on a determination to break the political union of Ireland and Great Britain. However, the Protestant majority in Belfast (and elsewhere in the north of the island) was resolutely opposed to any such secession. The consequences for Belfast's already divided ethnic geography were emphatic. Catholic–Protestant segregation increased further (the pattern in 1911 can be seen in Figure 4.15). Much of this came in short, sharp jolts associated with particularly active phases of the political argument over Home Rule for Ireland. In this instance, political turmoil was reproduced in the streets of Belfast in the form of intercommunal rioting, accompanied by the displacement of many Catholic and Protestant households living in neighbourhoods where their group was the minority.

In this phase Belfast clearly emerges as what has been called a frontier city[14] or a polarised city.[15] Joel Kötek's frontier city is a disputed city because of its location on fault lines between ethnic, religious or ideological wholes. A frontier city is 'a territory for two dreams'.[16] Meron Benvenisti's polarised city is similar. Here the focus is specifically on sovereignty claims: interethnic disputes are not only rooted in day-to-day bread-and-butter issues (such as housing, education or health care) but extend to and, indeed, are dominated by profound disagreements over which state is the legitimate claimant to the urban space in question.

If we see the beginnings of the *ethno-national city* in the second half of the nineteenth century, twentieth-century

FIGURE 4.15
Map of segregation, 1911

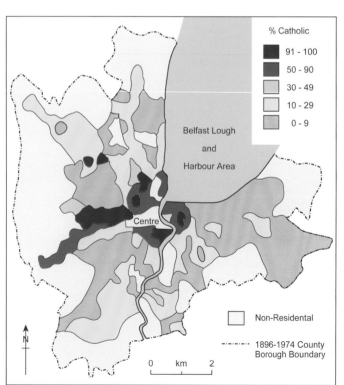

% Catholic

91 - 100
50 - 90
30 - 49
10 - 29
0 - 9

Belfast Lough
and
Harbour Area

Centre

Non-Residental

1896-1974 County
Borough Boundary

0   km   2

Belfast can be described as the *ethno-national city rampant* – our fourth phase. By 1920 the 'solution' to the ethno-national conflict in Ireland as a whole saw partition, whereby most of the island (mostly 'Irish' and Catholic) seceded from the UK, while the north-east corner (predominantly 'British' and Protestant) was granted a degree of local autonomy, but still within the broader political ambit of the UK.

Encapsulating the ethno-national conflict, Belfast experienced much communal violence in the early 1920s. This further sharpened segregation, as members of each ethno-national group were forced to seek the safety of their own enclaves (see chapter 13). The ethno-national 'earthquake' of the early 1920s in Belfast was followed by a long period of relative calm. However, the underlying ethno-national dispute remained unresolved as the Protestants consolidated their hold on the reins of government in Belfast and elsewhere in Northern Ireland, while the Catholics retreated into a sullen, alienated, and, to some degree, institutionally self-sufficient world. Thus segregation levels remained high, though there probably was some decline (see again Figure 4.14, and the pattern in 1951 as shown in Figure 4.16).

A second ethno-national 'earthquake' struck the city in 1969, rumbling on with recently decreased intensity ever since. Rioting, followed by paramilitary violence of unprecedented ferocity, gave a new twist to the segregation screw – the ratchet jerked up once again. Bombing, shooting, fire-raising, intimidation – all conspired to create a city almost overwhelmed by on-the-street manifestations of ethno-national struggle.

The unprecedented violence and the escalation of residential segregation to new heights produced a city more deeply divided than ever before (Figure 4.17). Into this fractured space was inserted a series of physical barriers – variously referred to as 'peace lines', 'peace walls', and 'environmental barriers' (Figures 4.18 and 14.19). These were constructed at 'interfaces' – locations where highly segregated Catholic and Protestant neighbourhoods butted uncomfortably against

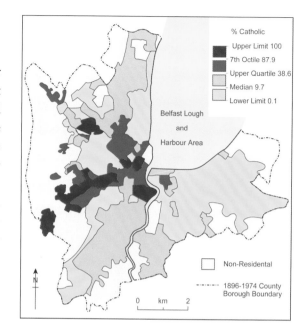

FIGURE 4.16
Map of segregation, 1951

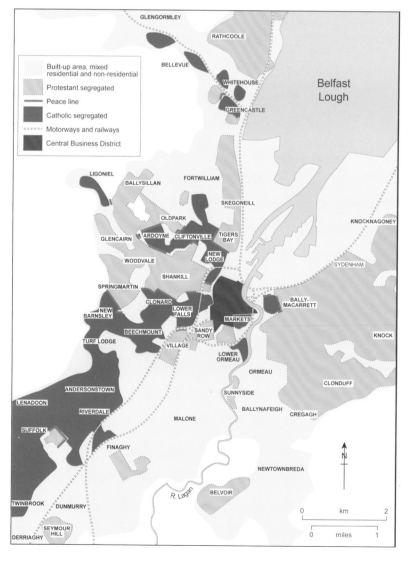

FIGURE 4.17
Segregation and peace walls, 2000

each other. Government-instigated, the peace walls were intended to reduce or eliminate localised neighbourhood-against-neighbourhood conflict. When first constructed in September 1969 it was hoped that they would be temporary expedients. However, not only are these walls still in place more than thirty years later, but others have also been introduced into the urban fabric.

Territoriality

The building of physical barriers between the competing ethno-national groups is nothing new in Belfast. Such were constructed in the early 1920s at what we would now refer to as interfaces; they have re-emerged and greatly proliferated since 1969. Their presence forcefully reminds us of the deep significance of territorial loyalties and behaviour in the city. Sometimes this behaviour is not very evident, at other times it bursts forth in quite stark ways. There is one location that can serve to illustrate this point – the interface between Catholic Clonard and Protestant Shankill in the west of the city. This was a conflict zone during the Troubles of the early 1920s (for instance, the 'Battle of Kashmir Road'). There followed a long period of quiet before the latent territoriality burst forth with renewed fury in August 1969. All this can be encapsulated in a series of photographs taken between December 1967 and January 1984 (Figure 4.20 a, b, c, and d). They are all taken from the same location in Kashmir Road, looking towards the Shankill neighbourhood. The first, taken in 1967, shows a woman returning from the Shankill to Clonard with some shopping – no obvious territorial restraints evident here; the second shows barriers erected by local people in August 1969 for defensive purposes after the re-emergence of aggressive territorial behaviour in that month; the third shows a relatively

FIGURE 4.18
Peace line in Bryson Street

STEPHEN A. ROYLE

FIGURE 4.19
The peace line between
Alliance Road and Ardoyne

IRISH NEWS

modest 'official barrier' erected by the government in September 1969, which was intended to be a 'temporary measure'; finally, the fourth shows the extended barrier present at the same location twenty-five years later. At the time of writing (July 2005) this barrier (the Cupar Street wall) is still in place, presenting to citizen and visitor alike a stark visual symbol of the ethno-nationally divided fabric of the city,[17] a division well rooted before the twentieth century began, but most sharply evident since the early 1900s.

FIGURE 4.20
The Shankill–Falls divide

(a) December 1967
(b) August 1969
(c) September 1969
(d) September 1994

FREDERICK W. BOAL

MIGRATION

People changing their residential locations can have a profound impact on the distribution of population in a metropolitan area. Such movements can contribute to the increase or the decrease in the numbers of people in an area, or if the inflows and the outflows are approximately in balance, they can contribute to a constancy in numbers. In addition, such flows can change the *composition* of the population in an area – for instance, older people may be moving in and younger people moving out, or members of one religious community may be moving in, while members of another may be moving out. Of course, as noted earlier, we must always remember that migration is only one of the two components of population change, the other component being 'natural' increase or decrease – the difference between the number of births and the number of deaths. With respect to the latter, we can note that in the City around the time of the 1926 census, there were 69 per cent more births than deaths, but by 2001 this had shrunk to 10 per cent. This change was due to a much younger population being present

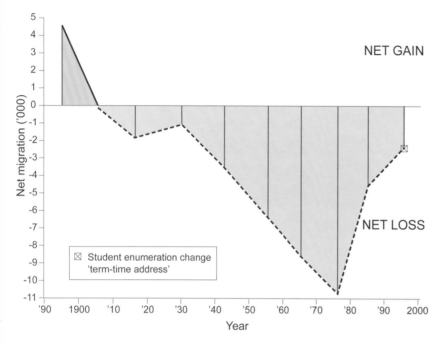

NET GAIN

NET LOSS

⊠ Student enumeration change
'term-time address'

Net migration ('000)

Year

FIGURE 4.21
Net migration, Belfast City

in 1901 with a much higher birth rate than was the case in 2001, when the population was older and the birth rate lower.

There are huge data limitations when we attempt to measure migration as it impacts on the Metro area. The only usable data that can be deployed right across the twentieth century refer to the City (as constituted between 1896 and 1973 and then as reconstituted between 1973 and the end of the century). Moreover, we can only measure migration as 'net migration' – that is, in the form of the balance between in-migration and out-migration.

Let us look at the net migration picture (Figure 4.21). This shows the net migration on an average annual basis (the averages having been calculated for each intercensal period). The data are drawn from each of the censuses from 1891 to 2001[18] (but excluding 1966; see Appendix A.2). What we see is that the City has been a net loser of population by migration throughout the twentieth century. However, we also see that the volume of this loss has varied greatly, from a miniscule average loss of 27 people per year between 1901 and 1911 to a massive 10,700 per year between 1971 and 1991.

The first intercensal period shown on Figure 4.21 (1891–1901) discloses the City gaining by in-migration. This seems to be the tail end of the great influx of people in the last few decades of the nineteenth century. From 1911 to 1937 the City became a loser by net migration, though the overall net movement was small (in part the picture is formed by the fact that the City could expand within its own boundaries (see Figures 4.8a and 4.8b). From the 1940s the situation begins to change quite radically. The City starts to run out of land for housing within its own boundaries, meaning that suburban expansion increasingly became part of out-migration. Housing redevelopment in the inner City in combination with large scale public and private housing development beyond the City boundary is the major contributor to an accelerating net out-migration in the 1950s and 1960s. Continued redevelopment 'thinning', with the additional push factor of the ethno-national violence of the Troubles then produces the peak of out-movement in the 1970s,[19] followed in the 1980s by a slowdown in population loss by migration; a further sign of this is evident between 1991 and 2001. In all this the roller-coaster nature of Belfast's twentieth-century population dynamics is once again most evident.

The only other data spanning the twentieth century that give any indication of the volume and nature of migration into or out of Belfast is provided by the birthplace figures (Table 4.9). The basic story here is that Belfast has drawn its in-migrant population overwhelmingly from the northern part of Ireland. The relatively high proportions born in the Irish Republic and Great Britain recorded in the censuses between 1926 and 1951 probably reflect the small but significant in-migration flows from those areas that occurred in the early part of the twentieth century and, indeed, in the latter part of the nineteenth. As the City became a population exporter in the second half of the twentieth century it clearly did not generate much of a countervailing in-migration from other parts of the world, unlike many major industrial centres in Britain. Thus at the end of the twentieth century Belfast had a very small but nonetheless important and now growing 'ethnic minority' population.

TABLE 4.9
Belfast City, Birthplaces, Census Years 1901–2001

Census Year	% born in Northern Ireland*	% born in Irish Republic**	% born in Great Britain	% born abroad
1901	89.3	3.2	6.6	0.8
1911	88.7	3.3	7.2	0.8
1926	87.7	5.5	6.1	0.8
1937	89.3	4.6	5.4	0.8
1951	90.2	4.0	5.0	0.8
1961	91.2	3.2	4.6	1.0
1971	90.6	2.7	4.6	1.0
1991	92.1	1.8	3.3	2.0
2001	91.4	2.3	3.4	1.8

SOURCE: Census of Ireland 1901 and 1911; Census of Northern Ireland 1926–2001

*1901 and 1911: nine-county province of Ulster
**1901 and 1911: Ireland less nine-county province of Ulster. For 1901 and 1911 the data are not available on a county basis. Consequently, the Northern Ireland figures for these two years will entail overstatement, while those for the Irish Republic will entail understatement. 'City' in 1991 and 2001 is the larger unit established in 1973. Data from the 1981 census are excluded.

THE OVERALL PICTURE

So what are the key features of Belfast's twentieth-century population? In terms of the numbers of people the century has seen two fundamental changes – a large growth in the Metro area overall, combined with a radical redistribution of the population, from a situation of high density concentration in the inner part of Metro (the City) at the beginning of the century to a much more dispersed lower density urban agglomeration at century end. These changes were evident in a large growth in the Outer Suburbs and Outer Metro populations and a remarkable decline in the City population. The interaction of the number of births, the number of deaths and migration flows lies at the heart of much of the population change we have recorded – and not only numerical change but change in composition as well.

Roughly paralleling the pattern of population change has been change in the number and spatial distribution of dwellings. Within this distribution there has also been a striking decrease in the number of people in the 'average' dwelling, so that by the end of the twentieth century Metro Belfast required a disproportionate number of dwellings to house its population relative to the situation in 1901. Our survey of the population of twentieth-century Belfast also notes changes in the composition of that population – a varying and spatially complex female majority, a varying and spatially complex Protestant majority and an age profile that has shifted from a youthful population to one with a much greater proportion of older people. In addition, we have noted increasing Catholic–Protestant segregation across much of the twentieth century.

The twenty-first century now beckons with demographic uncertainties potentially as great as those experienced by Belfast in the century just past.

APPENDICES

A.1. AREA FRAMEWORK

To enable analysis of the census material to be carried out on a consistent basis across the twentieth century, an area framework has been established, an approximately concentric system made up of three parts (see Figure 4.2):

i   the City of Belfast, defined by the boundary established in 1896

ii an Outer Suburbs area, lying between the City boundary and the edge of the built-up area as it existed at the end of the twentieth century

iii an area referred to as Outer Metro, lying between the Outer Suburbs boundary, on the one hand, and the outer edge of Metropolitan Belfast (Metro), on the other. The Outer Metro boundary lies approximately 13.7 miles (22 km) from Belfast City Hall.

In addition, the concentric zones are subdivided into sectors:

i   the City is subdivided into six Super Sectors. These Super Sectors are aggregates of the fifteen wards that existed between 1896 and 1973 and aggregates of the wards delineated and subsequently operational from 1973 onwards. The Super Sectors are referred to as East, South-East, South, South-West, West and North (see Figure 4.4).

ii the Outer Suburbs and Outer Metro are subdivided into seven sectors. Moving clockwise from the southern shore of Belfast Lough, these are: South Lough Shore; Dundonald–Ards; Breda–Saintfield; Lagan Corridor; Andersonstown–Crumlin; Carnmoney–Antrim; and North Lough Shore. The parts of the sectors in the Outer Suburbs are referred to as 'Inner', while the parts in Outer Metro are referred to as 'Outer'. For example, the inner part of the North Lough Shore sector is referred to as North Lough Shore Inner, NLS (*I*), and the outer as North Lough Shore Outer, NLS (*O*) (see Figure 4.2).

A.2. DATA BUILDING BLOCKS

Two sets of building blocks are used in this analysis:

i   the population census
ii small areas

The Census

For the twentieth century, censuses covering the six-county area that became Northern Ireland were held in 1901 and 1911, and censuses covering Northern Ireland itself were held in 1926, 1937, 1951, 1961, 1966, 1971, 1981, 1991 and 2001. The overall objective has been to hold a decennial census but it will be evident that this has not always been achieved. The difficulties in Ireland associated with civil war and partition prevented the 1921 census taking place, with 1926 serving as a substitute. No census was held in 1931, as it was thought too close to 1926, and a limited census was carried out in 1937 on the assumption that a full census would take place in 1941. The Second World War put paid to that and consequentially the next census was held in 1951. Since that time the decennial frequency has been achieved, with the addition of a limited census in 1966. However, there were difficulties with the 1971 enumeration and very major problems with that held in 1981, due to political factors and an environment dominated by ethno-national violence. For the present analysis we use data from all the censuses except 1966 and 1981. The 1981 census is not used (except for a few estimates) because of its considerable unreliability.

The Spatial Building Blocks

The areas used in this study (see Figure 4.2) are constructed from a series of smaller units. Table 4.10 provides information on the building blocks used. Our objective was to retain a consistent, comparable set of spatial data units for all nine censuses used in the analysis. One of the most important objectives was to retain a constant City boundary from 1901 to 2001. This was achieved by using the City boundary as established in 1896 as the standard line. The official city boundary was changed significantly in 1973, but for our purposes here the census data have been redistributed in such a way as to reconstitute the City along the line of the 1896–1973 boundary. This was done by allocating the wards to the appropriate side of the 1896 boundary. Where the boundary ran through a ward, the population of that ward was allocated according to the proportion of dwellings in the ward on either side of the line, creating what we refer to as 'ward fragments'. The dwelling counts were made using large scale Ordnance Survey maps.

Similarly with the construction of the Super Sectors in the City. Up to and including 1971 the Super Sectors were straightforward aggregations of the existing fifteen wards. For 1991 and 2001 the Super Sectors were built in the same way as the 1896 City boundary was retained – by using wards or ward fragments. Outside the City the sectors and their inner and outer segments were built using aggregations of district electoral divisions (up to and including 1971) and wards and ward fragments thereafter.

TABLE 4.10
Spatial Building Blocks for the Census Analysis

Census Year	City	Outer Suburbs and Outer Metro
1901, 1911	15 wards	64 district electoral divisions
1926–1971	15 wards	84 district electoral divisions
1971	52 wards/ward fragments	127 wards/ward fragments
1991	51 wards/ward fragments	153 wards/ward fragments
2001	53 wards/ward fragments	161 wards/ward fragments

SOURCE: District electoral division and electoral ward maps as appropriate

NOTE: 1971 census year: some of the data are available for the pre-1973 system of areal units, some for the post-1971 and some for both.

81

The 1973 changes to local government boundaries and the associated switch to a new system of wards places considerable stress on any attempt to retain a consistent data base across the twentieth century. Indeed, one is tempted to call the change the 'Great Disruption'. Compounding this has been a process whereby the new wards drawn up in 1973 have been subject to further revision up to and including 2001.

One irony should be noted. For the period from 1901 through 1971 it is possible to obtain census data on a much finer spatial scale for the area beyond the City boundary than for the area within it, even though in the first half of the century most of the population was located in the latter.

A.3. FURTHER POPULATION STATISTICS

Tables 4.11, 4.12 and 4.13 present further population statistics for Belfast and its surrounding area in the twentieth century and projections for the twenty-first century.

TABLE 4.11
Population of Metropolitan Belfast, Census Years 1901–2001

Area	1901	1911	1926	1937	1951	1961	1971	1991	2001
City	349,180	386,947	415,151	438,086	443,671	415,856	362,082	236,116	232,319
Outer Suburbs	48,329	52,295	58,716	68,088	103,976	162,570	240,309	244,435	265,541
Outer Metro	80,860	84,108	89,818	92,908	107,716	115,434	147,248	203,638	225,587
BUA*	397,509	439,242	473,867	506,174	547,647	578,426	602,391	480,551	497,860
Metro**	478,369	523,350	563,685	599,082	655,363	693,860	749,639	684,189	723,447

SOURCES: Derived from Census of Ireland 1901 and 1911; Census of Northern Ireland 1926–2001

*Belfast Urban Area (City plus Outer Suburbs)
**Metropolitan Belfast (City plus Outer Suburbs plus Outer Metro)
Data from 1966 and 1981 censuses are excluded.

TABLE 4.12
Number of Dwellings in Metropolitan Belfast, Census Years 1901–2001

Area	1901	1911	1926	1937	1951	1961	1971	1991	2001
City	77,786	80,257	84,667	106,535	110,619	118,003	119,755	102,346	102,906
Outer Suburbs	10,850	11,377	12,946	16,870	28,058	43,727	68,856	90,227	105,536
Outer Metro	20,056	20,702	22,404	26,195	31,036	34,781	47,157	76,318	89,257
BUA*	88,636	91,634	97,613	123,405	138,677	161,730	188,611	192,573	208,442
Metro**	108,692	112,336	120,017	149,600	169,713	196,511	235,768	268,891	297,699

SOURCES: Derived from Census of Ireland 1901 and 1911; Census of Northern Ireland 1926–2001

*Belfast Urban Area (City plus Outer Suburbs)
**Metropolitan Belfast (City plus Outer Suburbs plus Outer Metro)
Data from 1966 and 1981 censuses are excluded.

TABLE 4.13

Belfast City and Metropolitan Belfast Population and Projections, 1971, 1991, 2001, 2011 and 2016

Area	1971	1991	2001	2011	2016
Belfast City 1896 boundary	362,082	236,116	232,319	n/a	n/a
Belfast City 1973 boundary	416,679	310,100	279,237	263,313	258,858
Metro defined by 8 Local Government Districts	767,700	727,391	768,130	770,224	771,875
Metro defined in Figure 4.2	749,639	684,189	723,447	n/a	n/a

SOURCE: Derived from Census of Northern Ireland 1971, 1991 and 2001. Population projections for 2011 and 2016 from Northern Ireland Statistics and Research Agency (NISRA): www.nisra.gov.uk/publications

NOTES: n/a = not available. Population of Belfast City 1971–2001 as defined by the 1896 City boundary and by the 1973 boundary. Population of Metropolitan Belfast 1971–2001 as delineated in Figure 4.2 and as defined by Local Government Districts (Antrim, Ards, Belfast, Carrickfergus, Castlereagh, Lisburn, Newtownabbey, North Down). Projections for 2011 and 2016 (General Register Office Northern Ireland) are given for the 1973 Belfast City boundary area and for Metropolitan Belfast (as defined by the Local Government Districts).

NOTES

1   When 'City' is used in this chapter with a capital C, it refers specifically to the area delimited originally by the 1896 boundary.

2   See Appendix A.1 for discussion of the area framework.

3   The term 'Outer Suburbs', rather than just 'Suburbs', is used because the older suburbs of Belfast developed *within* the City boundary. Thus in the earlier part of the twentieth century suburbanisation was a within-City phenomenon.

4   From 1901 to 1951 inclusive, the count is of 'houses'. In 1961 the count is of 'buildings for habitation', while in 1971 the count is of 'private dwellings'. In 1991 the dwelling count is achieved by combining 'private households' and 'unoccupied dwellings'. Finally, in 2001 the count is of 'all dwellings'. At each census the 'dwelling' count includes unoccupied/vacant units.

5   Demolished dwellings numbered 8,809 in the redevelopment process in the 1990s; 3,724 were 'put back' (i.e. replacement dwellings).

6   The figures for 1901 apply to the 1896 City; for 2001 they apply to the more extensive Belfast City Council area.

7   John Brewer describes ethnicity as the most popular portrayal of the Catholic–Protestant dichotomy 'with the groups being seen as ethnic ones socially marked by religion', see Brewer, J. (1992) 'Sectarianism and racism, and their parallels and differences', *Ethnic and Racial Studies*, 15.3, pp. 352–64.

8   For 2001 the Catholic category used is that defined by the census as 'Community Background'.

9   Jones, Emrys (1960) *A social geography of Belfast*, Oxford University Press: Oxford.

10   See Doherty, Paul, and Poole, Michael A. (1995) *Ethnic residential segregation in Belfast*, University of Ulster Centre for the Study of Conflict: Coleraine.

11   Smith, David, and Chambers, Gerald (1991) *Inequality in Northern Ireland*, Clarendon Press: Oxford.

12   Boal, Frederick W. (2002) 'Belfast: walls within', *Political Geography*, 21, pp. 687–94.

13   Hepburn, Anthony C. (1996) *A past apart*, Ulster Historical Foundation: Belfast.

14   Kötek, Joel (1999) 'Divided cities in the European cultural context', *Progress in Planning*, 52, pp. 227–39.

15   Benvenisti, Meron (1987) Presentation at Salzburg Seminar 287 'Divided Cities', February 11, Salzburg, Austria.

16   Kötek (1991) 'Divided cities', p. 228.

17   Boal, Frederick W. (1978) 'Territoriality on the Shankill-Falls Divide: the perspective from 1976', in David A. Lanegran and Risa Palm (eds) *An invitation to geography* (2nd ed.), McGraw-Hill: New York, pp. 58–77.

18   The data used here for the years 1891–1971 are based on the City boundary as defined in 1896. For the subsequent years they are based on the city defined by the redrawn 1973 boundary.

19   The out-migration of the 1971–91 period must have been disproportionately Protestant to produce the changes observed in the relative numbers of Protestants and Catholics.

5

From Smokestacks to Service Economy

Foundations for a Competitive City?

Mark Hart

For many decades throughout the twentieth century the economy of Belfast was shaped and defined in terms of the fortunes of a particular sector and industry, and indeed by the decisions of a handful of boardrooms located in the city. From the heyday of the early years of the century to the continuing struggle for survival since the mid-1960s, the name of Harland and Wolff was never far from the lips of the people of Belfast (Figure 5.1).[1]

FIGURE 5.1
Harland and Wolff shipyard, 1973

CECIL NEWMAN

Whether to bemoan the passing of an industrial era and to demand, Canute-like, intervention to halt the inevitable, or simply to bear witness to the passing of a significant symbol of the sectarian divide in the city,[2] the 'yard' came to represent a statement about the way the city sought to cope with the increasing global nature of economic development. But the Belfast economy was always characterised by more than one firm and the shadow it cast over the fortunes of the city.

Indeed, Richard Harrison estimates that Harland and Wolff's value to the city and regional economy was actually much lower than shipbuilding in other regions such as Wearside and Clydeside.[3] This chapter develops a short narrative of the development of the economy of Belfast over the last 100 years and attempts to provide an assessment of its future in the context of the development of global connectivity in terms of the inter-connections of business and people. Many historical accounts exist which chart the progress of industrialisation in Belfast since the nineteenth century.[4] This chapter will not attempt to review this body of literature, but rather draw from it some understanding of its legacy for the future economic development of the city. The aim is to provide some assessment of the ability of the Belfast economy to provide a growing and sustainable city economy for its residents and indeed to become a key driver for the wider regional economy. The 'economic' reach of Belfast in the twenty-first century is rather different from that observed 100 years ago.

INDUSTRIAL GROWTH, DECLINE AND RETRENCHMENT

Two industrial developments of the nineteenth century provided the stimulus for the rapid expansion of Belfast to its position as a flourishing commercial and industrial city at the beginning of the twentieth century. These developments were the factory production of linen and shipbuilding.[5] From these basic industries came new opportunities for developments in engineering and, by the end of the nineteenth century, the production of textile machinery was the main branch of that industry in the city.

Further, the growth of population, from 75,000 in 1841 to 349,000 in 1901, due mainly to in-migration, produced a demand for a range of goods and services that resulted in a further expansion of the city.[6] At this time the character of Belfast was very similar

FIGURE 5.2
Workers leaving Harland and Wolff at the end of their shift, 1910 or 1911

ULSTER MUSEUM

to many northern industrial cities in Great Britain.[7] By 1910 three manufacturing trades dominated the industrial structure of Belfast: linen, shipbuilding (Figure 5.2) and engineering. Belfast at this time was clearly a proud and very prosperous industrial city, but this situation did not last for long. The goods in which the city specialised were in demand during the First World War, but in the postwar period Belfast underwent a radical economic change. Linen and shipbuilding suffered substantial decline and the growth in the engineering sector came to an end.[8] As Jonathan Bardon records, by 1932 the number unemployed in Northern Ireland stood at 76,000 (28 per cent), of which no less than 45,000 were in Belfast.[9] One of the primary reasons for this decline was related to falling pro-

FIGURE 5.3
The Belfast Ropeworks,
Newtownards Road, *c.* 1942

ULSTER FOLK & TRANSPORT
MUSEUM

ductivity levels in the UK shipbuilding industry associated with rapid technological change. Harrison describes this as the 'penalty' for having been first mover in an industry that for many years had led with major technological developments.[10] He argued that the speed and nature of the reaction to technological change in the UK shipyards was retarded by a combination of low investment, underdeveloped design capabilities, and poor labour practices and management.

However, the manufacturing base of Belfast was not completely eroded during the 1920s and 1930s. Some firms actually managed to expand their trade, the most notable being Gallaher's, Davidson's (tea machinery), the Belfast Ropeworks (Figure 5.3), and Neills, Andrews and White, and Tomkins and Courage (both milling). Also the rapid rise of the service sector, in particular wholesale and retail distribution, professional services, education and government, went some way towards compensating for the setbacks associated with the decline of Belfast's leading industries.[11] Indeed, by 1937 services provided 100,000 jobs in Belfast.

The Second World War saw prosperity temporarily return to the city as a whole and to the shipbuilding and linen industries in particular. However, the trends of decline identified in the 1920s and 1930s then re-established themselves. Once again the two most severely troubled industries were shipbuilding and linen. For the linen industry 1952 marks the major watershed of its changing fortunes with the end of the postwar boom in demand for textiles and the rise of competition from other, cheaper products.[12] Overall, the level of employment in the linen industry had fallen in Belfast by approximately 15,000 workers from its 1927 level of 45,000.[13] It has been estimated that at the start of the 1950s the total number of employees in the linen industry in Northern Ireland was 61,000, around half of which were located in Belfast.[14]

Employment in shipbuilding suffered a decline from 18,500 to 16,000 workers between 1949 and 1951 as a direct result of the shortage of steel at that time.[15] Nevertheless, the level of employment in the sector remained relatively stable throughout the 1950s but by the 1960s falling world demand began to seriously erode the industry's global position. In the immediate postwar years, therefore, the industrial city of Belfast was undergoing a period of transition. The two basic industries, which had contributed so much to its earlier prosperity, were in decline. Yet the number employed in the manufacturing sector in Belfast had increased during the period 1930–51, from 85,000 to 125,000 persons, located predominantly within a mile and a quarter (2 km) of Belfast City Hall.[16] Clearly the city's employment structure was beginning to diversify, with the expansion of other industries more than offsetting the decline in linen and shipbuilding. Together these two industries represented just over one-third (34.6 per cent) of total manufacturing employment in 1951.[17]

INDUSTRIAL DIVERSIFICATION AND RESTRUCTURING

Therefore, despite the decline of linen and shipbuilding, the economy of the city was buoyant in the 1950s. The fact that by the end of the 1950s only 10 per cent of Belfast's industrial employment was in its former staple industries did not diminish the dominance of Belfast in the regional economy. One of the most striking features of the distribution of industry in Northern Ireland was the marked concentration of manufacturing employment in Belfast. In 1951, approximately 58 per cent of employees in the sector were located in Belfast.[18]

Unemployment remained low as a direct result of the growing importance of firms new to Northern Ireland in completely new sectors, many of which were attracted by the industrial development (ID) legislation introduced by the Northern Ireland government.[19] In particular, the addition of modern engineering firms to the list of employers in the city strengthened the engineering sector. Industrial estates constructed under the ID legislation in the 1950s were the location for a number of major new firms engaged in such diverse activities as precision engineering, oil drilling, aircraft parts, food processing and toy manufacturing. These new industrial estates were developed on the boundary of the then Belfast County Borough in relatively sparsely developed areas such as Castlereagh in the east, Dunmurry in the south-west, and Carnmoney and Monkstown in the north.[20] Traditional inner-city-based industries were being replaced by new and relocated enterprises on the urban fringe and beyond (Figure 5.4). Tony Hoare demonstrated that over the period 1945 to 1973 between two-thirds and three-quarters of manufacturing plants supported with grant aid by the Ministry of Commerce chose sites within 30 miles (48.3 km) of Belfast, a large proportion of which were located in the large industrial estates of the Belfast Urban Area (BUA) – which included the contiguous district council areas of Castlereagh, Newtownabbey and Lisburn.[21]

Even well into the 1960s, these new developments had managed to offset to some extent the decline of Belfast's

FIGURE 5.4
Distribution of manufacturing industry in Belfast, early 1950s

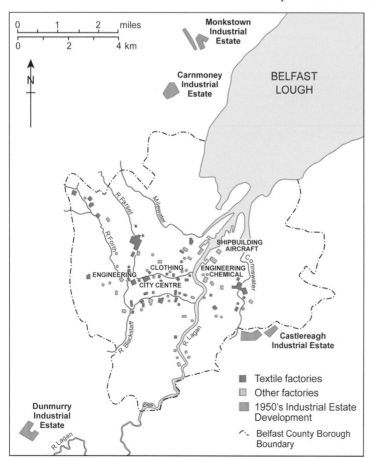

traditional industries. Throughout the 1960s, total ID employment, driven by the wider operation of UK regional policy, rose steadily at a rate varying between 3 and 7 per cent per annum, compared with a decline in what may be termed indigenous, locally controlled manufacturing employment.[22] Nevertheless, over the period 1959–71 the major feature of manufacturing employment change in Northern Ireland was the declining industrial base of Belfast, which experienced a net loss of 26.4 per cent of manufacturing employment.[23] This suburbanisation of the manufacturing base of the city was a key feature of the development of the sector in this period, which led to what can be termed a 'hollowing out' of the city economy.

Against this background total employment in Belfast had grown steadily since 1945 and reached approximately a quarter of a million by 1966, largely as a result of the growth of the service sector.[24] More specifically, in the 1959 to 1965 period total employment had increased by just under 5 per cent in the city, while the surrounding local authority areas making up the BUA were growing rapidly – in excess of 25 per cent in this six-year period.[25]

From 1965 to 1971 this process of industrial suburbanisation was replaced by a broader sub-regional shift in employment driven by the intra-regional planning strategy of the period based on the concept of 'growth centres' focused around the new towns of Antrim and Craigavon and the flow of inward investment into Northern Ireland.[26] As a result, the broader Belfast region and the BUA recorded employment growth rates of over 10 per cent, while Belfast city experienced a decline in total employment.

INDUSTRIAL TRANSFORMATION

The onset of the political conflict in Northern Ireland at the end of the 1960s was to provide a destabilising backdrop to the development of the city economy for the last three decades of the twentieth century. Belfast and Londonderry bore the brunt of the civil unrest, or 'Troubles', throughout this period and the effects on the attempts to develop a sustainable city economy were considerable.[27] Total employment declined in the BUA by 2.2 per cent in the period 1971–78, while in Northern Ireland as a whole there was an increase of 6.3 per cent.[28] While the service sector and, in particular, public services had continued to grow in Belfast throughout the 1970s, the further decline of the manufacturing sector meant that total employment in the city fell.

However, it would be wrong to suggest that the Troubles were solely to blame for the decline of manufacturing employment, as at the same time the world slump of 1974, together with the subsequent slump five years later, produced dramatic effects in Belfast and its broader region, as manufacturing expansion, through the growth of ID investment, almost disappeared overnight and the remnants of the traditional industrial base struggled for survival.[29] The process of deindustrialisation affected Belfast in very similar ways to other major industrial cities throughout the UK and the rest of Western Europe.[30]

Between 1973 and 1986 the rate of manufacturing employment decline in Belfast[31] was around 50 per cent, compared to just under 40 per cent for Northern Ireland as a whole.[32] This represented a loss of 38,400 jobs in firms that were trading in Belfast at the start of the 1970s, or, put another way, just over one in two of the 67,000 manufacturing jobs in the city in 1973 were lost in this thirteen-year period. Externally owned firms were responsible for 16,000 of these job losses, while medium and large scale enterprises (that is, firms with more than 50 employees) contributed a further 18,800, with the Harland and Wolff shipyard, Mackie's Engineering and Short Brothers aircraft manufacturers providing the bulk of these losses. In the face of this decline, job creation[33] through inward investment and new firm formation was only able to contribute 5,600 jobs with the majority (3,900 jobs) being created by locally owned small businesses.

This scale of manufacturing decline since the early 1970s served to break the link in the minds of the people of Belfast between their industrial past and their economic future (Figure 5.5). With the growth in employment in the service sector over the same period, that future seemed to have been caught up with the development of a 'white collar' city based upon a completely new set of skills. For example, between 1973 and 1984 service sector employment in the Belfast Travel To Work Area increased by 21 per cent (a net change of 36,200 jobs). However, the immediate effect was rising unemployment rates in the city (for example, 40 per cent in the constituency of West Belfast) as the scale of job loss in manufacturing exceeded that of job creation in the service sector. This, in turn, provoked major urban development initiatives to avoid the breakdown of the social and economic fabric of the city and also avoid the obvious and ominous consequences for the continuing attempts to resolve the ongoing political conflict.[34] These initiatives included the UK Enterprise Zone policy, which created the Belfast Enterprise Zone in 1981, and the European Commission Integrated Operations Programme for Belfast (also in 1981), as well as the Making Belfast Work initiative of 1988.[35]

FIGURE 5.5
DeLorean cars in receivership on the premises of Harland and Wolff in 1982

In the mid-1980s the size of the manufacturing sector in the Belfast City Council Area stood at 67,000 jobs and within a further fifteen years this had shrunk even further to around 16,000 – a net decline of 51,000 jobs. Over forty years, then, there has been a net loss of around 85,000 manufacturing jobs in Belfast (Figure 5.6). The decline has

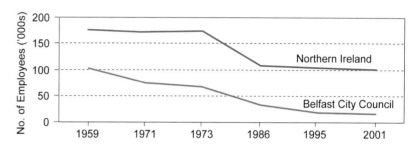

been steady in Belfast, as the traditional industries have been in long-term decline, whereas in Northern Ireland the sharp decline after 1973 represents the impact of the international recession and, more importantly, the disproportionate effect of the closure outside Belfast of the inward investment projects established in the 1950s and 1960s.

FIGURE 5.6
Manufacturing employment in Belfast and Northern Ireland, 1959–2001

By 2001 total employment in Belfast was 182,576, which meant that the manufacturing sector comprised around 9 per cent of total employment, which is amongst the smallest share of all the twenty-six district council areas (DCAs) in Northern Ireland. Thus, the transformation of the industrial structure of Belfast is almost complete by the end of the century. At the start of the 1970s, before the collapse of manufacturing, the manufacturing share of total employment in Belfast was just over one-third (34 per cent), by the end of the 1970s it was just over one-quarter (28 per cent). Even more striking is the fact that around one-third of total manufacturing jobs in the city are within one firm – Bombardier Aerospace (formerly Short Brothers), whose own future will be determined by global trends in the aerospace industry. Having employed over 20,000 persons at the start of the 1960s, Harland and Wolff commenced the twenty-first century with only 1,500 employees and a very different market presence, yet still it remains an important symbol of the city's industrial past as the company seeks to develop its future.

To summarise, in 2001 there were 637,533 persons in employment in Northern Ireland, of which just over one-quarter (28.6 per cent or 182,576 jobs) were in the Belfast City Council Area. The city and the wider Belfast Metropolitan Area[36] possess around two-fifths of the Northern Ireland population and almost half of Northern Ireland's jobs.[37] In brief, Belfast City Council dominates the economy of Northern Ireland – the second largest DCA in terms of the share of businesses and employment is Derry, with around 6 per cent of both businesses and employment.[38]

FIGURE 5.7
Total employment in Belfast City Council Area by sector, 2001

Figure 5.7 presents data on the sectoral distribution of total employment within the Belfast City Council Area. Not surprisingly, the public sector dominates with around one-third of total employment, and, in general, the service sector provides almost 9 out of every 10 jobs in the city. Indeed, over two-thirds (70 per cent) of the Northern Ireland civil service workforce are employed within the city boundary.[39] Since the Belfast Agreement (also known as the Good Friday Agreement) in 1998, Belfast has additionally benefited from the establishment of a number of major national service sector firms bringing substantial investment to the city.

The growth of the service sector in the last three decades has been a key feature of the economy of

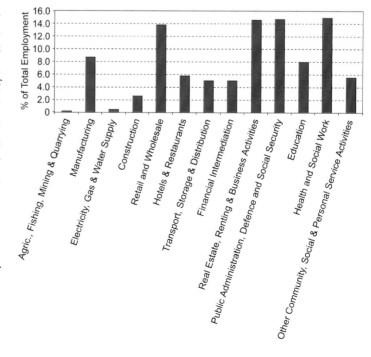

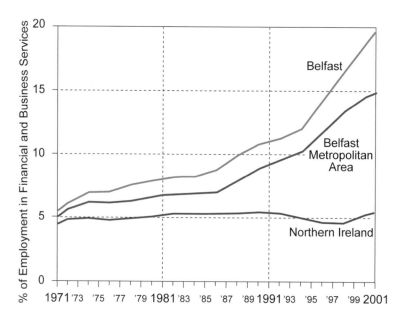

FIGURE 5.8
Business services share of total
employees, 1971–2001

FIGURE 5.9
Manufacturing and service
centre shares of total
employment in Belfast City
Council Area, 1901–2001

BELFAST CITY COUNCIL

Belfast and it is now very clearly a post-industrial city. In this respect it is very similar to the other 'core cities' of the UK,[40] which have all experienced the crossover to an employment structure dominated by services (see chapter 19). Since the mid-1980s the steady decline of employment in most UK cities, including Belfast, has been arrested and the last ten years has seen a growth in Belfast's total employment, which in relative terms has surpassed all other UK cities except Leeds.[41] Figure 5.8 illustrates this by showing the growth of Financial and Business Services in the city, especially since the end of the 1980s. The growth in this sector in Belfast has been the fastest of all the major UK cities by a considerable margin. As a result, the share of Financial and Business Services employment in Belfast has increased from around 5 per cent in 1971 to 20 per cent in 2001, although the proportion still remains small compared to other large UK cities such as Bristol and Manchester.[42]

The dramatic shift from manufacturing to services throughout the twentieth century is starkly illustrated in Figure 5.9, which presents aggregate census data on occupations in manufacturing and services for those resident in Belfast.[43] At the start of the century manufacturing constituted exactly 50 per cent of total employment in the city, a position it maintained for fifty years. The next fifty years saw the rapid growth in the service sector, especially public services, and in 2001 only 10 per cent of those resident in the Belfast City Council Area had an occupation in manufacturing activities.

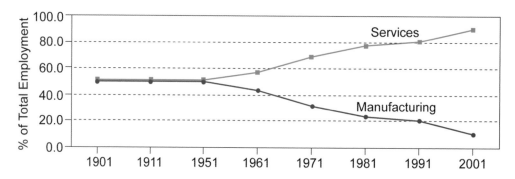

ECONOMIC FUTURES: PROSPECTS AND CHALLENGES

The Future is Services

Against a backdrop of a declining population, Belfast has added 35,000 jobs between 1993 and 2003 and it is estimated that this trend is set to continue for at least the next ten years, with 18,400 extra jobs being created – the vast majority (14,000) being in the Financial and Business Services sector.[44] The growth of this sector in Belfast will move the city up the league table of the UK core cities in terms of the sector's share of total employment. Other important growth sectors in Belfast in recent years have been Hotels and Tourism (Figure 5.10), and Retailing, with an additional 5,000 jobs and 3,500 jobs respectively in the last ten years. However, it is argued that this growth merely represented Belfast 'catching up' with other UK cities after a long period of underinvestment by major national retailers due to the poor image of the city created by the Troubles. Consequently it is estimated that the growth trajectory of this sector will be much slower in the next ten years. Since the Belfast Agreement in 1998 the increase in public sector employment in Belfast has been very marked, with an additional 10,000 jobs being created up to 2003, a large proportion of which were the result of the establishment of the Northern Ireland Assembly. This growth is not predicted to continue. Finally, the forecast for the manufacturing sector in Belfast is that it will undergo further decline in the next decade.

Interestingly this scale of actual and predicted job creation over the period 1993 to 2013, although impressive, would still leave employment levels in the city well below their mid-1960s peak when there were a quarter of a million employees. But is the growth of private sector services sufficient on its own to provide a competitive advantage for the city in the twenty-first century? Why are services, and especially Financial and Business Services, important in the drive to create a globally competitive city?

The rationale for this depends on the nature and scale of services being established in the city and their potential for service sector exports developed on the back of specialist activities. Added to this is the ability of the local service sector to provide 'better value' services in areas such as marketing, advertising, and consultancy finance to those organisations and businesses who have traditionally purchased them from outside the region (that is, through the mechanism of import substitution). The rapid growth of employment in Financial and Business Services in Belfast in recent years, at a rate considerably greater than most other major UK cities, suggests that the city has begun to develop a more sophisticated private service sector.[45]

FIGURE 5.10
Europa Hotel,
Great Victoria Street
SCENIC IRELAND

Manufacturing Matters!

Much of this chapter has documented the decline of the manufacturing sector and the rise of the service sector and therefore it is perhaps strange to revisit a question that seems to seek a return to the industrial legacy of the city. Why should we still care about manufacturing activity? Indeed, as we have just seen, recent economic forecasts for the city estimate that the manufacturing sector will continue to experience a net decline and will fall to less than 10,000 employees by 2013. However, important signs of life were observed in the sector in the late 1990s and these represent a potential opportunity for the city economy.[46] That opportunity, as reinforced in the Department of Trade and Industry's (DTI's) UK Manufacturing Strategy, focuses on manufacturing activity as a driver of economic growth, productivity and competitiveness through the processes of innovation, enterprise, jobs, skills and capital investment (that is, venture capital and private equity finance).

Despite the overall decline of the manufacturing sector in employment terms, it must be acknowledged that the sector represented 20 per cent of Gross Value Added (GVA)[47] in Northern Ireland (compared to 19 per cent for the UK overall), and that manufacturing GVA per head in Northern Ireland was relatively high in a UK context.

An examination of the gross flows of job gains and losses in manufacturing in Belfast over the period 1995 to 2001 shows that although the sector experienced a net decline of 13 per cent (a rate three times greater than in Northern Ireland as a whole) as employment fell to just under 16,000 jobs, this disguised an important dynamic that provides some grounds for optimism for those who still regard manufacturing as an important component of a competitive city (Figure 5.11).[48] Overall, almost 7,000 jobs (or almost two-fifths of the stock of manufacturing jobs in 1995) were lost in the six-year period to 2001, divided almost fifty-fifty between closures and contractions. Further, almost half (45 per cent) of the stock of manufacturing businesses that were trading in 1995 had closed or moved out of the city by 2001, with a loss of 3,477 jobs.

While large firms remain an important determining factor in the fortunes of the manufacturing sector in Belfast, the small firm sector (new starts and surviving businesses) exhibited 'vital signs', which will be an important feature of the future development of the manufacturing sector. Overall, there were 252 new manufacturing openings in the late 1990s, which had created 2,753 jobs by 2001, and a further 104 manufacturing establishments had created another 1,842 jobs at a growth rate of 8.5 per cent per annum. A significant number of these firms can be categorised as small hi-tech, value-added businesses in the engineering and printing sectors, which have the potential to provide both employment opportunities for skilled labour (thus contributing to increased earnings) and export sales outside the region.

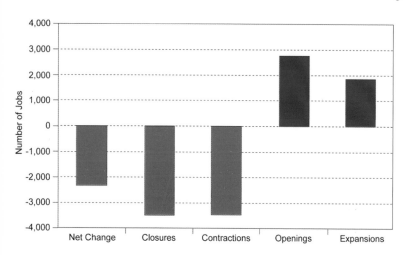

FIGURE 5.11
Components of employment change in Belfast City Council Area, 1995–2001

Belfast as a Twenty-first-Century Entrepreneurial City?

Having built the foundations of the prosperity and economic growth of Belfast in the first half of the twentieth century on enterprise and entrepreneurship, how well equipped is the population of Belfast to repeat that process and produce new business activity in either new firms or existing businesses? We have already seen that new firm formation in the manufacturing sector has been an important positive dimension of change in that sector in the late 1990s, with the creation of around 250 locally owned businesses employing 3,000 people.

Entrepreneurship and enterprise have been at the centre of economic and industrial policy in many countries belonging to the Organisation of Economic Co-operation and Development (OECD) since the 1980s, largely driven there by the presumed role of entrepreneurship and new firm formation in promoting economic growth. Certainly policy interest has sparked a series of attempts to model the links between entrepreneurial activity and the attributes of particular spatial units – local authority areas, cities, regions – the intent being to make the links between entrepreneurship and economic growth more transparent and unambiguous.

The UK government has chosen to focus on productivity as providing the key to enhanced economic performance and its approach focuses on improving the performance of the 'five drivers' (investment, innovation, enterprise, skills and competition) of productivity. Enterprise is expected to contribute to improving productivity, growing the economy and building prosperity, progress and social cohesion.[49] Moreover, since the announcement of the regional growth Public Service Agreement, the DTI, along with HM Treasury and the Office of the Deputy Prime Minister, have been developing policies whose aim is to stimulate the drivers in weaker cities and regions. However, it is now widely recognised that all five drivers are heavily interconnected and so it is difficult to devise policy instruments which target specific drivers. An alternative approach, favoured by the DTI, is to focus instead on 'common themes' which link the drivers and thereby exert leverage on regional productivity levels, and one theme that recurs in all regional productivity analyses is the need for new venture creation or start-ups.

A broad look at the evidence on enterprise formation can be obtained from the Value-Added Tax (VAT) statistics. Belfast had one of the lowest numbers of VAT registered businesses per 10,000 adult resident population (ARP) amongst all the DCAs in Northern Ireland at the start of 2003, and this pattern held for all sectors including Financial and Business Services.[50] In a wider UK context, Belfast had a similar number of VAT registrations per 10,000 resident adults in 2002 as Newcastle and Liverpool but fewer than the other six core cities, especially Bristol and Manchester (Figure 5.12). Only Bristol and Manchester have registration rates above that of the UK rate. Therefore, a broad picture emerges of a two-tier system of core cities. Overall, then,

FIGURE 5.12
VAT registrations per 10,000 adult resident population (ARP) by UK city (all industries), 2002

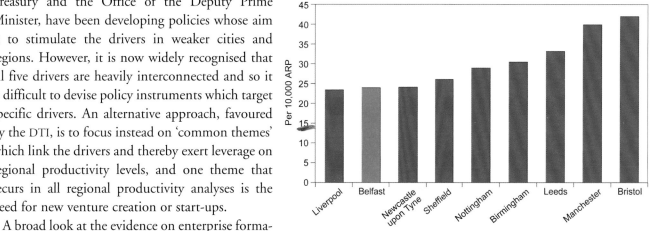

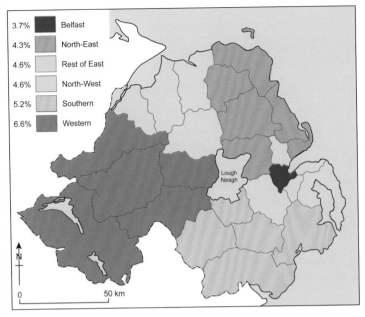

3.7%	Belfast
4.3%	North-East
4.6%	Rest of East
4.6%	North-West
5.2%	Southern
6.6%	Western

Lough Neagh

N

0   50 km

FIGURE 5.13
Total Entrepreneurial Activity (TEA)

it is possible to conclude that the level of enterprise and/or entrepreneurial ability in Belfast is low.

In 2004, for the first time, Belfast participated in the international Global Entrepreneurship Monitor (GEM) Programme, which seeks to assess the scale and nature of national and regional entrepreneurial activity. The key research questions at the core of the GEM project revolve around the objective of deriving a measure of how much entrepreneurial activity is taking place in the world, understanding the reasons for the differences and exploring the link between entrepreneurial activity and economic growth.

Figure 5.13 clearly shows that Belfast, and indeed the wider Belfast Metropolitan Area, lags significantly behind other parts of Northern Ireland in terms of its overall level of Total Entrepreneurial Activity (TEA) – the index in GEM to measure an area's scale of entrepreneurial capacity. The TEA rate for Northern Ireland as a whole was 5 per cent and within Northern Ireland this ranges from 3.7 per cent in the Belfast City Council Area to 6.6 in the western sub-region.[51] This pattern is broadly similar to that observed for VAT registration data over the last ten years at district council level.[52]

The level of entrepreneurial activity among men and women shows an even greater degree of variation across and within the six sub-regions and does not mirror the pattern for the overall TEA rate. The highest levels of female entrepreneurial activity are to be found in the 'Rest of the East' sub-region with a rate of 3.2 per cent, with the lowest level in the North West (1.1 per cent). The variation in male entrepreneurial activity is much greater across the sub-regions, from a rate of 13.1 per cent in the Western region to 6 per cent in Belfast City Council Area. Analysis of this wide variation in entrepreneurial capacity across the sub-regions of Northern Ireland reveals that when the demography (age and gender), attributes (income, education, employment status) and attitudes (towards risk, etc.) of the individual are taken into account, location emerges as a significant explanatory variable. In other words, controlling for differences in the mix of population across Northern Ireland, it is clear that 'Belfast' has a strongly negative and significant impact on the entrepreneurial capacity of people who live there. Does this suggest that the current configuration of employment and opportunity in the city is inherently creating framework conditions that are not conducive to enterprise and entrepreneurship? The role of the public sector and an employee mentality are dampening influences on creativity, which perhaps leads more people in the city, compared to elsewhere in Northern Ireland, to be more risk averse when it comes to starting their own business opportunity.

On a more positive note for Belfast, the highest levels of new business activity in the 18–24 age group are to be found in the city, along with the 'Rest of the East' and the North East. Allied to this is the fact that Belfast has one of the highest levels of graduate entrepreneurial activity in Northern Ireland, even though the actual proportion of graduates in the city is lower than in many other UK cities. This underlines the importance of attracting and retaining skilled people in the city – they are not only important for employers as they search for the skills to do business in the twenty-first century, but these individuals have the capacity to generate their own economic independence and wealth as they become employers in their own right.

Finally, it must be acknowledged that simplistic strategies designed to increase business start-ups, such as those currently being articulated in Northern Ireland through Invest Northern Ireland's Accelerating Entrepreneurship Strategy, without apparent recognition of the problems associated with them, do little to advance the objective of increasing a spirit of enterprise and competitiveness in the cities and regions of the UK. What is surely more important is a broader debate about the efficient use of scarce resources (public and private) to stimulate a dynamic and growing indigenous small business sector. Increasing the formation rate of new businesses or encouraging more people to move into self-employment per se should not be the sole focus of policy intervention. The importance of quality start-ups leading to enduring businesses and jobs, as well as the growth of existing small businesses, should be essential ingredients of an overall strategy designed to increase the level of 'enterprise' in Belfast.

CONCLUSION

The last 100 years have witnessed a roller-coaster ride of economic growth, decline and rejuvenation in Belfast, set against the backdrop of a society failing to come to terms with its divisive past. Although the economy has been a stage for some of the most important entrepreneurial feats of the twentieth century, it has been constantly buffeted by a series of less constructive external influences that have made it difficult for Belfast to maintain itself as a dynamic competitive city capable of providing security and a degree of wealth to all its citizens. The global trends in operation since the early 1970s proved to be a major challenge to all cities in the industrial developed economies but Belfast had to cope with the additional burden of a civil society seeking to implode. That it never actually did so speaks volumes for its people, and the evidence of recent years demonstrates that the city has the desire and skills to play its role once again in a wider national and global economy.

The strategic management of the city has changed dramatically in recent years with Belfast City Council now in the driving seat rather than faceless government departments and agencies. The development of the City Masterplan and the desire to understand more clearly the mechanisms by which sustainable economic growth can be maintained is a crucial development in enhancing the competitive position of Belfast, which, in turn, will offer opportunities, hope and pride for all its citizens. Will the narrative of Belfast in the twenty-first century provide a testimony to the vision and inherent entrepreneurial capacity of the city? It is impossible to answer this question with a degree of certainty. There is still much work to be done but what we can acknowledge is that there are important 'vital signs', which, if carefully nurtured, may yet provide the foundations of economic growth. What is critical in that objective is the need to generate income from outside the city and the region. Such generation depends on increasing the skills and confidence of the population through the twin processes of continuing education for the indigenous population hand in hand with attracting mobile, creative individuals who are prepared to exploit their entrepreneurial abilities on the Belfast stage.

NOTES

1 Moss, M., and Hume, J.R. (1986) *Shipbuilders to the world: 125 years of Harland and Wolff, Belfast 1861–1986*, Blackstaff Press: Belfast.

2 Throughout the twentieth century Harland and Wolff provided employment for primarily the skilled Protestant working class in the city. See O'Dowd, L., Rolston, B., and Tomlinson, M. (1980) *Northern Ireland: between civil rights and civil war*, CSE Books: London.

3 Harrison, R.T. (1990) *Industrial organisation and changing technology in UK shipbuilding*, Avebury: Aldershot.

4 Bardon, J. (1982) *Belfast: an illustrated history*, Blackstaff Press: Belfast; Beckett, J.C., and Glasscock, R.E. (eds) (1967) *Belfast: the origins and growth of an industrial city*, BBC: London; Beckett, J.C., et al. (1983) *Belfast: the making of the city*, Appletree Press: Belfast; Boal, F.W., and Royle, S.A. (1986) 'Belfast: boom, blitz and bureaucracy', in G. Gordon (ed.) *Regional cities in the UK 1890–1980*, Harper and Row: London; Coe, W.E. (1969) *The engineering industry of the north of Ireland*, David and Charles: Newton Abbot; Geary, F. (1981) 'The rise and fall of the Belfast cotton industry: some problems', *Irish Economic and Social History*, 8, pp. 30–49; Harrison (1990) *Industrial organisation*; Thomas, M.D. (1956) 'Economic geography and the manufacturing industry of Northern Ireland', *Economic Geography*, 32, pp. 75–86; Thomas, M.D. (1956) 'Manufacturing industry in Belfast, Northern Ireland', *Annals of the Association of American Geographers*, 76, pp. 175–96.

5 McCracken, J.L. (1967) 'Early Victorian Belfast', in Beckett and Glasscock (1967) *Belfast*, pp. 88–97; Harrison (1990) *Industrial organisation*.

6 Black, W. (1967) 'Industrial change in the twentieth century', in Beckett and Glasscock (1967) *Belfast*, pp. 157–68; McCracken (1967) 'Early Victorian Belfast'.

7 Bardon (1982) *Belfast*; Boal and Royle (1986) 'Belfast'.

8 Black (1967) 'Industrial change'; Bardon (1982), *Belfast*; Harrison (1990) *Industrial organisation*.

9 Bardon (1982) *Belfast*, p. 216.

10 Harrison (1990) *Industrial organisation*.

11 Black (1967) 'Industrial change'.

12 Black (1967) 'Industrial change'; Thomas (1956) 'Economic geography'.

13 Black (1967) 'Industrial change'.

14 Isles, K.S., and Cuthbert, N. (1957) *An economic survey of Northern Ireland*, HMSO: Belfast; O'Dowd, Rolston and Tomlinson (1980) *Northern Ireland*.

15 Thomas (1956) 'Economic geography'; Thomas (1956) 'Manufacturing industry'; Harrison (1990) *Industrial organisation*.

16 Thomas (1956) 'Economic geography'; Thomas (1956) 'Manufacturing industry'.

17 Thomas (1956) 'Economic geography'; Thomas (1956) 'Manufacturing industry'.

18 Thomas (1956) 'Economic geography'; Thomas (1956) 'Manufacturing industry'.

19 Bull, P.J., and Hart, M. (1984) 'Northern Ireland', in P. Damesick and P.A. Wood (eds) *Regional problems, problem regions and public policy in the UK*, Oxford University Press: Oxford, pp. 238–59; Harrison, R.T. (1982) 'Assisted industry, employment stability and industrial decline: some evidence from Northern Ireland', *Regional Studies*, 16, pp. 267–85; Hoare, A.G. (1981) 'Why they go where they go: the political imagery of Northern Ireland', *Transactions of the Institute of British Geographers*, 6, pp. 152–75; Hoare, A.G. (1982) 'Problem region and regional problem', in F.W. Boal and J.N.H. Douglas (eds) *Integration and division*, Academic Press: London, pp. 195–224; Thomas (1956) 'Economic geography'; Thomas (1956) 'Manufacturing industry'.

20 Thomas (1956) 'Economic geography'; Hart, M. (1985) 'The small firm: an evaluation of its role in the manufacturing sector of the Belfast Urban Area', unpublished PhD thesis, Department of Geography, Queen's University Belfast: Belfast.

21 Hoare (1981) 'Political imagery', p. 154.

22 Harrison, R.T. (1990) 'Industrial development policy', in R.I.D. Harris, C.W. Jefferson, and J. Spencer (eds) *The Northern Ireland economy*, Longman: London, pp 86–121.

23 O'Dowd, Rolston and Tomlinson (1980) *Northern Ireland*; Hart, M. (1990) 'Belfast's economic millstone: the role of the manufacturing sector since 1973', in P. Doherty (ed.) *Geographical perspectives on the Belfast region*, Geographical Society of Ireland: Special Publications No. 5.

24 Black (1967) 'Industrial change'.

25 Harrison, R.T. (1980) *Regional planning and employment location trends in Northern Ireland* (mimeograph); Hart (1985) 'The small firm'.

26 Harrison (1980) *Regional planning*; Hart (1985) 'The small firm'; Hoare (1981) 'Political imagery'; Matthew, R. (1964) *Belfast Regional Survey and Plan*, HMSO: Belfast; Wilson Report (1965) *Economic Development in Northern Ireland*, Cmd 479, HMSO: Belfast.

27 O'Dowd, Rolston and Tomlinson (1980) *Northern Ireland*; Rowthorn, B., and Wayne, N. (1988) *Northern Ireland: the political economy of conflict*, Polity Press: Cambridge.

28 Hart (1985) 'The small firm'.

29 Bull and Hart (1984) 'Northern Ireland'.

30 Fothergill, S., and Gudgin, G. (1982) *Unequal growth: urban and regional employment change in the UK*, Heinemann: London; Hart (1990) 'Belfast's economic millstone', pp. 37–53.

31 Defined as either the Belfast City Council Area or the broader Belfast Travel To Work Area (TTWA).

32 Hart (1990) 'Belfast's economic millstone'.

33 That is, jobs created in the period 1973 to 1986 that survived to 1986. This, therefore, does not include such high profile inward investment projects as Strathearn Audio or DeLorean, the sports car manufacturer, which were both set up in West Belfast in 1974 and 1979 respectively but did not survive to 1986.

34 Rolston, B., and Tomlinson, M. (1988) *Unemployment in West Belfast: the Obair report*, Obair: Belfast.

35 Hart (1990) 'Belfast's economic millstone'.

36 The Belfast Metropolitan Area includes the five District Council Areas of Carrickfergus, Castlereagh, Lisburn, Newtownabbey and North Down.

37 Gudgin, G., and Gibson, N. (2005) *Belfast: the economic future*, Belfast City Council: Belfast.

38 Hart, M. (2005) *Manufacturing matters*, Belfast City Council: Belfast.

39 Gudgin and Gibson (2005) *Belfast*.

40 In 1995 the city councils of eight major English regional cities began working together to set out a vision of the distinctive role that big cities must play in national and regional life in the new century. These cities – Birmingham, Bristol, Leeds, Liverpool, Manchester, Newcastle, Nottingham and Sheffield – subsequently agreed to formalise their association and become the English Core Cities Group.

41 Gudgin and Gibson (2005) *Belfast*.

42 Gudgin and Gibson (2005) *Belfast*.

43 These figures will be slightly different from those already reported in this chapter as they use the 'residence based' Census of Population data and not 'workplace based' Census of Employment data. For example, in 1951, although the Census of Population records 100,000 people working in manufacturing activities in the city, there were 125,000 jobs in firms operating within the city. The census data are used here to enable a broadly comparable data series on occupations over the 1901 to 2001 period.

44 Gudgin and Gibson (2005) *Belfast*.

45 Gudgin and Gibson (2005) *Belfast*.

46 Hart (2005) *Manufacturing matters*.

47 Gross Value Added (GVA) is a measure of regional income and productivity. In simple terms it is defined at firm level as sales less the cost of bought-in materials, components and services. Thus it is a measure of a firm's value and operating efficiency, which reflects both the price commanded by the product/service in the market place and the level of physical productivity the firm has achieved. Value added also provides a measure of the income generated by the firm and subsequently paid out to employees and shareholders as wages or profits.

48 Hart (2005) *Manufacturing matters*.

49 About the best, crisp, statement describing the 'five drivers' and the role of enterprise, with references to the documents which set out the detail, can be found in a document released with the Budget 2004, *Devolving decision making: 2 – meeting the regional economic challenge: increasing regional and local flexibility*, Office of the Deputy Prime Minister and the Department of Trade and Industry.

50 Hart (2005) *Manufacturing matters*.

51 O'Reilly, M., and Hart, M. (2005) *Global Entrepreneurship Monitor for Northern Ireland: 2004*, Invest Northern Ireland: Belfast.

52 Hart (2005) *Manufacturing matters*.

The rapidly changing skyline of Belfast has engendered much debate about the city as it attempts to meet the challenge posed by widespread deindustrialisation and the opportunities afforded by a fragile peace process. These and other highly visible changes to the built environment reflect the operation of a much more pervasive set of processes and forces impacting on land use and urban structure.

6
Belfast

Return from Motown?

Austin Smyth

FIGURE 6.1
Tramcars on Ann Street carrying shipyard workers home in the evening rush hour, 1948

Transport and the location of activities are mutually dependent (Figure 6.1). The structure of cities tends to be governed by the geography of the situation, the planning regime, dynamic factors often unique to the place but, above all, the relative accessibility afforded to locations within the city and its region. The transport system is vital both to the functioning of cities on a daily basis and to their long-term development and prosperity.

Over the last 100 years Belfast has experienced the complete transition from, in the terminology of Boal, and Schaeffer and Sclar, a 'walking city' via a brief interlude as a 'tracked city' or 'transit [public transport based] city' to an 'automobile city' or 'rubber city'.[1]

The contemporary lifestyles of many Belfast citizens would have been inconceivable 100 years ago. Fundamental to enabling this radical change to occur has been the emergence of widespread car dependency and lifestyles more characteristic of many United States cities rather than peer group European cities. Car dependency is higher in Belfast than in any other peer city in the British Isles or, indeed, Western Europe. Yet paradoxically the city itself exhibits relatively low levels of car ownership, suggesting severe mobility deprivation among substantial sections of the population, especially the elderly and less wealthy groups. The change to a car-dependent city is mirrored in population loss from Belfast, initially to adjacent suburbs but over the last two decades increasingly to a surrounding ring of dormitory towns and villages as well as a myriad of greenfield sites (see chapter 4).

Arguably, and almost without equal in Europe, Belfast in the early years of the twenty-first century faces the greatest challenge it has had to meet in the last 100 years if it is to prove to be an 'enduring city', and in particular if it is to seek a more sustainable future by attempting to reverse the almost ubiquitous car culture now permeating Northern Ireland. This culture, which encompasses not only travel behaviour but the importance locally of the car retail and wider motoring supply chain together with the prominence of motoring in the media and advertising, adds credence to the designation of Belfast as 'Motown', more often associated with centres of the car industry in the USA. How did we get to this state of affairs and is there anything realistic that can be done in the face of such levels of car dependency? This chapter will seek to address both questions.

Of course the precise nature of this challenge very much depends upon one's definition of Belfast, whether in terms of the core city within the District Council Area, the built-up area defined as the Belfast Urban Area (BUA), or the larger functional city region now designated as the Belfast Metropolitan Area (BMA).[2] We have noted that transport and the location of activities are interdependent. Transport, land-use trends and development have also contributed to social exclusion through the rundown of public transport on which many women, the elderly, the young and poorer sections of society are dependent. Transport can be expected to have made an important contribution to contemporary demographic, economic and ethno-religious spatial patterns so evident in Northern Ireland society. We cannot divorce the rapid transformation from extensive use of public transport and reliance on foot power or cycling (Figure 6.2) to a car-dependent society from the outbreak of

FIGURE 6.2
A cyclist on Victoria Street, c. 1915
ULSTER FOLK & TRANSPORT MUSEUM

community unrest and terrorism in 1969. The Troubles provided a major boost to car use, something reinforced by the policy responses both in land use and transport planning during the last three decades of the century. The chapter will consider the following matters:

1 the nature and scale of the relationship between ethno-religious segregation, residential patterns and job location, and the transport geography of the BMA

2 the evolution of transport policy, operational response and travel behaviour, with particular reference to the role of ethnic conflict and division since 1969

3 the impact of community tension and violence on travel patterns and the transport system

4 an evaluation of the implications of changes in the transport system in response to ethno-religious division

I will try to establish a benchmark for measuring the potential implications of 'normal' society, and identify and undertake a strategic review of policies, both land use and transport, designed to ameliorate inherent inefficiencies in current arrangements and limit further tendencies toward urban sprawl and ethno-religious segregation.

DEMOGRAPHIC TRENDS AND SEGREGATION IN BELFAST

From a population of just over 53,000 in 1831 the core city reached almost 350,000 inhabitants by the beginning of the twentieth century (see chapter 2). This growth was a product of rapid industrialisation. Migrants to the growing city were drawn in large part from the rural areas of the province of Ulster. In 1901 Belfast was home to some 30 per cent of the population residing in the six counties that were to become Northern Ireland. By 1911 the population within the city's then administrative boundary (Belfast County Borough) had reached almost 387,000. By then urban development was spreading beyond the limits of the city's administrative boundary and the pressures of urban concentration were beginning to be overtaken by those of decentralisation. Paul Compton suggested that the origin of this reversal in net population movement could be traced back to technological advances in urban transport at the turn of the century.[3] Nevertheless, the city's population continued to rise to 438,086 by 1937. However, the core city population began to decline from 1951 onwards. An enlarged Belfast City Council area saw its 1971 population total fall by more than a quarter between 1971 and 1981, two to three times the typical rate of loss of population experienced by other medium-size cities in Britain during the same period. For the BUA, population increase during the 1950s and 1960s brought a peak of around 600,000 residents in 1971 (see chapter 4).

In 1926, 90 per cent of the BUA's population resided in the core city. Little change occurred in the 1930s and 1940s. However, by 1951 the core city proportion dropped to 83 per cent, 74 per cent by 1961, and 60 per cent by 1971. Despite a boundary extension in the early 1970s, the core city population contained under 50 per cent of the BUA population by the end of the 1980s. Boal noted that suburbanisation into the BUA fringe reached a peak between 1951 and 1971.[4] Thereafter suburban growth decreased as urban

sprawl came up against a combination of topographic barriers and planning limitations. The BUA overall population decline over the subsequent twenty years can be attributed to population loss in the core city. Thus, while the latter decreased by 33 per cent between 1971 and 1991, the outer regional city, the commuter area beyond the BUA, grew by 39 per cent. Overall, the regional city, encompassing both the BUA and wider commuter area, declined by some 7 per cent during the same period.

Emrys Jones suggested that religious segregation may have been a characteristic of the city from its inception.[5] In the late eighteenth century Protestants formed 95 per cent of the then population of about 18,000. By 1861 Protestants made up 66 per cent of the population. As the nineteenth century proceeded relationships between Catholics and Protestants deteriorated. Periods of relative peace were punctuated by conflict. Further violence between 1920 and 1922 produced additional ratcheting up of segregation, although the less severe riots in the mid-1930s (Figure 6.3) did not produce significantly increased levels of this ethno-religious segregation. Then the period from the 1940s to the late 1960s saw little serious intercommunal violence and segregation levels remained stable until the outbreak of the Troubles in the late 1960s (see chapter 13).

Up to 12 per cent of the city's population moved house as a direct result of violence between August 1969 and February 1973. By 1972, 70 per cent of the population lived in highly segregated streets compared to 59 per cent in 1911 and 67 per cent in 1969.[6] The violence produced a marked resumption in the long-term trend of increased segregation, so that by 1991, at a ward level, segregation levels had risen almost 10 per cent since 1971. Of the 51 wards existing in 1991, 31 were highly segregated.

All this was occurring against the rapid decline in the population of the core city, and latterly that of the BUA as a whole, as Protestants, in particular, left the city for the dormitory towns and outer suburbs. The effect of the Troubles has been to act as a push factor for those able to afford to move to more settled towns and areas outside the city, reinforcing the overspill strategy adopted in the 1960s in line with the Belfast Regional Survey and Plan (the Matthew Plan). By 1991, 45 per cent of the population of the BUA lived in highly segregated environments (that is, more than 90 per cent one religion or the other). The percentage of Catholics in the core city rose from 28 per cent in 1971 to 39 per cent in 1991 (see chapter 4). During the 1980s, increasing levels of ethno-religious segregation reflected the emergence of independent housing markets not only between the two religions but also within each group. These trends have major implications on transport and have only been made possible by increasing levels of car ownership. Ethno-religious segregation has particular implications for public and private transport over and above any effects attributable to socio-economic segregation.

JOBS, SHOPPING AND LEISURE

People travel in order to get to work, to shop and to enjoy leisure activities. Where those jobs, shops and leisure facilities are located has a huge impact on travel patterns. By 1901 private residences in the city centre were being replaced increasingly by commercial premises. At the beginning of the twentieth century the Central Business District (CBD) supported five department stores (Figure 6.4) and this, with the rising number of office jobs, generated more journeys by shoppers and workers. As recently as the mid-1960s, 31.1 per cent of employment opportunities in the BUA were located in the city centre.

FIGURE 6.4
A view of J. Robb & Co. Limited showing the Castle Place and Lombard Street façades, *c.* 1912

ULSTER MUSEUM

The worldwide economic slump of the 1930s seriously threatened Belfast's core industries. This fuelled major population movements as well as heightening religious tensions. While high levels of wartime employment continued into the postwar years, the decline in shipbuilding and linen manufacture that had commenced in the 1930s re-emerged (see chapter 5). Large manufacturing plants were already in decline. Employment opportunities were growing in the fringe of the BUA. As with population, employment patterns in this area underwent radical change during the postwar period and particularly since 1969, with a considerable impact on transport demands and patterns.

THE GOVERNMENT'S RESPONSE

The Planning Commission, which was established to implement a plan set out in the government's *Preliminary Report on Reconstruction and Planning*, presented proposals in 1945 aimed at decentralising Belfast while recognising a need to limit the physical extent of the built-up area.[7] Population densities in inner Belfast at that time were as high as 677 persons per net residential hectare. Living conditions at such densities were thought unacceptable. The proposals envisaged rehousing many inhabitants of the high density areas elsewhere. High-rise flats for the whole population of the inner city area were thought to be unacceptable. The population within the city's administrative boundary, which reached 444,000 inhabitants in 1951, was expected to fall to about 300,000 people.

During the 1950s, little was done to implement the 1945 commission proposals. Urban sprawl manifested itself to an increasing extent while the core city was beginning to lose population. It was only with Sir Robert Matthew's 1962 *Belfast Regional Survey and Plan* that formal recognition was given to the relationship between the city and its commuter hinterland.[8] This plan envisaged accommodating the pressure for more development in growth areas elsewhere within the Belfast Region. It established physical limits to the Belfast conurbation by the delineation of a development stopline and formal planning for growth of Antrim, Ballymena, Bangor, Carrickfergus, Downpatrick, Larne and Newtownards, as well as the creation of a new city, subsequently named Craigavon (see

chapter 8). However, displaced families showed a marked preference for moving to Bangor and Newtownards (the inner growth centres), commuting daily to work and consequently encouraging further growth in the Belfast Region. The embryonic motorway system (Figure 6.5), intended to attract industry beyond the Belfast Region, had the effect of increasing accessibility to the centre, thereby extending the commuting sphere for workers.[9]

The Matthew Plan also set the scene for the Belfast Urban Area Plan (BUAP), prepared by Building Design Partnership in 1969.[10] By that time the population of the BUA had increased to 584,000, just short of Matthew's predicted 1981 limit of 600,000. Projections suggested that the latter would be breached by the end of the decade. Building Design Partnership's vision was a city with an integrated road network, district shopping centres and extensive renewal of a frequently sub-standard housing stock.[11] The plan also aimed to reduce employment in the Central Area (an officially designated area slightly larger than the CBD) in the period 1966–86. Growth was to be encouraged in twelve district centres in the BUA, as well as in growth centres outside this area. While the plan encouraged the city centre's role as a regional shopping centre, shopping was to be spread out from the CBD.

IMPACT OF THE TROUBLES AFTER 1969 ON JOBS, SHOPPING AND LEISURE

The impacts of these land-use strategies were compounded by changing population trends, economic decline and, not least, the effects of the terrorist bombing campaign in the 1970s and wider community unrest and instability. The percentage of retail turnover held by the Central Area decreased from 45.6 per cent in 1965 to 36.4 per cent by 1975, in contrast to trends for cities of similar size elsewhere in the United Kingdom. After 1975 there was even greater decentralisation. During the 1980s and into the 1990s, while some new investment brought about something of a renaissance in the city centre, overall market share fell further in response to large scale edge- and out-of-town shopping developments. By 2001 the CBD had become even weaker as a retail centre; its rank in UK terms having dropped dramatically since the 1960s.

The rate of dispersal of offices and retailing up to the mid-1980s was greater than that envisaged in the BUAP. Employment in the Central Area had already fallen 11 per cent to 74,430 by 1971; by 1985 it was 56,000. Today the CBD is under pressure not only from edge-of-town business parks but also from areas near the river developed by the Laganside Corporation as an alternative for office developments, with largely unrestricted parking facilities. Decline in recreational activity in the city centre was even greater than that experienced for shopping or employment. The early to mid-1970s represented the nadir as the effects of the Troubles made themselves felt on entertainment and leisure facilities. Regeneration aided by pump priming from government helped to re-establish the city centre in the late 1980s. As these changes in employment, shopping and leisure took hold, there was a switch from public to private transport. However, perhaps more fundamentally, they widened the gap – in terms of access to opportunities – between those members of society with and without access to private transport.

DEVELOPMENT OF THE TRACKED CITY: BELFAST'S TRAMWAY ERA

Let us now look at some transport history. Increases in Belfast's population and its expansion spatially led to an increase in the demand for travel. The first horse tramway running from Castle Place to Botanic Gardens was introduced in 1872. By 1885 the privately owned Belfast Street Tramways Company (BST) operated its six original routes mainly at a five-minute frequency. A twopenny ticket was the maximum fare and cheap workman's tickets were also issued at peak hours. The system carried 5.8 million passengers over its 12-mile (19.3-km) network. By 1895 it was carrying about 11 million passengers over about 24 miles (38.6 km) of track. The network had reached most of the then built-up area by the 1890s and had encouraged growth of some outlying districts. The vast majority of Belfast's working people, however, made limited use of trams. Tram fares were considered luxuries. Most people lived within walking distance of their places of work.

Belfast Corporation was anxious not to be left behind in tramway technology and as early as 1894 cable haulage was under consideration. The initial 21-year agreement between the Corporation and BST was subsequently extended to 1907, after which the local authority had the right of purchase. Pressure was placed on BST to electrify and expand (Figure 6.6). However, the Corporation and the tramway company were unable to agree upon the terms. Separate companies were therefore set up to build routes to Ligoniel, Sydenham (Strandtown) and into the Belfast and County Down Railway station. These companies raised capital and laid track, which they then leased to BST, which provided the cars and retained the fare receipts. These extensions were operated integrally with the rest of the system until purchased by BST. In 1896 the BST had a Bill drafted that would have allowed it to build electric tramways to Holywood, Newtownards, Comber, Carrickfergus and Lisburn. These proposals were not put into operation. However, the Corporation built lines, authorised by the Belfast Corporation Act of 1899, to Malone, Stranmillis, Knock, Ravenhill Road, Cliftonville and Springfield Road. These opened for traffic in 1900. BST owned the cars and horses, retained the receipts, paid a rental to the Corporation and operated the routes integrally with the remainder of the network.

The subsequent enactment of Belfast Corporation (Tramways) Act 1904 allowed the Corporation compulsorily to buy the BST and its assets. The Act also authorised further extensions, including those to Greencastle, Ligoniel, Dundonald, Queen's Road and Woodvale Road, as well as a number of connections between routes, together with electrification of

FIGURE 6.6
Laying of tracks for electric tramway at junction of York Street, Royal Avenue and Donegall Street, 1905

ULSTER MUSEUM

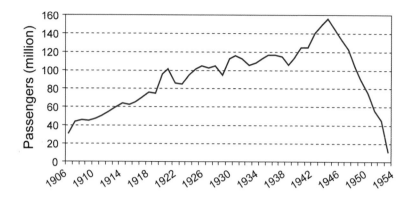

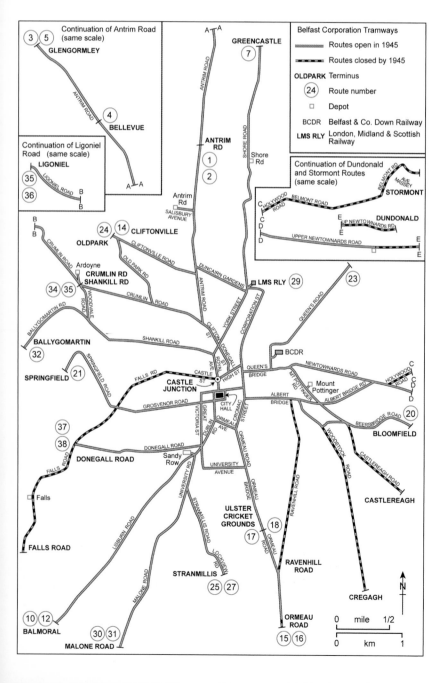

the system at a total cost of nearly £1 million. The newly electrified Belfast City Tramways became operational on 5 December 1905, the installation of electrification being one of the fastest in the UK at that time. Fourteen routes radiated from Castle Junction. In 1909 expansion was recommended, including routes to Donegall Road, Castlereagh, Bloomfield, Botanic Avenue, Oldpark, Holywood and McArt's Fort on Cave Hill, and extensions to Ligoniel and Stranmillis together with purchase of the Cavehill and Whitewell Tramway Company. Apart from McArt's Fort and Holywood, the other lines were built and opened on 28 January 1913.

In 1905 the trams carried about 30 million passengers, more than doubling by 1916 to 64 million (Figure 6.7). Although costs were rising, pressure existed for yet more extensions. The Belfast Corporation Acts of 1923 and 1924 authorised extension of the Belmont line to Stormont, the Knock line to Dundonald, and a link line joining Donegall Square North to Victoria Street, as well as a line along Ballygomartin Road to Forth River bridge. These various extensions helped to mould the shape of the city's suburbs during the 1920s in a way recognisable today in the middle city ring of residential areas. The rise of community unrest and terrorism in the early 1920s saw sporadic attacks on tramcars and depots, which had a significant, if short term, impact on patronage.

With development after the First World War, urban sprawl began to manifest itself. Belfast's tram network (see Figure 6.8 for the situation in 1945) did not adequately cover all parts of Belfast and increasingly had to be supplemented by bus routes, for with rapidly rising infrastructure costs the decision was taken that no further tramway routes would be provided after the extensions authorised by the 1923 and 1924 Acts. Belfast City Tramways henceforth became

Top left
FIGURE 6.7
Passenger journeys by tram in Belfast, 1906–54

Left
FIGURE 6.8
Belfast tram routes, 1945

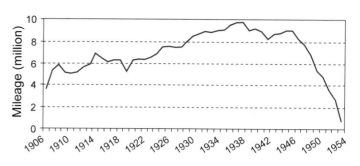

Belfast City Tramways and Motors Department, in turn foreshadowing the domination of rubber-tyred vehicles over track-bound public transport. The first bus route was the Cavehill Road service. A change in legislation transferred licensing of privately owned buses from Belfast Corporation to the new Ministry of Home Affairs. However, it also enabled the Corporation to frame bye-laws to protect its tramways, although the Corporation did not exercise these powers.

The success of the new bus service stimulated competition. Private bus operators such as the Belfast Omnibus Company and Catherwood and Imperial switched their focus from rural areas to compete with the city tramway system. During 1928 competition was particularly fierce between trams and buses, with adverse consequences for both modes of transport. The private operators formed the Ulster Motor Coach Owners Association. They opened negotiations with Belfast Corporation and reached an agreement which, in return for purchasing fifty buses from the private operators and employing a number of their drivers, gave the Corporation a monopoly to operate within its area and up to a quarter mile (0.4 km) beyond it. The essentials of this arrangement were inherited by Citybus in 1972, despite it being part of the same publicly owned holding company as the rural operator, Ulsterbus, and were a feature that determined patterns of bus service down to 2005. The introduction of the joint Metro branding of Citybus and a number of suburban Ulsterbus services in that year, allied to the network changes, represented the most significant shake-up in public transport arrangements in the city in the post-Second World War period.

FIGURE 6.9
Vehicle mileage operated by trams in Belfast, 1906–54

BELFAST: A PIONEER WITH TROLLEYBUSES

The early 1930s were some of the most stable years in the Belfast Corporation Transport Department's history. The number of tramcars and passengers carried, tramcar mileage and income all showed a sustained increase (see Figure 6.7 above, and Figure 6.9). A similar trend was evident in the bus operation. However, the latter provided less than 10 per cent of the total service. At this time consideration was being given to trolleybuses as an alternative means of public transport in the UK. On 28 March 1938 trolleybuses replaced tramcars on the Falls Road. The success of this pilot scheme led to a policy decision in 1939 to abandon tramcars in favour of trolleybuses throughout the city (Figure 6.10).

FIGURE 6.10
Trolleybus service in Donegall Place, 1938
BELFAST CITY COUNCIL

Although the Second World War slowed down the delivery of new trolleybuses and overhead equipment, the Cregagh route was converted to trolleybus operation in February 1941, Castlereagh in June of that year, Stormont in March 1942, and Dundonald via Queen's Bridge in November 1942 and via Albert Bridge in March 1943. This was to be the last wartime conversion. Although tramcar route mileage had been significantly reduced (see

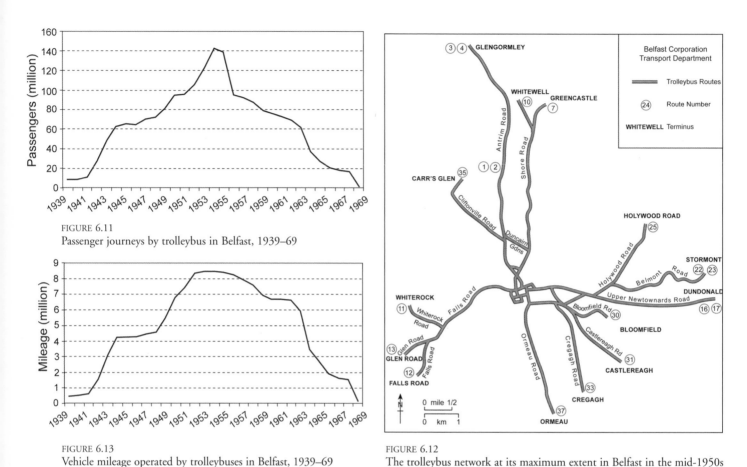

FIGURE 6.11
Passenger journeys by trolleybus in Belfast, 1939–69

FIGURE 6.13
Vehicle mileage operated by trolleybuses in Belfast, 1939–69

FIGURE 6.12
The trolleybus network at its maximum extent in Belfast in the mid-1950s

Figure 6.9 above), ridership continued to increase due to wartime restrictions on private transport and motorbuses (see Figure 6.7 above). One of the most noticeable measures taken in the early days of the war was bus service curtailment, but as fuel restrictions eased, services gradually reverted to normal hours. Blackout regulations were implemented, and adhesive strips to reduce the risk of flying glass from bombs were fitted. During the most recent Troubles, the bus operator was forced to introduce protection measures for passengers, including the installation of plastic windows.

By 1946, with the exception of the services to the shipyards, all routes in east Belfast were operated by trolleybuses. During the immediate postwar years the policy of replacing trams with trolleybuses continued, including Ormeau via Cromac Street (April 1948) Cliftonville (1947) and, in January 1949, Glengormley. By June 1951 the only routes operated by trams were Ligoniel, Ballygomartin, Springfield, Malone Road, Balmoral and Queen's Road. By 1953 the only ones remaining were Ligoniel via Crumlin Road, and Ligoniel via Shankill Road and Queen's Road. The official Last Tram Procession took place on Saturday 28 February 1954.[12] Coincidentally, the trolleybus, which had supplanted the tram in many areas of the city, saw its ridership peak in that year (Figure 6.11). Trolleybus mileage continued at a high level until the 1960s, when it plummeted; and the service ended in 1968 (Figures 6.12 and 6.13).[13]

Traffic congestion had been often blamed on trams, due to their dependence on track and overhead wires. Buses, on the other hand, were said to be able to alter route at short notice. It is ironic that reasons given for abandoning the tram (its high cost relative to the alternative transport and inflexibility of movement) were among those advanced to support the decision in 1958 to abandon further trolleybus investment in favour of diesel buses.

TABLE 6.1
Employment in Belfast and Numbers Commuting into the City, 1971–2001

Year	1971	1981	1991	2001
Number of jobs in Belfast city	184,991	151,566	146,917	173,070
Number of residents in jobs located in Belfast	115,785	85,012	69,138	77,341
Number of non-residents commuting to jobs in Belfast	69,206	66,554	77,779	95,729

SOURCE: Census data

THE RISE OF THE CAR/THE DECLINE OF THE BUS

The story of transport in Belfast in most of the postwar period is one of the decline of public transport and the rise of the private motor car. The rate of decline in Belfast's population was, until the 1980s, greater than the dispersal of employment, leading to a major increase in commuting, as reflected in Table 6.1.

FIGURE 6.14
Changes in the level of peak evening bus services, Belfast Urban Area, 1970–80

In Belfast an additional influence on public transport use both accelerated trends seen elsewhere and helped to create new ones. Religious and political differences, which for decades had tended to keep communities apart, erupted into widespread violence in 1969. In addition to the direct effects of violence – for instance, rioters burning buses and public transport going into free fall – there were worrying, widespread and long-lasting implications for transport services and travel behaviour. Throughout the Troubles, the transport companies operated in a very difficult environment. Eleven staff were killed on duty during the 1970s and 1980s and many more were injured, while some 1,200 buses were destroyed beyond economic repair. The reduction in peak evening services in the 1970s, as shown in Figure 6.14, reflects the onset of the Troubles.

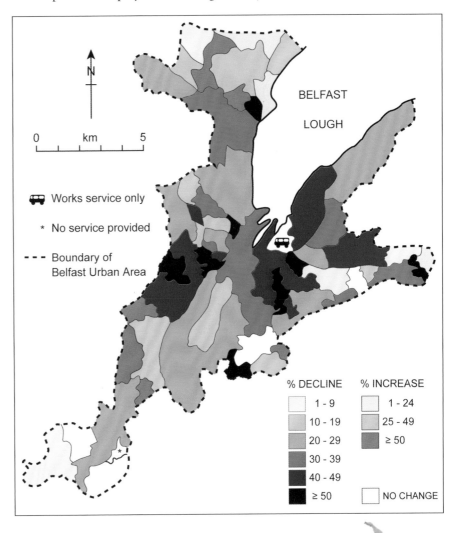

The decline in use of public transport in the peak hour (in 1966 over half of all peak-hour trips had been work trips) was unique in the UK and more closely accorded with the decline in use of public transport experienced in many cities in the US some twenty to thirty years earlier. The reasons for this change are complex. They include increasing car ownership, employment and residential dispersal, and a decline in the level of service offered by public transport. The Troubles certainly exacerbated these trends. In Belfast the car became the preferred mode of travel, dramatically illustrated in the trends in modal split for commuting seen in Table 6.2.

TABLE 6.2

Changes in the Pattern of Modal Split for the Work Trip into and within the former Belfast County Borough and Belfast City Council Areas, 1960–2001

Work trips by Belfast residents by:	1960	1966	1971	1981	1991	2001
Bus	–	77,908 (48%)	58,194 (43%)	32,561 (31%)	20,665 (22%)	16,052 (17%)
Car	–	32,019 (20%)	34,389 (26%)	43,572 (41%)	50,017 (54%)	56,513 (59%)
All private vehicles	–	35,429 (22%)	37,376 (28%)	44,930 (42%)	50,769 (55%)	57,503 (60%)
All work trips (including walking)	–	161,676	133,554	105,890	92,807	96,294
Commuter work trips to Belfast by:						
Bus	21,100 (48%)	–	25,103 (37%)	14,231 (22%)	10,848 (14%)	13,546* (14%)
Train	4,800 (12%)	–	4,237 (6%)	3,117 (5%)	2,418 (3%)	
Private vehicle	16,200 (40%)	–	39,111 (57%)	46,957 (71%)	62,241 (82%)	79,504 (84%)
Total motorised work trips	42,100	–	68,451	63,915	75,507	94,235
All work trips (including walking)			69,206	66,554	77,779	96,052

SOURCE: R. Matthew (1964) *The Belfast Regional Survey and Plan,* HMSO: Belfast; and census data.

*Figure for commuter bus count for 2001 (13,546) includes 2001 commuter train count. Percentages under residents of city refer to percentage of all trips. Percentages for non-residents refer to motorised trips. Figures to 1971 refer to Belfast County Borough, thereafter to Belfast City Council area.

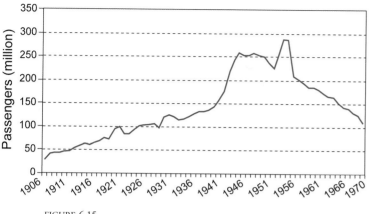

FIGURE 6.15
Total passenger journeys by public transport in Belfast, 1906–70

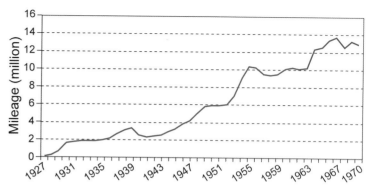

FIGURE 6.16
Vehicle mileage operated by buses in Belfast, 1927–70

The downward trend in bus use and the overall market share held by public transport continued right up to 2004, albeit at a reduced rate. The number of public transport passengers carried peaked in 1945 at 257 million (of which 155 million travelled by tram), and from then passenger numbers declined every year (Figure 6.15). The responses from the policy makers, in many cases, only served to make the plight of public transport worse. The upshot has been reduced access to travel for the marginalised in society. People have been deprived of opportunities for work, shopping and leisure.

Up to the late 1960s the changes in Belfast's bus use (Figures 6.16 and 6.17) were similar to those in other urban areas in the UK. During the final years of the erstwhile Ulster Transport Authority (UTA), Belfast Corporation negotiated the right to extend their bus services over several routes to the north of Belfast and in the east of the city. These had been accompanied by the transfer of several routes from the UTA to the municipal operator. However, during the period from 1969 the rate of decline far outstripped that experienced elsewhere in Britain. Total patronage declined by some 60 per cent between 1966 and the mid-1970s. After slowing down in the late 1970s, the rate of decline increased again. Recent years have witnessed greater stability, with a reduced level of absolute decline in ridership. Nevertheless, for every trip made today by bus in Belfast approximately eight were undertaken in the mid-1960s. In 2003–04 bus ridership in the area served by Citybus stood at 19.5 million journeys. The equivalent figure for the mid-1960s exceeded 150 million journeys.

For Ulsterbus BUA services, the decline in bus patronage since the late 1960s has been much more gradual, reflecting the significant population increases in the outer part of the urban area. While the decline in journeys per capita for Citybus in the period 1966–75 was 51 per cent, for Ulsterbus the equivalent figure was 42 per cent. Per capita use of Citybus remains higher than for Ulsterbus services. The relative stability in Ulsterbus suburban patronage enabled

FIGURE 6.17
Bus patronage, Belfast and the UK, 1965–79

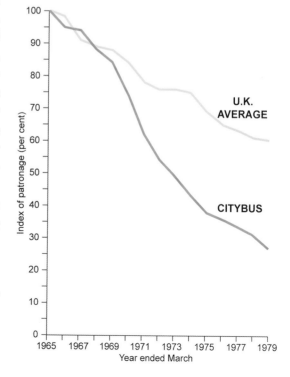

TABLE 6.3
Parking Supply in Central Belfast, 1966–2001

Year	Total number of parking spaces
1966	18,000
1967	12,500
1975	15,000 (5,500 private non-residential parking spaces)
2001	22,000 (10,000 private non-residential parking spaces)

SOURCE: official sources and other estimates

TABLE 6.4
Persons Travelling to/from Work in Northern Ireland by Train, 1966–2001

Year	Persons travelling to work by train
1966	4,694
1971	6,644
1981	5,268
1991	4,244
2001	5,920

SOURCE: census data

Ulsterbus service frequencies to be maintained to a greater extent than those of Citybus at the time, although, even after the Citybus cutbacks, Ulsterbus typically provided a lower level of service.

Passengers deserting the city's bus services created a financial crisis for the city's bus undertaking. This was exacerbated by the development of the so-called 'black taxi' services in the early 1970s, a system of 'paratransit' that had become established along the Falls Road and Shankill Road arteries in west Belfast during the height of the civil disorder when operation of the conventional bus services had to be suspended. Black taxi operations subsequently spread to the north-west and north Belfast. By 1974–75 it was estimated that 11 million journeys were being made by these services. Today the estimated figure is significantly reduced. The effect of this competition can be seen in the relatively greater bus service reductions in areas where the taxis are strongest. Bus patronage and revenues on the routes affected were severely curtailed. During 1972, Belfast Corporation ceased to exist and the bus undertaking, retitled Citybus Limited, was placed under common management with Ulsterbus. Moves to totally merge the operations were not pursued, and the two legal entities remained into the new century under the brand Translink.

An important factor in the steep decline of public transport during the 1970s and 1980s was increased car-parking provision. Total on-street and off-street car parking, which had declined in the late 1960s as a result of the introduction of a parking meter and clearway scheme, increased again towards the end of the 1970s (Table 6.3). Comparison with other medium-sized cities reveals a relatively generous provision of car parking and, in particular, a larger proportion of car parking in the private non-residential sector. The latter is mainly used by commuters, particularly those working in the public sector. The proportion of public sector workers in the labour market is particularly large in Belfast. Overall parking supply increased significantly in the subsequent period to the 1990s.

Northern Ireland vehicle registrations in 1971 numbered 382,728, of which 299,288 were cars. By 2003 registrations had increased to 852,742 (of which 712,835 were cars), increases of 123 per cent and 138 per cent respectively. In Belfast, however, car ownership is lower than for Northern Ireland as a whole, with concentrations of very low levels in west Belfast and other more economically disadvantaged areas. Traffic is currently increasing by an average of around 3 per cent per annum and shows no sign of diminishing. This has contributed to the increase in congestion and pollution, and the number and length of journeys also continue to increase.

RAIL TRAVEL

Rail travel represents only a small, if growing, proportion of public transport trips in the BUA (2 per cent of public transport trips in 1966 and 5 per cent by 1974–75). This is indicative of the stability in patronage since the mid-1970s. However, the disruption and deaths caused by terrorist incidents had a serious dampening impact on increases in

patronage in the 1970s and 1980s. In more recent years rail has been relatively successful in attracting additional commuters on journeys to Belfast city centre, following the construction of the cross-harbour rail bridge (Dargan Bridge) and the opening of the Great Victoria Street station (Figure 6.18) and associated spur line in the mid-1990s (Table 6.4).[14]

FIGURE 6.18
Great Victoria Street Station
STEPHEN A. ROYLE

PLANNING FOR TRANSPORT IN BELFAST TO 1970: DISPERSAL AND THE RUBBER CITY

Before the 1960s little strategic planning for transport in the BUA was undertaken. However, the railway network had been severely cut back by some 60 per cent and the entire future of the railways was being questioned. Furthermore, as government policy required public transport to be financially self-supporting, the effect was a declining level of service offered by all public modes. Central to both the Matthew Plan and the BUAP, however, was provision of an adequate transport system.

In April 1965 engineering consultants R. Travers Morgan and Partners were given the task of developing a transportation system incorporating past highway plans, notably the urban motorway system (see Figure 8.10).[15] They took on board and developed major road proposals first put forward in 1946 by the Planning Commission. The consultants proposed to link the city to the Matthew Plan's growth centres using an elevated inner motorway ring, two ground level ring roads and an upgrading of the three existing radial routes to dual carriageways.

Inner city housing had to be demolished to accommodate road construction, the occupants being rehoused in growth centres or in blocks of flats and maisonettes in the city. Given the terms of reference provided to the consultants, the policy output was inevitably a roads-based strategy, with expenditure on roads requiring 95 per cent of the total budget needed to implement the transportation plan. However, the one exception to this emphasis on roads was the recommended reopening of the Belfast Central Railway. To sum up, the period up to 1970 can be viewed as a phase when there was a general consensus on the need for new roads as an effective way of stimulating economic growth.

SAYING NO TO ROADS

By the early 1970s Belfast had already been suffering the effects of widespread civil disorder for several years. The violence and the demands for political reforms in Northern Ireland were having a very significant impact on the social, economic and political fabric of society. Furthermore, the direct effects of the violence on the implementation of road schemes were considerable, most notably forcing a rethink of the Belfast Urban Motorway through inner west Belfast adjacent to the CBD. The smaller scale Westlink along the western alignment of the Belfast Urban Motorway, completed in the early 1980s, reflected both the impact of the objections and the reality of a declining economy at that time.

Throughout Britain and Western Europe there was a growing realisation that unrestrained use of the private car in urban areas was not perhaps the best goal in relation to alleviating the urban transport problem. During this period a change in policy towards public transport in Northern Ireland as a whole became evident. In particular, much-needed new capital investment began to be made in the remaining rail services. As mentioned, the government gave the go-ahead for implementation of the Belfast Central Railway scheme.

A CHANGE OF HEART

In 1974 the government explained why it was reviewing the city's transport strategy. Attitudes to urban motorways had changed.[16] There was less money available because of a downturn in the economy. In any case traffic in Belfast was expected to be lower than previously forecast. After a public inquiry into the recommendations by R. Travers Morgan, the government decided to build an M1–M2 dual carriageway link, the Westlink, and a cross-harbour tangent to complete the Central Distributor Box of road links around the CBD. It also accepted the need to improve bus services to an unspecified level, and, in principle, the plan to build a rail link between York Road Station and Central Station. However, after April 1978 a number of events took place with important implications for the planning environment.

CUTS IN PUBLIC EXPENDITURE: A PERIOD OF RETHINK

The June election of 1979 saw a return of a Conservative government at Westminster, committed to reducing public expenditure. In the late 1980s a further review of transport policy in Belfast as part of a new *Belfast Urban Area Plan – 2001* broadly reaffirmed the 1978 strategy's philosophy and resulted in the construction of the cross-harbour road bridge and other more modest schemes.[17] However, against expectations and government thinking when the review started, new railway projects were also initiated,

including both the Belfast cross-harbour rail bridge (Figure 6.19) and the Great Victoria Street Railway Station and spur line. The Europa Bus Centre was also a product of this period. However, most bus measures had to be self-financing and in the prevailing political climate were thus limited. This was followed by other reports on the city centre and public transport.[18] Nevertheless, the emphasis on transport was changing largely under the influence of European Community/Union policy and financing mechanisms.

FIGURE 6.19
The cross-harbour road and rail bridge (on left)
ESLER CRAWFORD

THE ROLE OF THE EUROPEAN UNION AND ANOTHER RETHINK

European Union funding in Northern Ireland for transport infrastructure has been both substantial in financial terms and influential in informing policy development. Among the priorities identified was the need to reduce the effects of peripherality, a priority which reflected Northern Ireland's remoteness by land and sea from markets in the continental heart of the Community. In addition, the EU has been influential in establishing revenue support for rail services.

In January 1995 the then Minister for the Environment, Malcolm Moss, called for a rethink of transportation policies for Northern Ireland, intended to achieve a better balance between the economy, the environment, and individual freedom of choice. Seven principles to underpin transportation planning were:

1 minimise the effects of transport on the environment
2 recognise that it was no longer acceptable to seek to meet the full demands of traffic growth simply by building roads
3 improve the public transport system, including better co-ordination of bus and rail
4 maintain good strategic transport connections within Northern Ireland and with the rest of Europe
5 reduce, where possible, the need for travel
6 encourage the use of alternatives to the private car
7 provide an efficient, safe and accessible transportation system which offers better choice and mobility for all its users[19]

Publication of a policy/consultation document later in the year, *Transportation in Northern Ireland – The Way Forward*, sought to highlight the issues, identify the choices and explain what the government proposed to do in the short term. The government embarked on a programme of action to implement the new direction.[20] This included:

• bringing together the bus and rail companies under a single management
• an investment of over £100 million in the upgrading of the Belfast to Dublin rail service
• introduction of bus lanes in Belfast

- construction of several new bus stations in Belfast and other towns
- the proposed reopening of the more direct rail route between Belfast and Londonderry
- the introduction of new accessible services aimed at bridging the mobility gap suffered by those who find it difficult to use public transport

INTEGRATING TRANSPORT POLICY

The much-heralded and long-delayed White Paper on an integrated transport policy for the UK was published on 21 July 1998.[21] Northern Ireland had signed up to the principles of the new policy as set out in the original Green Paper. *The Way Forward* had already committed Northern Ireland to integrated public transport and integration of land use and transport planning, both intended to underpin the goals of sustainable development through reduced dependency on the private car.

It is generally agreed that progress on realising these goals locally has been slow. More recently, fundamental questions emerged about the coherence of the policy with the announcements of major new road developments coming in the wake of decisions to permit additional large scale out-of-town retail development on the edge of Belfast.

DEVOLUTION AND POLICY DEVELOPMENTS

The Northern Ireland Assembly confirmed a Regional Development Strategy (RDS) for the region in 2001. It seeks to achieve a strong and balanced economy, a good environment and an inclusive society.[22] It is consistent with British government thinking on sustainable development and wider European thinking on accommodating growth. The RDS outlined a spatial development strategy for future growth within the BMA core and along key transport corridors. The supporting Regional Transportation Strategy (RTS) seeks to establish a sustainable and safe transport system to the benefit of society, the economy and the environment.

The Belfast Metropolitan Area Plan (BMAP) of November 2004 and its associated Belfast Metropolitan Transport Plan (BMTP) are derived from the RDS and RTS thinking.[23] BMAP calls for a strengthening of the regional role of the BMA, promoting urban renewal, sustaining a living, working countryside, enhancing quality of life, supporting economic development and promoting equality of opportunity, developing an integrated inclusive transport system and encouraging protection of the natural environment.

The BMTP is founded on the RTS. The plan aims to encourage increased cycling, walking and use of public transport, and to accommodate an 'appropriate' level of car use. The plan contains proposals for significant expenditure on upgrading motorways

FIGURE 6.20
The former Belfast to Comber railway at North Road; at the turn of the century a nature reserve and path, potentially the Belfast–Comber E-WAY

STEPHEN A. ROYLE

and other key routes, along with improvements to local roads and traffic management measures. For slow modes, resources are recommended for expansion of walking and cycling facilities. For public transport, significant enhancement of local rail services is identified as a possibility, as are proposals for expansion of Quality Bus corridors and the first stage of a guided-bus-based rapid transit network. However, for many of the public transport measures the proposals did not represent definite commitments. For instance, the pilot rapid transit route (E-WAY, along the former Belfast–Comber rail line; see Figures 6.20 and 6.22) is intended for development as a private finance initiative. As yet there is little or no evidence of progressing the BMTP's flagship public transport measure.

PERSPECTIVES ON PLANNING AND TRANSPORT POLICY IN A DIVIDED SOCIETY

The transportation strategy pursued in Belfast throughout most of the postwar period, then, has been largely based on accommodating increased use of the private car. The original BUAP in the 1960s recognised that it was necessary to disperse some activities from the city's core to permit relatively unrestrained use of the private car. Dispersal was greatly reinforced by the bombing campaign of the 1970s, which was particularly concentrated on the city centre. The net result was a massive relocation of shops, offices and light industries to the suburbs and a significantly less important city centre in terms of employment, shopping and entertainment facilities. While the 1990s has witnessed some improvement in the fortunes of the city centre and the inner city, the pressure for dispersal remains strong.

Implementation of Belfast's transport strategy lagged significantly behind other cities in the UK from the beginning of the 1970s until the mid-1990s. In the main this can be attributed to the onset of the Troubles. Delay or abandonment of agreed public transport measures produced a transport strategy unparalleled elsewhere in the UK for its reliance on the motor car. This fuelled further 'rounds' in the spiral of decline in public transport. The dramatic decline in the fortunes of the public transport system helped produce increased demand for more road space and car parks. While the city's bus undertaking can boast a negligible subsidy requirement, the potential user over the last three decades has been faced with a low overall level of service. For some parts of the city this gap in conventional public transport is filled by the black taxis. However, of greater importance is the rapid growth in more conventional taxis/minicabs, which, in terms of journeys, now enjoy a market share approximately equal to bus travel in Northern Ireland as a whole. Taxis, including the black taxis, are more extensively used by disadvantaged groups in Belfast than equivalent cities elsewhere in the UK.

Against this background, the response of land-use and transport planners and public transport operators to the challenges raised by a segregated society can be summarised as follows: while planners did not seek to promote segregation, their policies of dispersal, coupled with road development, had the effect of reinforcing spatial separation and segregation, outcomes of which they seemed unaware. Transport planners for the most part executed policy that has facilitated/encouraged dispersal of population. Violence and segregation also reduced the likelihood of regulatory reform/privatisation of the transport system and promoted continued state-owned monopoly. Furthermore, planners presided over underfunding of public transport, leading to reinforcement of the classic spiral of decline. Moreover, the ambivalent attitude to black taxis encouraged part provision of public transport along segregated lines and threatened continued city-wide network provision.

Land-use planners, who up to at least very recently welcomed or permitted out-of-town retail developments, created the potential for increased socio-economic and religious segregation for those without access to private transport and reduced access to employment opportunities. The existence of greenfield-site-oriented housing development also tended to produce reinforcement of segregation by reducing effective access by public transport. By restricting access to residential areas for the purposes of promoting the principles of defensible space, planners deterred bus access. At the same time some high capacity roads have played a role as a barrier between communities.

Transport operators were forced to curtail services, while maintaining the network as a response to long-term market decline. The legacy of the intermix of the Troubles along with transport and planning policies has been the disruption of long-established travel patterns, making it difficult for conventional public transport to respond to new conditions.

A VISION FOR THE FUTURE: RETURN FROM MOTOWN?

During the last 100 years Belfast has moved from being an important industrial city of compact urban form with a population of almost 500,000 to one increasingly exhibiting many of the hallmarks of a rubber city, now the norm in the USA. The major difference from American cities lies in the fact that Belfast still retains a significant commercial centre, areas of relatively high population density and large pockets of relatively disadvantaged people with limited access to private transport. The similarity lies in the rapid expansion of new low density housing largely devoid of local facilities but exhibiting high levels of multiple-car households and widespread dependence on the private car (Figure 6.21).

Overall, Belfast is today the most car-dependent medium-size city in Western Europe.[24] The impetus for this was early postwar planning policy, greatly reinforced by thirty years of violence and political instability, and the unintended consequences of short-term policy responses to meet the security crisis from 1969. The movement out of residents and business has similarities with experience in many US cities in the 1960s. The effect has been to create an environmentally unsustainable urban structure with widespread inequities in access to opportunities. This prompts two questions: should, and can, such a state of affairs be reversed? The first of these has already been answered. UK national and Northern Ireland development and transport policies now promote a vision of more sustainable urban futures for our cities. Can Belfast translate the rhetoric into reality?

The recently published BMAP and BMTP are both in line with such thinking. Both plans reflect optimism in bringing about a more sustainable urban structure based on a balance between a compact urban core and controlled development in areas beyond the BUA. The reality is, however, that the pressures for continued decentralisation and urban

sprawl remain. The ability to mitigate these pressures, let alone control or reverse them, depends upon a strong planning system resistant to pressures for more low density residential and out-of-town commercial development, and one which successfully promotes more compact and denser urban forms while preserving quality built environments. A quality public transport system that offers a really competitive alternative to the private car for journeys that cannot be made on foot or bicycle is a fundamental requirement.

FIGURE 6.21
Traffic on Great Victoria Street
SCENIC IRELAND

Can we achieve such a future? In 1990 the answer would have been probably yes. In the early twenty-first century the answer is possibly yes. However, by the 2020s the answer is more likely to be no. As time moves on the conditions for a more sustainable future are becoming increasingly unfavourable with the result that the financial cost of improving matters is rising. The effect is to undermine the economic case for implementing increasingly expensive initiatives.

Transport initiatives in isolation will not produce a significant change in behaviour and thus bring about environmental and social benefits. Indeed, as the years go by the effectiveness of any public transport initiative tends to reduce. This is because the more car dependent a city becomes, the more expensive each journey attracted from cars onto public transport tends to become, even where it is technically possible to offer a competitive alternative. Thus Belfast, as Western Europe's most car-dependent medium-size city, faces a particularly acute challenge to reverse that position. In addition, the availability of future funding is at best problematic with the rundown in European grants for infrastructure in Northern Ireland consequent upon the expansion of the EU.

Initiatives that might address these challenges have been identified. In 1992, together with colleagues from the University of Ulster and Queen's University Belfast, I presented proposals to government for an integrated land-use and transport policy for what was termed the Belfast Metropolitan Region, the boundaries of which accord with the recently defined BMA. This research, entitled the 'Alternative Urban Transport Technologies (AUTT) study',[25] recommended the development of Belfast along key transport corridors in a star-shaped pattern, the arms of which would be designated for higher densities of development based on Scandinavian best practice and reflected in its classic form by the so-called Copenhagen Finger Plan. It also argued for the city to be tied together by a four-line high quality public transport system explicitly linking east (two lines) and west Belfast via the city centre, as well as a link to south Belfast feeding the already well-served northern corridor (Figure 6.22). The most ambitious proposal took the form of a Light Rail Transit system similar to the LUAS introduced in Dublin in 2004. The economic case for such a system in 1992 was justified after allowing for the inclusion of EU structural grant aid. A cheaper, albeit less effective, option along three of the corridors was to employ the guided bus technology. A critical argument in

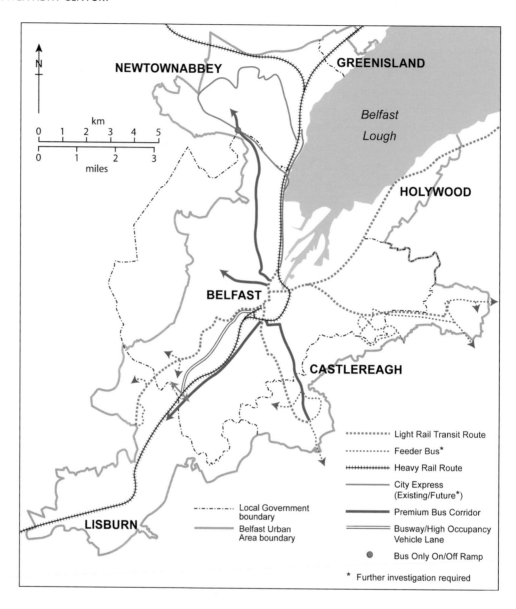

NEWTOWNABBEY

GREENISLAND

Belfast Lough

HOLYWOOD

BELFAST

CASTLEREAGH

LISBURN

km
0 1 2 3 4 5

0 1 2 3
miles

Light Rail Transit Route
Feeder Bus*
Heavy Rail Route
City Express (Existing/Future*)
Premium Bus Corridor
Busway/High Occupancy Vehicle Lane
Bus Only On/Off Ramp

Local Government boundary
Belfast Urban Area boundary

* Further investigation required

FIGURE 6.22
Alternative Urban Transport
Technologies (AUTT) proposals
for the Belfast Metropolitan
Area, 1992

support of these proposals was to reduce inequities in access to jobs revealed by the research suggesting that people in non-car-owning households had 25 per cent of the job opportunities available to neighbours with access to private transport. Both the guided bus proposal and the alignments recommended are virtually identical to the Rapid Transit system proposed in 2004 in the BMTP.

The AUTT study was extended in a subsequent study, which I undertook with support from the Engineering and Physical Sciences Research Council. This further study yielded detailed estimates of the implications of adopting densification and a high quality public transport system along transit corridors based on the finger plan concept. The results suggest that total distances driven by private cars could be reduced by up to a quarter by the year 2030, the planning horizon for the study.

The BMAP proposals are consistent with the concepts developed in the AUTT study over ten years earlier. However, realising that vision will depend upon an effective and consistent planning system and building control procedures as well as an upgraded transport system both to attract car users and underpin the physical, economic and social fabric of a more sustainable urban structure. The key proposals for public transport, even if there were whole-hearted commitment to implement them, appear too modest to bring about the change in behaviour required to meet the laudable land-use goals for the city set out in BMAP.

Belfast will endure in the years to come. However, under current conditions and the new plan's proposals it will be a city too weak to be able to withstand decentralisation pressures. We appear to have gone too far down the road to a rubber city for society and its decision makers to be able to justify, let alone have the confidence to take, the radical and expensive steps needed to grasp the opportunity that still presents itself to promote not only a city that endures, but one whose heart can flourish after decades of decay. Such a window of opportunity may no longer exist when BMAP is reviewed in 2015, and even if it does, it will certainly cost more to jump through.

NOTES

1   Boal, F.W. (1968) 'Technology and urban form', *Journal of Geography*, 67.4, pp. 229–36; Schaeffer, K.H., and Sclar, E. (1975) *Access for all: transportation and urban growth*, Penguin: London.

2   Boal, F.W. (1995) *Shaping a city: Belfast in the late twentieth century*, Institute of Irish Studies, Queen's University Belfast: Belfast.

3   Compton, P.A. (1990) 'Demographic trends in the Belfast region with particular emphasis on the changing distribution of the population', in P. Doherty (ed.) *Geographical perspectives on the Belfast region*, Geographical Society of Ireland: Dublin. pp. 15–27.

4   Boal, 1995, *Shaping a city*.

5   Jones, E. (1960) *A social geography of Belfast*, Oxford University Press: London.

6   Boal, F.W. (1982) 'Segregation and mixing: space and residence in Belfast', in F.W. Boal and J.N.H. Douglas (eds.) *Integration and division*, Academic Press: London.

7   Davidge, W.R. (1942) *Preliminary report on reconstruction and planning*, Government of Northern Ireland, Ministry of Home Affairs, HMSO: Belfast.

8   Matthew, R. (1964) *The Belfast regional survey and plan 1962 – a report prepared for the Government of Northern Ireland*, HMSO: Belfast; Ove Arup and Partners (2000) *The implications of segregation for transport within Northern Ireland*, prepared by A.W. Smyth at Ove Arup and Partners on behalf of and published by Community Relations Council for Northern Ireland: Belfast.

9   Forbes, J. (1970) 'Towns and planning in Ireland', in N. Stephens and R.E. Glasscock (eds.) *Irish geographical studies in honour of E. Estyn Evans*, Department of Geography, Queen's University Belfast: Belfast.

10 Building Design Partnership (1969) *Belfast urban area plan volume 1*, Building Design Partnership: London.

11 Hendry, J. (1984) 'The Development of Planning in Northern Ireland', in M. Bannon and J. Hendry (eds) *Occasional papers in planning no. 1 – planning in Ireland: an overview*, Department of Town and Country Planning, Queens University Belfast: Belfast.

12 Maybin, J.M. (1994) *A nostalgic look at Belfast trams since 1945*, Silver Link Publishing: Great Addington.

13 Anon. (1968) *Brochure to commemorate the termination of trolleybus operation 1938–1968*, Belfast Corporation Transport Department: Belfast.

14 Crockart, A., and Patience, J. (2003) *Rails around Belfast: an irish railway pictorial*, Midland Publishing: Leicester.

15 R. Travers Morgan and Partners (1969) *Belfast transportation plan. volumes 1 and 2*, R. Travers Morgan and Partners: London.

16 R. Travers Morgan and Partners (1976) *Transport for Belfast*, Department of the Environment for Northern Ireland: Belfast.

17 Building Design Partnership, *Belfast urban area plan*.

18 Department of the Environment for Northern Ireland (1994) *Belfast city centre: vision for the future*, HMSO: Belfast; Department of the Environment for Northern Ireland (1991) *Belfast city centre local plan 2005*, HMSO: Belfast; Ulsterbus (1993) *Southern approaches super-route: the public transport alternative*, Ulsterbus: Belfast.

19 Department of the Environment for Northern Ireland (1995) *Transportation in Northern Ireland – the way forward*, HMSO: Belfast.

20 Department of the Environment for Northern Ireland (1995) *Transportation in Northern Ireland*.

21 Department of the Environment, Transport and the Regions (1998) *A new deal for transport: better for everyone*, Department of the Environment, Transport and the Regions: London.

22 Department of the Environment for Northern Ireland (2004) *Belfast Metropolitan Area plan 2015, draft plan, parts 1–3, volume 1, plan strategy and framework*, Department of the Environment for Northern Ireland: Belfast.

23 Department of the Environment for Northern Ireland (2004) *Belfast Metropolitan Area plan 2015*.

24 Smyth, A.W. (2001) 'Contemporary lifestyles and the implications for sustainable development policy. Lessons from the UK's most car-dependent city, Belfast', *Cities*, 18.2, pp. 103–13 (with J. Cooper, E. Granzow and T. Ryley).

25 Smyth, A.W. (team leader) (1992) *Alternative urban transport technologies for the Belfast Metropolitan Area*, Transport Research Group, University of Ulster, and Faculty of Engineering, Queen's University Belfast: Belfast.

FIGURE S.3
Looking down the River Lagan towards
Belfast Lough in a north-easterly direction

ESLER CRAWFORD

Shaping the City

Early in the twentieth century local government was much less obviously subservient to central government than after the great expansion of the state's scope in the second half of the century. The functions of municipal authorities in Ireland were remarkably wide and, in addition, Belfast Corporation did not have the same ideological devotion to *laissez-faire* as so many British councils on the other side of the Irish Sea. Unlike Dublin, Belfast eagerly sought and obtained parliamentary permission to extend the borough area on several occasions, most notably in 1896 when it increased from 6,800 to 16,500 acres (2,751–6,677 ha). The White Linen Hall was demolished to make way for the sumptuous Belfast City Hall, opened in 1906, and the flamboyant magnificence of the building seemed an outward and visible manifestation of the confidence the city fathers had in Belfast's future (Figure 7.1). At the same time, when civil conflict was looming over Home Rule, there was something strained about the prevailing atmosphere of self-congratulation.

FIGURE 7.1
Belfast City Hall under construction, 1903

ULSTER MUSEUM

7

Governing the City

Jonathan Bardon

At the beginning of the century Belfast Corporation had 60 members elected from 15 wards – 15 aldermen and 45 councillors who retired from the Corporation in rotation. Fifteen councillors retired each year and 7 aldermen retired in 1901 and the remaining 8 stepped down in 1904 and so on, alternately, every third year. No alderman could remain in office for more than six years without being re-elected but all were eligible for re-election. Elections were held in the middle of January each year.[1]

Twelve years before the rest of Ireland, the £10 qualification to vote had been replaced by household suffrage. Irish Parliamentary Party MPs ensured that 2 of the 15 new wards, Smithfield and Falls, would have substantial Catholic majorities. In the first elections in 1897, 47,294 men were entitled to vote.

WIDE RESPONSIBILITIES

Standing committees did the main work of the Corporation and there were twelve of these in 1901. The Corporation seemed eager to add to its responsibilities, for example buying the Ulster Hall 'for the use of citizens' in 1902. A greater responsibility was taken on when, in August 1904, a private Bill sponsored by the Corporation to take over the tramways became law (Figure 7.2; see chapter 6). The Corporation paid the owners £307,500 and immediately set about spending another £617,620 to electrify some 40 miles (64 km) of track, a task completed by the end of 1905. A new service to Queen's Island proved a great success, but the purchase of the Cavehill and Whitewell Tramway in 1911 was an expensive decision: the acquisition included the Bellevue Pleasure Grounds which required great concrete buttresses to shore up the unstable slopes.

The Municipal Institute of Technology, opened in 1907, was a jewel in the Corporation's crown. It was dedicated to training engineers, designers, artists and apprentices of the principal skilled trades on which so much of Belfast's prosperity depended. No Catholic teachers were appointed and Catholic students were quick to find that they were entering an alien atmosphere – the Ulster Volunteer Force (UVF) bakery was based in the building in 1913–14, for example. The Catholic Church established its own technology centre in Hardinge Street, though its resources were extremely modest by comparison with the 'Black Man Tech'.

FIGURE 7.2
Tram workshop and forges
in Belfast, *c.* 1905

ULSTER FOLK & TRANSPORT MUSEUM

Belfast Central Library opened in 1888 in the newly completed Royal Avenue. The Corporation's Library Committee established branch libraries, the first one opening in Templemore Avenue in 1903. Thanks to the generosity of Dr Andrew Carnegie other libraries were erected on the Oldpark Road (built 1905–06, formally opened 1907), the Falls Road (1908) and on the Donegall Road (1909) (see chapter 3).[2]

By comparison with British cities of similar size, Belfast's Corporation's record in promoting elementary education was poor. Sir Otto Jaffe, lord mayor in 1899–1900 and again in 1904–05, felt compelled to build some schools at his own expense.

A severe blow to the Corporation's self-esteem was sharp criticism of its provision for public health. Anger at the failure of the Corporation to take remedial action permitted under existing legislation led to the formation of the Citizens' Association, which captured five seats in 1907. Thanks largely to agitation by the association and other opposition members of the Corporation, a Vice-Regal Health Inquiry was set up in 1906 and reported very unfavourably. Stung by its criticisms, the Health Committee energetically set about installing concrete culverts and a pumping station to remove sewage and drains water from roads. The infectious diseases hospital at Purdysburn, opened in 1906, reported in 1911 that typhoid cases had become 'quite rare'. The same vigour was not shown in combating the scourge of tuberculosis.[3]

Good public health depended heavily on the provision of a clean water supply, the responsibility of the separately elected Belfast Water Commissioners. New reservoirs at Woodburn, Lough Mourne, Stoneyford and Leathemstown proved insufficient. In 1893 parliament gave the commissioners the right to 9,000 acres (3,642 ha) of catchment in the Mourne Mountains and in 1901 the first water from there – so pure that no filtering was needed – flowed by gravity alone through 40 miles of pipe to Belfast. Plans for a holding reservoir in the Mournes were not to be put in effect for another three decades.

Belfast Corporation, by comparison with city authorities on the other side of the Irish Sea, was most reluctant to undertake any responsibility for the provision of housing for its citizens (see chapter 8). Builders, estate agents and property owners, such as Sir Robert McConnell (lord mayor in 1900–01) and Sir Daniel Dixon (lord mayor in 1892–94, 1901–04 and 1905–07), were reluctant to see the Corporation emerge as a rival in the housing market. The Corporation did not get around to building a single house until 1917.[4]

The new City Hall provided a splendid venue for wealthy entrepreneurs to display their civic munificence. Lord mayors were expected to fund their own civic expenses. Only men of substantial means, therefore, could head the Corporation. They vied with each other to provide lavish dinners and receptions – according to one contemporary, Belfast elected a 'much better class' of lord mayor than Dublin, which paid its civic leader a large salary.[5]

Many of the merchant families had been Liberal but when Gladstone declared his support for Home Rule in 1886, nearly all joined with the Conservative majority in the Corporation to become Unionists. Even the Citizens' Association was Unionist and its most active member, R.J. McMordie, was lord mayor between 1910 and 1914. The opposition of a variety of nationalist and labour councillors never threatened Unionist domination.

The Corporation did not hesitate to make the Ulster Hall, the City Hall (Figure 7.3) and the Technical Institute available for the campaign against the third Home Rule Bill. Leading members of the Corporation were also officers of the UVF, formed in January 1913, and they assisted in the landing, transportation and hiding

FIGURE 7.3
Unionist clubs and Orangemen marching to City Hall to sign the Solemn League and Covenant, 28 September 1912

ULSTER MUSEUM

of arms run in from Hamburg in April 1914. Then the civil war, which threatened in the early summer, was postponed by the outbreak of a general European conflict. Much of the Corporation's energy was absorbed in facilitating the recruitment of nationalists as well as unionists.

RULING A REGIONAL CAPITAL

Crawford McCullagh was not only the lord mayor between 1914 and 1916, he was also to become the longest serving lord mayor in the city's history. McCullagh was a farmer's son from Aghalee, County Antrim, who began work in Belfast at the age of fourteen in a large department store. He struck out on his own with such success that he eventually became the largest ratepayer in Belfast. First elected a councillor in 1906, he was knighted while lord mayor in 1915. Possessing great charm, and enormous energy and devotion to political life, he was regarded by his fellow Unionists as an ideal ambassador for the city, not least because his hospitality was lavish. He would not hear of a Corporation hospitality fund and preferred to fund civic entertainment out of his own pocket. Critics feared that he was turning the City Hall into his own personal fiefdom and that his clients were forming a party within a party.

FIGURE 7.4
State opening of Northern Ireland parliament by George V in Belfast City Hall, 1921

ULSTER MUSEUM

In 1920, just as Belfast was about to become a regional capital, the Corporation had to adjust to the new electoral system of proportional representation (PR). Westminster enacted the Local Government (Ireland) Bill with the aim of giving representation to minorities to find some middle ground between Unionists and Sinn Féin. Belfast Corporation had no choice but to produce a scheme for turning nine parliamentary constituencies into wards. It took three days to count the votes cast on 15 January 1920. The most striking change was the return of nineteen councillors from a variety of labour parties. In 1901, 55 out of 60 members of the Corporation could be described as upper middle class, while in 1920 the Corporation included 19 working-class councillors, 10 of whom were trade unionists.[6]

Northern Ireland elected its own parliament in May 1921 but had nowhere to meet. An arrangement was quickly made that it should use the City Hall when the Council was not in session. When the Council was in session, Parliament met in the Presbyterian Assembly College next to Queen's University. It was in the City Hall that King George V presided over the state opening of the Northern Ireland parliament on 22 June 1921 (Figure 7.4). Only Unionist MPs, senators and their wives were present, as both Sinn Féin and the nationalists refused to recognise the new regime. King George and Queen Mary had come to Belfast at considerable personal risk: the Anglo-Irish War had edged into Ulster and ferocious sectarian warfare had broken out in the city's industrial heartland in the summer of 1920 (see chapter 13). Sir William Coates, lord mayor throughout these Troubles, could do little more than issue appeals for calm and ensure that the city government continued to function. The outbreak of civil war in the Irish Free State contributed more than any other factor to the return of peace in the North – from the end of June 1922 Irish Republican Army activists moved south to join in the conflict over the Anglo-Irish Treaty of December 1921. So complete was the return to order that there was not a single sectarian murder in Belfast between 1923 and 1933.

In the City Hall Unionists pressed hard for the abolition of PR and, well represented in the Northern Ireland parliament, they succeeded in the autumn of 1922. Continued nationalist non-cooperation gave Unionists the opportunity to manipulate some of the local government electoral boundaries to their own advantage in many parts of Northern Ireland for the 1923 elections. Restraint was shown in Belfast, however, where the pre-1920 wards were restored along with the former comfortable Unionist majority.

During the interwar years, cities across the Irish Sea, particularly those dominated by the Labour Party, were eager to increase local authority spending to as high a level as government and ratepayers would permit in order to effect improvements. In Ireland, however, citizens had long been used to Dublin Castle rather than local bodies seizing the spending initiative. After the formation of Northern Ireland, central government was still expected to cover most costs and, in any case, voters were hostile to rate increases. Belfast Corporation councillors therefore risked electoral annihilation if they voted for expensive new commitments. The problem was that the Byzantine financial arrangements of the 1920 Government of Ireland Act had been worked out during the postwar boom and were then applied when Northern Ireland was assailed by two decades of unremitting depression following the Wall Street Crash. With a shrinking tax base, the Northern Ireland government frequently teetered on the edge of bankruptcy. Belfast Corporation could expect only limited help from the centre.

HOUSING SCANDAL AND THE COMMITTEE OF SIX

The most expensive new responsibility threatened to be the public provision of housing. The Corporation had to respond to an Act of 1919: a fourteen-member Housing Committee, with Sir Crawford McCullagh as chairman and T.E. McConnell as vice-chairman, prepared a modest scheme and built sixteen demonstration houses of different types. Then in 1924 Westminster revolutionised housing policy by virtually making it a social service: councils were to build houses for renting and an upper limit was to be placed on those rents. This solution was certain to be expensive – could Belfast afford such a policy?

To a majority in Belfast Corporation the British solution was quite unacceptable – an intolerable burden would be placed on the ratepayers. The views of the Corporation generally counted for more than those of backbench and opposition MPs, and of sixteen amendments to housing Bills between 1923 and 1936, eight were directly promoted by the Corporation or by Belfast MPs on its behalf. Provided subsidies were available, the Corporation believed private enterprise could cope adequately with the city's housing needs (Figure 7.5). Sir Hugh Pollock, the minister of finance, was only too happy to agree.

FIGURE 7.5
Belfast's poor children
in the early 1900s
ULSTER MUSEUM

The performance of the Housing Committee was to show that some of the city fathers were barely fit to undertake their new responsibilities. Evidence of failure to put contracts out to tender, malpractice and theft is abundant in the correspondence of the time. John McCormick, a member of the Housing Committee, wrote on 21 May 1926 to Sir Robert Meyer, the town clerk (Figure 7.6):

> … it had been discovered through Mr. Forbes that the man McDowell had misappropriated about £500 which had been paid to him by the City Chamberlain for the purpose of procuring stamps to be stuck on workmen's cards … I advised that there is no alternative but to institute a prosecution … there was a general expression of opinion by the Committee that if the money could be obtained and the prosecution legitimately abandoned this course should be adopted.

Clearly, the committee was attempting to avoid the embarrassment of a prosecution, pleading the 'delicate state of the accused wife's health'. McCormick added in a postscript: 'In view of the prevailing atmosphere of suspicion and distrust, I think it necessary to inform you that this letter is in the handwriting of my daughter.'[7]

Robert Megaw, appointed by the government to head an inquiry, reported in October 1926: he discovered irregularities on a wide scale – accounts had not been checked, inferior materials had been accepted, contracts had not been put out to tender and the city solicitor and members of the Housing Committee had a financial interest in the sites which had been chosen by consideration of 'profit to the vendor and not suitability for working-class housing'. He detected 'a feeling akin to fatalism as regards the chances of effecting any reform in the Corporation's management of its public duties'.

This was the first major incidence of corruption in Belfast since the 1850s. The question now was whether the Corporation could put its house in order. Under strong pressure from the government, Lord Mayor W.G. Turner got the Corporation to set up the 'Committee of Six', a special committee of five Unionists and one Nationalist to make recommendations on municipal reform. Arthur Collins, a distinguished London accountant, agreed to carry out a full-scale inquiry. Collins's report was damning: in particular, Corporation members were too involved in the appointment of staff and there were too many committees attempting to do work best left to professional staff. Included in his thirty recommendations were: staff appointment by competition rather than patronage; more meticulous financial control by the City Treasurer's Department; closer supervision by the town clerk over all departments; the adoption of British accounting practices; and the election of aldermen by the Corporation rather than by voters.[8]

FIGURE 7.6
Town Clerk Sir Robert Meyer
ULSTER MUSEUM

Following a much-publicised and somewhat chaotic Corporation meeting, the recommendations – which had already been accepted by the Committee of Six – were adopted, with the exception of a change in the way aldermen were elected. A private Bill to implement the changes was prepared and passed in 1930. Some of those implicated in the housing contracts were prosecuted and both the city solicitor and surveyor resigned. It remained to be seen whether or not enough had been done to root out corruption, patronage and inappropriate practice.

INTERWAR RESPONSIBILITIES

The Corporation's services were administered by a wide range of committees, each serviced by permanent staff. Sometimes committees were amalgamated and, usually as a consequence of government legislation, new ones were created. There is little wonder that outside observers were to report that there were too many committees.

The committee with the most daunting task was the Public Health Committee. Belfast's health record during the interwar years is particularly bleak (see chapter 14). Maternal mortality actually rose by one-fifth between 1922 and 1938, and the city had the highest death rate from tuberculosis in the British Isles. A government commission, reporting in 1927, had advised that there should be a complete overhaul of the chaotic system of health services inherited in 1921. Craigavon's government had to admit that it could not pay to implement the commission's 153 recommendations.

Lacking specialist staff and with government support largely restricted to laying down standards and obligations, the Public Health Department had a great deal expected of it. Food, milk, the abattoir and ships coming into port had to be inspected. In ice-cream shops ingredients had to be 'effectually covered and protected against dust and flies'. There was a bye-law 'for securing the Good and Orderly Conduct of Persons Resorting to Ice-Cream Shops' with penalties up to £5. One inspector was actually disguised as a dosser in the Common Lodging Houses, keeping 'at least one eye open' for 'migrating "Ne'er do wells" who are lousy and might "light up" the city if not watched'. As for venereal disease, the medical officer, Dr Charles Thomson, commented: the 'Public Health department is at one with the theologians. People should keep a grip of themselves …'[9]

By the end of the 1930s the Public Health Department had a staff of 30 medical officers, 8 of them part-time; 51 health visitors; 21 sanitary sub-officers; 1 port inspector; 5 food and drugs officers; 4 meat inspectors; 1 disinfecting officer, and 39 clerical staff. Mosquito control staff were involved in oiling and larviciding breeding grounds in the Bog Meadows, the Shore Road marshes and at Sydenham. Dr Thomson organised campaigns such as a 'Health Week' and a 'Rat Week', and gave lectures himself four or five times a week to mothers at child welfare centres.[10]

The Baths and Lodging Houses Committee opened Carrick House for homeless men in 1902 and added another building opposite in 1930, bringing the accommodation to 369 beds. In a city where so many homes did not possess anything more than a portable tin bath, the provision of public baths was a vital municipal duty (Figure 7.7). The Ligoniel 'Bathing Establishment' had to be closed for lack of support but the 157 private baths and 8 swimming pools at Peter's Hill, Ormeau Avenue, the Falls Road and Templemore Avenue, which had all opened in the late nineteenth century, were fully

FIGURE 7.7
Corporation Public Baths,
Falls Road, 1905

ULSTER MUSEUM

utilised. Foam baths had been introduced at Ormeau in 1935 for the 'alleviation of rheumatism and allied conditions' and all baths had their own laundries where towels and bathing costumes could be disinfected and washed. There were reduced charges for the unemployed and pupils of public elementary schools had free use of the swimming pools four days a week.[11]

When the Belfast Education Committee came into being in October 1923, it effectively had responsibility only for schools attended by Protestants. There is little doubt that this was the most dynamic and progressive of the Corporation's committees. Alderman James Duff, the first chairman, was remembered by one of his officials as 'a real dynamo supplying the energy to get local control off the ground'. In the first five years of the committee's life fifty schools were closed down, so there was no appreciable reduction in overcrowding in spite of the construction of a new cohort of well-designed schools.[12]

The committee began to provide school meals for necessitous children from 1926 and the School Medical Service was taken over from the Public Health Department. Dr T.F.S. Fulton, head of the School Medical Service, did what he could with insufficient staff but his annual reports became ever more despairing as he attempted to rouse public concern (see chapter 15).

The achievement of the Education Committee contrasted with that of the Housing Committee. Scandal notwithstanding, it was in the 1920s that most houses were built: under the subsidy scheme, 913 kitchen houses and 88 parlour houses at Whiterock, Donegall Avenue and Seaview; 584 parlour houses and 518 kitchen houses under a Corporation unemployment relief scheme at Woodvale, Ulsterville, Stranmillis, Skegoniel and the Donegall Road; and under a government assisted scheme, 363 parlour houses and 96 kitchen houses at Wandsworth, Cherryvalley, Dundela and Rosebery Road. The junior minister of home affairs, G.B. Hanna, believed these houses to be perfect for three or four children, a 'clean and tidy wife', and a father who 'does not want to go out either to a public house or to a Local Option meeting, he wants his *Evening Telegraph* and having patted the children on the head and said good night to them he sits down in that house which is his own or becoming so more and more every day'.[13]

The problem was that the average working-class family could not afford to buy or rent these houses. The last large scale building for artisans was in Glenard, Ardoyne, which reached completion in 1934–35: no bathrooms were included and the living space was little more than had been provided fifty years before. Still, they provided a desperately needed refuge for Catholic families driven out of the York Street area in 1935 following intense sectarian conflict at the close of the Twelfth parade. In all, Belfast Corporation built only 2,600 houses in the interwar years.

McCullagh was elected lord mayor again in 1931 and held office without a break until 1942. As the economic crisis worsened he received a blizzard of letters requesting help. Hugh Campbell from the Crumlin Road wrote: 'I think I am not getting fair play … as a Champion Side Drummer and the most known man in the procession I think I should get a start somewhere.'[14]

Captain R.L. Clements wrote from London: 'I called before I left Belfast fitting my Second Wife out at your Premises Belfast. I am both Orange and Freemason and I have been done down by Crooks (Business Crooks) in about £30,000 … I am almost starving a sick wife and I am appealing to you Sir Crawford for your help … I am without food both Wife and myself for these past Four days.'[15]

Unwilling to increase the rates, the Corporation left the responsibility of providing relief to the Belfast Board of Guardians – niggardly relief that precipitated the Outdoor Relief riots of October 1932, which briefly united Catholic and Protestant unemployed in opposition to the Board of Guardians and the government.[16]

The Children Act Committee was responsible for the Balmoral Boys' Industrial School for 'neglected, wayward, or destitute orphan boys'. In December 1926 it had a total of 129 boys, one of them 'a Poor Law case', 2 on remand, 4 'time expired', and 119 'under detention'. Four pigs raised by the boys were ready for sale. The Markets Committee in the same month sympathetically considered an application 'for Mess Room Accommodation and other facilities for men employed in Tripe Dressing and Gut Scraping' at the abattoir.[17]

FIGURE 7.8
Belfast Museum, College Square North, 1911

ULSTER MUSEUM

Around 170,000 animals were slaughtered in 1936–37. The Captive Bolt Pistol replaced the maul for stunning cattle in 1932 and an electric stunner for pigs, sheep and goats was introduced in 1933. A singeing plant was installed in 1934 to facilitate pork producers in the production of the Wiltshire cure (vigorously promoted by the Ministry of Agriculture to compete with the Danes in the British market).

The interwar period saw Belfast Corporation involved in a number of constructive developments. In 1924 the Corporation built a new airport – the first municipal aerodrome in the United Kingdom – on the Malone Road. The Surveyor's Department constructed an automatic electrically operated pumping station near the Queen's Bridge in 1930 to deal with storm water, and a new outfall culvert in 1932. In 1934 the Works Department was employing 4,043 men on relief schemes – mainly to resurface the city's streets, which had increased from 265 miles (427 km) in 1901 to 410 miles (660 km) in 1938. By 1938 the length of pebble-paved carriageways had been reduced from 133 miles (214 km) to 62 (100 km) (partly because 'kidney pavers' were all too easily prised up for use as ammunition during the 1932 and 1935 riots). In 1938 the Cleansing Department had 75,566 galvanised dustbins on hire and had purchased gully emptiers 'displacing much manual and insanitary handling'. Public conveniences with attendants were 'gradually replacing obsolete urinals'.[18]

The Electricity Department started life with a generator in Chapel Lane in 1895, and went on to open a much larger station at East Bridge Street (which then supplied to tramways), and a sub-station in the harbour area in 1923. By 1938 the city's Gas Works had 120,000 consumers using 4,522 million cubic feet a year (128 million cubic metres). On the main site at Ormeau vertical retorts were replacing horizontal ones; the North of Ireland Chemical Company had been taken over in 1923 and the Holywood Gas Company in 1937. There was a ready sale for by-products, including tar, ammonia, benzol and coke.

The Museum and Art Committee received the entire collection of the Belfast Natural History and Philosophical Society as a gift in 1910 (Figure 7.8). A site in the Botanic Gardens for a new museum was given by the Cemeteries and Parks Committee in 1912, but it was not until 1924 that the foundation stone was laid, and the Municipal Museum and Art Gallery was opened in 1929 (see chapter 3).

The Police Committee was largely concerned with traffic control. Traffic lights were first introduced in 1930 and by 1938 thirty junctions were controlled by them. By 1938 there were also 38 one-way streets (instituted in 1927) and roundabouts, and accommodation for 1,000 vehicles in official car parks. The committee first licensed taxis in 1910 and by the end of the 1930s there were 150 plying for hire and only 13 hackney carriages and jaunting cars (there had been 700 in 1888). The Police Committee also decreed in 1928 that all omnibuses had to stand at official stances and follow prescribed routes: this followed a disastrous experiment in deregulation earlier that year, which was accompanied by congestion and confusion. The Corporation recovered complete control by the end of the year. In addition to trams, the Corporation had fifty omnibuses and began an experimental trolleybus service on the Falls Road route in 1938 (see chapter 6).

WARTIME IGNOMINY AND POSTWAR RECOVERY

The complacency of the Corporation reached its height during the first years of the Second World War, though it was no worse than in the Cabinet room at Stormont. References to civil defence are extremely sparse in the Corporation minutes and papers of this time. Approximately only 2,000 civil defence volunteers were trained and only 4 public air-raid shelters made of sandbags were put up adjacent to the City Hall – the view was that citizens could use the under-street toilets in Donegall Square and Shaftesbury Square in the event of an air attack (Figure 7.9). It was not until July 1940 that a scheme was adopted to take 17,000 children out of the city: when implemented, only 7,000 children turned up, followed by 1,800 six weeks later, and more than half the evacuees had returned by the spring of 1941.

FIGURE 7.9
Public toilets being sandbagged, Donegall Square North, c. 1940

MARGARET CAMPBELL

Over 1,000 citizens were killed during the air raids of 1941 and by the end of May around 200,000 had left Belfast (not counting those who slept each night in the open outside the city). Some 40,000 citizens who had not fled to the countryside had to be given meals every day in emergency feeding centres. The Belfast Education Committee, opening schools as rest centres and providing food and other essentials, appears to have been the most energetic branch of the Corporation in its response to the crisis.

The German air raids revealed to public gaze, in a way that cold statistics could not, the appallingly low standard of health in much of Belfast. In

September 1941 the Corporation invited Dr T. Carnwath, former deputy chief medical officer of the Ministry of Health in Britain, to report on the state of the city's health. He condemned poor chlorination of piped water; low standards of meat inspection; 'the use of raw milk in the feeding of infants and growing children'; and 'people living in indescribable filth and squalor' in 'mere hovels'. His report, published in 1941, also observed:

> A good deal still requires to be done to make the treatment of Venereal Disease in Belfast effective ... There appears to be a law in operation in Belfast which forbids reference to a 'loathsome disease' in any public place such as a urinal. This surely carries prudery to foolish limits and the Council might well consider the question of having it rescinded ...
>
> Midwifery is a whole-time profession, and cannot be safely entrusted to obstetrical dilettanti ...
>
> In its personal services ... Belfast falls far short of what might reasonably be expected in a City of its size and importance, and I believe the reason is that the Council is not quite certain what it is doing in this field, whether it is worth doing or whether they are the people to do it.[19]

Standards were raised rapidly thereafter mainly by transferring many of the Corporation's public health functions to regional bodies.

It was also during the darkest days of the war for Belfast that evidence of further corruption and malpractice was surfacing. During a rigorous inquiry, John Dunlop of the Ministry of Home Affairs encountered an almost complete lack of co-operation from elected representatives in the City Hall. His report, published on 15 June 1941, censured the medical superintendent, charged the City Treasurer's Department with 'complete laxity' and called for the dissolution of the Tuberculosis Committee, which had bought an inappropriate and over-priced site for the Whiteabbey sanatorium and purchased 'totally unsuitable' blackout material. Once more a 'Big Six' special committee was formed and Messrs. W.B. Keen & Co. of London was engaged to investigate. The inquiry revealed many improper procedures and there was much comment on the wasteful use of petrol in wartime by the Corporation's 23 cars:

> In a number of cases officials of the Corporation are conveyed from their houses to the City Hall in the morning, and to and from their houses at lunch-hour. Several of the cars are kept at the homes of the officials using them, on the assumption that, in the case of an enemy Air Raid, they would be accessible for the conveyance of these officers. As the officers all referred to all live at some distance from their place of employment, this practice entails an appreciable amount of dead mileage in the course of a year.

Public interest in the activities of the Big Six was considerable, fuelled by detailed newspaper reports.[20]

The special committee's report at the end of the year recommended sweeping changes to ensure probity but the report was thrown out by the Corporation. When the Ministry of Home Affairs gave the Corporation two months to effect real improvements McCullagh stepped down as lord mayor. The new lord mayor, G.R. Black, made proposals so weak that Stormont passed an Act placing Belfast Corporation into administration for three and a half years. McCullagh (seen in 1945 with General Eisenhower in Figure 7.10) returned as lord mayor and remained in office until he retired from public life in 1946. Meanwhile, the real work of the Corporation was being administered by the three commissioners, C.W. Grant from the Ministry of Home Affairs and two former presidents of the Belfast Chamber of Commerce, C.S. Neill and W. Robinson.

The impact of these disruptions over control led to delays in Stormont's plan to mirror the 1944 Butler Education Act. Legislation was not on the statute book until 1947, and it took two years for the Belfast Education Committee to devise a scheme to put the 120 provisions of the Northern Ireland Education Act into effect. It was not until 1952 that the first new secondary school was built. Further education provision expanded and by the time Rupert Stanley College was opened in 1965 the Education Authority was spending £3 million a year.

The period between 1945 and 1972 witnessed a massive increase in welfare expenditure and, while most of the cost was met by the government with rising subventions from the Treasury in London, a high proportion of the spending was administered by local authorities. A crash programme of house building seemed to be Belfast's most urgent need. The main task would have to be done by the Corporation Housing Committee – dubbed 'Hustle the Houses Committee' by the press. The prefabricated bungalows put up at Beechmount, Shore Crescent, Annadale Embankment, Upper Malone and elsewhere proved much more popular and durable than anticipated. The rapid spread of postwar housing led Councillor A. Cleland to warn in January 1949 that 'unless steps are taken to extend the City boundary – and taken early – we shall be without building land and be unable to plan any further building beyond the present programme'. Nearly three-quarters of the land surface of Belfast Borough was built over.

The 1960s and 1970s was a particularly energetic period in relation to planning in Belfast. Two plans were especially significant: Robert Matthew's Belfast Regional Survey and Plan and Thomas Wilson's economic study that followed it. The Matthew Plan had three main features: a Stop Line was to be drawn around the city and no new building could take place outside this line; new towns were to be created at Antrim and Lurgan-Portadown (Craigavon) and people were to be encouraged (even paid) to move to them; and a number of small towns around Belfast, such as Bangor and Newtownards, were to be designated as growth centres and people were to be paid to move to them also. The Wilson Plan endorsed Matthew's proposals and, above all, sought a more vigorous drive to bring new firms to Northern Ireland. Many members of the Corporation had grave reservations about both of these, believing that outside enterprises would be happiest in Belfast and that the restriction on the growth of the city was unnatural. The Corporation's position was weak because it did not have a fully-fledged planning department to argue its case until 1965. The councillors reluctantly accepted the Belfast Urban Area Plan and the Belfast Transportation Plan in 1970.

136

LOCAL GOVERNMENT REFORM

As these plans were being adopted, much of the city was convulsed by violence. One out-come was a major alteration in the way that Belfast was governed. Under strong pressure from Westminster, Stormont appointed a review body, chaired by Sir Patrick Macrory, to plan local government reform. The Macrory report was published in 1970 and accepted by Major James Chichester-Clark's government: Unionist councillors from Belfast were amongst its strongest critics. Local government bodies were stripped of important powers in the 1973 reorganisation. Now social services, health care, housing services, education and libraries were to be controlled by area boards: councillors were entitled to be mem-bers but board members nominated by the government would outnumber elected representatives.

Belfast Corporation was replaced by Belfast City Council elected, as in 1920, by a PR system. Its functions were reduced to little more than the collection and disposal of refuse, the burying of the dead, the maintenance of public parks, the administration of commu-nity and leisure centres, and commenting on applications for planning permission. In addition, the City Council transferred powers in urban transport to the Northern Ireland Holding Company. Many staff left the service of the Council to work for the new area boards and the Northern Ireland Housing Executive (NIHE). On the shoulders of those who remained behind rested heavy burdens: the maintenance and improvement of serv-ices in conditions at times approximating civil war, and when elected representatives refused on occasion to carry out their duties. The original twelve committees were reduced to five: General Purposes and Finance; Town Planning and Environmental Health; Technical Services; Gas; and Parks and Recreation.

'BOGS, BINS AND BODIES'

'The Council is not limited to the narrow role of providing a series of services to its area but has within its purview the overall economic, cultural and physical well-being of that community.' Such was the advice given to elected representatives by the Association of Local Authorities of Northern Ireland in 1981.[21]

Perhaps this was a slight exaggeration of the scope of a councillor's responsibilities but the duties certainly extended beyond 'bogs, bins and bodies'. A relatively new function of the City Council was the provision of community services; that is, the creation and upkeep of community centres and small scale provision for community groups and local voluntary organisations. Alone of the twenty-six district councils in Northern Ireland, Belfast had its own building control and public health services. Staff were assigned to examine plans for building works and to inspect the work on site; in short, to enforce building regulations. Public health inspectors carried out environmental health functions not only for the City Council but also for area boards, government and the NIHE. Thus there was a continued responsibility for detection of contamination, inspecting abattoirs and food premises, and monitoring water quality and effluents from sewage disposal. Growing new responsibilities included control of air pollution and the creation of smoke control areas, and the enforcement of legislation designed to control noise.

Technical Services generally absorbed around one-half of the Council's annual budget. The most obvious service was public cleansing, which involved the cleaning of streets and public places, the collection and disposal of refuse, and recycling. This work by its nature was essential, labour intensive and continuous. Professional Services advised on construction projects and redevelopment of sites. Other tasks included management of the abattoir and maintenance of plant equipment, and Council properties. By the end of the century the Council committees were: Policy and Resources; Client Services; Contract Services; Development; Health and Environment Services; and Town Planning. The working environment of the staff was very much enhanced when the Cecil Ward Building in Linenhall Street became operational in the 1990s.

A significant slice of the City Council's budget was set aside for recreation and leisure services. The Parks and Recreation Committee had responsibility for parks (Figure 7.11), playing fields, leisure centres, baths, playcentres, cemeteries and the crematorium, and it continued to maintain school grounds on behalf of the Belfast Education and Library Board (Figure 7.12). The Parks Department alone employed 83 white-collar workers and almost 600 manual staff. It acquired the Mary Peters Track from Queen's University in 1985 and created Belfast's only true municipal golf course at Mallusk in the same year. The number of playcentres was increased from 4 in 1980 to over 30 by the end of the century. The zoo at Hazelwood was redeveloped at the end of the 1970s (Figure 7.13) and the complete restoration of Belfast Castle (given to the city by the earl of Shaftesbury in 1934) was finished in November 1988. Other restorations included Malone House (fire-bombed in 1976) in Barnett's Park, and the Palm House and the Tropical Ravine in Botanic Gardens. With the help of government funding, leisure centres were built across the city in the late 1970s and the 1980s. Though most attracted steady custom, the expense of staffing and maintenance was a constant source of anxiety to members of the Council.[22]

FIGURE 7.11
Drumglass Playcentre in the 1980s
ROBERT SCOTT

FIGURE 7.12
Hammer playground, west Belfast, 1975
BELFAST CENTRAL LIBRARY

TRANSFORMING A DIVIDED CITY

The paramilitary ceasefires in 1994 offered fresh opportunities for the City Council to increase the attractiveness of the city to both its citizens and its visitors. Nowhere was the transformation of Belfast more apparent than by the banks of the river (see chapter 9). The Council played its part in regenerating the riverside by implementing a project conceived in the 1970s: on the site of the old cattle and fish markets the Waterfront Hall was built to give citizens a concert hall and conference centre without rival in Ireland. The enterprise cost £33 million and seeking sufficient income to cover running and maintenance costs was the primary concern of the Waterfront Hall Board attached to the Client Services Committee. In March 2004, when the overall deficit exceeded £5.6 million, it was proudly reported to Council nevertheless that the hall 'has won fifteen national and international awards including worldwide runner up in the prestigious "Association des Palais de Congress – World's Best Congress Centre 2002" placing the Waterfront Hall as Europe's number one conference centre'. Upstream at Cromac, the Council won more awards by transforming, with the assistance of Laganside Corporation and European Regional Development funds, the Gas Works, 'once one of the most heavily contaminated sites in Ireland', to provide an additional 3,000 jobs for the city.[23]

Health and Environment Services wrestled with the problem of waste management, seeking to move from older civic amenity sites to more strategically located and larger centres with recycling facilities. For example, it considered using the methane gas burned off in two flare units at the Dargan Road landfill site (opened in 1974) to generate electricity. It also participated in an Interagency Working Group on Bonfires to minimise damage caused by Eleventh Night celebrations.

The divisive passions raging in the city spilled over into the Council chamber and bitter exchanges intensified after the election of the first Sinn Féin councillor, Alex Maskey, in 1983. In June 1988 journalist David McKittrick concluded a report of a City Council debate with this description:

> The sides sit, implacable and irreconcilable, just feet away from each other, each regarding compromise as defeat. Together they make up a bitter frozen little tableau, a microcosm of political life in Northern Ireland.[24]

Following the signing in 1985 of the Anglo-Irish Agreement, Unionist councillors pursued a policy of non-cooperation. This meant that governing the city fell to an exceptional degree to the Council staff, in particular the town clerks Cecil Ward, Brian Hanna and Peter McNaney. Lord Mayor John Carson, for all his dislike of the 1985 agreement, played a leading role in persuading the Council to end its adjournment protests in May 1986.

The paramilitary ceasefires of 1994 ushered in a new era of compromise and acceptance of change. In any case, significant demographic shifts were bringing the exclusive rule of Unionists to an end. David Cook, the Alliance councillor elected lord mayor in 1978, was the Council's first civic leader to come from a cross-community party; Alban Maginness, the Social Democratic and Labour Party councillor elected in 1997, was the city's first-ever nationalist lord mayor; and the election of Sinn Féin's Alex Maskey as lord mayor in 2002 was accepted with more equanimity than anyone would have dared to hope a decade earlier.

NOTES

1 *Belfast and Ulster Directory 1901.*
2 Libraries, Museums and Art Committee memorandum (1938) Public Record Office of Northern Ireland (hereafter PRONI), LA/7/3C/11.
3 Blaney, R. (1988) *Belfast: 100 years of public health*, Belfast City Council and Eastern Health and Social Services Board: Belfast, p. 27.
4 Cleary, P.G. (1980) 'Spatial expansion and urban ecological change in Belfast 1861–1917', unpublished PhD thesis, Queen's University Belfast, p. 419.
5 Corbett, R., and Montgomery, I. (2003) 'A civic record: the Belfast City Archive Project', Belfast: draft, p. 8.
6 Budge, I., and O'Leary, C. (1973) *Belfast: approach to crisis*, Macmillan: London, pp. 139–40.
7 Town Clerk's Correspondence (1926) 21 May, PRONI, LA/7/12AA/4.
8 Budge and O'Leary (1973) *Belfast* pp. 147–48.
9 Minutes of the Public Health Committee (1927) January, PRONI, LA/7/2EB/104 and Anon. (1929) *The Belfast book: local government in the city and county borough of Belfast*, Carswell: Belfast, p. 89.
10 Memorandum from Dr Charles Thomson to John McKinstry, PRONI, LA/7/3C/16.
11 Memorandum by W.J. Crossley, Superintendent of Public Baths for *Northern Whig* (1938), PRONI, LA/7/3C/11.

12 McNeilly, N. (1974) *Exactly fifty years: the Belfast Education Authority and its work 1923–73*, Blackstaff Press: Belfast, p. 12.
13 Bardon, J. (1982) *Belfast: an illustrated history*, Blackstaff Press: Belfast, p. 211.
14 Lord Mayor's correspondence (1933) PRONI, LA/7/3A/20.
15 Lord Mayor's correspondence (1932) PRONI, LA/7/3A/6.
16 Memorandum of conference in the Lord Mayor's Parlour 5 October 1932, PRONI, LA/7/3A/6.
17 Memorandum by John Carlisle for *Northern Whig* (1938), PRONI, LA/7/2EB/104.
18 Markets Committee memorandum (1938) PRONI, LA/7/3C/11.
19 Carnwath Report (1941) PRONI, LA/7/3C/14.
20 First Interim Report, PRONI, LA/7/3C/13; Lord Mayor's correspondence (1932), PRONI, LA/73A/6; Third Interim Report, PRONI, LA/7/3A/92.
21 Association of Local Authorities of Northern Ireland (1981) *The councillor's handbook*, Association of Local Authorities of Northern Ireland: Belfast, p. 9.
22 Scott, R. (2000) *A breath of fresh air: the story of Belfast's parks*, Blackstaff Press: Belfast, pp. 145–70.
23 Belfast City Council minutes (2004) 1 March.
24 *Independent* (1988) 4 June.

As Belfast entered the twentieth century the natural growth process of urbanisation was at its most powerful. The city had become a potent engine of growth for the island of Ireland as a whole (Figure 8.1). Indeed, Belfast had established itself as a modern industrial city, ready to take on the world. What had been achieved by the Victorian city fathers in the last fifteen years of the nineteenth century was, in development terms, nothing short of astonishing. Belfast had become bigger and stronger than Dublin; and the physical transformation of the city centre was spectacular (see chapter 2).

8
Planning the City; Planning the Region

Bill Morrison

FIGURE 8.1
View across Belfast from the Castlereagh Hills, 1906, by J.A. Carey
PATRICK DALTON

Make no mistake, the development of Victorian Belfast was carried out in accordance with a well thought-out vision. There was no master plan – certainly no plan such as we think of today – but there was a vision, one that was shared by men with common purpose. It was sufficient to rely upon the commitment of civic leaders, the patronage of the landowning classes and the motivation of a dedicated cadre of entrepreneurs who shared common values and understood the dynamics of growth and development. Their vision was to promote wealth and transform the physical appearance of the city as a symbol of prosperity, which would endure for 100 years. Belfast was not unique in this respect, although the sheer scale of its development in the late nineteenth century was without equal. The completion of Belfast City Hall in 1906 was but the final jewel in the crown of a city centre that had now come of age.

There had also been a boom in house construction in Belfast in this period – to the extent that as the twentieth century began there was a significant housing surplus in the city. The terraced houses were built to a standard that pushed up rents but reflected the more recent reforming measures in health and sanitation that gave birth to modern town planning. In common with other parts of the UK, however, there was also a legacy of older dwellings, where rows of terraced houses with narrow frontages had been built in exploitation of earlier minimum bye-laws in order to crowd as many houses as possible into the city streets.

THE EMERGENCE OF TOWN PLANNING

FIGURE 8.2
'Group of Slumless Smokeless Cities',
from *To-morrow: A Peaceful Path to Real
Reform* (1898) by Ebenezer Howard

Town planning is a twentieth-century ideal, based on the notion that the world would be better for everyone if processes of urbanisation could be harnessed. The concept of 'planning towns' emanated from the professional classes as a reaction to the less attractive features of the Victorian city. The early town planners, a body of architects and surveyors, began in the first decade of the twentieth century to develop ideas about urban form, building on concepts such as the city evolution theories of Scots biologist Patrick Geddes and the garden city visions of Ebenezer Howard (Figure 8.2). The years leading up to the First World War had seen the emergence of Belfast's much-treasured Edwardian suburbs reaching out to the extended city boundary and the limits of the tramway system. This nineteenth-century investment was, indeed, intended to encourage the development of low density housing to meet the growing aspirations of the burgeoning middle classes.

While Edwardian entrepreneurial activity was profitably directed to the fringe of the expanding city, living conditions were declining both within the heart of the city and beyond the city limits. Inner areas were receiving ever-increasing numbers of people in search of employment and opportunity. This influx accelerated through the First World War, with more and more people coming in from the countryside in search of work in the

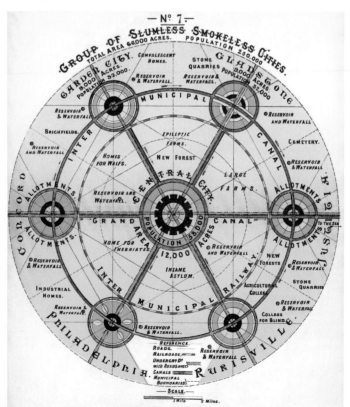

booming factories. Such new citizens usually found their way into the poorest backstreet terraces of Belfast.

Overcrowding became doubly acute as house building came to a standstill during the war. In Great Britain, meanwhile, the density standard for working-class housing was becoming a political issue. In 1917, national government received a report on housing that was far-sighted and to become a major influence on future urban form.[1] The Tudor Walters Committee, welcomed by David Lloyd George with the slogan 'homes for heroes', called for better designed housing layouts at reduced densities. It established an enduring link between housing and town planning.

Working-class housing was not, however, seen as a priority for Belfast Corporation at this time. Much of the housing in the city was relatively new, and the Corporation rejected the principle of building council houses for rent, introduced by the government in Britain in 1924 (see chapter 7). Rent subsidy was seen to be an intolerable burden on ratepayers, and the Corporation prevailed upon the newly formed Northern Ireland government not to follow the British model but to opt instead for an alternative approach of subsidising private house building.

Following a wartime boom, the city suffered from an economic decline that set in soon after hostilities ended and progressively deepened over the next twenty years. The combination of low incomes, unemployment and a failure to improve working-class housing meant that by the onset of the Second World War, Belfast had come to be widely regarded as the most disadvantaged industrial city in the UK. With no priority given to working-class housing, the link to town planning did not take hold in Belfast as it did in Britain during the interwar years. Nor did town planning particularly commend itself to the new regional administration, which was endeavouring to secure the economic survival of the northern state in a period of general economic downturn through support for the private sector. The government did, however, introduce in 1931 the Planning and Housing Act (Northern Ireland), which allowed local authorities to produce planning schemes and regulate development if they chose to do so. Belfast Corporation put in place some preliminary administrative arrangements in the expectation of financial assistance. None was on offer.

POSTWAR RECONSTRUCTION

During the Second World War, town planning became widely accepted throughout Europe as one of the essential factors in any future postwar reconstruction (Figure 8.3). From 1941 the administration of Belfast was assumed by Stormont and the city remained under its control until 1946. It was during this period that a vision of postwar Britain emerged, based upon town planning principles. The vision was firmly predicated on a fuller and better life for the people, sound housing and the provision of all the

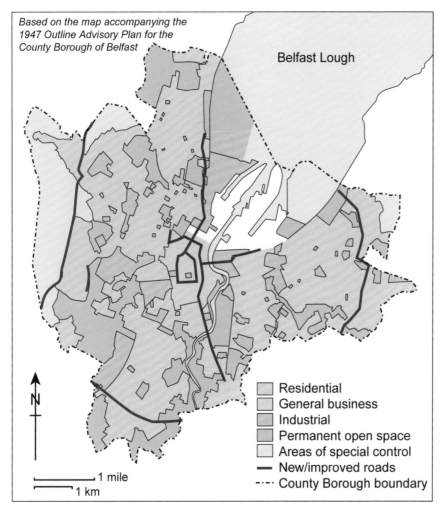

Based on the map accompanying the 1947 Outline Advisory Plan for the County Borough of Belfast

Belfast Lough

N

1 mile
1 km

Residential
General business
Industrial
Permanent open space
Areas of special control
— New/improved roads
---- County Borough boundary

FIGURE 8.4
Redrawn version of the map that accompanied the 1947 Outline Advisory Plan, showing allocation of land for development in Belfast County Borough

MAURA E. PRINGLE

services needed to support proper economic and community welfare.

Picking up on the nationwide consensus, the Stormont government in 1942 invited W.R. Davidge, a former president of the Town Planning Institute, to produce a preliminary report on reconstruction and planning in Northern Ireland. Davidge recommended the setting up of a representative advisory board, and a technical planning commission.[2] The Ministry of Home Affairs did so, and recommended that local authorities appoint architects to fulfil the new town planning function.

As John Hendry has noted,[3] the reports over the following decade of the Planning Advisory Board and the Planning Commission are remarkable for their breadth of coverage and for the way in which they foretold how planning would take hold and shape the future development of Northern Ireland.[4] The planning proposals, however, met with considerable opposition. While the doctrine of state planning won all-party political support in Britain after the war, no such consensus emerged in the northern state.

The 1944 Interim Development Act (Northern Ireland) made it obligatory for local authorities to prepare planning schemes. Without the equivalent of Britain's 1947 Town and Country Planning Act, however, there was no comprehensive basis for the control of development and land use. Until the mid-sixties there were no powers in Northern Ireland to create new towns, no means of controlling suburbanisation or protecting the natural and built heritage.

The German bombs of 1941 left Belfast in particular need of effective town planning. Almost 57,000 houses were destroyed or damaged and over 1,000 people killed (see chapter 13, addendum). Davidge had called for a plan that would lead reconstruction and at the same time establish a green belt as a backdrop for the city. But it was housing conditions in the heart of the city and the scale of the problem of reconstruction and redevelopment that gave rise to greatest concern. An Outline Advisory Plan – advisory in the sense that Belfast Corporation had not initiated it – was produced for the city in 1947, based on planning standards used in the City of Manchester Plan.[5] Land was zoned in a broad way for residential, general business, industry and open space uses, and proposals included an outer ring road and a new bridge across the River Lagan (Figure 8.4).

Rapid suburban expansion of Belfast, meantime, was taking place beyond the city limits, eating up the surrounding countryside at an alarming rate. New jobs were created in factories built on greenfield sites to modern standards. With increased wages, the prospect of owning a semidetached suburban house came within the reach of many in middle-class society.

The return of democracy to Belfast's municipal government after the Second World War led to renewed calls for a boundary extension to allow the city to benefit from the suburban development. But the Stormont government was not prepared to countenance expansion of Belfast Corporation's electoral power base under any circumstances. Suburban expansion was perceived to be evidence of people continuing to be drawn to the city from the rural hinterland, but it was, in fact, an acceleration of the long-established drift of people and jobs away from the crowded inner city. The population within Belfast's municipal boundary had peaked in 1951 (see chapter 4). Industrial employment outside the city limits increased as new factories were built with government assistance aimed at boosting industrial production. The Stormont government's development policy at this time was focused on the Ministry of Commerce, investing in roads and transport and offering financial inducement to attract new industry to Northern Ireland.

Belfast Corporation's record on house building after the war proved to be no better than during the interwar period – other than taking advantage of the prefabricated emergency housing and development of blitzed sites. A generous standard for housing development had been set by the Northern Ireland Housing Trust, which was established as an agency to assist local district councils with their housing projects. The Housing Trust produced many attractive schemes under the guidance of Scottish architect James Cairncross. Housing developments were carefully planned around open spaces, retaining trees and hedgerows to a high standard of landscape planting and maintenance. Tenants were provided with gardens in suburban estates such as Belvoir (Figure 8.5) and Seymour Hill, which were developed at this time. Newtownabbey emerged as a new urban municipality on the edge of Belfast, consolidating a number of villages to the north of the city, between which the Housing Trust built enormous estates. There is no evidence today that sound principles of town planning, by now well established in Britain, were seriously applied to what became Northern Ireland's first 'new town' since the Plantation.

Meanwhile, little was done to limit urban growth or to tackle the physical infrastructural problems of the inner city. The Housing Act of 1956 enabled the Corporation to start planning for a programme of inner-city development. Almost 100,000 dwellings were identified as unfit and earmarked for redevelopment in published documents, but it would be years before action took place on the ground. The consequence of designating redevelopment areas without any programme of action was 'planning blight'. There was no interest on the part of investors either to initiate new development or to undertake maintenance of existing buildings.

Town-planning thinking across the UK in the1940s and 1950s was focused on how to reduce inner area overcrowding and how to rebuild to new space standards. The high-rise building of the 1950s and 1960s was a pragmatic response to

FIGURE 8.5
Belvoir Estate, October 1979
NIHE

this. The only positive consequence of Belfast Corporation's postponed redevelopment programme was that fewer high-rise and deck-access housing structures were built in inner Belfast than in the inner areas of comparable cities elsewhere in the UK.

THE MATTHEW PLAN

FIGURE 8.6
The Matthew Plan (1964) – a New City, the creation of a Stop Line around Belfast, and a centralised planning regime were key components of the plan to stimulate growth in centres away from Belfast.

ORDNANCE SURVEY OF NORTHERN IRELAND

As Prime Minister Harold Macmillan was telling the nation that it had 'never had it so good', the Stormont government was undergoing what John Oliver describes in his book as a period of 'most unhappy relations' with Belfast Corporation.[6] Political tensions between a large city Corporation and a small government once again came to a head in 1960 over the matter of an extension of the city boundary. Officials in the Ministry of Heath and Local Government saw an opportunity to appoint an independent planner, Robert Matthew of Edinburgh, to arbitrate. Matthew offered something more, according to Oliver: 'For a mere twenty-five thousand pounds, I recall, he undertook to set up an office in Belfast under the care of that most talented, versatile and meticulous planner, Cecil Newman, and within a couple of years to produce for us all a Belfast regional plan. This he did.'

The Matthew Plan, formally named the Belfast Regional Survey and Plan,[7] brought Northern Ireland back from the wilderness to embrace, almost wholeheartedly, the

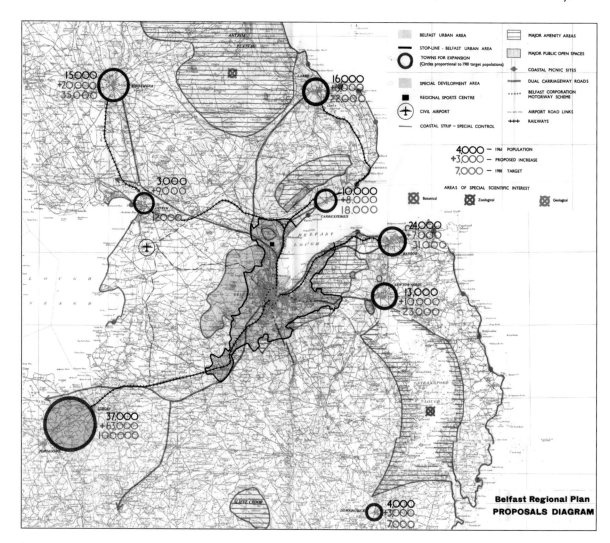

British planning ideal – and set out along the path of a positive, activist approach to the physical and economic problems of the region (Figure 8.6). The plan was by no means universally popular, but the exercise reflected the public mood and attitudes during the 1960s. Criticism would come from those who felt the plan should have encapsulated the whole region, and from those who felt it wrong to devise such a physical strategy ahead of the parallel economic study by Thomas Wilson that followed.[8]

Matthew established a Stop Line around the urban area to prevent further urban sprawl, and called for the development of a group of eight growth centres within a 30-mile (48.3-km) radius, each with a defined target for population and industrial provision. One of these centres was to be upgraded to the status of a 'new regional centre' of 100,000 people based around the existing boroughs of Lurgan and Portadown. This new city was subsequently named Craigavon (Figure 8.7).

Matthew made specific proposals for visual and recreational amenities arising from analysis of the survey carried out in Belfast under the direction of Cecil Newman (Figure 8.8), and included an important section on administrative and legislative provisions which he thought necessary for the implementation of the Regional Plan. This, in the words of Chief Planner James Aitken addressing the Town and Country Planning Summer School held in Belfast in 1967, was an 'unexpected bonus'. These proposals met with a considerable measure of approval in parliament during the debate on the Matthew report and led to a series of enactments that within the decade would move Northern Ireland to the forefront of British town planning.

The Matthew Plan may have represented a high point in the history of regional planning, but regrettably it was not the result of enlightened thinking in the highest levels of government – it was largely devised to defuse a power struggle between Belfast Corporation and regional government. It was based on a range of assumptions that subsequently proved false. It was cavalier in the way it dealt with people forced to move to the new regional centres and it relied too much on public funding. But the Matthew Plan proved to be a wake-up call, rediscovering the wartime visions for town planning in Northern Ireland.

Meanwhile, Belfast Corporation was facing an urban crisis, having failed to deal effectively with urban renewal, housing, industrial overspill and traffic problems in the postwar years. In 1965 the Corporation commissioned consultants to work together on a city plan and traffic study – the new Ministry of Development entering into an agreement with the Corporation to extend (and pay for) the planning exercise to cover the entire urban area. In 1967 Belfast Corporation recruited its first city planning officer. Geoffrey Booth was tasked with setting up a new town planning department.[9]

The London-based planning consultants Building Design Partnership[10] devised a plan based on a strategic concept to promote greater choice and convenience through a

FIGURE 8.7
The New City Planning team that shaped Craigavon – led by former Cumbernauld New Town chief architect-planner Geoffrey Copcutt *(seated centre, with cigar)*

BELFAST TELEGRAPH

FIGURE 8.8
Cecil F.S. Newman, a champion of town planning and countryside protection whose passion proved to be a key influence in winning acceptance of the Matthew Plan proposals

MOLLIE NEWMAN

concentration of services in twelve district centres in various parts of the city. A scale model left no doubt as to the audacity of the architectural vision for the central area (Figure 8.9). The engineering consultants R. Travers Morgan[11] endorsed an equally bold road-based transportation strategy, the main component of which was an elevated motorway ring around the central area (Figure 8.10). The Belfast Urban Area Plan (BUAP), incorporating traffic and transportation proposals, was published in 1969 – a significant year for Belfast in the context of the political history of Northern Ireland as a whole. The 1960s were heady days for all levels of town planning in Northern Ireland, leading to the enthusiastic adoption of ambitious plans drawn up by consultants from Britain. But the enthusiasm was short-lived and ended in disappointment, both at a community level in Belfast and at a regional scale.

THE TRAUMA OF THE 1970s

In a move floated by the wartime planning advisory bodies and heralded in the Matthew Plan, the opportunity was taken under the 1973 reorganisation of local government to lift planning to a regional level as an executive function of the Ministry of Housing, Local Government and Planning. Belfast Corporation was no more. Top-tier local government powers had all been taken to the centre, leaving the members elected to the City Hall in Belfast with a much-reduced role. Indeed, the introduction of Direct Rule following the proroguing of the Stormont parliament in March 1972 meant these local government functions were transferred along with other legislative and executive powers to the Westminster parliament and to a Westminster Cabinet minister – and with them the obligation and opportunity for successive British governments to translate urban policies of regeneration into direct action on the ground in Belfast.

Belfast City Council, however, retained a powerful voice reflecting the views and aspirations of local people. Few developments took place in Belfast in the last quarter century that did not have the support of the Council, reflecting general consensus within the community. But the government was also forced into rethinking large scale planning proposals by the emerging realisation that the country could no long afford to pay for them. Many urban infrastructure proposals, including the proposed motorway ring around the centre of Belfast, were abandoned or put on the long finger. By the time the BUAP had been published in 1969, the economic outlook was decidedly less promising. Very soon the combined effects of international recession, intercommunal violence, declining population growth in Northern Ireland as a whole and increasing outward migration resulted in a rejection of most of the optimistic assumptions of the 1960s.

For inner-city local communities, already roused by sectarian conflict and political developments, the published proposals seemed to be a further threat to their existence. While the BUAP development proposals were mostly shelved, a major proposal to build a road through the city to link the motorways was given the go-ahead in the face of bitter opposition. Wholesale clearance of areas awaiting long-promised redevelopment left the inner city looking like a barren wasteland. Town planning as such was held to blame for the destruction of entire communities. It fell to the newly formed Northern Ireland

Housing Executive (NIHE) to rise to the challenge of urban renewal and the planned redevelopment of substantial areas of the inner city.

At one level, the inner-city problems facing Belfast in the 1970s were common to most UK cities. The added dimension for Belfast in the 1970s was the fear and intimidation experienced by its citizens, which led to mass movements of population within the city into what were perceived to be 'safe' areas. The outbreak of violent ethnic conflict in 1969, which continued for the following twenty-five years, provided what Fred Boal has described as the 'final jolt to the urban system and to extant urban strategies'.[12] No longer was the city planning for growth – Belfast was a city endeavouring to halt catastrophic decline. In the seven years after 1971 when the conflict was at its height, 77,000 people – almost one-fifth of the population of municipal Belfast – were recorded to have moved from and within inner city areas. The Catholic population crowded into traditional heartlands. The pattern within the Protestant community, on the other hand, was to accelerate and accentuate the outward drift from the inner city. Young and mobile Protestants fled the troubled central areas to what were formerly mixed estates in the sub-urbs, leaving behind a rapidly collapsing local community structure and a distorted population profile comprising mainly the elderly and those no longer of working age.

Town planners now had to recognise two parallel cities – an overcrowded and youthful Catholic inner city interwoven with a sparsely populated and elderly Protestant inner city. To ease the overcrowding in Catholic west Belfast, the Department of the Environment (as it now was) proposed a geographical extension into the green belt at Poleglass. But to implement it was a brave political decision, as it amounted to the relocation of 10,000 Catholics from inner Belfast into the green fields of the Protestant-controlled and locally elected Lisburn District Council. Nearby Twinbrook was cited as a glaring example of a problem estate and a prime source of sectarian trouble. It was acknowledged at the highest levels in government that success would depend on good planning and design, notably absent at Twinbrook, and systems were put in place to ensure that the expenditure plans of each implementing agency were 'skewed' to deliver

FIGURE 8.10
R. Travers Morgan's urban motorway proposals, disparagingly known as 'the spaghetti proposals' – the blighting effect of which became a cause célèbre within the community in the 1970s.

BUILDING DESIGN PARTNERSHIP

facilities at Poleglass strictly in accordance with the planned programme of development.

The bombing campaign, at its most intense in the early 1970s, had a devastating impact on the commercial centre of the city (see chapter 13). While businesses demonstrated remarkable resilience, few buildings escaped bomb blast. The central city was not fulfilling its role as a regional retail centre and nightlife was almost non-existent. The city centre was deprived of investment for over a decade. By the end of the 1970s Belfast was a city in danger of collapsing outward. The heart had been ripped out of the city centre and the inner city was an extensive building site as renewal got under way. Commercial investors and private house-builders turned their attention away from the city to surrounding towns that were within commuting distance of the city itself.

The collapse of inner-city communities, however, was also a consequence of successive generations – those who were in a position to do so – voting with their feet and heading for the middle city, outer estates and beyond. Wages and salaries had fallen below the national average, but with house prices significantly lower than elsewhere in the UK, the property market was kept buoyant and there was a measure of disposable income to spend in shops, mainly in out-of-town locations. The city was continuing to function in its wider regional context.

HOUSING-LED REGENERATION IN THE 1980s

The Planning Service sensibly reviewed the Stop Line from time to time to facilitate the release of land for development in appropriate locations. The most significant allocation was in 1982 at Cairnshill in Castlereagh District, where a new road into the city was on the drawing board. This occasional release of greenfield land, later disparagingly branded as 'predict and provide planning', worked well for a time, moderating the excesses of market-led development by the prudent eking-out of housing land in areas of high demand. But by the early 1980s it was evident that what Belfast needed were projects, not plans. Large scale planning was discounted in favour of government-led investment and targeted action programmes – focused on the inner areas and the city centre.

The economy was in recession and Belfast had little prospect of surviving the economic decline without special assistance from the Westminster government. The shutdown of the DeLorean factory at Dunmurry, which had offered such promise in one of the worst unemployment blackspots of the city, was a bitter disappointment. But the scale of the government investment that had brought DeLorean to Northern Ireland was a measure of necessary government commitment.

The thrust of government policy generally in the UK was by now geared to the 'leverage' of private sector investment in the city centre and in disadvantaged areas. The outer city continued to generate employment in service industries and information technology, with new industrial areas around the city sited to take best advantage of access to the motorway network. In an attempt to target the disadvantaged, Belfast was accorded the opportunity to participate in the Enterprise Zone experiment

FIGURE 8.11
The Northern Ireland Housing Executive built ten thousand new houses in the 1980s, hoisting standards of living in the inner city.

NIHE

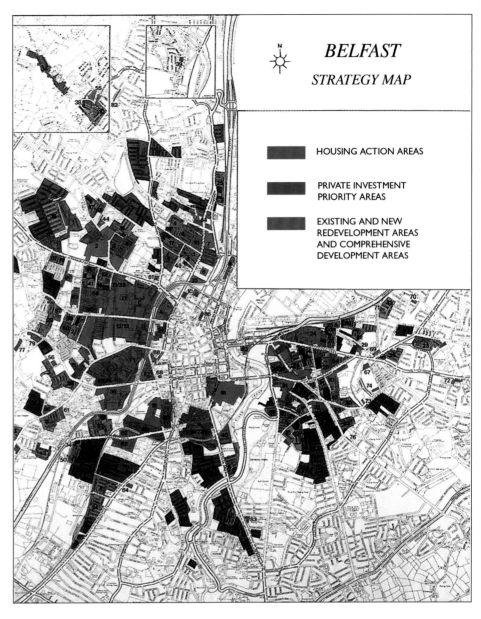

FIGURE 8.12
The Belfast Housing Renewal Strategy, 1982, represented a massive programme of social housing unmatched in the UK.

NIHE

and private investment was levered by financial incentive into the north foreshore and redundant mill buildings in the western inner city. But while jobs were created in these areas of high unemployment, the benefits did not accrue to the jobless in adjacent disadvantaged areas. Jobs created in flourishing enterprises were on offer and accessible to everyone, no matter where they lived in the city region.

In 1981 the government specifically identified housing in Belfast as its prime social priority. While every other local authority in the UK was being denied money for council housing, the government committed something in the order of £100 million every year towards social housing in the 1980s[13].

The NIHE built no high-rise flats and the 10,000 new homes that it produced in Belfast during the 1980s are virtually all two-storey terraced or semidetached dwellings (Figure 8.11). Working closely with local communities, the NIHE placed emphasis on the delivery of two-storey houses built in traditional materials to generous space standards. Most of the inner-city housing developments were served by 'shared surface' courts, where the pedestrian has priority – a good concept sometimes used to excess. The quality of those new homes owes much to the standards insisted upon by Charles Brett during his time in as chairman of the NIHE.[14] Critics of the extensive housing regeneration programme argued that it reinforced sectarian territory and contributed to the polarisation of communities, but there was no practical alternative. People felt safe only if rehoused within their own community. Of the many ways and means at the disposal of government to target social need and lift quality of life in the poorest areas, none can be of such lasting impact as a new home. The housing regeneration programme in Belfast was a huge planning achievement (Figure 8.12).

TOWARDS THE END OF THE TWENTIETH CENTURY

At this time Richard Needham, the longest-serving minister under Direct Rule, played an important role in the commercial regeneration of Belfast. As an under-secretary in the Northern Ireland Office, Needham's responsibilities after 1988 embraced both the

FIGURE 8.13
The Laganside Corporation's achievements in improving the river and its environs will be cherished by the future citizens of Belfast.

FREDERICK W. BOAL

FIGURE 8.14
Demolition of Red Hall in east Belfast's Circular Road, where C.S. Lewis played as a child – one of many fine houses pulled down for more intensive development as suburban land values soared at the end of the century

ULSTER ARCHITECTURAL HERITAGE SOCIETY

Environment and Economic Development. He was given special responsibility as 'Minister for Belfast' to ensure that the actions of government were focused and co-ordinated in line with the aspirations of the City Council. During his time in office, Belfast saw the arrival of CastleCourt (the first significant city centre retail investment for more than a decade), and the creation of the cross-harbour road and rail links. The road link proved particularly important, as it significantly eased traffic flows in the city centre and opened up development opportunities on redundant land in the harbour, making it accessible to all the citizens of Belfast. The construction of a weir downstream of the Queen Elizabeth Bridge was a bold decision to create development value through the elimination of unsightly mud flats (see chapter 9). Laganside Corporation was set up under the able chairmanship of the duke of Abercorn to exploit the opportunities. It proved difficult. Only after the Provisional IRA ceasefire announcement in 1994 was there any serious interest in major private investment in the heart of the city.

Belfast City Council, acting in association with government through the Laganside Corporation, gave a massive lift to waterfront Belfast, setting the stage for exciting developments in the twenty-first century. The Council's Waterfront Hall at Lanyon Place, and its development on the former Gas Works site, set the standard. By century's end the city's waterfront had been transformed (Figure 8.13). The Organisation for Economic Co-operation and Development (OECD), reporting to the international community in the year 2000, declared that the Laganside regeneration achievement had 'redefined a sense of what is possible in Belfast'.[15] Meanwhile, civil servants were picking up on national government thinking on urban containment. In January 1996, Environment Minister Malcolm Moss announced the publication by his department of a consultation document to provoke debate about a strategic vision for the Belfast city region.[16] History appeared to be repeating itself. While its status as a planning document was unclear, it emerged as a timely assessment of the dynamics of the city region that would have informed a broad range of urban policy.

But the city region debate was short-lived. A newly appointed environment minister, Lord Dubs, was immediately challenged to proceed instead with a strategic plan for Northern Ireland as a whole. The primary purpose of what became the Regional Development Strategy was to give effect to the aspiration of spreading development opportunity evenly across Northern Ireland. In line with the emerging compact city doctrine, the strategy also called for more intense development in existing settlements.[17] Greenfield land supply was allowed to dry up in order that house-builders would turn their energies to building on land within the existing urban footprint.

By the end of the century the biggest planning issue in Belfast in the eyes of its citizens was what they believed to be 'town cramming'. The purpose of cutting off the supply of land for greenfield development had been to force house-builders to look for brownfield sites. But as the planning net tightened, a plot in the leafy suburbs would become more valuable than the house that occupied it. Vacant inner-city sites were not attractive to developers and the property market, buoyed up by speculative investment from the Irish Republic, focused attention on well-looked-after property in the Edwardian suburbs. Property values in these areas escalated with the prospect of replacing fine houses with blocks of apartments (Figure 8.14).

Thus the century ended with planners under increasing pressure to protect the natural and built heritage. Regulatory town planning came to be seen by government as capable of delivering development that is sustainable – taken to mean that which is undertaken without detriment to the physical or social welfare of the community at large. A new doctrine of state planning appeared to be taking hold – every bit as forthright as its fifty-year-old predecessor in determining where people should live. This time there were no carrots to drive it forward. Just sticks.

THE LEGACY

The legacy of the Matthew Plan is positive, in that it established the principle of a Stop Line around Belfast – a simple, easily understood regulatory device that effectively preserved the setting of the city. The Matthew Plan also stressed the importance of lasting protection for the natural landscape of the Lagan Valley. This concept was developed in Belfast Corporation's 1969 BUAP, and by the end of the century the citizens could access a green lung reaching far out from the heart of the city through Belvoir Forest to the unspoiled landscapes of the Lagan Valley Regional Park. This regional park is self-evidently a town planning achievement of significance to the city.

The housing programme of the 1980s saved Belfast from an urban catastrophe, and the transformation of the river environment in a few short years at the end of the century was extraordinary (see chapter 9). The centralised doctrine behind the Matthew Plan was then cast aside as the actions of government became progressively more responsive to the aspirations of local communities. The street challenge 'Whose city is it anyway?' opened up a new debate on the purpose of planning. The voice of the community was heard by Belfast City Council, which led visioning exercises and participated in a range of initiatives to promote dialogue between the statutory agencies, the private sector and the voluntary sector. Wholehearted engagement was promised to communities through partnerships involving government officials, elected representatives and community leaders.

By the end of the century, centralised doctrine was back – this time with urban containment as the goal. The Regional Development Strategy for Northern Ireland was a popular document. It was applauded through Stormont by members of the Northern Ireland Assembly in late 2001. Its indicative policies were given effect in 2004 with the publication

FIGURE 8.15
A view of the city
from Cave Hill

SCENIC IRELAND

of the draft Belfast Metropolitan Area Plan (BMAP), which clamps down firmly on the availability of development land.[18] Guided by the Regional Development Strategy (with which BMAP must in law be in general conformity), the plan allocates no new edge of city land for development to 2015.[19] Acknowledging the pressure on the Edwardian suburbs, BMAP also offers protection for areas of townscape character, further restricting available development opportunities.

Regulatory planning at the hands of the regional Planning Service achieved much in the last quarter of the twentieth century in holding at bay undesirable development trends. But the future of the city, and of the greater Belfast area, was shaped more through ad hoc development initiatives and the occasional, and often unplanned, release of funds for investment in strategic infrastructure. The town planning ideal was for something more than that. Only Matthew came close. While the Matthew Plan may not have got it right, planning on that city regional scale was, and continues to be, the right approach.

The destiny of the city calls for studies at the scale of the city region. Belfast city region is a spatial unit that shapes the behaviour of people and organisations (Figure 8.15). A city region defines itself: a self-contained housing and labour market. Planning is essential for the welfare of the citizens. There should be a better world. Things have moved from no planning as such in 1950 to a statutory planning system today with substantial resources allocated to it. But regulatory planning on its own is not enough. It has to be directly associated with action planning for the community and a strategy for integrated investment in infrastructure – effective plans pave the way for development as well as harnessing it (see also chapter 19).

NOTES

1   Tudor Walters Committee (1918) *Report of the Tudor Walters Committee appointed by the Local Government Board 'to consider questions of building construction in connection with the provision of dwellings for the working classes in England and Wales, and Scotland and report upon methods of securing economy and despatch in the provision of such dwellings'* (Cmd 9191), HMSO: London.
2   Davidge, W.R. (1944) *Preliminary report on reconstruction and planning*, HMSO: Belfast.
3   Hendry, J. (1985) 'The development of planning in Northern Ireland', by M. Bannon and J. Hendry (eds) *Occasional papers in planning no. 1 – planning in Ireland: an overview*, Department of Town and Country Planning, Queen's University Belfast: Belfast.
4   Planning Advisory Board (1944) *Water supply and sewerage* (Cmd 223), HMSO: Belfast; Planning Advisory Board (1944) *Housing in Northern Ireland* (Cmd 224), HMSO: Belfast; Planning Advisory Board (1944) *Location of industry in Northern Ireland* (Cmd 225), HMSO: Belfast; Planning Commission (1945) *Planning proposals for the Belfast area* (Cmd 227), HMSO: Belfast; Planning Advisory Board, (1946) *Tourist industry in Northern Ireland* (Cmd 234), HMSO: Belfast; Planning Commission (1946) *Road communications in Northern Ireland* (Cmd 241), HMSO: Belfast; Planning Advisory Board (1947) *Provision of recreational and physical training facilities in Northern Ireland* (Cmd 246), HMSO: Belfast; Planning Advisory Board (1947) *The Ulster countryside: report on amenities in Northern Ireland*, HMSO: Belfast; Planning Commission (1952) *Planning proposals for the Belfast Area* (Cmd 302), HMSO: Belfast.
5   The Manchester Plan, formally attributed to Rowland Nicholas, the city's chief surveyor and engineer, was based on the American concept of a neighbourhood unit of 5,000–10,000 people, coinciding with the catchment area of a typical urban primary school, and thought capable of supporting an adequate range of local services.
6   Oliver, J.A. (1978) *Working at Stormont*, Institute of Public Administration: Dublin.
7   Matthew, R. (1964) *Belfast Regional Survey and Plan 1962*, HMSO: Belfast.
8   Wilson, T. (1965) *Economic development in Northern Ireland* (Cmd 479), HMSO: Belfast.
9   Geoffrey Booth went on to become the first director of the regional Planning Service. In 1979 he was elected president of the Royal Town Planning Institute.
10 Building Design Partnership (1969), *Belfast Urban Area Plan*, Building Design Partnership: London.
11 R. Travers Morgan and Partners (1969) *Belfast Transportation Plan*, R. Travers Morgan and Partners: London.
12 Boal, F.W. (1995) *Shaping a city: Belfast in the late twentieth century*, Institute of Irish Studies, Queen's University Belfast: Belfast.
13 Morrison, J.W.O. (1990) 'Making Belfast work', paper published in the *Report of Proceedings of the Town and Country Planning Summer School*: London.
14 Charles Brett's 1986 book – *Housing a divided community*, Institute of Public Administration: Dublin, in association with the Institute of Irish Studies, Queen's University Belfast: Belfast – provides insight into his personality, his dedication and commitment to high standards. Under his chairmanship, NIHE insisted on retaining the Parker Morris standards, which were introduced in 1961 to establish common understanding of minimum space standards that families should expect of new housing, based on occupancy and furniture layout, and which had been abandoned by the Conservative government in 1980.
15 Organisation for Economic Co-operation and Development (OECD) (2000) *Urban renaissance: Belfast's lessons for policy and partnership*, OECD: Paris, p.93.
16 Department of the Environment (1996) *The Belfast city region: towards and beyond the millennium. A paper for discussion*, Department of the Environment: Belfast.
17 Department for Regional Development (2002) *Shaping our future – the Regional Development Strategy for Northern Ireland 2025*, Department for Regional Development: Belfast.
18 Department of the Environment (2004) *Belfast Metropolitan Area Plan 2015 Draft Plan*, Department of the Environment: Belfast.
19 The Planning (Amendment) (Northern Ireland) Order 2003 gives the Department for Regional Development a statutory obligation to provide a statement on the conformity of development plans with the Regional Development Strategy.

To Belfast's salty waters where her lonesome journey ends.

'My Lagan Softly Flowing', NOEL McMASTER[1]

Let us do a little time travelling. We will take two trips, from the sea up to the great green wedge of countryside that we know today as the Lagan Valley Regional Park. The first trip we take is in 1900,[2] the second in 2000.[3]

9
Back to the River

The Lagan and Belfast in the Twentieth Century

Frederick W. Boal

FIGURE 9.1
The barge *Shamrock* being drawn along the Lagan at Drumbridge, in the early 1900s
ULSTER MUSEUM

UP THE LAGAN IN 1900

Our first journey is by rowing boat. It will be a hard pull for our two study oarsmen, but at least there is a light north-easterly breeze and the tide is just on the turn, so we can expect some help from the incoming flow. On our left, as we face towards the bow (the port side for those of a nautical bent), is the County Down shore; on our right (starboard) lies County Antrim. Particularly noticeable are the large expanses of mud, the Holywood Bank on the County Down side, the West Bank on the County Antrim shore. Of course, these will be hidden as the tide comes in, but at the moment they are fully exposed.

Ahead we can see two stone-faced islands. These are the East and West Twin Islands, constructed in the 1840s as part of the process of creating a straight channel from the quays near Queen's Bridge to deep water. In 1849 the channel was officially opened and named the Victoria Channel. So it is the Victoria Channel we are now entering, our first landfall being almost 2 miles (3.2 km) from the Queen's Bridge. The two Twins are very low lying, though on the West Twin there is a smallish building called (according to our map) the Intercepting Hospital for Contagious Diseases, presumably there to accommodate any mariners arriving at the port of Belfast who may have been suffering from such illnesses.

We continue up between the two Twin Islands for some distance. As we do so we begin to see ahead the first signs of one of Belfast's great industries – shipbuilding. There are shipyards on both the County Antrim and the County Down shores, presenting themselves in the form of forests of bare tree trunks. These are the wooden frames formed round a number of ships under construction on the slipways. The first two shipyards we see belong to Workman Clark – the North Yard on the County Antrim shore, the South Yard on the County Down.[4] We are told that most of the ships under construction at the moment are cargo vessels: *Cauldron, Mechanician, Indian, City of Athens, Carrigan Head*, and others.

The Victoria Channel now begins to narrow a bit. More shipbuilding activity appears on the County Down side (the North Yard of Harland and Wolff[5]) but this is not duplicated on our right, where we now see a long stretch of quayside lined with coal yards and cranes and with a number of coal boats tied up alongside. This is the Albert Quay. A second set of slipways appears on the County Down side – Harland and Wolff's South Yard. As with Workman Clark, here also evident is a forest of timber frameworks around ships under construction – vessels such as *Saxon, Minneapolis, Commonwealth, Devonian, Runic* and *Cedric*. Notably, the *Celtic*, one of the ships at the North Yard, will be the largest vessel in the world when she is completed.

As we clear the last of the shipbuilding activity at the Abercorn Basin we have to hold back to let a small passenger ferry cross our course – crowded literally to the gunwales with shipyard workers returning from their day's work at Harland and Wolff or Workman Clark. We have now reached a stretch of the river where the County Antrim side is lined with goods sheds and a string of large steamers at Donegall Quay. These ships are ferries that ply to Liverpool, Heysham, Ardrossan and Glasgow. Opposite the ferries, on the County Down side, is a quay dominated by coal imports – a mass of

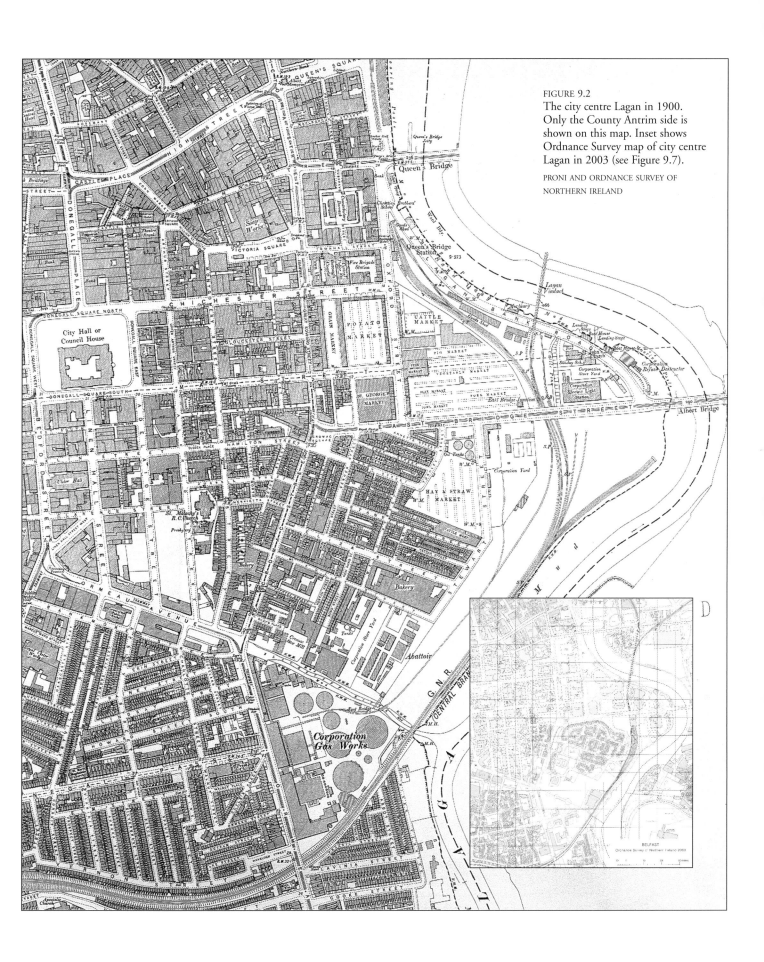

FIGURE 9.2
The city centre Lagan in 1900.
Only the County Antrim side is
shown on this map. Inset shows
Ordnance Survey map of city centre
Lagan in 2003 (see Figure 9.7).
PRONI AND ORDNANCE SURVEY OF
NORTHERN IRELAND

cranes, coal yards and coal boats. The names Kingsberry, Neill, Craig and Hinde are evident on the sheds. Tucked rather uneasily between the coal yards is the Queen's Quay station of the Belfast and County Down Railway (BCDR).

Ahead lies the first bridge over the Lagan – the Queen's Bridge. This is placed on the line of the old Long Bridge and was opened in 1835 and later widened in 1880. A paddle steamer is taking on passengers at a wooden jetty attached to the bridge. This is the famous Bangor Boat (see chapter 16, Figure 16.2) and it will soon be departing for the County Down resort.

Having passed under the bridge, we come on a new set of riverbank activities (Figure 9.2, with inset [see Figure 9.7]). A number of barges (known as lighters) are tied up at the Canal Quay, while another is unloading material at the Sand Quay – the material, not surprisingly, being sand brought down from Lough Neagh on the Lagan Canal. Upstream from this we can see some trains moving on a branch line of the Great Northern Railway (GNR), while nearby there are a number of other premises tucked close to the riverside, including the City Mortuary and the Corporation Refuse Destructor Works. Amongst all this is found a small church and Sunday school (St John's) and the boathouse and landing slip of the Belfast Rowing Club.[6] So religion and recreation are not totally excluded from an area dominated by commercial activity, transport systems and some of the less seemly components of urban function.

FIGURE 9.3
The Electric Light Station
was opened on East
Bridge Street in 1898.

ULSTER MUSEUM

Immediately behind the quays and the railway line lies a large expanse of markets – selling cattle, pigs, vegetables, flax, fowl, pork, potatoes and fish. One wonders whether Belfast is a great industrial centre (after all, we have just passed the shipyards), or a market town dealing in farm produce, or is it in a transitional stage between the two? And

we do get a sign of changing technologies when we spot the Belfast Corporation Electric Light Station (Figure 9.3) just behind the Refuse Destructor. Opened just two years earlier in 1898, the building, according to the *Belfast Directory*, 'marks an epoch in the history of the progress and development of Belfast'.

All this is on the County Antrim side of the river. The County Down side again provides a contrast. Here we see an iron foundry, Richardson's Chemical Manure Works and, most importantly, Davidson and Company's Sirocco Works, with its own quay on the river.

The tide is still quite low and we can observe extensive mud banks. (I see the word 'mud' printed on my map of the river in eight places.) We go under a railway viaduct that carries the Central Branch of the GNR across to join up with the BCDR system. Ahead lies the second bridge across the Lagan – the Albert Bridge (opened in 1890) – and just downstream we see the first sign of housing close to the river. This is the edge of Short Strand, though from our vantage point on the river it might be called 'Short Mud'.

Above the Albert Bridge we enter a section of the river even more dominated by mud banks, this being the case as far up as the confluence with the Blackstaff. The County Antrim bank in this stretch is dominated by the close proximity of the railway line, behind which (my map tells me) are located oil storage tanks, a hay and straw market, and an abattoir. Again the city seems to have commandeered the lands close to the river for some of its less appealing activities.

What of the County Down side? Again housing is kept well away from the river; the bankside locations here are occupied by the Lagan Engine Works, ('engineers, millwrights, iron and brass founders, boilermakers'), and McConnell's Cromac Distillery and Brewery. Immediately upstream from this industrial riverside there is a sharp change as the northern edge of Ormeau Park impinges directly on the river bank, with trees, grass and a 'riding and cycling track'. As we take in the greenery of the park after so much urban activity we have to pull over towards the ever present but now receding mud bank to allow the passage of a string of coal-laden lighters being pulled by tug to the Blackstaff Quay, there to feed the insatiable appetite of the city's Gas Works.

The Gas Works are an extraordinary manifestation – towering gasholders, chimneys, large industrial buildings and everywhere clouds of smoke and 'steam'. The Gas Works have been located here since 1823. Just as Belfast was proclaiming the presence of the largest shipyard, the largest ropeworks, and so on, in the world, so the city directory trumpets the gasholders – 'the largest of them is of greater capacity than any similar storehouse in Ireland, containing when full 2,600,000 cubic feet [*c.* 73,600 cubic metres] of gas. It stands 106 feet [32.3m] high from the level of surrounding ground to top of framing.'

Upstream from the Gas Works the contrast between the two banks of the Lagan is still evident. On the County Down side Ormeau Park continues to impinge directly on the river, with pathways and lines of trees. On the County Antrim side the dominant features are areas of tightly packed red brick terraced houses. But for much of this stretch the houses are not directly on the riverside, but are stepped back some yards, with a scatter of indeterminate commercial buildings intervening. Thus the river is not seen as an

FIGURE 9.4
Side on to the river:
Holyland gable ends

FREDERICK W. BOAL

attractive feature to align dwellings along. Indeed, even where housing does encroach close to the high tide mark, it is the gable ends that face the river, not the fronts of the terraced houses. On the other hand, this orientation is not at all surprising since the river here (except at high tide) is fringed by the almost inevitable mud banks.

We now reach the third road bridge across the Lagan – Ormeau Bridge (1863). We are tempted to stop here to give our oarsmen a rest and for all of us to take the opportunity to partake of some refreshments at Mr Boyce's Confectionary and Coffee Stand, which is conveniently located at the County Down end of the bridge. This we do before continuing upstream, our next destination being the Stranmillis Lock, which marks the beginning of the Lagan Canal. What do we observe on our way up? The County Down side is dominated by large chimneys and great round brick structures signalling the presence of four very substantial brickworks – the Haypark, the Marquis, the Prospect and the Annadale. Any housing here is well away from the river, as the brick-makers have commandeered the underlying clays to provide the raw material for their manufactories.

On the County Antrim side above Ormeau Bridge seven streets of houses approach the river, but at right angles to it. Thus, just as with part of the area below the bridge, the houses are sideways to the river, presenting us with a view of fourteen gable ends (Figure 9.4). This area, known as the Holyland, is clearly not oriented to the river, whose bank is admittedly low lying, offering the usual mud banks except at high tide. Beyond the Holyland the County Antrim riverside is open and undeveloped, though there is a narrow tree-lined walkway (known as the River Promenade) running back to the extensive and long-established Botanic Gardens, these having been purchased five years earlier by the Corporation from the Royal Belfast Botanic and Horticultural Society.

Ahead we can now see the entrance to the Stranmillis Lock, closely attended by the lockkeeper's house and the premises of the Belfast Boat Club (Figure 9.5). Immediately back from this, more industrial activity is evident – the Lagan Brick and Terra Cotta Works (echoing the activity on the other side of the river), an asphalt works and a paper mill.

We need to enter the Lagan Navigation here to proceed further up the river. Fortunately several lighters laden with coal are tied up waiting to be hitched to horses and then to be towed upstream to one or more of the industrial premises in the Lagan Valley.[7] These particular loads are bound for John Shaw Brown at Edenderry. We manage to squeeze our rowing boat in with the commercial traffic and wait for the water level in the lock to rise. When this is complete we can leave the lock and re-enter the river, which also serves here as the canal. We are now really in the countryside, with some low lying meadows to be seen between the plentiful trees. On the County Antrim side we are accompanied now by the towpath, and ahead we can see the last of the lighters that we shared the lock with being hauled by one of the stalwart horses.

At this point our 1900 journey up Belfast's Lagan terminates, though not before we come on four people in a small boat out for a gentle row from the Boat Club. The ladies are attired in their Sunday best. We note that in this stretch of the river above the Stranmillis Lock there are no mud banks to be seen. This is the non-tidal river now, with the water upstream ponded back by the Stranmillis Weir, which is part of the control works associated with the Lagan Canal.

FIGURE 9.5
The boathouse at Stranmillis in the early twentieth century
LINEN HALL LIBRARY

What, then, are the salient features of Belfast's Lagan in 1900? First, the lands in proximity to the river are commandeered for industrial and transportation purposes, with the marked exception of the rural-oriented markets. Second, the absence of riverside housing attests to the unattractiveness of the river itself. Third, the presence of large areas of mud flats in the river bed above Queen's Bridge is striking. And finally there is the reclamation dynamic that pushes dry land further out across the mud flats at the head of Belfast Lough, at the same time extending the river seawards in the shape of the Victoria Channel.

UP THE LAGAN IN 2000

It is now time to revisit the river, but 100 years on from our first journey. This time we have the comfort and the motive power of the *Joyce Too*.[8] As before, we will describe what we see, but we will also take advantage of 'memory' extending over 100 years to note any significant changes that have taken place.

FIGURE 9.6
Claiming the lough, extending the river: land 'reclamation', 1750–2000

As we approach the entrance to the Victoria Channel we see a large area of flat ground edged by stone revetments. A scatter of apparently abandoned containers is the only feature of note. The extensive mud banks of 1900 have disappeared. We also note that we are entering the river at least one and a half miles (2.4 km) further out from the Queen's Bridge than we did in 1900. Immediately upstream from this container graveyard is an area dominated by large horizontal transporters, busily unloading containers off a boat and stacking them on top of each other. This is the Victoria Terminal, totally dedicated to the handling of containers, either by 'lo-lo' (lift-on/lift-off), as here, or by 'ro-ro' (roll-on/roll-off) a little nearer the city.

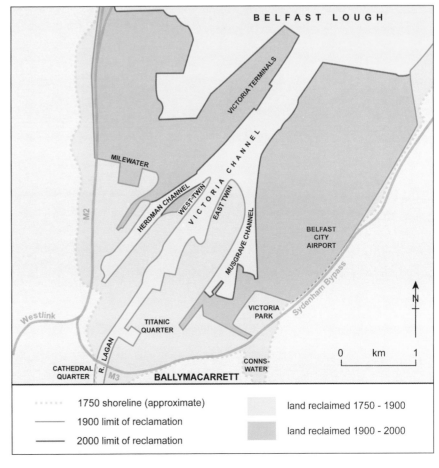

1750 shoreline (approximate)
1900 limit of reclamation
2000 limit of reclamation
land reclaimed 1750 - 1900
land reclaimed 1900 - 2000

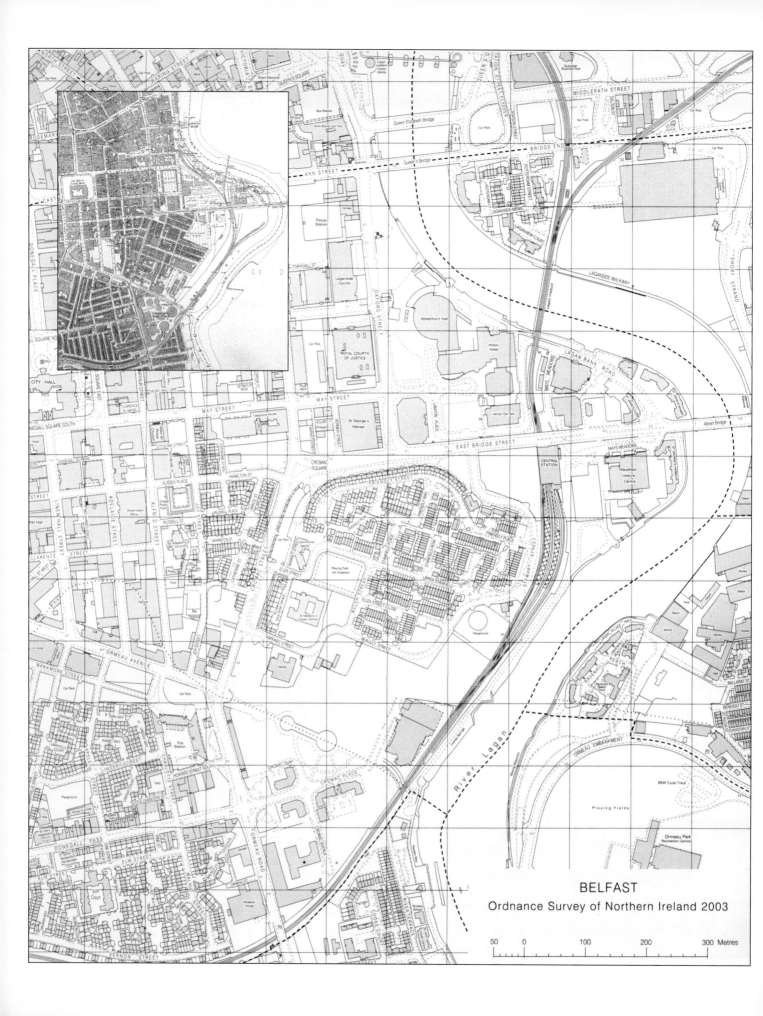

BELFAST

Ordnance Survey of Northern Ireland 2003

50   0   100   200   300 Metres

As well as the container boat we see the Liverpool ferry, which now docks about 3 miles (4.8 km) further down from the Queen's Bridge than it did 100 years earlier.

On the County Down side the mud banks have also disappeared under the surging reclamation[9] of the twentieth century (Figure 9.6). On this new land we see an extensive area of multicoloured plastic sacks, then a smaller sized area that is fringed by a vegetation cover of low bushes and trees. Our map (Figure 9.7, with inset [see Figure 9.2]) tells us that this is actually an embanked area of shallow water known as the Harbour Lagoon, which now functions as a bird sanctuary under the management of the Royal Society for the Protection of Birds (RSPB). Next to this, tied up at a jetty, we see a tanker unloading refined petroleum products, which are then piped to an extensive 'tank farm' inland from the bird reserve. Back from the lands in immediate proximity to the Victoria Channel can be seen a line of new office blocks and behind them we see a large passenger jet lifting out of the Belfast City Airport in the Harbour Estate.

Though we have already seen all sorts of activities and structures we have not yet reached the first point of land that we encountered on our journey in 1900. All this did not exist 100 years ago – seagoing container traffic, petroleum delivery and storage, offices and a busy airport (not to forget the RSPB reserve, see Figure 9.8), and perhaps most significant of all, the land itself.

As we head upstream we can see in the distance that the skyline has changed. There are no longer any forests of wooden frames where ships are a-building, but we do see some very tall cranes and, further inland, two yellow horizontal structures on huge tripod-like legs. More on this when we get further upriver.

We now reach the location where we first met land in 1900 – the outer tips of the East and West Twin Islands. On the County Antrim side we no longer have a narrow strip of land, but a much more substantial though still narrow promontory. First we see a tall grain silo, then a long low shed at the quayside where a vessel is unloading. Beyond this there is an open area with piles of stone aggregate, while looming behind is the three-chimneyed bulk of the West Twin electricity generating station. Though an impressive structure, it appears to be inactive. We are reminded that electricity as a power source has come a long way from the Corporation Electric Light Station at the Albert Bridge to the West Twin Station that we now see, to much further out on the north shore of Belfast Lough where the massive single chimney of the Kilroot Power Station presents its widely visible landmark. Finally, on the West Twin we see a large area of coal. This is where the

Opposite page
FIGURE 9.7
The city centre Lagan in 2003. Inset shows city centre Lagan in 1900 (see Figure 9.2).
ORDNANCE SURVEY OF NORTHERN IRELAND AND PRONI

FIGURE 9.8
Looking over the RSPB Belfast Lough Nature Reserve towards the Cave Hill
ROBERT SCOTT

much-diminished importation of coal now occurs, having been moved downstream from its earlier location near the Queen's Bridge.

The East Twin Island is much more developed that it was in 1900, but there is also considerable evidence of reduced activity. There is a large dry dock at the end of the island and a long quay with two monstrous, somewhat rusty oil rigs undergoing maintenance work. Next we see the entrance to a second dry dock – the Thompson – constructed originally for the fitting out of vessels such as *Olympic* and *Titanic* but now quite unused. But something else is under way here – a sparkling new building with the sign 'Innovation Centre' and plans for an ultra-modern building for Queen's University's Institute of Electronics, Communications and Information Technology (ECIT), as the University extends its reach from south Belfast into what is to become the Northern Ireland Science Park.[10] Thus, on the East Twin we see the greatly shrunken relics of Belfast's shipbuilding era providing a location for the development of some of the cutting edge technologies of the early twenty-first century as Belfast strives to turn round the fortunes of its rust-belt modernism. Not only is the technological change massive, but the English language seems to be undergoing a transformation as well, for we are told in the promotional literature for ECIT that it will 'incubate spin-off and spin-in start-up companies'.

The channel narrows further and the sense of industrial change becomes even starker. The South and North Yards of Workman Clark are no more, neither are the North and South Yards of Harland and Wolff. What we get instead are huge expanses of concreted space almost stripped bare of any structures whatsoever – bar Harland and Wolff's former Paint Hall, though we are told that even it will not be around much longer. It is difficult to envisage fully the degree of change that has gone on here. This was where, in 1900, there was a multitude of wooden frames embracing the many ships under construction and where, in 1911–12, *Titanic* and *Olympic* were built, as well as Harland and Wolff's last passenger liner, the *Canberra*, in 1960. In 1969 this area was abandoned – shipbuilding moved to the Building Dock, the home of the great yellow 'Samson' and 'Goliath' cantilever cranes that we first spotted as we entered the Victoria Channel.

Much of this area, with its considerable sense of abandonment and its tiny but significant sense of rebirth, has recently been designated the Titanic Quarter. Located on a major part of the redundant shipyard lands, Titanic Quarter offers (according to its publicity documentation[11]) a land-use pattern that will be 40 per cent residential ('waterfront apartments and family townhouses'), and over 50 per cent employment (the employment being 'high-tech, office/administrative and industrial'). Titanic Quarter will also have a 'heritage' section to include the *Titanic* slipway and the Harland and Wolff Design Office. It will also have an element of leisure and tourism – 'cruise liner berth, media facilities, hotels … boulevards'. All this is a long way from the harsh grind of labour-intensive heavy industry that dominated the site 100 years ago, but it also provides, rather intriguingly, a throwback to the middle of the nineteenth century when Queen's Island was a pleasure park.

Ahead we now see more change; a huge domed complex – the Odyssey – where the coal quays and storage areas dominated the scene in 1900; a massive concrete bridge – the Lagan Bridge – with continuous streams of traffic, the Dargan rail bridge nuzzled against it; and then through the arches of the two bridges a striking structure that appears to block our progress up the river – the Lagan Weir.

Before exploring the weir, we need to turn our attention to the County Antrim side of the river. Where there had been a long line of coal sheds followed by goods sheds and their attendant cross-channel steamers right up to the Queen's Bridge in 1900, now we observe the latest in high-speed sea transport – the Stena HSS ferry rapidly disgorging its cargo of goods trailers, vans and cars (as well as foot passengers), and just as rapidly loading a replacement set of vehicles for the return journey to Scotland.[12] Near the Lagan Bridge there is a second ferry terminal where the more modest but still nippy Seacat is gathering its share of cross-channel traffic. In between the two ferry terminals, again where coal quays dominated in 1900 (the Albert Quay), we now see an array of office blocks clearly oriented towards the visual delights of the river frontage.

The Lagan Weir turns out not to be the total obstacle to navigation that it first appeared. It is basically a device to control the level of the river from this point to the foot of the Stranmillis Weir (a distance of some 2.9 miles [4.7 km]). Once the incoming tide has reached the same level as the water impounded upstream, the weir gates are lowered, permitting navigation up (and down) stream for small vessels such as the *Joyce Too*. This can only be achieved for a period of about two and a half hours either side of high water.

As we slide upstream over the weir we note that the goods sheds that once lined the Donegall Quay have disappeared. The river bank is now quite open except for the Lagan Lookout, a round building that serves as an educational and information centre focusing on the river and its related activities (both past and present). Straight ahead of us is another bridge that was not present in 1900 – the Queen Elizabeth Bridge (1966) – and immediately beyond that we see an old friend, the Queen's Bridge.

Emerging from under the Queen's Bridge, we come upon a section of the Lagan that has probably undergone a greater transformation than anywhere else on Belfast's river. The all-pervasive mud banks of 1900 are nowhere to be seen. Perhaps they have just been covered by the rising tide? But we are reliably informed that this is not the explanation. Rather, it is the contribution made by the Lagan Weir in retaining a relatively high water

Top
FIGURE 9.9a
Upriver view of Lagan from Queen's Bridge, 1930

ULSTER MUSEUM

Middle
FIGURE 9.9b
Upriver view of Lagan from Queen's Bridge, 1990

LAGANSIDE CORPORATION

Bottom
FIGURE 9.9c
Upriver view of Lagan from Queen's Bridge, 2005

STEPHEN A. ROYLE

FIGURE 9.10
The remnant piers of the
former McConnell Weir,
with the Halifax call
centre at the Gas Works
site behind, Cave Hill
forming the backdrop

FREDERICK W. BOAL

level that makes the difference, in conjunction with a pro-gramme of dredging (see section titled 'A Tale of Two Weirs' below).

If the river itself has changed radically, this is perhaps truer still for the lands in proximity to the Lagan. The cat-tle, fish and vegetable markets are all gone, as is the bankside railway. There is no mortuary, no Corporation Refuse Destructor Works. Instead we see the striking glass-clad Waterfront Hall, backed by the towers of the Hilton hotel and the Northern Ireland headquarters of British Telecom. The very name Waterfront Hall emphasises the now powerful attraction exerted by the transformed river. Activity looks to the river rather than turning its back to it, as was the case 100 years ago (and indeed much more recently than that). This new sense of 'back to the river' is further emphasised by the presence of tall apartment blocks (on both the County Antrim and County Down sides), carrying names such as Gregg's Quay, Laganview and St John's Wharf[13] (see Figure 9.9a, 9.9b and 9.9c).

We note other changes from 1900 – St John's church is no more, nor is the premises of the Belfast Rowing Club, the latter now to be found well upstream near the Stranmillis Weir. Gone also on the County Down side is the Sirocco Works, the site currently exist-ing in a transitional state between deindustrialisation and the service economy (not to mention the prospect of more riverside apartments). The only real reminder of the former presence of a significant element of Belfast's industrial past is a plaque on a wall that demar-cates the newly named Sirocco Quay. Amongst all this change the Lagan Railway Viaduct is still in place, carrying trains to and from the relatively new Central Station. However, a pedestrian bridge has been built onto the viaduct, linking the riverside walkways.

We now pass under the Albert Bridge, familiar enough from 1900, now sparkling in its new paint. Immediately upstream (on the County Antrim side) there are more apart-ments (St George's Harbour this time) and the Maysfield Leisure Centre, with a glimpse of the Central Railway Station behind. There then follows a narrow, grassy bank and a riverside walkway with a belt of trees almost screening the railway track. However, it is just upstream from here that we come on another of the massive riverside transforma-tions. The huge gasholders of the Gas Works are nowhere to be seen. Also absent is the channel of the Blackstaff River that used to serve as a coal quay for the gas company. Instead we have a glistening new office block (a call centre for Halifax Bank of Scotland), together with a number of other red brick office structures. Just as downstream, the activ-ities of the industrial era, which dominated in 1900, are gone and the service economy has taken over.

There has been less apparent change on the County Down side upstream from the Albert Bridge. Buildings are still tightly squeezed against the river, with evidence of ware-housing and industry. However, the presence of Lagan Watersports, an architect's office and another cluster of riverfront apartments with a river-oriented name (Ravenhill Reach) signals that the dynamic we have observed elsewhere is active here as well.

All the way up from the Albert Bridge the absence of mud banks is evident, but upstream from the confluence with the Blackstaff we note a pair of rather odd-looking structures – two brick piers rising up in midstream, all that is left of the McConnell Lock and Weir (see Figure 9.10, 'A Tale of Two Weirs' below and, again, Figure 9.12). A second change from 1900 is the much more sharply defined river edges from here at least up to the Ormeau Bridge – stone-faced revetments on both banks, with a road on the Ormeau Park side and a widened strip of land between the lower Ormeau housing and the river. All this is evidence of changes that took place at this location in the 1920s and 1930s, as part of the major 'improvements' carried out on the river. We are looking here at the embankments, which we later observe to be continuous almost all the way to the Stranmillis Weir.

Upstream from the Ormeau Bridge we see changes other than those that are a product of the embanking process. On the County Down side the four brickworks of 1900 have been replaced by flat-roofed apartments dating from the1950s and, further upstream, by new townhouse complexes, some of which are still under construction. On the County Antrim side the Holyland houses still butt gable-on to the river, but now there is a substantial strip of land between them and the river itself – again a product of the embanking process. Upstream from the Holyland a rather ugly and quite massive, grey, box-like structure intrudes onto the flat expanse at the foot of the Botanic Gardens. This is the Queen's University Physical Education Centre.

Ahead we see another bridge that was not present in 1900 – the King's Bridge,[14] built in the 1920s; and further ahead, another new bridge – the Governor's Bridge, opened in 1973. And still further ahead, yet more riverside apartments (Stranmillis Wharf), but no sign of the entrance to the Lagan Canal. Instead, on the site of the lock sits a squat building that declares itself to be a riverside restaurant and bar, and we can see folk sitting out on the terrace enjoying their refreshments. The lock itself is gone and the canal has ceased to function as a navigable waterway. So the *Joyce Too* can take us no further. Consequently we land and walk upstream, past various boat clubs (including the Belfast Rowing Club on its third relocation from where we saw it in 1900). As in 1900 we now depend on muscle power for our upriver progress as we board a small rowing boat on the last leg of our journey. No coal barges, no horses on the canal towpath, but plenty of people walking, some with their dogs, and others jogging and cycling. The commercial water highway of 1900 has become the sedate river spine of the Lagan Valley Regional Park, a great green lung that thrusts its refreshing rurality into the fabric of the bustling city.

A TALE OF TWO WEIRS

The alterations we have observed between our two journeys up the Lagan were driven to a very considerable extent by technological and economic change over the twentieth century. However, we must note another process that has had a huge impact – what we may call 'improvement'. Today 'improvement' may seem a rather old-fashioned term, but it effectively encapsulates several key contributions to change on the river. Symbolically as well as functionally, improvement can be summarised as a 'tale of two weirs' – the McConnell Weir, opened officially in 1937, and the Lagan Weir, opened in 1994.

The McConnell Weir, 1937

In August 1923 Belfast Corporation, sitting in committee, gave consideration to the promotion of a Bill to obtain powers for, among other matters, 'the construction of locks on the River Lagan at Albert Bridge'.[15] The Bill reached the statute book in May 1924 as the Belfast Corporation Act (Northern Ireland). The Act was divided into ten parts; Part II, 'Works on the River Lagan', concerns us here. These works were of great importance for that part of the Lagan between the confluence with the Blackstaff and Stranmillis Weir,[16] but quite remarkably they also gave a major foretaste of the works to be carried out on the river almost seventy years later. The 1924 Act referred to eight works:[17]

> Work No. 1 – A widening and deepening of the River Lagan on the right or eastern side thereof between the confluence of that river with the Glentoran stream and a point 1 furlong 9.3 chains [388 m] or thereabouts south of the said confluence.
>
> Work No. 2 – A lock and weir across the said River Lagan above the confluence of the River Blackstaff with the river.
>
> Work No. 3 – A wharf or landing place partly on the left bank of the said River Lagan and partly on the bed of that river.
>
> Work No. 4 – A wall or embankment partly on the right bank of the said River Lagan and partly on the bed of that river.
>
> Work No. 5 – A wall or embankment partly on the left bank of the said River Lagan and partly on the bed of that river.
>
> Work No. 6 – A new road commencing by a junction with Ravenhill Road and terminating by a junction with Annadale Avenue.
>
> Work No. 7 – A new road commencing by a junction with Stranmillis Road and terminating by a junction with Ormeau Road.
>
> Work No. 8 – A towpath along the left bank of the said River Lagan.

The objectives of these works were to sharpen up the rather indeterminate banks of the Lagan from the Blackstaff confluence to the Stranmillis Weir and also to maintain a level of water in the river that would cover the unsightly mud banks previously exposed at low tide. Since there was still significant canal traffic, it was also necessary to insert a lock at the weir to enable the passage of barges. The decision to locate the weir upstream from the Blackstaff confluence rather than at the Albert Bridge, as earlier proposed, was driven by a need to avoid interrupting the flow of coal barges from the coal quays to the Gas Works. The embanking of the river was also a very significant improvement, narrowing the channel and providing new land for the construction of a series of 'boulevards' – the Stranmillis, Ormeau and Annadale embankments. Photographs taken by A.R. Hogg in 1929 clearly illustrate the embanking process in action and the early results (Figures 9.11a and 9.11b). To enable this to take place, the 1924 Act gave Belfast

Top
FIGURE 9.11a
Lagan Embankment construction under way, 1929, looking downstream towards the Ormeau Bridge from the Stranmillis Embankment

PRONI

Bottom
FIGURE 9.11b
Lagan Embankment looking upstream to Stranmillis Lock, 1929 (note the brickworks' chimneys on both sides of the river)

PRONI

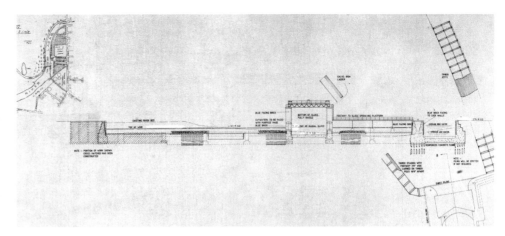

Corporation the powers to 'dredge, deepen or otherwise alter the said River Lagan as will be on the landward side of the walls or embankments'.[18] These manipulations of the physical characteristics of the river were to be repeated by Laganside Corporation in the 1990s.

Although powers were given to the Corporation in 1924 to construct a lock and weir and plans were drawn up in 1926 (Figure 9.12a), it was not until 1937 that the 'McConnell' Lock and Weir was declared open (Figure 9.12b). However, the weir itself was completed as early as 1932. Why there was such a long gestation period for the lock is not entirely clear, though depression economics may have had an impact, while the construction technology available at the time could not produce results with the rapidity of those achievable in the late twentieth century.

Top
FIGURE 9.12a
McConnell Weir
construction plan, 1926

LAGANSIDE CORPORATION

Bottom
FIGURE 9.12b
McConnell Weir: the
completed works, 1937

PRONI

The improvements to the Lagan upstream from the Blackstaff were not greeted with universal acclaim. Writing in 1944, the geographer Estyn Evans noted that the 'provision of riverside promenades on both sides of the Lagan is greatly to be desired',[19] but he went on to record that the distinguished school architect Reginald S. Wilshere (see chapters 3 and 15) had described the results as 'aesthetically really little better than a flooded railway cutting'.[20] Since then, of course, the 'raw edge' of the embanking process has been greatly softened by mature trees and grassy slopes (see chapter 8, Figure 8.13).

A second problem arose from the improvements, in this case from the presence of the weir itself. An unpleasant odour emanated from the river during spells of warm summer weather. It was only in the 1970s and 1980s that survey work disclosed that in the impounded stream there was a major problem caused by a surface freshwater layer overlying denser salt water, the latter being introduced into the impoundment by the tidal flood. This led to the entrapment of seawater near the bottom of the river, the subsequent blocking of the exchange of oxygen from the overlying freshwater and the consequent generation and emission of hydrogen sulphide gas from the bottom muds. It was not until the early 1990s that action would be taken to tackle this unfortunate state of affairs.

The McConnell Lock and Weir and the embankments were introduced as improvements to the upper part of the Lagan in Belfast. However, the critical section between the weir and the Queen's Bridge remained 'unimproved' – a place where the city continued to turn its back to the river. Only over a prolonged period after the Second World War would attention be turned to that part of the Lagan in proximity to the heart of the city.

The Lagan Weir, 1994

Early Planning for the River

In August 1942 the Northern Ireland Minister for Home Affairs, Sir Dawson Bates, appointed a commission to examine matters relating to physical planning. This action suggests considerable foresight, as 1942 cannot have been a particularly encouraging time, though the tide of war was beginning to turn in the Allies' favour. In 1945 the Planning Commission presented its preliminary proposals for the 'Belfast Area'.[21] A section of the document focused on the Lagan Valley, reporting as follows:

> [An] … area of supreme importance is the valley of the Lagan which from Stranmillis to Lisburn provides a natural parkway of great beauty enjoyed by increasing numbers of walkers and holiday makers. The Lagan valley is one of the few well-wooded regions in the Province and it has the great advantage of penetrating deeply into the built-up area, thus forming a natural, health-giving lung of immeasurable value to the city. This great asset should be preserved at all costs and improved by the gradual clearing of the Lagan banks between Stranmillis and the Queen's Bridge to form a continuous green embankment strip linking the city centre with the open country. Belfast has an opportunity here open to few other towns of its size in the world; it would be a catastrophe if this opportunity was lost by lack of the necessary control over future development.

The commission also noted that it hoped to see the Lagan banks improved by new buildings. Thus were sown the seeds that markedly came to fruition in the last decade of the twentieth century.

Although the Belfast Regional Survey and Plan 1962[22] (the Matthew Plan – see chapter 8) did not focus on detailed planning measures within the city itself, it did make a number of references to the Lagan – expressing concerns about matters such as 'the deplorable environment for landing [boat] passengers (down-at-heel out-of-datedness and depressingly unattractive to progressive visitors)', while noting that urban development should not be permitted to intrude on the Lagan Valley between Belfast and Lisburn. The Matthew Plan did not make any direct reference to the river between Stranmillis and Queen's Bridge, though the document did include a two-page appendix entitled 'Notes by the Architectural Group on Lagan Bank Development Proposals'.[23] This provided a reinforcement to the thinking presented by the Planning Commission nineteen years earlier, while also foretelling some of the changes to come thirty years later.

The follow-up to the Matthew Plan was the Belfast Urban Area Plan (BUAP) of 1969.[24] This was tasked to fill in the detail within the broader regional framework of the earlier document. The River Lagan received specific attention:

> The river has a potential comparing favourably with any in Europe. This may seem optimistic in view of its present condition but opportunities are present on this scale in the redevelopment of the quayside and city centre sections of the river that are also related to the concept of the Lagan as a major landscape feature in the Urban Area as a whole extending from the Harbour to the proposed Lagan Valley Country Park.[25]

The proposals included the redevelopment of the river from the Queen's Bridge to the Gas Works, to include a leisure centre and a government office complex. A weir was to be built downstream from the Queen Elizabeth Bridge to 'ensure the covering of the present mudflats, enable the use of the river for pleasure boating and provide a fine setting for riverside development in the Maysfield and May's Market areas'. Here again hindsight enables us to foresee the basic components of what was to become 'Laganside'.

Moving towards 'Laganside'

Nine years later (1978), another report was issued, but this time the focus was *entirely* on the river. Entitled, rather unglamorously, *River Lagan: Report of a Working Party*,[26] it highlighted the problems facing the river: 'The unsightly accumulation of mud and silt have a highly detrimental effect on the river's already-impaired visual quality. They are particularly obtrusive downstream from the McConnell Weir where they are exposed twice daily. Viewed from the Queen's and Albert Bridges at low tide they convey a strong impression of neglect' (Figure 9.13a – and compare with 9.13b).[27] Moreover, the report stat-

ed: 'From the Queen's Bridge to the Ormeau Embankment on the east bank, and to Ormeau Bridge on the west bank, urban and industrial development extends almost or right to the water's edge. Little or no regard has been paid to environmental amenity.'[28] To tackle these problems the Working Party proposed:

1 a water control structure [weir or barrage] near the Queen Elizabeth Bridge

2 the reclamation of land on both sides of the river to permit the insertion of a green corridor from the Blackstaff confluence to the Queen's Bridge

3 dredging of the mud

The second proposal, the narrowing of the river, was actually limited to a slender strip on the west bank between the Blackstaff and the Albert Bridge. The first and third of these proposals became key elements of the Laganside action in the 1990s. The Working Party, very significantly, stressed the need for a co-ordinated effort to carry forward their recommendations, either by the creation of a specific river authority or by the formation of a special group representative of all the public bodies with an interest in the river. In all of this the Working Party concentrated on the river and its immediate banks. It emphasised 'amenity' and had little to say about possible developments on the lands in proximity to the river.

Published in March 1987, the Lagan Concept Plan[29] was commissioned as input to the Belfast Urban Area Plan but clearly stands as a key document in its own right. Parliamentary Under-Secretary of State at the Department of the Environment Richard Needham wrote in his Foreword to the document: '[This study of Laganside] describes the potential which exists to transform completely the environmental quality of a vital part of the city, and by this means to help transform perceptions of Belfast at an international level. The proposals

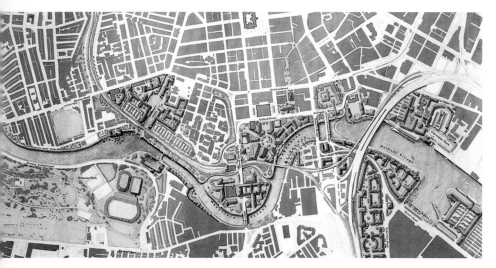

FIGURE 9.14
The Lagan Concept Plan, 1987

SHEPHEARD, EPSTEIN AND HUNTER
(LONDON) AND BUILDING DESIGN
PARTNERSHIP (BELFAST)

of the study are visionary. They are ambitious in scope and concept but are also pragmatic.'

As with the earlier reports and plans, the several problems associated with the river and its proximate lands were rehearsed, and the fact that the city had not yet realised the development opportunities offered by reuniting buildings and spaces with the water was underlined. However, most significantly, the document stated that 'the Lagan could become one of the most attractive rivers in Europe'.

The Concept Plan outlined each of six major development sites – the Blackstaff Quays (at the site of the McConnell Lock), the Gas Works, Maysfield Island, Laganbank, Queen Elizabeth Bridge and Abercorn Basin, Albert Square/Custom House Square and Corporation Square/Clarendon Dock (Figure 9.14). The first four of these sites are upstream from the Queen's Bridge and their designation implied the removal of previously existing developments; the rest are effectively in the inner part of the harbour and their redevelopment would be largely dependent on the migration seawards of the marine activities located there.

For the upstream development sites to be attractive, a key infrastructure innovation would be an imperative – the construction of a new weir to enable a constant high water level to be maintained in the river to cover the much-maligned mud banks, thereby providing an attractive stretch of waterfront in the heart of the city. In addition, the Concept Plan called for the construction of a new cross-harbour road and rail bridge (or bridges), thereby relieving the surface routes near the river banks of very high volumes of traffic. Finally, and also of the highest importance, the plan called for the establishment of a unitary authority to implement the infrastructure and land management aspects of the overall scheme.

The Laganside Era

The unitary authority called for in the Concept Plan was established in 1989 as the Laganside Corporation.[30] The Corporation had a single, if widely embracing, objective – 'to secure the regeneration of the designated area'. To achieve this, it was permitted to 'acquire, hold, manage and dispose of land and other property'. It was also given leave to 'carry out building and other operations', and, indeed, to 'do anything necessary or expedient for the purposes of the object'.

The corporation's report for 2003–04 stated: 'It may be hard to believe that only ten years ago the Lagan was a rank, polluted river; devoid of life in its waters and along its shores. Its dark, ominous form repelled visitors at high tide, and at low tide the river retreated to reveal foul-smelling, rubbish-strewn mudflats.'[31] The report went on to paint a glowing picture of the river at the beginning of the twenty-first century. Though the language used might be considered rather overenthusiastic, there can be no denying that a huge transformation had taken place. The lynchpin of this transformation is the Lagan Weir,[32] opened in 1994 (Figure 9.15; see also chapter 19, Figure 19.6). This weir has the same basic function as that intended for the McConnell Weir opened in the 1930s. However, there are important differences between the two weirs:

1 The Lagan Weir provides an impoundment over a significantly longer stretch of the river. Moreover, this extended impoundment includes the city centre segment of the river.

2 Rather than being a static structure, the Lagan Weir is comprised of five 'fish belly' gates that can be raised and lowered.

3 Navigation across the line of the weir is not by lock, but by lowering one of the gates during the higher part of the tidal cycle.

4 Pipes were inserted into the base of the weir to allow withdrawal of the poor quality denser seawater, the impoundment of which had been an unfortunate feature of the McConnell Weir.

5 An aeration system was installed on the river bed to help oxygenate the impounded waters, again countering a problem that had been associated with the McConnell Weir.

6 Dredging of the mud banks, entailing the removal of 100,000 tons of sludge. Thus not only did the impounded waters cover any remaining mud banks, but the mud banks themselves were greatly reduced in extent.

7 Changes were made to Belfast's 'combined' waste-water management system, as well as to that of the upstream communities. In consequence, water quality between the Stranmillis Weir and the Lagan Weir was improved.

8 The gates on the weir can be raised to create a bar-rage that can be used to prevent possible flooding in the low lying city centre, which could otherwise be generated by storm surges in the Irish Sea.[33]

FIGURE 9.15
The Lagan Weir at work: flowing right to left, the river discharges to the sea at low tide.

JASON APSLEY

BACK TO THE RIVER

For most of the twentieth century Belfast turned her back to the Lagan. The river was not seen as an attraction – rather as a back yard. This, of course, was not true for the section of the river downstream from the Queen's Bridge, where the Lagan and its extension in the shape of the Victoria Channel has been a fundamental functional focus since 1900 and, indeed, well before that – most specifically with shipping and shipbuilding (Figure 9.16). However, the city has positively refocused on the river in a highly dramatic fashion, particularly in the last decade of the twentieth century (Figure 9.17). Two sets of observations can be offered, though stated briefly.

FIGURE 9.16
Belfast's Lagan from the south-west, 1953. Note the mud
banks downstream from the McConnell Weir (foreground).

SIMMONS AEROFILMS

FIGURE 9.17
Belfast's Lagan from the south-west, 2004

ESLER CRAWFORD

1 Factors Driving the Dynamics of Change

i Changes in the nature of employment – 'from smokestacks to service economy' (see chapter 5).

ii Fundamental changes in the technology of sea transportation and the port handling of goods and vehicles – containerisation, roll-on/roll-off ('ro-ro') and lift-on/lift-off ('lo-lo') – starting in the 1950s but developing rapidly as the century wore on. Most importantly, the container 'revolution' and the roll-on/roll-off innovations called for much greater areas of land in immediate vicinity to ship berths. For instance, as a rule of thumb, traditional cargo handling required 9.9 to 12.3 acres (4–5 ha) of land for each ship berth, containerisation 34.5 to 37.1 acres (14–15 ha).

iii Large scale reclamation of the estuarine mud flats, creating substantial expanses of 'new land'[34]. This new land offered the area necessary for the space-extensive activities of the container revolution (ii above).

iv The physical transformation of the river itself by major infrastructural innovations, creating, in turn, a riparian environment of attraction rather than repulsion.

v Changes in the nature of the provision of gas for domestic and industrial uses, making the massive Gas Works redundant (1963) and consequently releasing the associated lands for alternative uses.

2 Slow Gestation, Followed by Rapid Implementation of Change

With the exception of the McConnell Lock and Weir and the associated embanking activities of the 1920s and 1930s, change came slowly to Belfast's Lagan. However, there has been a quite astonishing acceleration in the rate of change since the late 1980s. Two questions arise – why did this acceleration occur, and why did it occur when it did?

i The 1980s and the 1990s saw a very significant decline in the levels of violence associated with the Troubles. Thus the future could be perceived in a much more optimistic way.

ii General economic growth created both a financial and a psychological environment conducive for major investment, both governmental and private sector.

iii The cumulative impact of many years of reports, proposals, committees and consultants finally led to 'lift-off'. One would also like to think that the much earlier 'improvements' on the river, concluded in 1937 with the official opening of the McConnell Lock and Weir, would have provided an encouraging background stimulus for the new wave of change.[35]

iv The formation of Laganside Corporation in 1989 provided a degree of focus for improvement not previously available. The concept of an infrastructure-led approach funded by government drawing down a much larger stream of private sector investment was also very significant.

v Waterfront redevelopment became increasingly widespread and increasingly well known in the 1980s in a large number of other cities (perhaps most notably in Baltimore, Maryland, and the London Docklands). This provided Belfast with a considerable stimulus and a range of models for possible adoption or adaptation.

Observing Belfast's Lagan over the twentieth century has given us a physical and economic time-extended cross-section through the city itself. The changes we have seen have been driven by forces much more extensive in their operation than the mere municipal bounds of the city. Yet these forces have been given a distinctive Belfast imprint and as we move through the first decade of the twenty-first century we can expect the river not only to be subject to the pulses of tide and river flow but to those of politics, economics and social forces in general. But most importantly, the last decade of the twentieth century has bequeathed to Belfast's river a future prospect that is bright indeed.

NOTES

1   http://bakerloojunction.mysite.wanadoo-members.co.uk/page5.html, accessed 11 February 2006.
2   The descriptions apply to the period around 1900, not strictly to the year.
3   The descriptions apply to the period around 2000, not strictly to the year.
4   Lynch, John (2004) *Forgotten shipbuilders of Belfast: Workman Clark 1880–1935,* Friars Bush Press: Belfast.
5   Moss, Michael, and Hume, John R. (1986) *Shipbuilders to the world: 125 years of Harland and Wolff, Belfast 1861–1986,* Blackstaff Press: Belfast.
6   Mitchell, Walter F. (1994) *Belfast Rowing Club, 1880–1982,* Belfast Rowing Club: Belfast.
7   The Lagan Canal was originally extended through to Lough Neagh so that coal from the east Tyrone coalfield could be shipped down to Belfast. As things turned out, the coalfield was never much of a commercial success and the canal's dominant function was to provide a routeway for the *importation* of coal from England and Scotland. So the coal travelled upstream rather than down.
8   The *Joyce Too* is a small vessel that provides sightseeing trips on the river.
9   The term 'reclamation' is not strictly correct. This is not really land *reclaimed* from the sea. Rather it is *claimed* from the sea.
10 The Institute of Electronics, Communications and Information Technology (ECIT).
11 Titanic Quarter (n.d.) *The rebirth of a city; the launch of a metropolis,* Titanic Quarter Ltd: Belfast.
12 All this directly across the river from the slipway where the *Titanic* was launched in 1911.
13 St John's Wharf serves as a reminder of the church we saw there in 1900.
14 Belfast has had a tendency to give its bridges a royal flavour – Queen's, Albert, Queen Elizabeth, King's, Governor's. Only the Ormeau from an earlier time breaks from this 'tradition', together with the recent Lagan and Dargan.
15 Minutes, Council in Committee, Monday 13 August 1923.
16 As noted, the original proposed location for the lock was at Albert Bridge, but clearly a subsequent decision led to its being sited above the Blackstaff. This relocation took place to allow coal barges to continue to have uninterrupted passage from the harbour to the coal quays at the Gas Works.
17 Belfast Corporation Act [14 and 15 Geo. 5] (Northern Ireland), 1924.
18 The Act also stated that 'the lands filled in and levelled shall … be vested in the Corporation and the Corporation may hold and use or dispose of the same for such purposes as they may think fit'. One piece of this land was made available to the Chinese community in 2005 to build a new community facility.
19 Evans, E. Estyn (1944) 'Belfast: the site and the city', *Ulster Journal of Archaeology,* third series, 7, p. 13.
20 Quoted in Evans (1944) 'Belfast: the site and the city'. Original in Wilshere, R.S. (1944) 'Town planning in Northern Ireland', in *The Irish Association, Town Planning in Ireland. The Irish Association Pamphlets on Irish Affairs,* 2, p. 44.
21 Government of Northern Ireland (1945) *Interim report of the Planning Commission: planning proposals for the Belfast area,* HMSO: Belfast, p. 13.
22 Matthew, Robert H. (1964) *Belfast Regional Survey and Plan 1962.* HMSO: Belfast.
23 Matthew (1964) *Belfast Regional Survey.*
24 Building Design Partnership (1969) *Belfast central area,* Building Design Partnership: Belfast.
25 Building Design Partnership (1967) *Lagan Valley Country Park,* Building Design Partnership: Belfast.
26 Department of the Environment for Northern Ireland (1978) *River Lagan: report of a working party,* Department of the Environment for Northern Ireland: Belfast.
27 Department of the Environment for Northern Ireland (1978) *River Lagan,* p. 19.
28 Department of the Environment for Northern Ireland (1978) *River Lagan,* p. 25.
29 Shepheard, Epstein and Hunter and Building Design Partnership (1987) *A Concept Plan for Laganside,* Shepheard, Epstein and Hunter and Building Design Partnership: London and Belfast.
30 Laganside Development (Northern Ireland) Order, 1989.
31 Laganside Corporation (2004) *Annual report and accounts, 2003–2004,* Laganside Corporation: Belfast.
32 Cochrane, S.R., and Weir, D. (n.d.) *The development and operational control of the Lagan Weir and its impoundment, 1987–1997,* Laganside, School of Civil Engineering, Queen's University Belfast, Construction Service Department of the Environment for Northern Ireland: Belfast.
33 In October 1995, when the highest tide ever recorded in Belfast Lough occurred, severe flooding of the city centre was averted by use of the weir as a tidal barrage.
34 Material for the reclamation came from four sources: dredged material from the shipping channel, material from the excavation of new docks, waste material (so-called 'landfill', but in this case more appropriately 'seafill'), and material from the dredging of the river channel mud flats.
35 In 1944 R.S. Wilshere noted, somewhat begrudgingly, that 'the formation of the Boulevards to the River Lagan in 1924 might have been Belfast's most interesting and impressive Town Planning improvement', see Wilshere [1944] 'Town planning in Northern Ireland', p. 34.

FIGURE S.4
On 9 February 1996 the IRA ended its 17-month ceasefire by bombing Canary Wharf in the Docklands area of London. This peace rally took place in Belfast on 12 February – hundreds of people gathered outside the City Hall holding cut-out doves of peace.

EMPICS

Together and Apart

FIGURE 10.1
Raglan Street, 1970. The twin spires of St Peter's dominate the skyline, with the Divis Tower
on the left and the crane involved in building the Divis Flats on the right.

While the contemporary religious landscape in Belfast is in many respects markedly different from Victorian times, there remain ways in which the religious geography of the city continues to manifest itself in the twenty-first century. Although scattered signs, then and now, show that Belfast is not solely a Christian city, a threefold religious division between the established Church of Ireland, Presbyterianism and Catholicism (Figure 10.1), which mapped itself onto the city's socio-political topography, persisted through a range of controversies rotating around penal restrictions, educational provision, employment structure, and residential accommodation. Periodic rioting continued throughout the nineteenth century, reinforcing religious boundaries and politicising faith.[1] Religious segregation thus greatly intensified on account of violence and the movement of people, the consequences of which still affect Belfast in the twenty-first century.

10
Landscape of Spires

John D. Brewer, Margaret C. Keane and David N. Livingstone

FIGURE 10.2
East Belfast gable wall

STEPHEN A. ROYLE

Figure 10.3
Sinclair Seaman's Church,
Corporation Square

SCENIC IRELAND

THE VICTORIAN HERITAGE

Protestantism in Victorian Belfast gave the impression of unity, as witnessed by the coalition between Reformed theology, industrial power – manifested in the impressive shipyards, docks and mills – and working-class Protestant interests (Figure 10.2). However, the ecclesiastical landscape of Protestants was characterised by its diversity. An 1898 volume entitled *Illustrated Belfast*, prepared for the National Christian Endeavour Convention, noted that 'Belfast has been described as a "city of churches"' and recorded details of 31 Episcopal congregations, 49 Presbyterian, 18 Methodist, 3 Congregational, 2 Moravian, 3 Baptist, 1 Society of Friends, 6 Mission Centres, 5 Unitarian, 4 Catholic, and 1 Synagogue.[2] It prefaced this inventory with the observation that it did 'not take into account quite a large number of smaller mission halls … erected for the benefit of the very poor, who will not, as a rule, attend any regular church until their circumstances are bettered'.

This denominational variety made itself manifest in the visible landscape. St Anne's, Belfast's first Church of Ireland parish church, for example, had been completed in 1776 and remained in existence until 1904 when it became the site of St Anne's Cathedral. As the cathedral developed, a more 'Hiberno-Romanesque' style replaced the old Georgian style of the parish church. Gothic arches and stained-glass windows were features of St Thomas's church on the Lisburn Road built during the Victorian period, a style then favoured not just by Church of Ireland but by all the denominations. By contrast, the mission halls, some independent, others connected with various denominations, displayed a far more humble architectural presence. Presbyterian congregations came in a range of styles. While Sinclair Seaman's church in Corporation Square (Figure 10.3) displayed a distinctively nautical motif in its interior design, Church House at Fisherwick Place, the denomination's headquarters, with its clock tower at a height of 131 feet (40 m), was built in the form of a Scottish baronial castle. All Souls Non-Subscribing Presbyterian church at Elmwood was constructed in 1896 in a fourteenth-century style that became associated with Anglicanism. Other denominations were also present. While Methodists had been in Ireland from the 1740s, the Methodist Church was only established as a separate denomination in 1878. Baptist history in the island goes back to at least 1640, but the denomination remained congregationally small with an estimated thirty-one churches in all of Ireland by the end of the nineteenth century.[3] The oldest Belfast congregation, Great Victoria Street, dates back to 1811, though its building was not opened until 1866.

Churches often moved location or were established in response to the changing human geography of the city. Among Presbyterians, for example, Rosemary Street, originally established in 1723, eventually moved away from the city centre in 1929; Fitzroy, begun in 1813 as the Alfred Place meeting house, moved to the university area in 1874; Great Victoria Street church was opened in 1860 specifically to serve the growing populations of Sandy Row and Donegall Pass. With respect to educational provision, the Presbyterian Church made its mark on the landscape with the establishment of the Assembly's College in 1853 for the training of ministers. In an era of cultural, religious, and scientific upheaval, the new college found itself weaving a way through the storms of political controversy surrounding its first principal, Henry Cooke; differences of opinion regarding the religious revival that swept through Ulster in 1859; and the intellectual challenges of the controversial 1874 Belfast meeting of the British Association for the Advancement of Science.[4] The Methodists, too, provided for their educational needs with the establishment of the Methodist College in 1865. In 1920 Methodist ministerial training moved to Edgehill College in Lennoxvale, south Belfast.

Catholic religious infrastructure in early nineteenth-century Belfast amounted to no more than three churches – the city centre network of St Mary's (1784), St Patrick's (1815) and St Malachy's (1844; see Figure 10.4) – one religious community and a handful of priests trained in a very inadequate seminary.[5] The Catholic Church was ill equipped, then, for the profound social changes that were in train as the numbers of Catholics in Belfast rose rapidly, from 2,000 in 1800 to 41,000 in 1861. Most were rural and landless and were moving to Belfast's mills and factories in search of work. At the same time, a significant Catholic religious revival coincided with enthusiastic Protestant evangelical crusades in the rapidly industrialising city. The 'devotional revolution' that occurred in Catholicism was linked to the trauma caused by famine death and emigration, which split up families and uprooted them from the land, and encouraged Catholics to turn to the Church both for solace and ethnic identity.[6] Its effects began to be felt in Belfast after the appointment of Bishop Patrick Dorrian in 1865.[7] Mass attendance amongst the urban poor increased dramatically, and missions were made a strong part of the effort to evangelise the Catholic labourers who migrated to Belfast. This devotional transformation was Ultramontanist in form, characterised by the adoption of Roman-style liturgy and devotional practices like novenas, the rosary, perpetual adorations, benedictions, devotions to the Sacred Heart and to the Immaculate Conception (promulgated in 1854), and processions and retreats, all largely unknown before the mid-nineteenth century.[8] New devotional tools were used, such as beads, scapulars, medals, missals, catechisms, and holy pictures,[9] and the head of the Catholic Church in Ireland, Cardinal Paul Cullen, determined that papal authority would replace Celtic traditions and placed Ireland under the patronage of the Blessed Virgin rather than St Patrick.

Initially Catholic development in Belfast was restrained by Bishop Cornelius Denvir's fear of unsettling the tense relations with Protestants in a climate that was punctuated by rioting and intermittent attacks on Catholic churches and property, but the changing circumstances that confronted the Catholic Church inevitably became set in stone and mortar. The 'craze for church building' that occurred in Belfast after the famine had to be, Cardinal Cullen insisted, in the ornate Roman style in order to demonstrate Catholic

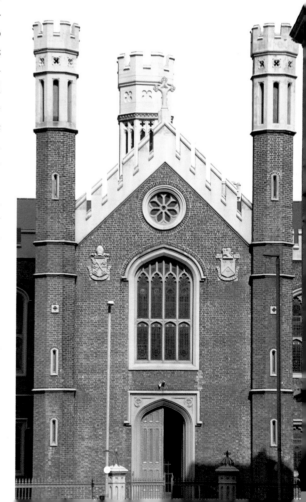

FIGURE 10.4
St Malachy's Catholic Church, Alfred Street

SCENIC IRELAND

FIGURE 10.5
St Peter's Cathedral,
St Peter's Square,
Albert Street

STEPHEN GALLAGHER

self-confidence and victory over adversity.[10] He wished to equal in architecture 'many of the Roman churches ... we are determined to be very grand'.[11] The impressive neo-Gothic exterior of St Peter's (1866) fitted well with this vision and its twin spires, added in 1885, now dominate the lower Falls (Figures 10.1 and 10.5). A church-building programme started in 1869 with the renovation of the simple barn-like St Mary's in Chapel Lane. It continued with churches in the Romanesque style to replace St Patrick's, Donegall Street, and Holy Cross, Ardoyne, which had pillars, mosaics and frescoes more reminiscent of continental, not Irish, cultures. When the church at Clonard Monastery was built at the turn of the century, to serve the Catholic mill workers crowding into the Falls area,[12] the architects returned to the popular neo-Gothic style.[13] The needs of the rapidly growing dockland community were met by St Joseph's Church, which was built in 1884. As the pastoral role of the Church extended to include education, welfare and health care, the Catholic landscape in Belfast included a network of schools, hospitals and orphanages. St Mary's Teacher Training College was built on the Falls Road in 1900 and the Mater Infirmorum Hospital on the Crumlin Road in 1884. Staffed by clergy and members of religious orders, whose dress reinforced the continental look to local Catholicism – Cullen insisted priests around Belfast wear soutanes and Roman hats – the numbers within religious orders in Belfast increased. So too did the variety in the orders permitted to work in Belfast, the demand having to be met in part from outside Ireland. Therefore, presbyteries, convents and monasteries complemented the programme of church building.[14] As the twentieth century opened, the denominational infrastructure represented a visible and confident Catholicism.

THE DENOMINATIONAL LANDSCAPE

The changing geography of Belfast churches throughout the twentieth century is recorded in Figures 10.6, 10.7 and 10.8. These maps show the locations of Catholic, Church of Ireland, and Presbyterian churches as well as those of other smaller denominations for the years 1906, 1960 and 1996 respectively, and are largely, but not exclusively, based on street directories for the years in question. As can be seen, the distribution of the city's churches progressively spreads out from the centre in response to its initially growing and then dispersing population. The general story that these maps disclose is plain: for each time period the Presbyterians have the largest number of churches, followed by the Church of Ireland. What is also clear is that while the number of Presbyterian and Church of Ireland churches remained stable or declined between

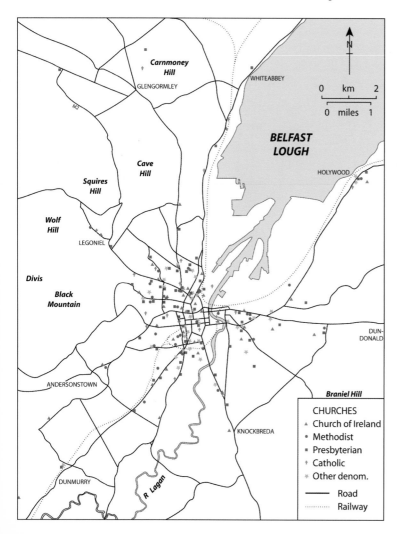

FIGURE 10.6
Distribution of churches in Belfast, 1906

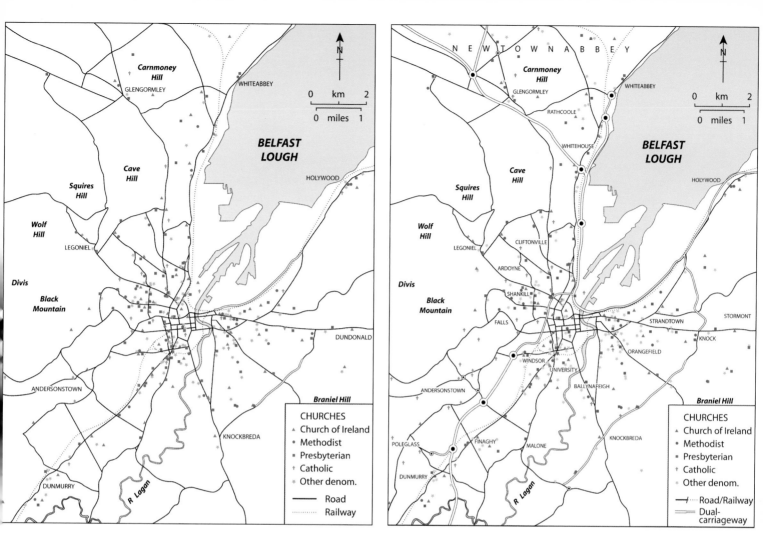

1960 and 1996, the number of Catholic churches continued to increase from less than 20 in 1906 to around 30 in 1960 and well over 40 in 1996. The figures for Methodist churches remained relatively constant – in the thirties – throughout the century, though this is complicated by the city mission hall tradition. Taken overall, of course, the largest increase was in 'other denominations', which include Free Presbyterians, Baptists, Evangelical Presbyterians, and so on.

Church building marked the tide of Catholic population growth and movement. The location of Catholic churches provides a spatial framework around which to understand the growth and progress of Belfast Catholics. After initially clustering in or near the city centre, geographical and social mobility in the nineteenth and twentieth centuries largely accounts for the founding of parishes in the west and north of the city and onward to the suburbs. Churches went westward from St Mary's, northwards from St Patrick's and southwards from St Malachy's. Young women in domestic service and the emerging Catholic professional and business class formed the backbone of new churches along the Antrim Road and in the south of the city. Comparison of the 1960 and 1996 maps makes plain that later Catholic churches were mirroring the drift to both suburban semi-detached dwellings and large public sector housing developments in the outer north, especially Newtownabbey, as well as the outer west, sometimes using nineteenth-century churches as the nuclei before new churches were built.

Geographical location of Catholic churches mattered in another way. Churches are

Top left
FIGURE 10.7
Distribution of churches
in Belfast, 1960

Top right
FIGURE 10.8
Distribution of churches
in Belfast, 1996

185

powerful symbols of community identity and, not surprisingly, plans to erect Catholic churches often led to contention. There has also been a history of attacks on churches. Few outside the west of the city were unscathed during the civil unrest after 1968, although only one small church in Sydenham in the east of the city had to close. There are, however, a number of congregations, such as St Anthony's, Willowfield, and St Mary's, Star of the Sea, at Whitehouse, whose numbers have plummeted as parishioners have moved away.[15] The movement of Catholics to the west has been accompanied by the building of new churches; ten have been added since 1969. Transfers from other denominations – St Matthias's Church of Ireland church on the Glen Road was reconsecrated a Catholic church in 1970 – reflect that Protestant churches have suffered in the same way. Even though a new, larger St Matthias's, dedicated in 2004, now sits alongside, the old church survives (Figure 10.9).

The 1996 map also demonstrates the intensification of 'other denominations', especially in the east of Belfast and Newtownabbey, reflecting their roots still in the Reformed tradition. The growth of independent fellowships and house churches, it should be noted, is not geographically marked, for these represent 'hidden spaces' with no visible landscape. Belfast, however, was never a city entirely of Christians. By 1906 it had two Jewish synagogues, mostly serving Jews fleeing pogroms in the Russian Empire. Other Jewish spaces – schools, cemetery, social centre and shops selling kosher products – were concentrated in the north of the city, and when the Somerton Road synagogue was built in 1965, it served around 1,500 members. Belfast's Jewish community has dwindled to around 200, although other world religions now feature on the religious landscape. The former Carlisle Circus Memorial Methodist church hall houses a Hindu temple where over 1,000 people worship, and the Muslim community has a small mosque and cultural centre in the south of the city.[16] The 2001 census enumerates 13 non-Christian faith communities with more than 10 members, and 1,651 people with 'other religions and philosophies', although this may well be an underestimate.

This general story, then, highlights a number of factors that need to be considered in understanding Belfast's ecclesiastical landscape. First, recording the number of churches has to be interpreted in tandem with location. In many cases city centre buildings have been vacated and corresponding new churches opened up in suburban contexts. Second, there are several situations in which church buildings have transferred from one denomination to another. Third, the growth in independent fellowships and house churches is not reflected in the visible landscape, but their presence needs to be registered in understanding the sociology and social geography of faith in the city. Fourth, the mapping of church buildings does not tell us anything about attendance, and there are many places where tiny congregations are now struggling to maintain buildings that once flourished, as we shall see below. Nevertheless, the presence of a large number of dedicated religious spaces in Belfast and its immediate environs is a conspicuous feature of a cityscape that can appropriately be designated a 'landscape of spires'.

BENEATH THE SPIRES

Ulster Protestantism discloses a long history of theological and denominational division.[17] Brewer has shown that these old identities survive as cultural relics into the modern era in patterns of marriage or cohabitation between Protestant denominations, with 68 per cent of Church of Ireland respondents in the 1998 *Northern Ireland Life and Times Survey* still having partners inside the denomination, and 72 per cent of Presbyterians.[18] While it is true that evangelical theology developed hegemony from the mid-nineteenth century as the dominant sacred canopy[19] and as successive religious revivals took increasingly conservative moves,[20] evangelicalism is itself fractious.[21]

Left
FIGURE 10.10
Fisherwick Presbyterian
church, Malone Road

STEPHEN A. ROYLE

Ulster Protestantism has always been more united politically than theologically.[22]

To place some order on the variety of denominational life underneath the spires, we can draw broad divisions within Protestantism. The Church of Ireland, formerly the Established Church, represents the Episcopalian tradition with roots in English rather than Scottish Protestantism, structured around dioceses and with control embedded hierarchically in bishops. Its cathedrals are normally symbols of the state, aping the perpendicular style of medieval England, with the flags of regiments adorning the inside, although Belfast's St Anne's Cathedral is not in this ancient style. The Presbyterian Church dominates the Reformed tradition, and while it has been subject to several schisms, it is the largest single Protestant denomination. Based around local presbyteries, authority in the Church is decentralised; many of its Belfast churches were built grand and imposing, irrespective of the culture of austerity that characterised Presbyterianism, reflecting the prosperity of the city at the time of their erection, Fisherwick church on the Malone Road being an obvious example (Figure 10.10). The Methodist Church has a small presence and together these three denominations comprise what might be called the mainstream Protestant tradition.

FIGURE 10.11
Martyrs Memorial Free
Presbyterian Church,
Ravenhill Road

SCENIC IRELAND

This is complemented by more conservative evangelical Churches in the Reformed tradition, like the Brethren, Baptists, and schismatic Presbyterian Churches such as the Evangelical Presbyterians and the Free Presbyterian Church, whose church buildings often reflect the small scale of their membership, although the expansion of Martyrs Memorial church on the Ravenhill Road reflects the growth and self-confidence of the Reverend Ian Paisley's Free Presbyterian Church (Figure 10.11). There is also a growing Pentecostal and Charismatic tradition, with emphasis on the gifts of the spirit and the personal experience of God above liturgy, doctrine and formal worship. Examples are the Elim Church on the Ravenhill Road, and the independent new Churches like Christian Fellowship Church in Sydenham, City Church in the university area, and Whitewell Metropolitan Tabernacle in north Belfast. Both sets of groups are normally subsumed for social survey purposes into 'other Christian', which tends to conceal the marked difference in style, authority and theology between the conservative evangelical groups and the Pentecostal/Charismatic tradition.

We can use these broad categories to demonstrate the relative balance of identification with these groupings across Northern Ireland as a whole, since figures for Belfast only are not available. The 1998 *Life and Times Survey* revealed that 38 per cent of the sample described themselves as Catholic, 39 per cent 'mainstream Protestant', which breaks down as 15 per cent Church of Ireland, 21 per cent Presbyterian and 3 per cent Methodist; 'other Christians' comprised 12 per cent and was the only category in which there had been growth since the 1991 survey, although it remains the case that the growing Churches are still numerically small and the declining ones big.[23]

Religious commitment, observance and practice are declining for all denominations but especially mainstream Protestant Churches and this has been evident since the beginning of the twentieth century.[24] The trends disclose falling numbers in the main Protestant denominations over and above demographic changes, particularly in the Belfast area, and the loss of membership amongst the young and the ageing population of its churchgoers. For example, the Belfast synod of the Presbyterian Church in Ireland witnessed a drop in personal membership of 62.6 per cent between 1963 and 1999. The figure for the Belfast District of the Methodist Church is 53 per cent, while the Church of Ireland's Diocese of Connor, which includes Belfast west of the River Lagan (as well as its rural hinterland), saw a decline of 35.3 per cent between 1969 and 1985. Some of this reflects the flight of people from Belfast, but the ageing nature of Protestant churchgoers in Northern Ireland discloses the extent of the change in membership amongst the young. As younger people leave the Protestant Churches, they are increasingly disinclined to get married according to their rites – in 1995, just over half of marriages in Greater Belfast suburbs like Carrickfergus and in north Down were celebrated in church and two-thirds in Newtownabbey – or bring up the next generation within it. The number of young people baptised Protestant is declining throughout Northern Ireland. Baptisms fell in the Presbyterian Church by 68.7 per cent between 1959 and 1999, to just over 2,000 a year, and Sunday school numbers declined by 49 per cent in the same period. The equivalent figure for Sunday school numbers in the Church of Ireland's Diocese of Connor is a drop of 47 per cent to nearly 8,000, which declining birth rates cannot entirely explain.

Whereas churchgoing Protestantism expresses itself through a range of denominations, Catholicism is a universal, self-contained entity that traces its doctrine and organisation directly to the Apostles. By the beginning of the twentieth century Irish Catholicism had settled '… into a mould that has only been broken in recent years'.[25] However, it has adapted, if slowly, to the renewal of its structures that emanated from the Second Vatican Council.[26] The encouragement of liturgical participation by lay people affected the layout and shape of church buildings. Altars facing the people were installed and newly built churches gathered the faithful around

FIGURE 10.12
Our Lady Queen of
Peace, Kilwee
STEPHEN GALLAGHER

the ritual centres (Figure 10.12). The excessively legalistic moral theology on which Catholicism in the first half of the twentieth century was based has generally been replaced by a pastoral theology that stresses involvement of the church in communities and sees parish congregations as faith communities.[27] The Catholic parish system has a strong geographical focus, and assists in fostering a sense of community in each of Belfast's thirty-five Catholic parishes. These parishes are repositories of custom and tradition, which furnish a sense of place and identity for parishioners; in some of them are rooted long-established networks of community engagement, charity and voluntary work.[28]

FIGURE 10.13
Decorations in a street off the Falls Road celebrating the Eucharistic Congress of June 1932

DOWN AND CONNOR DIOCESAN ARCHIVES

Like Protestantism however, the Catholic Church faces changing times, and the secularism of the modern world is impacting on the regularity of Mass attendance and reducing identification with the Church amongst the young. F.W. Boal, M.C. Keane and D.N. Livingstone show that only 7 per cent of Belfast's churchgoing Catholics are under twenty-five and that loyal churchgoing Catholics tend now to be middle-aged or elderly, and female.[29] Less than half a century ago there was almost universal attendance at religious services. James Grant remarks on the lengthy queues for confession and the huge attendances at pilgrimages, novenas and confraternities, and describes throngs at celebrations to mark the Eucharistic Congress in 1932 (Figure 10.13), the Holy Year in 1950 and the Marian Year in 1954.[30] Many Catholics may have left behind, in one generation, traditions that have endured for more than a century. As the 1990s began, 75 per cent of Belfast Catholics were attending Mass weekly and this downward trend continues. A decade later A. Hanly reports weekly attendance levels in Northern Ireland of 57 per cent, yet only 4 in 10 of 25–34-year-olds are regular Mass-goers,[31] while Patrick McCafferty points to working-class Belfast parishes where attendance at weekly Mass is now only 1 in 10, and falling.[32] Nonetheless, attendance at pilgrimages is flourishing and popular piety is holding its own.[33] The drop in vocations to the priesthood and religious orders since the 1960s is blamed on cultural changes in society, and many large presbyteries and convents have opted for smaller premises.

THE CONSERVATIVE–LIBERAL SPECTRUM

Crucial though the denominational lens is for visualising the cartography of religious observance in Belfast, this institutional filter is not the only, or perhaps even the best, means of grasping the dynamic of religious experience and practice in the city. Among Protestants the spectrum of belief from evangelical to liberal has been of critical significance in shaping religious life. While it is difficult to be precise about definitions, evangelicalism is routinely associated with a number of central convictions including an emphasis on the infallibility of the Bible, the need for a conversion experience, and an impulse toward evangelicalism, while liberalism has been less committed to these particular theological convictions. While some, mostly smaller, denominations and independent fellowships are massively positioned on the conservative evangelical end of this spectrum, the larger denominations have different proportions of those with evangelical leanings. In a major survey of Belfast churchgoers conducted in 1993, the Church of Ireland returned 27 per cent of Belfast members with distinctively conservative evangelical convictions; for Presbyterians the figure was 38 per cent and for Methodists 43 per cent.[34] Amongst Baptists, the proportion soared to 83 per cent, and to 87 per cent among Pentecostal/Charismatic Churches.

These differences of outlook are not merely theological, of course; rather, they shape the attitudes of churchgoers on a wide range of cultural and political affairs. The survey, for example, revealed that while 70 per cent of those with a liberal outlook favoured greater social and religious co-operation with Catholics, the figure dropped to 30 per cent among conservative evangelicals. On attitudes to Protestant–Catholic intermarriage, this spectrum again manifested itself. While 27 per cent of Protestant liberals were not opposed to such unions, a mere 7 per cent of conservatives approved of mixed marriage. It also mapped onto party political preference. Support for the Democratic Unionist Party was substantially drawn from the conservative evangelical wing of the churchgoing population, with liberals dominating the Alliance Party's church constituency (the Ulster Unionist Party drew support much more evenly from both conservative and liberal wings). Similar patterns were discernible in attitudes to female clergy, integrated schools, abortion, divorce and the constitutional future of Northern Ireland. Thus, while denominational affiliation counts for a good deal in understanding the religious landscape of the city, the evangelical–liberal polarity persistently reasserts itself in the religious, cultural, social, political and moral realms.

It would be a mistake to assume that the Catholic denominational label refers to a monolithic bloc, for any impression of solidarity is fractured by the range and level of theological convictions between what are popularly called in the wider Catholic world 'traditionalists' and 'modernisers'. From the beginning of the twentieth century there was always 'a small rump determined to be more Catholic than the Pope'.[35] The persistence of orthodoxy was revealed in a survey of over 3,000 Belfast Catholic churchgoers which showed that just under half followed all Church teachings compared to 14 per cent who showed high heterodoxy.[36] Heterodoxy was most prevalent amongst the young and educated, but clearly the bulk of churchgoers lay somewhere between these extremes. The conservative–liberal polarity in theology, while real in Catholicism, cannot be impressed upon Catholics to the same extent as Protestants, although there is a small charismatic movement amongst Belfast Catholics that has its roots in the modernisation promulgated by the Second Vatican Council. The council's emphasis on self-understanding and the interpersonal dimensions of spiritual life resonated with the charismatic movement in the 1970s and, although this has faded, L. Power reports that there are 450 charismatic groups meeting throughout Ireland, with a few in Belfast.[37] The origins of Belfast's Nazareth Community lie in the charismatic movement. The Neo-Catecumenal Way communities, which have Spanish roots, respond in a different way to the Second Vatican Council through sharing their lives and faith.[38] According to Vincent Twomey, these movements are 'conservative'.[39]

If not in theology, there is clear evidence of marked divisions between Catholics in attitudes towards wider moral and social concerns. Desmond O'Donnell suggests that in

FIGURE 10.14
Interior of the Whitewell
Metropolitan Tabernacle,
Shore Road

SCENIC IRELAND

moral judgements on sexuality and marriage, educated young Catholics inhabit a different world to their parents.[40] The desire for exclusivity is greatest among the more orthodox no matter the context: marriage, schooling or place of residence. The more liberal are four times as likely to marry a Northern Ireland Protestant and three times as likely to live in a mixed neighbourhood.[41] Shades of religious opinion may condition the moral, social and cultural spheres, but when it comes to politics and ethno-national identity there is broad agreement among Catholics. Doctrinal and attitudinal differences have little bearing on support for nationalist/republican parties, which come from all sections of Belfast Catholic churchgoers. A 1998 survey found that only 1 per cent of Catholic respondents supported 'unionist' parties and 2 per cent did 'not know'; 63 per cent were 'nationalist' supporters and 33 per cent neither unionist nor nationalist, a category that would include substantial support for republican parties.[42] Nationalist support amongst Catholics has risen from 51 per cent in an equivalent 1991 survey.[43]

NEW SPIRITUAL PLACES

As buildings, churches embody the patterns of belief, practice and observance at the time of their erection and, correspondingly, also measure the extent of change in religiosity as depopulation and other shifts alter the composition of an area. The immense social change and population relocation that has affected Belfast has put some churches out of place. The idea of a local church serving the adjacent neighbourhood survives with the parish structure in the Catholic Church but has diminished for many Belfast Protestants with suburbanisation and commuting back to city churches. Protestant churches in interface areas are particularly vulnerable to decay; the boards and grilles to protect windows conceal emptying churches that are struggling to clutch onto life. Very few have become secular spaces, however, for their elderly members mostly sustain the witness, although they may have to share a minister. There is little evidence of the use of deconsecrated spiritual places as family residences because of the grandeur of Victorian churches in Belfast; they make better commercial premises. By contrast, some new church buildings have been erected in the suburbs as church plants, both by the independent Churches as they grow and by the mainstream Protestant denominations, in order to catch up with their geographically mobile members. Some of the new independent Churches are resplendent as a material demonstration of growth and their doctrine of the prosperity gospel, such as Whitewell Metropolitan Tabernacle (Figure 10.14); this is perhaps a throwback to the great Victorian church buildings in Belfast.

New spiritual places are evident also in the religions new to Belfast's tapestry of beliefs, such as Islam. Although there is no purpose-built Mosque, as previously mentioned,

Muslims hold services in the Islamic Centre that occupies a Victorian three-storey building in south Belfast. In addition to the Hindu temple housed in the Indian Community Centre at Carlisle Circus, there is a Hare Krishna temple in Dunmurry, a Chinese Christian church in south Belfast and a Baha'i Spiritual Assembly in suburban Dundonald. Most occupy former secular spaces and offer good examples of how new spiritual places may recolonise secular space, such as disused mills, industrial premises, furniture shops and the grand Victorian terraces, in preference to new church building. Many of the independent house churches that wished to break away from institutionalised religion have reinstitutionalised around their own purpose-built premises or the reoccupation of identifiably spiritual spaces from the past. Thus on some occasions, growing churches have recolonised former churches, taking over the buildings of congregations long disappeared, recapturing vibrancy with newer forms of worship and observance. City Church's occupancy of the old Congregational Church premises in south Belfast is an excellent example, the former church hall of which, however, is now a block of flats.

CROSSOVER SPACES

Divided political spaces result in divided churches, so that the peace and reconciliation mission of churches requires the negotiation of crossover spaces where divided congregations can come together, even if only momentarily.[44] This can take the form of voluntarily entering the other's space to display a willingness to enter their social world, so that ecumenical and other reconciliation work involves entering the other's domain as a way of communicating a willingness to share the wider society. The Fitzroy–Clonard group, for example, makes a point of rotating meetings between each other's premises and most of the clergy groups from local areas alternate meetings, although a Presbyterian minister was forced to resign from a Belfast clergy group in 2004 because the local newspaper captured him in Rome as a member of the group; some spaces are clearly still too hostile to share. It is for this reason that most crossover spaces are neutral ones. They are neutral in one of two ways. They are spaces in mixed areas or in areas with fewer incidences of conflict, which means that south Belfast, for example, is home to several peace and reconciliation initiatives of a religious and secular kind, such as Restoration Ministries, Women for Peace Together, Protestant and Catholic Encounter (PACE), The Way In, Mediation Network, and so on. They are neutral in a second sense in that while some may occupy space in a partisan area identified with one community or the other, they de-sensitise their presence, neutering any markers that may indicate it is crossover space. Cornerstone Community, for example, in Catholic west Belfast, looks from the outside like any Victorian terrace; only from within is it evident that this is a spiritual place for divided communities to share.

There are also crossover spiritual spaces of a slightly different kind. Churches have occasionally been used as spaces of reconciliation for bringing political parties, groups and community activists together on their premises as an informal setting away from public attention. This has been particularly useful for groups which could not be seen to meet together. Clonard Monastery

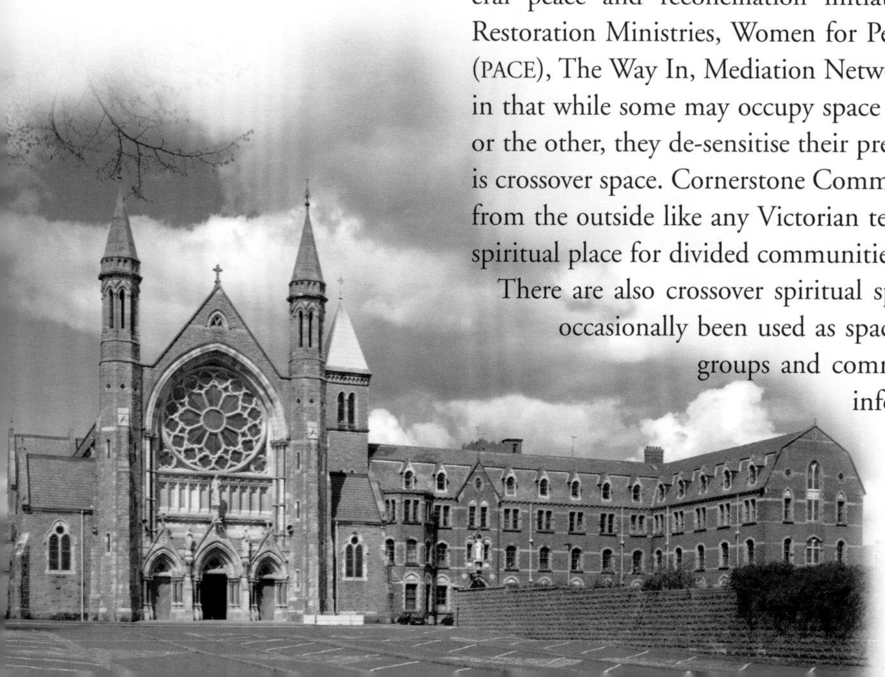

FIGURE 10.15
Clonard Redemptionist Church
and Monastery, Lower Falls

SCENIC IRELAND

LIGHT V.

DARKNESS

○ White spots shew Churches and Mission Halls

"Light shineth in darkness"

NEW CITY BOUNDARY

• Public Houses
◉ Spirit Grocers
■ Distillers

"He maketh a shew of them openly"

in west Belfast (Figure 10.15), Fitzroy Presbyterian church in south Belfast and Christian Fellowship church in east Belfast have all been used as secret crossover spaces to allow those who are considered publicly beyond the pale to meet in private. Of these, Clonard Monastery stands proudest in the annals of Belfast's peace initiatives, all the more surprising, perhaps, because it is sited solidly in Catholic west Belfast . Sitting right on the peace line as a space more recognisably crossover, the ecumenical communities of Cornerstone and Currach have joined with the Springfield Road Methodist church and the Middle Springfield Community Association to form Forthspring, a new venture in reconciliation and cross-community outreach.[45] In making creative use of crossover spaces for dialogue and meeting, churches and para-church organisations have required vision and courage, and demonstrate the trust and legitimacy some spiritual spaces still retain.

PUTTING SECULARISATION IN ITS PLACE

The competing forces of Light and Darkness have long been dominant in the psyche of Belfast churchgoers. In his 1898 story of the Shankill Road Mission, William Roome presented this epic battle in cartographic form. The map of light, symbolised by the locations of churches and missions, stood in contrast to the darkened sites of public houses, spirit grocers and distillers (Figure 10.16). The anxiety about beacons of light in the midst of spaces of darkness continues among all the denominations, with the progressive forces of secularisation biting ever more deeply into churchgoing populations. And yet simplistic conceptions about progressive and inevitable secularisation in the wake of societal modernisation are troubling in several respects. Whatever may have been occurring among intellectual élites, modernisation *per se* has simply not had the universal secularising effect on mass populations that theoretical prescription has diagnosed. Widespread religious belief in the United States, for example, does not seem to have diminished in

FIGURE 10.16
Light versus Darkness: William Roome's 1898 representation of the battle being fought on the streets of Belfast between the church temperance movement and the evils of alcohol.

pace with modernity. Moreover, while there is evidence that Protestant denominational Church membership discloses significant decline, the rise of house churches and independent fellowships of the sort discussed above makes the interpretation of official statistics difficult. However, levels of identification with their religion remain very high for both Catholics and Protestants and there is no evidence of any immediate rise in unbelief. Comparisons over long time periods inevitably throw up greater change. In the 2001 census, 17 per cent registered 'no religion' or refused to state an identification; a century before it was only 0.17 per cent. Although levels of strict observance have fallen markedly, survey data indicate that Northern Ireland people remain religious, with 85 per cent claiming to 'draw comfort and strength from religion' and 61 per cent defining themselves as 'religious'. It would be foolish to underestimate the depth of spirituality. We may be witnessing the transfer of spiritual allegiance from the communal to the private sphere, with church buildings remaining as beacons of light but reflecting less intense devotion within. It remains clear that the urban fabric of Belfast continues to present itself as a landscape of spires.

NOTES

1 Heatley, Fred (1988) 'Community relations and the religious geography 1800–86', in J.C. Beckett et al. (eds) *Belfast: the making of the city*, Appletree Press: Belfast, pp. 129–42.

2 National Christian Endeavour (1899) *Illustrated Belfast: prepared for the National Christian Endeavour Convention, Belfast 1899*, John Adams: Belfast.

3 Vedder, Henry C. (1891) *A short history of the Baptists*, American Baptist Publication Society: Philadelphia.

4 See the discussions in Holmes, R. Finlay (1981) *Henry Cooke*, Christian Journals: Belfast; Brooke, Peter (1994) *Ulster Presbyterianism: the historical perspective 1610–1970*, Athol Books: Belfast; Livingstone, David N. (1997) 'Darwin in Belfast: the evolution debate', in John W. Foster (ed.) *Nature in Ireland: a scientific and cultural history*, Lilliput Press: Dublin, pp. 387–408.

5 Corish, Patrick J. (1985) *The Irish Catholic experience*, Gill and Macmillan: Dublin.

6 Larkin, E. (1972) 'The devotional revolution in Ireland, 1850–75', *American Historical Review*, 77, pp. 625–52.

7 Macauley, Ambrose (1987) *Patrick Dorrian, Bishop of Down and Connor, 1865–1885*, Gill and Macmillan: Dublin.

8 Nic Ghiolla Phadraig, M. (1995) 'The power of the Catholic Church in the Republic of Ireland', in P. Clancy et al. (eds) *Irish society: sociological perspectives*, Institute of Public Administration: Dublin.

9 Larkin (1972) 'The devotional revolution'.

10 Rafferty, Oliver P. (1994) *Catholicism in Ulster 1603–1983: an interpretative history*, Gill and Macmillan: Dublin, p. 150.

11 Quoted in Bowen, Desmond (1983) *Paul, Cardinal Cullen and the shaping of modern Irish Catholicism*, Gill and Macmillan: Dublin, p. 146.

12 Macauley (1987) *Patrick Dorrian*.

13 Grant, James (2003) *One hundred years with the Clonard Redemptorists*, Columba Press: Dublin.

14 Rafferty (1994) *Catholicism in Ulster*.

15 Macauley, Ambrose (1988) *St Anthony's, Willowfield, Belfast 1938–88*, Ulster Journals: Belfast.

16 Richardson, Norman (ed.) (2002) *A handbook of faiths: a brief introduction to faith communities in Northern Ireland*, Northern Ireland Inter-Faith Forum: Belfast.

17 See Megahey, Alan (2000) *The Irish Protestant Churches in the twentieth century*, Macmillan: London.

18 Brewer, John D. (2003) 'Are there any Christians in Northern Ireland?', in A. Gray et al. (eds) *Social attitudes in Northern Ireland: the eighth report*, Pluto: London.

19 See Brewer, John D. (1998) *Anti-Catholicism in Ireland*, Macmillan: London.

20 See Hempton, David, and Hill, Myrtle (1992) *Evangelical Protestantism in Ulster society 1740–1890*, Routledge: London.

21 Jordan, Glenn (2001) *Not of this world? Evangelical Protestantism in Northern Ireland*, Blackstaff Press: Belfast; Mitchel, Patrick (2003) *Evangelicalism and national identity in Ulster 1921–1998*, Oxford University Press: Oxford.

22 For a review of denomination differences in Northern Ireland, see Richardson, Norman (ed.) (1998) *A tapestry of beliefs*, Blackstaff Press: Belfast.

23 Brewer (2003) 'Are there any Christians'.

24 See Brewer, John D. (2004) 'Continuity and change in contemporary Ulster Protestantism', *Sociological Review*, 52, pp. 264–82.

25 Corish (1985) *Catholic experience*.

26 Crilly, O. (1998) 'The Catholic Church in Ireland' in Richardson, *Tapestry of beliefs*, pp. 23–44.

27 Fuller, Louise (2002) *Irish Catholicism since 1950: the undoing of a culture*, Gill and Macmillan: Dublin.

28 See Bacon, Derek (2003) *Communities, churches and social capital in Northern Ireland*, Centre for Voluntary Action Studies: Coleraine.

29 Boal, F.W., Keane, M.C., and Livingstone, D.N. (1997) *Them and us? Attitudinal variation among churchgoers in Belfast*, Institute of Irish Studies, Queen's University Belfast: Belfast.

30 Grant (2003) *Clonard Redemptorists*.

31 Hanly, A. (1998) *Religious confidence survey: Northern Ireland*, Maynooth Council for Research and Development: Maynooth.

32 McCafferty, P. (2001) 'Republicanism/nationalism, culture and faith' in E.G. Cassidy, D. McKeown and J. Morrow (eds) *Belfast: faith in the city*, Veritas: Dublin, pp. 39–42.

33 Fuller (2002) *Irish Catholicism*.

34 Boal, Keane and Livingstone (1997) *Them and us?*

35 Rafferty (1994) *Catholicism in Ulster*, p. 187.

36 Boal, Keane and Livingstone (1997) *Them and us?*, p. 24.

37 Power, L. (2001) *Irish Catholic*, 20 September.

38 Murray, J. (2001) 'A conversation on the Way', in Cassidy, McKeown and Morrow (eds) *Belfast*, pp. 76–84.

39 Twomey, D. Vincent (2003) *The end of Irish Catholicism?* Veritas: Dublin, p. 216.

40 O'Donnell, D. (2002) 'Young educated adults: a survey', *Doctrine and Life*, 52, pp. 3–79, on p. 71.

41 Boal, Keane and Livingstone (1997) *Them and us?*, pp. 104–05.

42 Brewer (2003) 'Are there any Christians', p. 28.

43 Brewer (2004) 'Continuity and Change'.

44 Brewer, John D. (2003) 'Northern Ireland', in M.A. Cejka and T. Bamat (eds) *Artisans for peace: grassroots peacemaking in Christian communities*, Orbis Books: Maryknoll, Y, p. 280.

45 See Livingstone, Shelagh (2001) 'The Forthspring Initiative', in Cassidy, McKeown and Morrow (eds) *Belfast*, pp. 110–15.

For life is at the start a chaos in which one is lost. The individual suspects this, but he is frightened at finding himself face to face with this terrible reality, and tries to cover it over with a curtain of fantasy, where everything is clear. It does not worry him that his 'ideas' are not true; he uses them as trenches for the defence of his existence, as scarecrows to frighten away reality.

JOSÉ ORTEGA Y GASSET[1]

11
Past and Future

Imagining and Visioning the City

William J.V. Neill

FIGURE 11.1
Still the heart of the city: Belfast City Hall in the early twentieth century
ULSTER MUSEUM

A city is not just bricks and mortar. It is also a focus of identification, aspiration, longing and dreams. It has been well said that a city must be founded in the imagination as securely as it is founded upon the earth.[2] In the twentieth century Belfast as a place of the imagination rested on shaky foundations. As the new millennium dawned, the civic republican vision of the United Irishmen, who had climbed to McArt's Fort at the summit of Belfast's Cave Hill in the closing years of the eighteenth century, had long faded. The pledge taken on the rock appealing to Catholics, Protestants and Dissenters to combine in the common pursuit of Irish independence fell on stony ground as Irish nationalism increasingly took a cultural turn in the nineteenth century. A divided imagination was to be the enduring legacy in Belfast throughout the twentieth century, with no common vision for the city's future. This chapter traces the schizoid disposition of Belfast through the decades. Recognition is given to the fact that the city of the spirit and imagination is not something abstract. Rather it crystallises in various spatial manifestations as places, and the natural and built fabric of the city are imbued with meaning and significance. The chapter proceeds by way of a focus on various emblematic spatial reference points in Belfast's twentieth-century journey. In short, attention is placed on the fractured spatial imagination of Belfast, involving how people identified with the city and sought to represent it.

EMPIRE CITY

Belfast city centre at the beginning of the twenty-first century continues to be identified with the image of Belfast City Hall (Figure 11.1), despite many newly built third-rate impostors. Completed in 1906 and described as 'one of the most important examples of the Baroque Revival anywhere in the British Isles',[3] the new municipal heart of Belfast, more than any other building of the Victorian or Edwardian era, symbolised civic pride in Belfast's place within the strength and enormity of the British Empire. Belfast at the beginning of the twentieth century was a powerful industrial city. With its shipbuilding, linen and engineering output and with one of the most important ports in Europe, Belfast was part of the famous 'workshop of the world'.

This vision of Belfast as part of Britain's greatness was not shared by all. When the foundation stone was laid for the City Hall in 1898, the vision of the city's future was not that of Wolfe Tone a century before. Rather, the Home Rule question had divided the people of Belfast and the north of Ireland into the competing allegiances that remain to the present. While the 1901 census showed that 24 per cent of the total population of Belfast was Catholic (see chapter 4, Table 4.8),[4] the ethos of the city was a Protestant one, with Protestants dominating 'the aristocracy of labour'. The famous 1907 Dock Strike, led by labour leader Jim Larkin, appealed for a time to a common Belfast worker identity,[5] but political aspirations were to prevail, with the city becoming, as the heart of the unionist north-east of Ireland, the focal point for opposition to Home Rule. This was symbolised above all else by the signing, in September 1912, of the Solemn League and Covenant by anti-Home Rule leader Sir Edward Carson and thousands of others at Belfast City Hall. Belfast City Council (formerly Belfast Corporation) was to be under the control of unionist parties until 1997 when, with the changing demography of the city, 'the jewel in the unionist crown'[6] would henceforth be shared with nationalists.

The thought lingers that perhaps the image of Victorian splendour expressed by the City Hall was too pretentious to be entirely convincing, even to itself. It has recently been observed that the 'restrictive spatial visions of Irish nationalism and unionism [are] both rooted in a rural idealism that limits representations of place and society in Irish culture'.[7] By way of possible recompense, Belfast was not to produce a James Joyce to invoke a mythology of the city. It was not to his native Belfast so much as to the Glens of Antrim that the 'planter poet' John Hewitt was attracted in search of identity and meaning.[8] Combine these cultural predispositions with the loss of Harland and Wolff's *Titanic* in April 1912, the ultimate symbol of human hubris, and one is better able to understand even a certain Protestant ambivalence towards taking pride in past stupendous technological achievements. Sometimes pride is left to poets of lesser rank to express. The last line of 'The Ballad of William Bloat', attributed to Raymond Calvert, touches on a distant but deeply felt connection expressed with typical Belfast black humour, which many still feel towards the early twentieth-century city of Empire. The poem concerns William Bloat from the Protestant Shankill Road who tries to kill his wife, regrets it and hangs himself with her bedclothes. She survives:

FIGURE 11.2
Battle of the Somme: Attack by the Ulster Division, 1 July 1916 by J.P. Beadle, which hangs in Belfast City Hall
BELFAST CITY COUNCIL

> For the razor blade was German made,
> But the sheet was Belfast linen.

CITY OF SACRIFICE

The gravesite of the *Titanic*, in the abysmal depths of the North Atlantic, is but one facet of a sunken and brooding Belfast imagination,[9] existing as it does in the collective Ulster mind alongside the trenches of the Somme (see chapter 12). While the remains of 'Belfast's own', approximately 400 miles (644 km) off the coast of Newfoundland, call to memory a calamity and unspoken guilt that lie close to Belfast's heart, an even greater tragedy is embraced by a collective memory that has a spatial imagination centred on the Somme and the fields of Flanders. The 36th (Ulster) and 16th (Irish) divisions fought side by side on the Western Front. The former, subsuming the Ulster Volunteer Force (UVF), saw the outbreak of war as an occasion to demonstrate loyalty to the Crown. The latter, the Irish Volunteers, saw fighting for the Crown as, *inter alia*, ensuring the right to Home Rule without secession by any of the Ulster counties.[10] While both experienced heavy losses during the First World War, commemorated only since 1998 by a common Irish memorial at Messines in Belgium, it is the losses of the 36th (Ulster) Division in the Somme campaign of 1916 that burn especially deep in the imagination of Ulster Protestants. J.P. Beadle's famous painting *The Battle of the Somme, the Attack of the Ulster*

Division hangs in Belfast City Hall (Figure 11.2). In the first two days of the battle it is estimated that over 5,500 men of the Ulster Division were killed or wounded in the face of blistering machine-gun fire and shelling. The death columns spiralled in the pages of the *Belfast Telegraph*.[11] The Belfast headquarters of the UVF framed the events at Thiepval on 1 July 1916 in the lines:

> And where the fight was fiercest,
> And the sternest task was set,
> Ulster Struck for England,
> And England will not forget.[12]

The sacrifice finds much pictorial representation, sometimes of a dubious kind, on murals in Protestant Belfast in the twenty-first century. New symbolic ground was broken on 1 July 2002 when the first Sinn Féin lord mayor of Belfast, Alex Maskey, laid a simple wreath on the war memorial outside City Hall in commemoration of the Somme dead, thus holding out hope for psychic suture in a city where remembrance of war continues to divide.

CAPITAL CITY

After the armistice in 1918, the *Belfast Telegraph* reported King George V's praise of the citizens of Belfast for their contribution to the war effort. Edward Carson's message was also featured, reminding the Empire of the debt that would be called upon if the Home Rule Bill, in abeyance during the war years, proceeded any further.[13] In the event Belfast

FIGURE 11.3
Rebranding of Stormont by a republican mural, Short Strand, 1998

WILLIAM J.V. NEILL

found itself, subsequent to the Government of Ireland Act 1920, as capital city of a newly created Northern Ireland. Denying legitimacy to the new local parliament, no elected nationalist or republican members attended the first sitting in Belfast City Hall on 7 June 1921. It would be 1928 before the foundation stone was laid for what is now the dominant, internationally recognised symbol of both Northern Ireland and its capital – Parliament Buildings at Stormont. The place-vision of Belfast, embodied in the plinth of Mourne granite and the classical claims of Portland stone, is solidly cast in terms of a British identity and future. The construction of Parliament Buildings was constitutive of a partially successful unionist project asserting the legitimacy of the division of Ireland. From the top of the edifice a large statue of Britannia, flanked by two guardian lions, looks over the city's eastern suburbs. On the pediment below, another group of statues 'represents Ulster presenting the golden flame of loyalty to Britain and the Commonwealth'.[14] This loyalist ensemble looks down upon a large monumental sculpture of Northern Ireland's founding father, Lord Edward Carson, representing 'the expressive personification of the challenge which was mounted to an ascendant Irish nationalism.'[15] In terms of a place-vision Stormont as an edifice thus jars with both the civic republican tradition of the United Irishmen and Gaelic-Catholic Irish nationalism. Sinn Féin members taking their seats in a post-Belfast Agreement (also called Good Friday Agreement) Executive in 1998 was consequently presented as the frontal assault and occupation of another unionist citadel in the city (Figure 11.3).

While Stormont stands on a plinth of solid granite from the local Mourne Mountains, its imaginative foundations are less secure. It has been astutely pointed out that the single most important weakness of the unionist cause 'arguably lies in its failure to develop – through the creation of a specific heritage – a separate place consciousness'.[16] The greatness of the British past is an insufficient substitute.

CITY OF DEPRESSION

When the Prince of Wales visited Belfast to open Stormont in November 1932 many in the city had other more pressing concerns. The whole of the Western world was suffering from the depression following the Wall Street Crash, with unemployment, poverty and hardship reaching epic proportions on both sides of the Atlantic (Figure 11.4). Jonathan Bardon reminds us that the Outdoor Relief provided begrudgingly by Belfast's Board of Guardians to the hard-pressed unemployed was the lowest of any city in the UK.[17] In such desperate circumstances, for a brief moment in the city an intercommunity vision of shared class interest was to flicker into life. This took the spatial form of an Outdoor Relief strike, when on 3 October 1932 Outdoor Relief workers from nationalist and unionist neighbourhoods of Belfast came together in protest.[18] Over 60,000 people from both religious communities marched to Custom House Square, the Belfast equivalent of London's Speakers' Corner, for a strike meeting, thus symbolically appropriating the city through a common act of movement and congregation. In the revamping of this historic public place in 2004–05 this significant symbolic event in Belfast's twentieth-century history unfortunately went unremembered. The march, demanding improvements in the relief system, was led by bands, that, to avoid giving offence to either side, played (in a story well told in Belfast) the neutral tune 'Yes We have No Bananas'.[19] While opinion differs as to the strength of Protestant and Catholic workers' unity in the Outdoor Relief strike and the potential of worker solidarity in tackling sectarianism in the city, what is certain is that soon after the strike had passed old fears and divisions continued to endure. By 1935 sectarian rioting had returned to the streets of Belfast. One historian in this context refers unfavourably to the stance of the Belfast City Corporation:

> The city's Unionist dominated council perpetuated its habitual and malignant record of municipal corruption. Favouritism rather than ability determined the pattern of appointments. Its political composition and its practice of discrimination against the city's Catholic population in the allocation of jobs and contracts served to deepen sectarian division and further alienate the minority community (23.8 per cent of the total in 1937).[20]

CITY AT WAR

Collective vision for the vast majority of the city's population during the Second World War centred on survival and the mobilisation necessary for victory. Nothing symbolised more the bonding of the city to Britain's struggle in its

FIGURE 11.4
The queue for food outside the Ker Hall in Glengall Street during the outdoor relief crisis in 1932

BELFAST CENTRAL MISSION

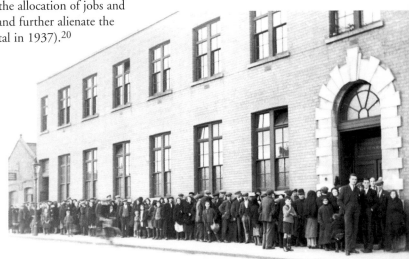

hour of need than the destruction of the Belfast blitz in which almost 1,000 citizens perished, many were injured and 100,000 were made homeless (Figure 11.5; see also chapter 13). The *Belfast Telegraph* produced a booklet in 1941 with photographs of the physical devastation. Called simply *Bombs on Belfast*, this would be raw material for the constructed memory of the city to be sedimented during many a 1950s childhood. The Foreword to the booklet states:

> In April and May 1941, as the price of loyalty to the British Empire, the Ulster capital endured the severest ordeal in its history. For several hours without interruption on the nights of the heaviest raids relays of the Luftwaffe rained fire and bomb on a semi-defenceless city.[21]

Despite the gratitude for fire engines sent from Dublin to help put out the Belfast fires and despite the service of many southern Irish volunteers in the Allied cause, the enduring image of committed Belfast versus neutral Dublin forms an important part of the identity of the city to the present. Unionists in particular took sustenance from the words of Winston Churchill in 1943: 'the bonds of affection between Great Britain and the people of Northern Ireland have been tempered by fire and are now, I firmly believe, unbreakable.'[22]

While, as Bardon points out, there is evidence to suggest that some feeling of togetherness did grow up between Catholics and Protestants as the war progressed, the conclusion, nevertheless, is reached that 'the shared experience of blitz and privation had only papered over intercommunal divisions'.[23] David Harkness concurs:

FIGURE 11.5
Annadale Street, off the
Antrim Road, after
German air raids

BELFAST TELEGRAPH

> despite some common experience of the terror of bombing, some common determination to see the defeat of Hitler and nazism, little had yet been done to heal the divisive sectarian breach. The IRA had failed to rouse support, but many Catholics were no more reconciled to being within a polity not of their own choosing than they were before the war started.[24]

COASTING CITY

In the 1950s Belfast had no vision. It coasted. The allusion is drawn from John Hewitt's poem 'The Coasters', which reflects on the birth of the Troubles in 1969. His subject matter was chickens coming home to roost from the lack of development of civic-minded unionism especially among the Protestant middle class, whose Ulster Unionist Party representatives were amply reflected in the composition of the Belfast Corporation:

> … You coasted along
> and the sores suppurated and spread.
>
> Now the fever is high and raging;
> who would have guessed it, coasting along?
> The ignorant-sick thresh about in delirium
> and tear at the scabs with dirty fingernails.
> The cloud of infection hangs over the city,

a quick change of wind and it
might spill over the leafy suburbs.
You coasted too long.[25]

While the coasting spilled into the 1960s, the evoked image of complacency before the whirlwind has its roots in the outwardly peaceful city of the 1950s. Looking back, the now sadly missed Smithfield Market can be seen as the spatialisation of this illusory calm. Growing up in Belfast during these years and exploring the labyrinthine alleyways of this popular city market (Figure 11.6) was to be transported, as Robert Johnstone aptly describes it,[26] to a temple of exotica (and some erotica too), where the gathering winds of sectarian strife lay beyond the enchanted enclosure. The present-day appeal to a common identity as shoppers in modern Belfast temples of consumption does not quite fire the imagination in the same way. The following fragment from an early twentieth-century writer – Herbert Moore Pim – goes some way to capturing why Smithfield, for many, is part of the lost soul of the city:

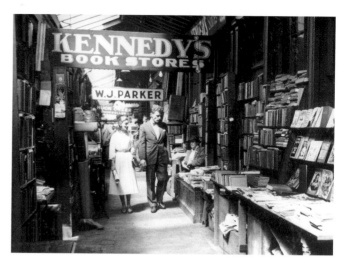

> One there is in Smithfield who gathers about him the scum of our sphere: crutches and corset-busts, turbines and teapots, sewing-machines and Salvation Army tambourines, weigh-bridges and whetstones, yard-rules, and Yule-logs, zithers and Zulu-shields. And beside him there are strange old men who stew before stoves, and draw about them tyres and tubes … In Smithfield, breathing as it does the majestic maxim, 'Man know thyself', we have a storehouse of splendours, for the loss of which nothing could compensate this city of success.[27]

Nothing has.

MODERNISING CITY

As prime minister of Northern Ireland in the 1960s, Terence O'Neill became a standard-bearer for a modernising and reforming unionism, which was to make haste too slowly before the Troubles engulfed in 1969. The vision of a more inclusive society in Northern Ireland was for many symbolised by the historic handshake between Irish Taoiseach Seán Lemass and Terence O'Neill outside Stormont on 14 January 1965. Belfast and its region in this vision was seen and endorsed in major planning studies as the driver of economic prosperity, drawing particularly on the possibilities afforded by multinational investment offsetting the decline in traditional industries. Spatially this was represented quintessentially by the building of major motorways converging on Belfast, firstly the M1 from Belfast to Lisburn, opening in 1962, followed by the M2 motorway to the north, opening in 1966 (Figure 11.7). This spatial vision in later years would be deemed to be flawed, drawing as it did on standard regional economic theory imported from Britain

Top
FIGURE 11.6
The enchanted enclosure of old Smithfield Market in the 1950s. It was destroyed by fire in 1974 and replaced with a pale substitute bearing its name.
ULSTER MUSEUM

Bottom
FIGURE 11.7
The A2 (M) motorway, 1966
ULSTER MUSEUM

to advocate the concentration of growth plans in the predominantly Protestant east of Northern Ireland. The ghost of the main physical planning study of the 1960s led by Sir Robert Matthew, now considered to be ethnically insensitive, continues to reside in the background of virtually all strategic spatial planning in Northern Ireland (see chapter 8). Such debate, however, would seem more abstract as the vision horizon of Belfast in the 1970s contracted to that of grim endurance and sheer survival.

FORTRESS CITY

The city of the imagination called to the fore of international television viewers' consciousness in the 1970s was that of a fortress braced against attack. Between 1970 and 1975 a Provisional IRA bombing campaign destroyed a quarter of retail floor space in Belfast city centre.[28] Radical defensive security measures ensued, including the 'ring of steel' security cordon at entrances to the city centre where pedestrians and vehicles were

Top left
FIGURE 11.8
Security gates in the city centre
BILL KIRK

Top right
FIGURE 11.9
In March 1972 a bomb exploded in the busy Abercorn restaurant in Castle Lane, killing two young women and injuring around seventy people, some severely.
BELFAST TELEGRAPH

searched (Figure 11.8). The government's *Review of Transportation Strategy* in 1978 recommended the construction of a motorway link running to the north and west of the city centre and canyoned through part of its length. The decision to depress the motorway was a reversal of thinking from the late 1960s when an elevated structure was preferred on the basis of less severance to communities lying on either side of the motorway and the considerably reduced cost of not having to construct retaining walls through Belfast sleech.[29] The Westlink acted as a moat cutting off the city centre from the Catholic and Protestant housing areas of the Falls and Shankill, with access much curtailed to the centre from the many small backstreets of the once more permeable residential area. Where the road formed a flyover or was at ground level, access to the city centre was in strategic locations at North Queen Street and the Grosvenor Road, guarded by heavily fortified police stations like bastions in medieval walled towns. Other spatial evocations of siege appearing enduringly in the landscape of the city during these years included so-called peace lines at ethnic interface zones, with the retreat of many inner city neighbourhoods into fortified residential camps. A brutal fortress landscape, not just of security force installations but of commercial and government buildings constituting an architecture of fear, physically pockmarked a city ravaged by conflict over two competing and zero-sum place-visions for Belfast as either Irish or British (Figure 11.9).

RE-IMAGED CITY

In the 1980s Belfast dared to articulate a new vision of a more normal city. If Belfast inhabitants could not work through their cultural differences and come together as citizens, the city of shopping and consumption offered some basis for common and more neutral ground. In the decade of the 1980s the city centre became an official symbol of a possible shared and prosperous future in opposition to the perceived wanton destruction of terrorism. New corporate logos led the way, with no building being more emblematic than the new CastleCourt Shopping Centre (Figure 11.10) on the site of Belfast's old landmark General Post Office on Royal Avenue. Richard Needham, the British Northern Ireland environment minister most closely associated with this period, characterised himself in 'rebuilding Belfast' as 'battling for peace'. The new CastleCourt, Needham insisted, should be faced in glass, thus throwing down a gauntlet to terrorism through 'the defining landmark of the city's new confidence'.[30] In the publicly pump-primed development of Belfast in the 1980s, the general emerging place-promotion imperative of the time dovetailed with the political management of the Troubles.

A new development corporation was established to lead the physical transformation of Belfast's riverfront, now renamed as Laganside and based on ideas from Baltimore in the United States and Salford Quays in England (see chapter 9). A concept plan for the River Lagan in 1987 can be interpreted as extending an invitation to leave behind sectarian space with its antagonistic ethnic identities and to identify with the 'anywhere' of post-modernist space. A Belfast Urban Area Plan (BUAP) published in 1990 can again be seen as a consensus-inducing document holding up a vision of a future shared city. Here positive images of newly built or planned developments in the 'new Belfast' were projected, counterpoised with anaemic-toned panoramas of the 'old' backward-looking city.[31] Any reference to the sectarian divisions with which Belfast is ridden was avoided.[32]

This re-imaging of Belfast was criticised on a number on fronts.[33] First, in embracing almost any development as good, much third-rate architecture and design has been accepted in a city that deserves better. Second and more importantly, 'lipstick on the gorilla' seems an apt metaphor for this

FIGURE 11.10
CastleCourt: the Royal Avenue shopping centre opened in 1990.

STEPHEN A. ROYLE

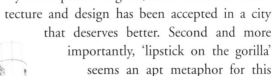

planning and visioning period, given its ultimately cosmetic approach and the failure to deal at a deeper level with cultural identity and conflict. Identity remains important in Belfast, as it does everywhere, because consumption is not enough.

LOOKING TO THE EMERALD CITY OF OZ

In the closing decade of the twentieth century active visioning for the city of Belfast was to move into high gear as political initiatives in a conflict-weary city and society held out the tantalising possibility that 'parity of esteem' for both cultural traditions was perhaps a realisable goal as an alternative to interethnic strife. A pessimistic view might conjure to the imagination *The Wizard of Oz* and Dorothy's disconsolation when she discovers the secret of the Emerald City. Or perhaps a rainbow city truly lies at the end of the trials of the yellow brick road of the peace process. On this matter the twenty-first century will tell its own story. Dealing with the known, what is certain is that Belfast in the 1990s and beyond, along with many other cities, promoted 'visioning' as the main approach to making plans for the future. Vision documents were to abound, merging with mainstream place promotion in the competitive world of urban entrepreneurialism. Compared to the turn of the previous century, however, Belfast had fallen substantially down the economic pecking order and much promotion seemed like bluster. On 11 May 1995, Malcolm Moss, minister for the environment in Northern Ireland, addressed a meeting of Belfast City Council. He appealed for civic leadership to formulate 'a strategic vision' that would define 'the sort of city which we could proudly hand over to future generations'.[34] A follow-up ministerial statement, involving an exhortative retreat to the future in a city that has difficulty advancing from the symbolic landscapes of the past, promised the establishment of a City Partnership Board to facilitate the creation of the vision. 'Vision setting,' this document declared, required an act of faith: 'By stepping out into the future, say 20–25 years from now, envisaging what Belfast should look like, and working backwards from there, it can be possible to bridge the many differences and obstacles that currently hold back development.'[35]

FIGURE 11.11
Taoiseach Bertie Ahern, George Mitchell and Prime Minister Tony Blair after the signing of the Belfast Agreement at Stormont in April 1998

EMPICS

A massive IRA bomb at Canary Wharf in London on 9 February 1996, in reaction to the fact that inclusive political talks on the future of Northern Ireland had failed to materialise following an IRA ceasefire on 31 August 1994, for a while took the steam and euphoria out of place-visioning in Belfast. With a reinstated ceasefire in 1998 and particularly with the signing of the Belfast Agreement on Good Friday of that year, euphoria was justifiably reborn (Figure 11.11). However, in the relaunch of Belfast's place-vision on 15 June 1998, a school choir and glitzy promotional videos could not hide the fact that the core issue of identity in this exercise continued to be avoided. It was reported that respondents to a questionnaire on how Belfast people felt about their city shied away from discussion on issues of identity, with the disappointing and naive conclusion drawn that 'it will be necessary for the vision to demonstrate that it goes beyond issues of cultural identity to the core shared values which emerged for a future Belfast'.[36] This notion, that there can be some escape into a transcendent civic or even cosmopolitan culture where values and meanings are held in common without confronting, negotiating and compromising over identity conflict rather than 'going beyond' or avoiding it, seems well meaning but misplaced. The Belfast vision when published in June 2000 looked forward with optimism to a twenty-first-century city:

> Moving beyond respectful tolerance of each other to a more common civic identity, we will celebrate the full range of our cultural affiliations. And enriched with such confidence, we will have enough goodwill left over to attract and embrace 'outsiders' … Such arrivals will add to our ethnic groups; Chinese, Indian, Jewish etc. who will no longer exist at the margins of the city, relatively invisible. A more multicultural view of the city will be expressed at every level.[37]

The problem with such aspirations in the dimming afterglow of the Belfast Agreement is that, to paraphrase Humpty Dumpty in *Through the Looking Glass*, they mean just what people choose them to mean – neither more nor less. Meanwhile, in the real city as the new century opens, the accommodation and recognition of cultural difference proceeds with smaller steps along a difficult road. In September 2002, Alex Maskey, in the name of 'parity of esteem' and in a highly symbolic act that caused much unionist consternation, installed the Irish tricolour alongside the Union flag in his mayoral office in City Hall. The act also of necessity reflected the simple reality of Belfast at the turn of the millennium as a dual city where division has endured. In Belfast more than half the population currently lives in wards that comprise 90 per cent or more of a single religious group.[38] A study in 2002 showed that internal sectarian partitioning in fact seems to be getting worse, with growing numbers of people wishing to live and work within the safety of their own community.[39]

Against this background, Belfast at the close of the century turned its visionary thoughts to obtaining from the European Union the designation of European Capital of Culture. A bid document, produced by an offshoot of Belfast City Council calling itself Imagine Belfast, resulted in an eclectically lyrical but unsuccessful submission entitled: *One Belfast: Where Hope and History Rhyme*.[40] In a context where to criticise the bid was likely to be misinterpreted as 'doing down the city', the main problem with the re-imaging venture was its lack of authenticity, failing, as it did, to keep at least one foot on the ground. The appropriate posture in a city with such an enduring, antagonistic and sometimes murderous gulf between the main local cultures should be one of some shame and a commitment to the work at hand and not the hollow hyping of visionary mantras. The sentiment was well captured by David Trimble in his Nobel Peace Prize lecture when he was rightly critical of what he called 'the kind of rhetoric which substitutes vapour for vision': 'Vision in its pure meaning is clear sight. That does not mean I have no dreams. I do. But I try to have them at night. By day I am satisfied if I can see the furthest limit of what is possible'.[41] Or as they thankfully continue to say in the real Belfast of lived experience: 'away and catch yerself on'.

NOTES

1   Ortega y Gasset, José (1932) *The revolt of the masses*, W.W. Norton: New York.

2   Rykwert, J. (1988) *The idea of a town*, MIT Press: Cambridge, MA.

3   Larmour, Paul (1987) *Belfast: an illustrated architectural guide*, Friar's Bush Press: Belfast, p. 60.

4   Bardon, Jonathan (1982) *Belfast: an illustrated history*, Blackstaff Press: Belfast, p. 157.

5   Gray, J. (1984) *City in revolt: James Larkin and the Belfast Dock Strike of 1907*, Blackstaff Press: Belfast.

6   Ó Muilleoir, Máirtín (1999) *Belfast's dome of delight. City Hall politics 1981–2000*, Beyond the Pale Publications: Belfast, p. 213.

7   Allen, Nicholas, and Kelly, Aaron (2003) Introduction, in Nicholas Allen and Aaron Kelly (eds) *The cities of Belfast*, Four Courts Press: Dublin, p. 8.

8   Dawe, Gerald, and Foster, John Wilson (1991) 'The poet's place: introduction', in Gerald Dawe and John Wilson Foster (eds) *The poet's place: Ulster literature and society. Essays in honour of John Hewitt*, Institute of Irish Studies, Queen's University Belfast: Belfast.

9   Foster, John Wilson (1997) *The Titanic complex: a cultural manifest*, Belcouver Press: Vancouver, p. 75.

10 Messenger, Charles (1985) *Northern Ireland: the Troubles*, Hamlyn, Bison Books: London, p. 41.

11 Brodie, Malcolm (1995) *The Tele: a history of the Belfast Telegraph*, Blackstaff Press: Belfast, p. 34.

12 Quoted in Killen, John (1985) *John Bull's famous circus: Ulster history through the postcard 1905–1985*, O'Brien Press: Dublin, p. 13.

13 Brodie (1995) *The Tele*, p. 36.

14 HMSO (no date) *Parliament Buildings Stormont*, HMSO: Belfast.

15 Officer, D. (1996) 'In search of order, permanence and stability: building Stormont, 1921–32', in Richard English and Graham Walker (eds), *Unionism in modern Ireland*, Gill and Macmillan: Dublin, p. 142.

16 Graham, B.J. (1994) 'Heritage conservation and revisionist nationalism in Ireland', in G.J. Ashworth and P.J. Larkham (eds) *Building a new heritage: tourism, culture and identity in the new Europe*, Routledge: London, p. 141.

17 Bardon, Jonathan (1999) *Belfast: a century*, Blackstaff Press: Belfast, p. 66.

18 Gillespie, Sandra, and Jones, Gerry (1995) *Northern Ireland and its neighbours since 1920*, Hodder and Stoughton: London, p. 43.

19 Devlin, Paddy (1981) *Yes we have no bananas: Outdoor Relief in Belfast 1920–39*, Blackstaff Press: Belfast.

20 Barton, Brian (1989) *The Blitz: Belfast in the war years*, Blackstaff Press: Belfast, p. 9.

21 *Belfast Telegraph* (1941) *Bombs on Belfast: the blitz 1941*. (reprinted by Pretani Press: Belfast, 1984).

22 Harkness, David (1983) *Northern Ireland since 1920*, Helicon Press: Dublin, p. 102.

23 Bardon (1982) *Belfast,* pp. 240–41.

24 Harkness (1983) *Northern Ireland*, p. 103.

25 From 'The coasters', *The collected poems of John Hewitt* (1991), ed. Frank Ormsby, Blackstaff Press: Belfast. Reproduced by kind permission of Blackstaff Press.

26 Johnstone, Robert, and Kirk, Bill (1983) *Images of Belfast*, Blackstaff Press: Belfast, p. 25.

27 Craig, Patricia (1999) *The Belfast anthology*, Blackstaff Press: Belfast, pp. 416–17; quote from Herbert Moore Pim (1917) *Unknown immortals*.

28 Brown, S. (1985) 'Central Belfast's shopping centre', *Estates Gazette*, 19 October.

29 R. Travers Morgan and Partners (1967) *Report on the Belfast Urban Motorway*, R. Travers Morgan and Partners: Belfast.

30 Needham, Richard (1998) *Battling for peace*, Blackstaff Press: Belfast, p. 171.

31 Greer, John, and Neill, William J.V. (1990) 'The plan as symbol: a case study of Belfast', paper delivered at conference entitled Planning Theory: Prospects for the 1990s, Oxford Polytechnic, 2–5 April.

32 Department of the Environment for Northern Ireland (1990) *Belfast Urban Area Plan*, Department of the Environment for Northern Ireland: Belfast.

33 Neill, William J.V. (1993) 'Physical planning and image enhancement: recent developments in Belfast', *International Journal of Urban and Regional Research*, 17.4, pp. 595–609.

34 Moss, M. (1995) 'Opening remarks' to Belfast City Council, 11 May (minutes).

35 Moss, M. (1995) *A strategic vision for Belfast*, Department of the Environment: Belfast.

36 Belfast City Partnership Board (1998) *What the people said*, Belfast City Partnership Board: Belfast, pp. 3–4.

37 Belfast City Partnership Board (2000) *Belfast city vision*, Belfast City Partnership Board: Belfast.

38 Blease, Victor (2002) *Developing competencies for the next decade*, Northern Ireland Housing Executive: Belfast.

39 Hughes, Joanne, and Donnelly, Caitlin (2002) *Life and times survey*, School of Policy Studies, University of Ulster: Belfast.

40 An allusion to the much-quoted line ('And hope and history rhyme') from Seamus Heaney's *The Cure at Troy*. Belfast City Council – Imagine Belfast (2002) *One Belfast, Belfast's bid for European Capital of Culture, 2008* Belfast City Council: Belfast.

41 Trimble, David (2001) *To raise up a new Northern Ireland: articles and speeches 1998–2000*, Belfast Press: Belfast, p. 61.

Life springs from death; and from the graves of patriot men and women spring living nations.[1]

This quotation is drawn from Patrick Pearse's renowned oration of 1915 at the Dublin graveside of Fenian leader Jerome O'Donovan Rossa and it reminds us of the powerful political and symbolic role of public commemoration in the politics of everyday life. The links between cultural identity, remembrance and nationhood have been long established but continue to carry significance in contemporary society.

12
Memorialising and Marking the Great War

Belfast Remembers

Nuala C. Johnson

FIGURE 12.1
Gassed by John Singer Sargent
THE ART ARCHIVE/IMPERIAL WAR MUSEUM

From the toppling of statues of Lenin in the post-communist states of Eastern Europe to the erection of a memorial to the victims of the terrorist attack on the World Trade Center in Manhattan that took place on 11 September 2001, acts of public remembering and marking retain their importance across a variety of cultural contexts.

In Belfast, too, rituals of commemoration and the creation of landscapes of remembrance have played a key role in the making and remaking of cultural identities. In particular, the celebration of St Patrick's Day on 17 March and the remembrance of the Battle of the Boyne on 12 July form important parts of Belfast's commemorative calendar, although historically they have been divisive rather than unifying moments. Rather than looking at either of these two significant dates and the rituals surrounding them, I will instead focus on Belfast's acts of remembering the Great War (Figure 12.1). I have chosen the First World War because it affected families of all social classes and religious denominations around the city. Second, it represented the single most significant loss of life of Irish men and women in the twentieth century. Third, the rituals and sites of memory established in the immediate postwar period continue to have an important place in the life of the city and are visible in the landscape of everyday life.

IRELAND AND REMEMBERING THE FIRST WORLD WAR

Commemorating the dead who had served in Irish regiments in the First World War would challenge cultural allegiances in Belfast, both in nationalist and unionist quarters. The peace parades of July 1919 established the initial framework for commemoration. Although 11 November would become the main day for remembering war dead, it was 19 July that was the dedicated official public holiday devoted to marking the final arrival of peace in Europe in the year immediately after the conflict ended. The public spectacle staged in cities and towns around Ireland in 1919 provides insights into how the war registered in the popular imagination at a moment when the Home Rule crisis was not yet resolved and the Easter rebellion of 1916 (Figure 12.2) was fresh in the public's memory. Although the war has been treated by some scholars as a deciding moment in provoking a modern memory, in the Irish case popular interpretations of the conflict cannot be easily disentangled from the prewar political conditions on the island. For one historian 'honouring the dead was not simply a matter of paying due respects – it forms a potent element in the endorsement of a particular political culture or the creation of an alternative one'.[2] The mapping of commemorative space in Ireland in 1919 was a controversial exercise from the outset. While all participating states had to face the challenge of confronting the loss endured during the war and dealing with the inadequacy of traditional forms of remembrance, in the Irish case the exercise of social memory rubbed up

FIGURE 12.2
The corner of Abbey Street,
Dublin, shelled in the
Easter Rising

NATIONAL LIBRARY OF IRELAND

against a whole suite of immediate, conflicting allegiances, and these allegiances would find material expression in the geographical location and distribution of 'national' icons.

In this chapter I will focus on how the memory of the dead of the First World War in Belfast was articulated, through an analysis of the Peace Day parades of 1919 and the creation of memorial sites at the City Hall and Queen's University. Irish men and women participated in significant numbers in the war, particularly among the Protestant community. I will argue that the prewar circumstances (the Home Rule crisis) against which Irish people chose to participate in the war partly explain the significance they subsequently attached to it. The Peace Day parades represent the first attempt to add significant cultural and political meaning to the war and, as such, they laid the foundations for the manner in which future generations would make sense of the war. While remembering the dead is often seen as a private, personal affair, the commemoration of the war dead became a public, collective event, which implicated the society as a whole. Through analysing commemoration as large scale spectacle, I wish to suggest that public memory is maintained as much through a geographical lens as a historical one. Spectacle constructs the geographical and temporal limits to popular understandings of the past and, in so doing, it underlines how universal principles of bereavement are locally mediated through the actual symbols and patterns used in public spectacles.

Representations of the war and the construction of a collective memory of the conflict have also been subject to diverse analyses. Literary historians have claimed that the war represented a critical juncture in the evolution of an ironic modernism, particularly expressed in the visual arts and literature. They have suggested that writers' attitudes and depictions of the war were filled with anxiety, irony, despair and a mistrust of the notion of a 'just cause' perpetuated at the time by politicians and military leaders. These studies, however, have focused on élite expressions of the war, for instance through analysing the image of war in fine art, poetry and fiction. Alternative views stress the linkages between postwar memory and the cultivation of nationalist politics, especially in Germany and Italy.[3] One historian claims that 'Modern memory was born not just from the sense of a break with the past, but from an intense awareness of the conflicting representations of the past and the effort of each group to make its version the basis of national identity.'[4] Geographers, too, have examined landscapes of war and memory where they have stressed the debates underpinning the commemoration of war dead and the construction of national or regional identities.[5]

THE SPECTACLE OF MEMORY

Unlike formal academic histories, where an account of the past is conventionally structured around the linking together of episodes into a narrative, public memory may be more suitably articulated as a spatial arrangement of objects around a spectacle. Joep Leerssen puts it as follows: 'one way of unifying history [is] to rearrange its consecutive events from a narrative order into a spectacle, a conspectus of juxtaposed "freeze-frame" images'.[6] The memory of four consecutive years of war, for instance, can be foreshortened into a single commemorative event. The collapsing of time into space through the annual rehearsal and repetition of a spectacle provides a framework not only for under-

standing remembrance but also for the public enactment of forgetfulness.

The strength of this approach to the study of remembrance of the Great War is that it was popularly represented precisely through large scale drama or theatrical performance. The construction of a spectacle of remembrance translated individual responses to loss and victory into a collective response, where the relationship between the 'actors' in the spectacle, the audience viewing it and the geographical setting which framed it, all created the context for interpretation.

The question of the intelligibility of death, and in this case the prodigious loss of life, is germane (Figure 12.3). Each death was simultaneously a private moral matter (for family and for friends) and a public one (for states and for armies). The response of a civilian audience to that which they themselves did not experience directly raised questions about the moral and political meaning of modern warfare. European society, in the aftermath of the war, attempted to present and reconcile these questions through staging annual parades and creating commemorative landscapes. By treating these as ritual spectacles, albeit considerably different in kind to more orthodox spectacular events, we begin to unravel the ways in which large scale death could be culturally and morally harmonised in a peacetime environment.

An account of the past relayed through public spectacle, like narrative history, is partly mediated through the lens of current political preoccupations. In the case of Belfast this involved constructing a commemorative spectacle when the pre-1914 divisions were not eliminated, the constitutional position of Ireland within the Union was uncertain and the Easter rebellion was still fresh in the public mind. These facts add a specific dimension to Belfast's acts of remembrance that differentiate it in important ways from the fashioning of memory in Britain and France. The manner in which the spectacle was produced and received across the city varied considerably.

PARADING TRADITION IN BELFAST

In Belfast the spectacle of parades has a long genealogy and thus the development of remembrance rituals for soldiers killed in the First World War extended that practice of public commemoration for military victory. In particular, the success of William of Orange at the Battle of Boyne and his accession to the throne provided the centrepiece of Protestant commemorative practices. From the eighteenth century onwards, Orange parades have been at the heart of the commemorative calendar of Protestant identity (Figure 12.4). The central role of the 36th (Ulster) division in the Battle of the Somme in 1916 anchored the memory of the war around that single battle. In the first two days of the offensive the Ulster Division lost 5,500 (killed, missing or wounded) from a total of 15,000 soldiers. The fact that the first day of the battle – 1 July – coincided precisely with the Battle of the Boyne in 1690 was recognised at the time. The commanding officer of the Ulster Division, on the eve of the offensive, wrote: 'We could hardly have a date better calculated to inspire national traditions amongst our men of the North.'[7] The losses of the first days of the Somme focused Belfast minds on the personal bereavement experienced by close-knit communities. It also cemented a sense of the social nature of Belfast's sacrifices in the war. The Battle of the Somme became the archetype of Ulster's loyalty and defence of the Crown (Figure 12.5).

FIGURE 12.4
An Orange Order procession in Shaftesbury Square, 1923

LINEN HALL LIBRARY

Although many thousands of other Irish soldiers lost their lives during the course of the war, the intensity and catastrophic strategy associated with this battle was particularly acute in the formation of Ulster's collective memory of the war. Indeed in 1916, for the first time in its history, the Orange Order cancelled its annual 12 July parades and observed a five-minute silence for those killed. The temporal proximity of the Somme to 12 July helped to link the war in Belfast memory along a historical trajectory that emphasised Ulster's continued sacrifice for a greater British cause. As Neil Jarman has noted: 'Opposition to Home Rule was no longer couched solely in references to seventeenth century battles or in abstract politico-religious ideals; it was securely anchored in the events of the recent past.'[8]

In terms of the July 1919 Peace Day celebrations the *Belfast News Letter* claimed that 'local considerations' (the celebrations associated with 12 July Orange parades) would mean the postponement of the civic celebrations until 9 August. This date would also allow Ireland's viceroy, Lord French, to take the salute in Belfast and honour Ulster's contribution to the war effort in an event separate from his role in the Dublin parade. The city did observe the day with an official pageant of military personnel, which was comprised exclusively of English and Scots regiments. More significantly, in the Orange parades of 1919 the connections between the Somme and the Boyne were first displayed. The Hydepark Loyal Orange Lodge 1067 unveiled their banner portraying King William on one side and the Battle of the Somme on the other.[9] The inclusion of the Somme in the iconography of the Orange Order extended the sightlines of Protestant social memory while simultaneously narrowing the focus of the war in Catholic consciousness in Ulster.

FIGURE 12.5
Loyalist paramilitary mural on the Newtownards Road, commemorating the 36th (Ulster) Division at the Battle of the Somme

STEPHEN A. ROYLE

The public display of memory in the social space of Belfast that mimicked the geography of the Orange Order's parades would have serious consequences for the possible creation of a collective memory that would have transcended the sectarian divisions of this part of the island. The introduction of mini-parades by the Orange Order on 1 July, to commemorate the Somme, would institutionalise the interpretation of the war in Ulster and codify it in ways that deviated from the official day of national remembrance on 11 November. The idiom of the memory-makers' calendar underscored Protestant desire to celebrate British identity while simultaneously marking this identity through localising discourse. The dispute over the routing of the parade from Drumcree Church of Ireland parish church to the centre of Portadown in recent years ironically is a conflict over the use of public space for the remembrance of the Battle of the Somme rather than the Battle of the Boyne. But the fact that this parade is associated with William of Orange by both sides in the dispute reinforces the aggregation of the two events into a single motif of identity.

FIGURE 12.6
Peace Day parade route in
Belfast, 9 August 1919

BELFAST'S PEACE DAY PARADE, 9 AUGUST 1919

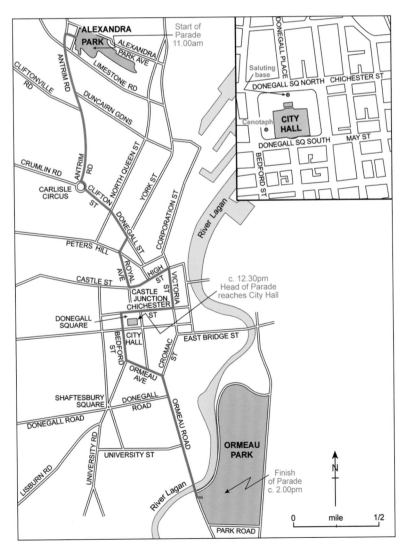

We are today in Belfast joining with our fellow citizens of the British Empire in expressing our heartfelt thankfulness to Almighty God for complete triumph over an arrogant and remorseless enemy.[10]

As already noted, Belfast postponed its Peace Day celebrations until August 1919, so as not to conflict with the Orange parades of July. While 9 August had been designated for the civic celebrations by the Unionist councillors in Belfast Corporation in July, decisions to participate in the parade were largely reserved until August. At a special meeting in Derry of the local branch of the Nationalist Veterans' Association, led by Alderman J.M. Monagle, the attitude of nationalist ex-servicemen towards the parade was debated. Regarding the proposals surrounding the parade as focusing almost exclusively on the 36th (Ulster) Division, the following motion was passed unanimously: 'We believe it is being held for political motives, which are contrary to the rights and principles of freedom we, Nationalists, fought for, and we call on all Nationalist ex-servicemen to refrain from participation in it.'[11] The editorial of the *Belfast News Letter* denied any political motives and stated that the complaint came from 'those whose acquaintance with loyalty is not of the most

intimate nature'.[12] In a sideswipe at Dublin's efforts the previous month, the paper claimed that 'No such demonstration as that which will salute His Majesty's representative [Lord French] has ever been organised in Ireland, nor, we imagine, have so many people ever been brought together for entertainment at one time.'[13] Those eligible to apply to participate in the parade included the following: Ulstermen who had served during the war; all others who served in Ulster units; all demobilised officers and men now residing in Ulster and all Ulster ladies who took up service during the war and all others with service now living in Ulster. While the organisers anticipated about 20,000 applications, in the final account numbers swelled to somewhere between 30,000 and 36,000 participants.

The parade was organised around a route of approximately 4 miles (6.4 km), beginning in north Belfast and ending at Ormeau Park, south-east of the city centre (Figure 12.6). The symbolic keystone of the route was the City Hall, itself a building with many unionist associations, where Lord French took the salute. He had made the journey by car from Dublin to attend the event. The City Hall, located in Belfast's central square and housing the city's Corporation, formed the local centrepiece of the parade. Invited guests occupied the stands specially erected for the occasion. They included Field Marshal Sir Henry Wilson and other senior military personnel; Ulster Unionist Party MPs, such as Sir Edward Carson (MP for Belfast Duncairn) and G. Hanna (MP for East Antrim); city councillors headed by the lord mayor, J.C. White; and a variety of members of the local aristocracy.[14] Sir Edward Carson had arrived in Belfast the previous day to unveil a roll of honour at the Workman Clark shipyard, where some 2,600 men had volunteered for service. The death of soldiers along the battlefront was not ideologically separated from the status of the Union. In a tribute to the men who had fallen during the war, Carson declared:

> I myself came in at the head of the first Volunteer regiment which formed the nucleus of the Ulster division and marched with them to the recruiting office ... I never doubted that they would acquit themselves on the field of battle as great soldiers, loyal to their king and country, and that our old motto of the province, 'No surrender', would be the guiding ideal when they came in contact with the Hun aggressor.[15]

Clearly identifying a lineage with the will to defend the nation, Carson's comments trace an ideological link between prewar conditions in Ulster and the conclusion of the war.

The parade began at 11.10 a.m., departing from Alexandra Park in the north of the city and travelling along the Antrim Road and into the city centre. The Royal Navy and auxiliary forces were given the post of honour. While most of the demobilised men were from Ulster, many from the Munster Fusiliers and Connaught Rangers were also present. Flags decorated the main thoroughfares (Figure 12.7). They included a Japanese flag and an American flag. The Irish Rifles (11th Battalion) were led by Captain C.C. Craig, Unionist MP for South Antrim, and he was loudly cheered when recognised. Along the

Antrim Road 'Tipperary' was sung by the crowd and played by the band of the Irish Guards. Wounded soldiers were conveyed in motor vehicles, charabancs and lorries, prompting the *Belfast News Letter* to comment that 'they were so merry and boisterous, and so resolutely bent on sustaining the festive spirit of the occasion, that commiseration would have been glaringly out of place'.[16]

While spectators lined the entire route, the real concentration was at the viceroy's saluting point in front of the Queen Victoria statue at the City Hall. A temporary cenotaph to the memory of the dead had been placed on the west side of the building. A guard of honour, comprised of four soldiers with bowed heads, stood around the cenotaph. Many wreaths were laid there and the whole area was ablaze with bunting. Behind lines of armed soldiers who managed the route of the parade was a thick fringe of spectators. At noon the parade reached the saluting point and took three hours to pass. When the 36th (Ulster) Division reached the saluting point there was a

> prolonged outburst of cheering. The men made a very fine show. The greater proportion of the men was in civilian attire and they marched with true soldierly bearing. Many wore the ribbons belonging to certain decorations and the spectators' hearts filled with pride as they gazed upon those men who have brought so much credit to their Province and to Ireland.[17]

When the procession had passed, the Irish Guards' band played the national anthem and Lord French was cheered. The greater public enthusiasm, however, was extended to Sir Edward Carson, where the crowds sought handshakes and a speech that he willingly supplied. He said, 'I never was prouder of Ulster and her heroes than I was today. May God bless Ulster and may God bless the King.'[18]

Afterwards there was a luncheon at the City Hall for Lord French and the other invited guests, while at Ormeau Park marquees had been erected to feed and entertain the thousands of soldiers who had taken part in the parade. During the luncheon, Lord French made a speech of thanks to the people of Belfast, noting that

> In spite of the absence of military weapons and uniforms the spectacle was magnificent with a grandeur which no military environment could have created. It was rendered so by the bearing of victorious soldiers who had fought their way through bloodstained paths by deeds of unparalleled heroism over the bodies of the flower of their country's manhood to victory.[19]

The lord mayor honoured His Majesty's representative in Ireland, 'who after a rite of toil and danger, was now in stormy and difficult times, the staunch guardian of peace and order among them'.[20] The fragile political position of Ireland in the summer of 1919 was ironically reminiscent of the summer of 1914. While the course of the war may have blurred political allegiances in Ireland, divisions were to resurface quickly once the conflict was concluded.

The spectacle in Belfast, although sharing some of the characteristics of the parades held elsewhere in Ireland, differed in important respects. The length of the route and the number of participants and spectators exceeded what happened elsewhere. One commentator stated that 'As a spectacle the march was magnificent, but its true significance lay in the powerful appeal which it made to the emotions.'[21] These emotions were aroused through the iconography of the parade and through the narrative that subsequently came to reflect it. The links between physical prowess, 'race' and regional identity were repeatedly used to represent the parade in Belfast. The *Belfast News Letter* employed phrases such as 'brave clansmen of Ulster', 'our sturdy population' and a 'great and imperially-minded race' to situate Ulster's position in the larger theatre of war.[22] The *Irish Times* also remarked that the celebrations in Belfast were 'a striking demonstration ... of Ulster's loyalty and adherence to the Throne and the Constitution. It was at the same time convincing proof of the noble part played by the Northern province in the Great War.'[23] The nomenclature of individual and 'national' heroism reinforced in the minds of Ulster Protestants, in particular, the significance of their sacrifice in the broader political arena of Anglo-Irish relations. The more nationalist-leaning newspaper the *Irish News and Belfast Morning Post* offered more reserved comment on the day's events. Unlike the glowing reports of other newspapers, it stressed what it regarded as a lack of splendour and pageantry due to the 'proportion of those in ranks who wore civilian dress', and the disorganisation at Ormeau Park, where many soldiers, who had travelled long distances, received no food or drink.[24] Similarly, although making front-page news in the Dublin-based *Saturday Herald*, the column there was a brief and descriptive account of the day's events.

THE CENOTAPH, BELFAST CITY HALL

While parades were one way in which memories could be evoked and maintained, memorials in the form of statues and monuments became permanent reminders on the landscape of the city. In the years following the war big efforts were made to create sites of memory within churches but also in public spaces across Belfast. One of the most significant church memorials was erected in St. Anne's Church of Ireland Cathedral in Belfast, where the west portals were dedicated 'to the men of Ulster who fell in the Great War'. The placing of Belfast's main memorial within the grounds of the Protestant-dominated Corporation offices at the City

FIGURE 12.8
The cenotaph, Belfast City Hall
STEPHEN A. ROYLE

Hall (Figure 12.8), ironically, was to make the connections between the war and politics in ways that were being wholly resisted in Dublin. In Dublin the placing of a First World War memorial adjacent to a seat of local or national government aroused strong opposition across a range of political opinions. However, this was not the case in Belfast. Designed by Sir Alfred Brumwell Thomas, the architect of the City Hall, and constructed by W.J. Campbell between 1925 and 1927, the cenotaph is framed by a colonnade, consisting of Greek order columns and an encircled cornice and balustrade. The classical design and the use of a cenotaph as a memorial icon found favour across Europe. The one in Belfast was unveiled on Armistice Day 1929 and has remained the focal point of official remembrance in the city ever since.

Top
FIGURE 12.9
A temporary UVF hospital at
Queen's University, 1916

PRONI

Bottom
FIGURE 12.10
The duke of York (*right*),
accompanied by Lord
Londonderry (*left*),
inspecting a guard of honour
drawn from the Queen's
University Officers' Training
Corps on the occasion of the
war memorial unveiling
ceremony in the grounds of
the university, 21 July 1924

BELFAST NEWS LETTER

Daniel Sherman reminds us that 'Monument sites prompted strong reactions, more-over, because they entailed a kind of geographical superposition of memories: memories of individuals had to share mental space with the memories attached and attributed to places.'[25] As the epicentre of local government in Belfast, the City Hall may have been an uninviting venue for commemoration among the city's Catholics, with the iconogra-phy of unionism evident in other statues surrounding the building (for example, Queen Victoria). The ritual of remembrance was pronounced in Belfast, with the Armistice Day programme of 1926 listing thirty-nine representative bodies laying wreaths at the (still temporary) cenotaph at the City Hall. These included the lord mayor, prime minister and governor of Northern Ireland.[26] The unveiling of the cenotaph in 1929, according to Keith Jeffery, was 'almost exclusively a Protestant affair'.[27] The 16th Irish Division was omitted from the invitation list, although the Italian Fascist Party was included. The fol-lowing year, however, the 16th Irish Division was invited.

The choice of a cenotaph as the symbolic representation of loss perhaps reflected a desire to replicate the pattern in London, although the anonymity of identity implied through the use of an empty tomb may not have had the intended impact of inclusivity in a heavily religiously seg-regated city.[28] Although the tomb was to represent all soldiers killed in the war irrespective of class, creed or eth-nicity, its location within a space regarded as unionist in political complexion may have implied remembrance of a Protestant soldier in the eyes of Catholic families.

QUEEN'S UNIVERSITY MEMORIAL

Like other institutions in Belfast, Queen's University made a significant contribution to the war effort. As well as expanding the Queen's University Officers' Training Corps and providing facilities for training on the univer-sity campus, the college also provided space for the extension of the Ulster Volunteer Force hospital in the Botanic Gardens (Figure 12.9). But the greatest impact of the war on the university was the number of members who volunteered for service. Both staff and students enlisted in the armed services and many lost their lives.[29] Consequently, once the war was ended the university was keen to honour its dead through the erection of a memo-rial on the campus grounds. Sir Thomas Brock was commissioned to design the statue and by 1923 a clay mould of the monument was completed. In addition, the university provided funding for the alteration of the roadway where the statue would be placed and the instal-lation of appropriate entrance gates opposite it. The

university hoped that the 'entrance gates [would be] commensurate with the dignity of the university and the beauty of the noble statuary which would commemorate their brothers'.[30]

By early the following year, plans were well afoot for the unveiling of the memorial on 21 July 1924 by the duke of York. Emanating initially from a private invitation to the duke from Lord Londonderry (chancellor of the university), this breach of protocol resulted in the visit becoming an official royal visit, with all the attendant organisation and ceremony. Indeed, this visit was to become the template for subsequent visits by members of the royal family to Northern Ireland.[31] Included in the official visit was the awarding of the freedom of the cities of Derry and Belfast, the conferring of an honorary degree at Queen's, the unveiling of the memorial and a garden party at the governor's residence at Hillsborough. The day of the visit was declared a public holiday and this added further significance to the unveiling ritual at the university.

The royal procession arrived at Queen's just after noon on 21 July to be welcomed at the entrance gate by a guard of honour drawn from the Officers' Training Corps. Greeted by Lord Londonderry, the duke proceeded to inspect the guard of honour (Figure 12.10). Then, having been appropriately robed, the duke and duchess of York joined the procession to the library, where they were both conferred with honorary degrees of LLD. Among those present at the ceremony were the lord mayor and members of Belfast Corporation, as well as university personnel. This was followed by the centrepiece of the visit, the principal royal duty of unveiling the war memorial.

The Brock memorial, executed by Arnold Wright, represents 'Sacrifice'. It consists of a female allegorical figure of Victory, supporting a wounded youth and holding upright a laurel crown (Figure 12.11). At the base of the figure lies a German shield on top of a helmet. Drawing on classical motifs, the statue is cast in bronze and stands on a granite pedestal. The overall height is 24 feet (7.3 m) and it occupies a key space at the main entrance to the university, in front of the impressive neo-Gothic Lanyon building built between 1847 and 1849. In geographical terms it occupies a prime location and this reflects the importance the university attached to the project. The inscription states that it had been erected 'To the memory of members of this University and its Officers' Training Corps who gave their lives in the Great War, leaving their successors a perpetual example of self-sacrifice and loyal service'. The names of the dead are contained on panels recessed into the pedestal (Figure 12.12).

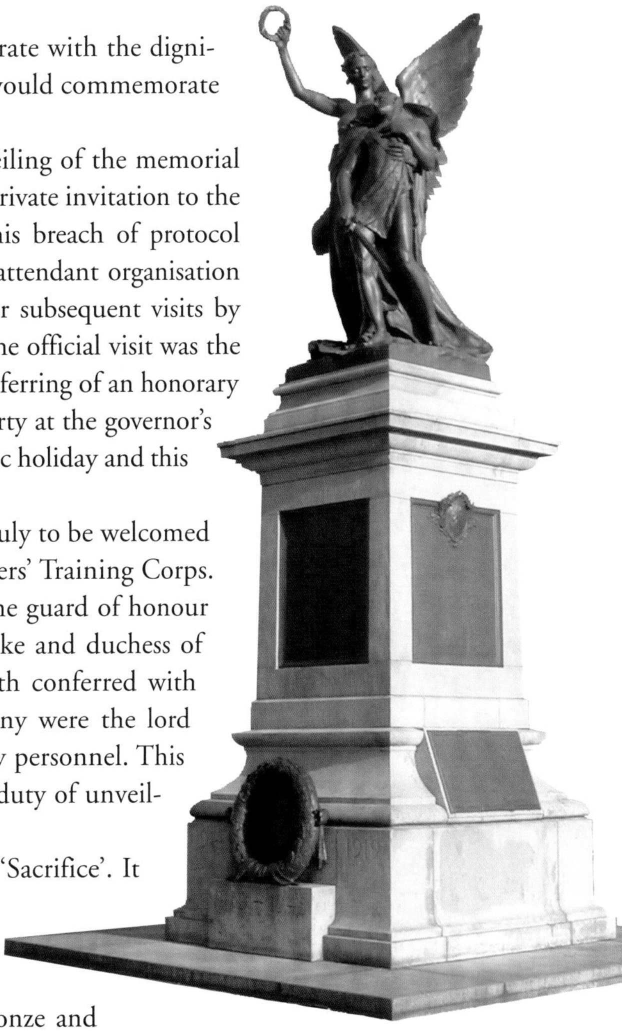

Above
FIGURE 12.11
Queen's University Belfast war memorial

NUALA C. JOHNSON

Left
FIGURE 12.12
Roll of honour plinth, Queen's University Belfast war memorial

STEPHEN A. ROYLE

FIGURE 12.13
The duke of York unveiling Queen's
University Belfast war memorial,
21 July 1924

BELFAST NEWS LETTER

Seats were reserved in front of the memorial for the royal party. The unveiling proceedings began with the singing of 'O God Our Help', accompanied by the band of the 1st Lincolnshire Regiment. The chancellor opened the ceremony, stating that:

> The Roll of Honour … contains names which are obviously closely identified with Ulster, bearing as they do an eloquent and pathetic tribute to the sentiments which actuate the citizens of Northern Ireland in common with the sentiments of the best of the British race.[32]

The duke of York then performed the unveiling, followed by the playing of the reveille, and a prayer offered by Reverend Doctor Simms. Then the hymn 'For All the Saints' was recited and the national anthem sung. The duke and duchess consecutively placed wreaths and floral tributes at the base of the memorial and the chancellor and other representatives proceeded to lay their wreaths (Figure 12.13).

Once the unveiling was completed, the royal couple proceeded to visit the Ulster Volunteer Force hospital located on the university grounds, and then attended a lunch hosted by the chancellor in their honour in the Great Hall. Guests included the governor of Northern Ireland and other political dignitaries from local and national government, as well as senior members of the university. In his welcoming speech, Lord Londonderry said that he and the people of Northern Ireland wished to 'express our loyalty to a dynasty which so fully and adequately represents the best and highest ideals of the British race – and at the same time, is enshrined by feelings of respect and affection in the hearts of a loyal and devoted nation'.[33] He also commented on the close connections between Ulster and Scotland and the duchess's close Scottish links. In his reply, the duke noted the appropriateness of his first public duty in Northern Ireland being the unveiling of a memorial to those 'who gave their lives in our Empire's cause'.[34]

After the lunch the royal party left the university for other engagements. The statue that they unveiled in 1924 became the centrepiece of the university's annual Remembrance Sunday commemorations and it continues today to be the pivot of Queen's University's dedication to those killed in military service. Indeed, in 1950 the memorial was rededicated to include those killed in the Second World War (Figure 12.14) and each November the base of this statue is adorned with wreaths remembering those who died.

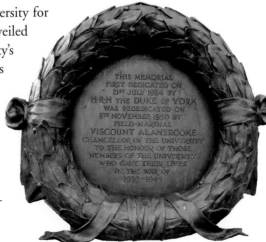

FIGURE 12.14
Plaque rededicating the Queen's
University Belfast war memorial to
include the dead of the
Second World War

STEPHEN A. ROYLE

CONCLUSION

Overall, in the decade following the armistice, Belfast and Northern Ireland created a series of commemorative spaces to the war that inscribed it onto the landscape and memorial record – both those described above and others, such as the grove of cedar trees in the grounds of Stormont (Figure 12.15). While there were some instances of inclusive rituals of remembrance, the narrative undergirding the overall exercise tended to highlight and reinforce the exceptionality of Ulster within the island and replicate the divisions found in a prewar Irish context. The fact that the political boundaries of the island had changed since the war's end added weight to the battle of ideologies that had characterised the earlier decades.

While the First World War was important for the construction of a social memory throughout the United Kingdom, it took on some special characteristics in Belfast. First, the war almost immediately became foreshortened and summarised by a single battle, the Battle of the Somme, and thus four years of conflict were compressed into a few days of July 1916. The significance of this battle continues in popular memory today and is represented in Frank McGuinness's play *Observe the Sons of Ulster Marching towards the Somme*. In addition, the Somme Heritage Centre in Newtownards, County Down, has opened as an arena for understanding Ulster's role in the First World War by presenting a 'virtual' experience of trench life. This centre also includes a substantial consideration of the role of the 10th Irish and 16th Irish divisions in the war. Second, for the memory-

FIGURE 12.15
Cedar grove, Stormont, commemorating the 36th Ulster Division

STEPHEN A. ROYLE

makers the significance of July could not be ignored and thus the commemoration of the First World War through the Somme battle shifted to some degree the dates of remembrance. The inclusion of the Battle of the Somme in the iconography and calendar of the Orange Order gives the First World War a specificity in Belfast and Northern Ireland as a whole. Although 11 November is the United Kingdom's official day of remembrance, in Belfast July may be just as significant as November. The mini-parades held by the Orange Order on the Sunday closest to 1 July in memory of the Somme marks out Northern Ireland's commemorations as different to those that take place elsewhere in the United Kingdom. The visual representation of the battle in Orange Order banners, as well as on loyalist murals, indicates its continued significance in the identity formation of Belfast Protestants. And the idea of a public memory acted out through ritual parades and embedded in the landscape in sculpture and statuary indicates the enormous role that marking and remembering plays in the overall life of this city.

NOTES

1   From Patrick Pearse's graveside panegyric delivered at the funeral of Jerome O'Donovan Rossa in Glasnevin Cemetery in 1915; see Mac Aonghusa, P., and Ó Réagáin, L. (1967) *The best of Pearse,* Mercier: Cork, p. 134.

2   Travers, P. (1990) 'Our Fenian dead: Glasnevin Cemetery and the genesis of the republican funeral', in J. Kelly and U. MacGearailt (eds) *Dublin and Dubliners*, Helicon: Dublin, p. 52.

3   See Mossé, G. (1990) *Fallen soldiers: shaping the memory of two world wars,* Oxford University Press: Oxford.

4   Gillis, J.R. (1994) 'Memory and identity: the history of a relationship', in R. Gillis (ed.) *Commemorations: the politics of national identity,* Princeton University Press: Princeton, NJ, p. 8.

5   Johnson, N.C. (2003) *Ireland, the Great War and the geography of remembrance,* Cambridge University Press: Cambridge; Winberry, J. (1983) '"Lest we forget": the Confederate Monument and the southern townscape', *Southeastern Geographer,* 23, pp. 107–21; Clout, H. (1996) *After the ruins: restoring the countryside of northern France after the Great War,* Exeter University Press: Exeter.

6   Leerssen, J. (1996) *Remembrance and imagination: patterns in the historical and literary representation of Ireland in the nineteenth century,* Cork University Press: Cork, p. 7.

7   Quoted in Jeffery, K. (2000) *Ireland and the Great War,* Cambridge University Press: Cambridge, p. 56.

8   Jarman, N. (1997) *Material conflicts: parades and visual displays in Northern Ireland,* Berg: Oxford, pp. 71–72.

9   Jarman (1997) *Material conflicts.*

10 *Belfast News Letter* (1919) Editorial, 9 August.

11 Cited in *Freeman's Journal* (1919) 9 August.

12 *Belfast News Letter* (1919) Editorial, 9 August.

13 *Belfast News Letter* (1919) Editorial, 9 August.

14 *Irish Independent* (1919) 11 August.

15 Quoted in *Belfast News Letter* (1919) 11 August.

16 *Belfast News Letter* (1919) 9 August.

17 *Irish Times* (1919) 11 August.

18 *Irish Times* (1919) 11 August.

19 *Irish Times* (1919) 11 August.

20 *Irish Times* (1919) 11 August.

21 *Belfast News Letter* (1919) 11 August.

22 *Belfast News Letter* (1919) 11 August.

23 *Irish Times* (1919) 11 August.

24 *Irish News and Belfast Morning Post* (1919) 11 August.

25 Sherman, D. (1999) *The construction of memory in interwar France,* University of Chicago Press: Chicago, p. 218.

26 Gregory, A. (1994) *The silence of memory: Armistice Day 1919–1946,* Berg: Oxford.

27 Jeffery (2000) *Ireland and the Great War,* p. 132.

28 See Larmour, Paul (1987) *Belfast: an illustrated architectural guide,* Friar's Bush Press: Belfast.

29 Moody, T.W., and Beckett, J.C. (1959) *Queen's Belfast 1845–1949: the history of a university,* Faber and Faber: London.

30 Quoted in the *Belfast News Letter* (1923) 20 December.

31 This matter is discussed in more detail in McIntosh, G. (n.d.) 'From decadence to decay: Northern Ireland's governors', unpublished paper kindly loaned to me by the author.

32 Quoted in the *Belfast News Letter* (1924) 22 July.

33 Quoted in the *Belfast News Letter* (1924) 22 July.

34 Quoted in the *Belfast News Letter* (1924) 22 July.

It is a sad fact that for many outsiders, Belfast, like Beirut and Baghdad, is known as a city of violence. The Troubles since 1969 is only the latest, albeit the bloodiest, episode in the city's twentieth-century history. This chapter gives an overview of that violence, especially the deaths that have resulted from it.

13
Belfast
The Killing Fields

Russell C. Murray

FIGURE 13.1
Street rioting at the corner of York Street and Donegall Street, Belfast, 1920
BELFAST TELEGRAPH

Belfast entered the last century no stranger to communal violence. The latter half of the nineteenth century saw numerous clashes between the two communities as the tensions of the struggle for and against Irish Home Rule spread to the city. There were serious outbreaks of rioting resulting in deaths in 1857, 1864, 1872, 1886, and 1898.[1] In the opening years of the new century, the preparations for armed conflict were intensified with the formation of the Ulster Volunteer Force (UVF) on the unionist side and the Irish Volunteers (later Irish Republican Army [IRA]) on the nationalist side. With the outbreak of the Irish War of Independence in 1919, it was inevitable that conflict would break out again in a Belfast still riven by sectarian divisions and spatially segregated after a world war which 'seemed to accustom men to the regular use of violence to advance a cause, redress grievances and enforce the will of government'.[2]

THE TROUBLES, 1920–22

The communal violence in the north began in Londonderry in April 1920, but soon spread to Belfast (Figure 13.1). The first fatality in Belfast was a policeman killed by a Protestant mob in June. (Ironically, the first police officer killed in the post-1969 conflict was also killed by Protestants in Belfast.) In the violence that beset the city until nearly the end of 1922, 489 people were to die.[3] Of these, 444 were civilians (266 Catholics, 178 Protestants), 10 were members of the IRA, and 35 were members of the Crown forces (the contemporary collective term for the army and police).[4]

The catalyst for the start of intensive sectarian violence in Belfast was the decision by Protestant shipyard workers, at a meeting on Tuesday 21 July 1920, to expel all 'disloyal' workers (this included socialist Protestants). Their attack on workers in and around the shipyards sparked off communal violence throughout the inner areas of the city. Some of this took the form of hand-to-hand fighting, especially along the interfaces. However, unlike the situation in 1969, paramilitary groups on both sides were well armed and there were numerous shooting incidents. Troops were deployed to restore order, but lacking any of the relatively non-lethal alternatives available in the latest Troubles, they frequently resorted to gunfire (including machine-gun fire). By the time some order was restored at the weekend 18 civilians were dead (10 Catholics, 8 Protestants); at least 13 of these were shot by soldiers and 1 by the police. There were two particular 'hotspots': the lower Falls, especially around Kashmir Road, and the Short Strand in east Belfast, particularly around St Matthew's Catholic Church at the corner of Newtownards Road and Bryson Street.

Even worse was to follow at the end of August after the IRA killed a police inspector as he left church in Lisburn. There was almost continual violent disorder from 25 August until 1 September. The death toll was 34 (15 Catholics, 19 Protestants), but now the killing had taken on a more sectarian character. Only 14 of the victims were killed by the army (including the first army fatality); 9 were Protestants. This time there was more violence in the north of the city, particularly between the Crumlin Road and the Oldpark Road (the 'Bone') and the area around the north end of York Street.

By the end of 1920, 69 people had died; most of them civilians (31 Catholics and 33 Protestants). In nearly one-fifth of cases it was not possible to identify the group responsible (usually because they died in situations where at least two groups were firing into the area). Where responsibility could be attributed, 41 victims were killed by Crown forces, 8 by loyalists, 10 by republicans. Most were killed almost at random during widespread disturbances.

These patterns changed as the violence continued into 1921. The extensive, almost indiscriminate shootings continued; almost one-third of the deaths were unattributable. Gun battles between opposing areas could last for days on end, with or without the intervention of the Crown forces, with people caught up in the crossfire. However, there were two significant new factors. One was that some Catholics were now singled out for assassination. In 1920 there was only one incident of this, on the night of 26 September when three Catholics were killed in their homes in reprisal for the IRA killing of a police officer; it is almost certain that the killers were police officers. There were three similar incidents in 1921; as before, the victims were usually Catholics with IRA or Sinn Féin connections. The other group to be targeted were Catholics employed in bars or spirit groceries (later called off-licences) in Protestant areas. The second, and more important, new factor was that 1921 saw the deployment of the Ulster Special Constabulary on the streets of Belfast. Formed almost entirely of Protestants, including many members of the UVF, it took over from the army the main responsibility for policing Belfast's Catholic areas. Also, after the partition of Ireland and the establishment of a Unionist government in the north, the new Royal Ulster Constabulary (RUC) quickly became a predominantly Protestant force.

Another new feature in 1921, but still of minor significance, was the use of explosives – hand-thrown devices (usually improvised) rather than the much larger bombs seen since 1969. The first was thrown by Protestant rioters on 11 June, killing a Catholic. By the end of the year another 10 people had been killed by bombs. These included 4 Protestants killed when a bomb was tossed into a Shankill Road tram in Royal Avenue. As Alan Parkinson has commented: 'Trams, exhibiting distinctive destinations and mainly transporting people of one particular religious denomination through "hostile" districts, were easy and regular targets for those determined to maim and kill.'[5]

There were more deaths in 1921 than 1920: 120 civilians (65 Catholics, 55 Protestants), 5 IRA men, and 14 policemen. Where responsibility could be attributed, 28 per cent of deaths were caused by the Crown forces (unlike 1920, mostly by the police), 38 per cent by loyalists, 34 per cent by republicans. However, 1922 was worse still with 281 deaths: 260 civilians (170 Catholics, 90 Protestants), 3 IRA men, 2 soldiers, 16 policemen. Most of the attributable deaths were caused by loyalists (56 per cent); republicans were responsible for 25 per cent, and the Crown forces for 19 per cent (again, mostly killed by the police).

There were two especially notorious incidents in 1922, in Weaver Street and in Kinnaird Terrace. In the former, 6 Catholics (3 women and 3 girls) were killed when a bomb was thrown into a group of girls playing skipping games. The second, the so-called 'McMahon Massacre', saw 5 men of the McMahon family and their lodger shot in their home by police officers. Generally, by 1922 the killings were more organised than spontaneous. In January 1922 a government report stated: 'These outrages were not so much the outcome of party rioting on an organised scale, but were chiefly the result of sniping and cold blooded assassination of innocent victims … These … were committed by organised bands of hooligans as reprisals for deeds previously committed by the other side.'[6]

Mapping the Deaths

The deaths in 1920–22 and in 1969–99 were mapped onto the 51 electoral wards of Belfast District Council, as used by Paul Compton[7] (Figure 13.2). (Cases occurring on ward boundaries were assigned to one or other at random.) The spatial distribution of deaths during the 1920–22 period is shown in Figure 13.3. The most striking feature is that nearly half of the deaths (210) occurred in the Central ward, mostly in the streets north of Great George's Street. This was an area where the close proximity of Catholic and Protestant streets facilitated intercommunal violence; 119 Catholics died here, 73 Protestants. It was also the area that saw half of the police deaths. The lower Falls area (the wards of Falls, Clonard, and Grosvenor) saw over 60 deaths, but here three-quarters of the civilian victims were Catholics. East of the river, most of the deaths were in and around the Short Strand; in the Island and Ballymacarrett wards the majority (37) of the 66 civilian victims were Protestants. On the other hand, the more suburban (and middle-class) areas saw little or no fatal violence.

The deaths mark only the extreme end of the violence spectrum. There was widespread 'ethnic cleansing', especially of Catholics living within or adjacent to Protestant areas. In the riots of August 1920 alone, for example, about 400 Catholic families were forced out.[8] On several occasions entire Catholic streets were burned out. Over the three years as many as 23,000 Catholics may have been driven out;[9] 'the objective … [was] to drive the Catholics more and more into the Falls Road ghetto'.[10] Catholic businesses, especially spirit groceries, were looted and destroyed. At the same time, the IRA undertook a campaign of attacks on Protestant businesses. Again, solely in August 1920 there were '180 major fires, causing nearly £1 million worth of damage'.[11]

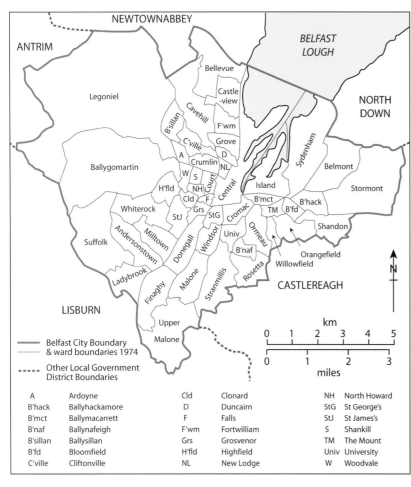

FIGURE 13.2
Belfast: wards used to map
conflict-related deaths

THE 1935 RIOTS

Although many of the underlying tensions remained, Belfast was peaceful for over a decade after the end of the violence in 1922. However, when sectarian violence did recur, in the 1930s, the focus was again the area around the docks, north of Great George's

Street. Here, as in the 1920s, 'Protestants and Catholics were intermixed to a greater extent than in most working-class areas of Belfast, but micro-level segregation was intense'.[12] There was trouble in the area in the early summer of 1935, but the main rioting was triggered by an Orange march along York Street on 12 July. There followed ten days and nights of violence marked by attacks on homes (on the night of 13 July alone 56 Catholic houses were torched) and shootings; 10 people were killed.

Although most of the conflict centred in the Dock area, there were also outbreaks of rioting and 'cleansing' in the Old Lodge and Village areas. Many of the Catholic families forced out of these areas (usually by their Protestant neighbours) moved into a new estate still under construction at Glenard in Ardoyne; in the process, as well as occupying empty houses, they displaced Protestants who had recently moved into what was intended to be a Protestant area. As Anthony Hepburn observed: 'In social terms the riots were a phase in the process, partly ongoing and partly cyclical, of ethnic segregation in the city.'[13]

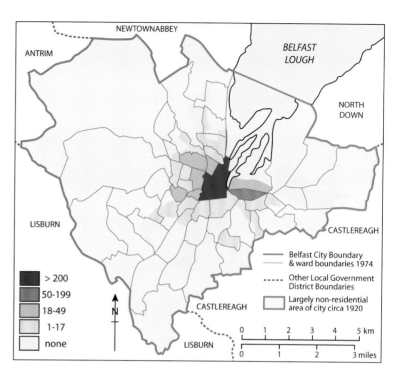

FIGURE 13.3
Belfast: conflict-related deaths, 1920–22

THE 'TROUBLES'
1969–1999

The most recent outbreak of social violence began, in Belfast, in August 1969 (Figure 13.4). From then until the end of 1999 some 1,527 deaths occurred in the city.[14] It should also be noted that almost two-thirds of these deaths occurred in the eight-year period 1970–77, and indeed almost 20 per cent in the one year – 1972 (Figure 13.5). Table 13.1 shows the distribution of deaths in four categories. These figures immediately indicate one significant difference from the 1920s. In the earlier period civilians accounted for 90 per cent of the victims, whereas in 1969–99 they constituted only 67 per cent. By contrast, in the earlier period security forces personnel accounted for only 7 per cent of the victims, in the latter they accounted for 18 per cent.

We also see a different picture when we try to make some assessment of the direct responsibility for the deaths. In both periods there were deaths that were unattributable because those killed were victims of crossfire (that is, at least two, and sometimes three, groups were firing into or through the area) and not (as far as could be ascertained) directly targeted. In the 1920s such deaths

FIGURE 13.4
Corner of Falls Road and Conway Street after rioting, August 1969

IRISH TIMES

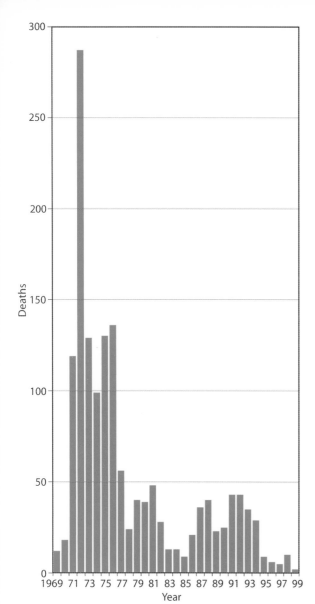

FIGURE 13.5
Conflict-related deaths per
annum, Belfast, 1969–99

TABLE 13.1
Conflict-related Deaths, 1969–99

Civilians	1,018 (661 Catholics, 338 Protestants, 18 other, 1 unattributed)
Security forces personnel	274 (201 army, including UDR; 73 RUC)
Other government appointees	20 (e.g. prison officers, judges)
Paramilitaries	215 (136 republican, 79 loyalist)

SOURCE: see endnotes 3 and 14

accounted for 22 per cent of all deaths, but in the period since 1969 for only 5 per cent.[15] Where deaths could be attributed, again a difference emerges (Table 13.2). A key difference between 1969 and 1920 was the almost total absence of firearms amongst the civilian protagonists at the later date. When violence broke out in 1920, the paramilitary groups on both sides had access to stocks of rifles and pistols. One of the reasons for the split in the IRA that led to the formation of the Provisionals in December 1969 was the almost total lack of weapons available to the IRA in Belfast to defend Catholic areas.[16] However, the same applied within the loyalist community, where the UVF had only been re-formed, on a very small scale, in 1965.[17] Thus, although the sectarian rioting in the city from 14–16 August was very extensive, 5 of the 7 who died were killed by the police; most of the firearms that were used by civilians appear to have been shotguns.

However, both sides were quick to acquire new weapons and to adopt new tactics. Although rioting – both sectarian and that directed mainly against the security forces – continued after 1969 (with very intense outbreaks in Catholic areas associated with the introduction of internment without trial in 1971 and the hunger-strike deaths in 1981), its significance as a context for killing diminished significantly. Whereas in the 1920s most deaths occurred against a simultaneous background of other violent events, the dominant pattern since 1969 was one where deaths tended to happen out of the blue. If the archetypal sectarian victim of the 1920s was someone killed when gunmen fired into a residential area, the victim of the later period was assassinated.

Moreover, there has been a greater complexity to the patterns of violence since 1969. In addition to sectarian violence, there has been a significant element of intra-communal violence; for example, feuds within and between paramilitary groups (more republican and loyalist paramilitaries have been killed by their own side than by their opponents) and the killing of informers. Second, the IRA (largely freed by the security forces from its traditional role of defending Catholic areas against loyalist attacks) waged a much more extensive guerrilla war against the security forces.

These differences are reflected in different spatial patterns to the violence since 1969. The overall pattern of deaths is shown in Figure 13.6. As in the 1920s, most deaths have

TABLE 13.2
Percentage of Conflict-related Deaths Attributed to Security Forces, Republicans, and Loyalists, 1920–22 and 1969–99

Deaths (%)	1920–22	1969–99
Attributed to:		
Security forces	29	12
Republicans	26	45
Loyalists	45	43

SOURCE: see endnotes 3 and 14

been in the Central ward. However, the 144 deaths here are significantly less than the 210 in the same area in the 1920s, and account for only 9 per cent of all deaths, compared with over 40 per cent in the earlier period. Another difference is the distribution within the Central ward. Previously most deaths were in the north of the ward, the result of sectarian violence. Since 1969 only 33 deaths have been in this area, and nearly half of these were the result of the loyalist bombing of McGurk's bar in North Queen Street when 15 people were killed, including 3 women and 2 children (the worst act of violence in Belfast in the entire century). A major reason for this shift was the IRA bombing campaign in the city centre.

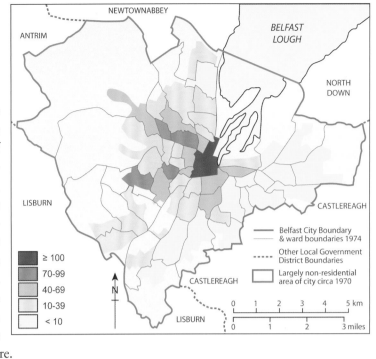

Another difference from the 1920s is that the area around Short Strand, while still a violent area, has not figured as prominently. More significant have been the Ardoyne, Crumlin, Clonard, and Whiterock wards. Marie-Thérèse Fay, Mike Morrissey and Marie Smyth,[18] looking just at the deaths of residents and taking into account ward populations, found that the Falls, Ardoyne, St Anne's[19] and Clonard wards had the highest death rates within Belfast. It is also clear from a comparison of Figures 13.3 and 13.6 that the violence since 1969 has been more widespread; only the Stormont ward has been free of deaths. Clearly a major factor in this has been the growth of Belfast since the 1920s, especially the construction of public housing in the west.

Given the changes in the forms of violence, from rioting to assassination and guerrilla warfare, we might expect to see a change in the spatial patterns. Figures 13.7 and 13.8

FIGURE 13.6
Belfast: conflict-related deaths, 1969–99

Bottom left
FIGURE 13.7
Belfast: ten wards with highest numbers of conflict-related deaths, 1969–79

Bottom right
FIGURE 13.8
Belfast: ten wards with highest numbers of conflict-related deaths, 1980–99

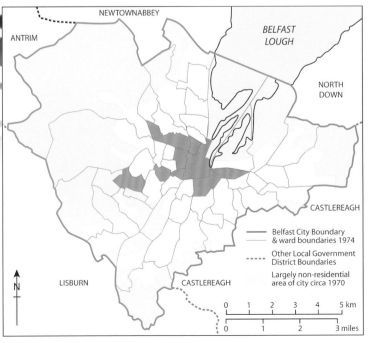

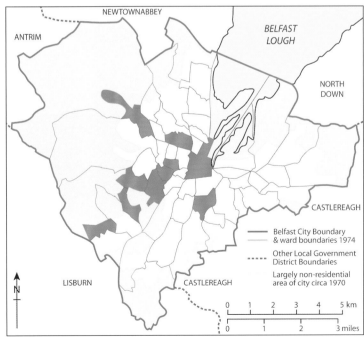

show the 10 wards with the highest number of deaths in 1969–79 and in 1980–99 respectively. Most noticeably, they show a shift from centre to periphery, particularly in the Catholic wards fanning out from the Falls Road. The prominence of Ligoniel is linked to loyalist assassinations of Catholics; it was a common area to which victims were taken before they were killed.

We can also look at the spatial patterns generated by the two main components of the violence: between republicans and the security forces; between republicans and loyalists (Figures 13.9 and 13.10). Figures 13.11 and 13.12 try to capture the former dimension. First, Figure 13.11 shows the distribution of deaths resulting from republican attacks on the security forces. Broadly speaking, the wards with the highest values form a map of Catholic Belfast. Second, Figure 13.12 shows the distribution of deaths of people killed by the security forces. As most occasions on which the security forces have used deadly force are linked to their campaign against the IRA, not surprisingly the pattern of the wards with the highest incidence is also largely a map of Catholic areas.

The next pair of figures (13.13 and 13.14) shows the ward distribution of Catholics killed by loyalists and Protestants killed by republicans respectively.[20] They demonstrate, with one exceptional ward in each case (Ballymacarrett), the extent to which sectarian violence has been concentrated west of the Lagan. Broadly, these are interface areas.

If we combine the results of Figures 13.12 to 13.14, we can identify two particular 'zones of violence' within the city, shown in Figure 13.15. First, North Belfast, comprising Bellevue, Cavehill, Castleview, Fortwilliam, Crumlin, Cliftonville, Grove, Duncairn, New Lodge and Ardoyne wards. Second, the Falls, comprising North Howard, Falls, Clonard, St James, Grosvenor, Milltown, Suffolk, Andersonstown, Whiterock and Ladybrook. A key difference between these two zones is that while the latter is very highly ethnically homogenous, the former is a patchwork of Catholic, Protestant and mixed areas.

Bottom left
FIGURE 13.9
Republican memorial,
Joy Street, Belfast

STEPHEN A. ROYLE

Bottom right
FIGURE 13.10
Loyalist memorial, Lower
Newtownards Road, Belfast

STEPHEN A. ROYLE

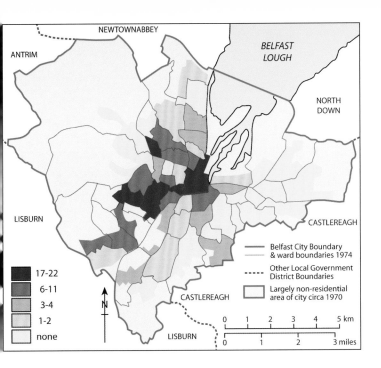

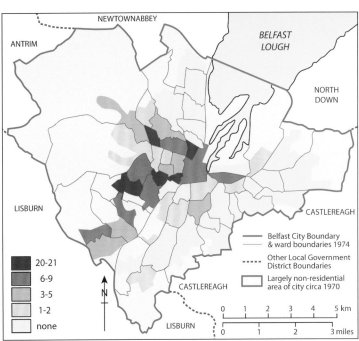

Over half of the deaths from 1969 onwards have occurred in these two zones; 362 in North Belfast, 440 in the Falls. However, the nature of the violence has differed between them. Firstly, in terms of the relative involvement of the three parties to the conflict, in North Belfast, the security forces were responsible for 13 per cent of the deaths, republicans for 34 per cent, loyalists for 44 per cent. By contrast, in the Falls, the security forces were responsible for 18 per cent of the deaths, republicans and loyalists for 58 per cent and 18 per cent respectively (with the latter being concentrated at the inner-city end of the zone). These differences are matched by differences in the characteristics of the victims. In the Falls, 28 per cent of the victims were members of the security forces, 46 per cent were Catholics (including paramilitaries), and 8 per cent were Protestants. By contrast, in North Belfast, 19 per cent were members of the security forces, 47 per cent were Catholics, and 20 per cent were Protestants.

Essentially North Belfast is a zone of communal conflict (with a degree of guerrilla warfare in the Ardoyne area). Over much of the city, the patterns of ethnic segregation have

Top left
FIGURE 13.11
Belfast: deaths resulting from republican attacks on security forces, 1969–99

Top right
FIGURE 13.12
Belfast: deaths attributed to security forces, 1969–99

Bottom left
FIGURE 13.13
Belfast: Catholics killed by loyalists, 1969–99

Bottom right
FIGURE 13.14
Belfast: Protestants killed by republicans, 1969–99

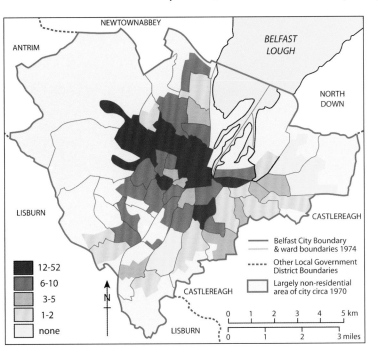

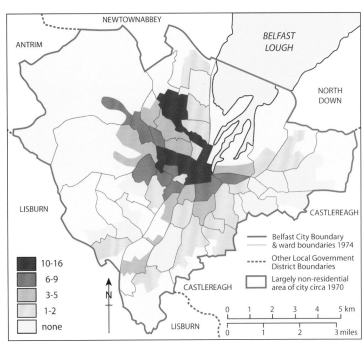

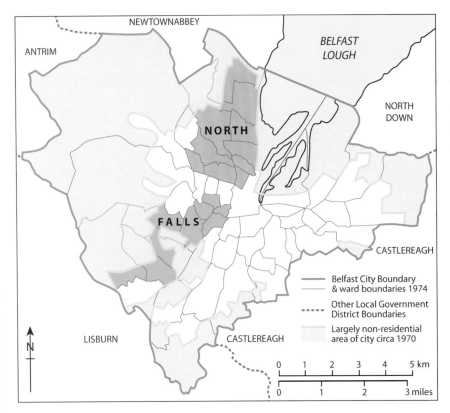

FIGURE 13.15
Belfast: zones of violence, 1969–99

been fairly static since 1969; population movements have tended to reinforce, not change, the existing distribution. North Belfast, on the other hand, is in flux; in particular, the Catholic population is expanding into formerly Protestant areas. This change is resented, and resisted, by many local Protestants. Moreover, the patchwork pattern of settlement facilitates violence. In our essay on residential mobility in Belfast, Fred Boal and I pointed out: 'Firstly, the areas are relatively easy to penetrate; their smallness means that they are quickly traversed … Secondly, all possible target areas are near to secure areas such as the Shankill or Ardoyne. Murderers can very soon be back in the safety of their own territory.'[21]

The Falls, by contrast, is the zone (within Belfast) where the guerrilla war between republicans and the government has been focused (with an element of communal violence along the periphery in the inner city). It is the area with the largest and most homogenous Catholic population that can provide the 'water' for the paramilitary 'fish'.[22] It is the area that combines the most targets for republican paramilitaries, in terms of security forces' patrols and bases, with the most secure refuges.

EXPLOSIONS

In terms of the weapons deployed by the paramilitary groups, the most striking development since 1969 has been the widespread use of explosive devices of all sizes and forms. In the 1920s all that seems to have been available to the paramilitaries on either side was improvised hand grenades (no doubt familiar to men who had made them in the trenches of World War I); buildings were destroyed by arson, not by bombing. From the 1970s onwards the paramilitaries acquired (albeit with a fatal learning curve) the means and the skills to deploy a wide range of explosive devices in a variety of situations. Consequently 17 per cent of the deaths in Belfast between 1969 and 1999 were caused by explosions (265 in all, including 7 in an explosion in Lower Donegall Street in 1972; see Figure 13.16), compared with only 6 per cent in the 1920s.

Broadly, we can identify three main dimensions to the use of explosives in the conflict. First, sectarian, with attacks on buildings (especially public houses) and residential areas. Second, economic, with the IRA's campaign against commercial and business premises intended to increase the British government's financial costs through having to compensate the owners. Third, military, with attacks by the IRA on security forces personnel and installations.

Not surprisingly, the sectarian attacks were the most deadly; they were intended to kill and were launched against 'soft' targets. In all, 115 people were killed, most of them

(78 per cent) in attacks on public houses (the carnage at McGurk's bar has already been mentioned). The attacks on military and police targets killed 58 people, 17 of them civilians. The commercial campaign caused the fewest fatalities, 33 people. (In fact, more deaths, 52 [mostly paramilitaries], were caused by accidental or premature explosions.) Generally, the attacks on commercial targets were accompanied by clear warnings that minimised casualties. However, this was not always the case, the most notorious example being 'Bloody Friday' (21 July 1972) when 9 people were killed and 130 seriously injured in a wave of IRA bombings across the city.

The spatial distribution of these three dimensions has differed because of the distribution of potential targets. The initial focus of the commercial bombings was the city centre with its high status, high profile targets. (The Europa Hotel in Great Victoria Street was reputedly the most bombed building in Europe in the 1970s.) When the government responded by erecting a security fence around the central core, attackers were forced to switch to using much smaller, incendiary-type devices in this area and to range more widely across the city, especially along the main roads such as Antrim Road and Lisburn Road. However, most (nearly 80 per cent) of the deaths from property attacks have been in the city centre.

FIGURE 13.16
The aftermath of an explosion caused by an IRA car bomb in Lower Donegall Street in March 1972, which killed 7 and injured 150

Because of the attackers' reliance on cars to deliver the bombs and then escape, the sectarian attacks have been concentrated along the main roads, in particular Newtownards Road, Ormeau Road, Shankill Road and North Queen Street. This is especially true of attacks on public houses. Bomb attacks on the security forces have been most common in the Falls zone, with most of the fatalities occurring in the inner wards.

POPULATION MOVEMENTS

As in earlier outbreaks of sectarian violence, people living in 'border' areas between segregated areas and those in mixed areas (especially those in the minority in the area) have been threatened or attacked.[23] For many, the response has been flight. This, in turn, can lead to a knock-on effect whereby other households are displaced to accommodate the refugees. Even in the absence of overt violence, the possibility of it can be enough to persuade people to move to what are perceived as safer areas.[24]

John Darby and Geoffrey Morris estimated that

> the total enforced movement in the Belfast area between August 1969 and February 1973 is between 8,000 families (minimum) and approximately 15,000 families (maximum). Based on an average family size of four, the figure suggested by our investigation, this indicates a total of between 30,000 and 60,000 people who were forced to evacuate their homes – roughly between 6.6 per cent and 11.8 per cent [sic] of the population of the Belfast urban area.[25]

In peaceful times there tends to be a lessening of segregation in Belfast, particularly as Catholic households move into areas that were predominantly Protestant.[26] Violence reverses this trend. Paul Doherty and Michael Poole,[27] using census data from 1971, 1981 and 1991 found that ethnic segregation in the city had risen strongly since the start of the Troubles, especially in the 1970s. Although the rate of change may have declined (mainly because most of those 'at risk' areas have already been consolidated), it has not ceased, especially in north Belfast where territory continues to be contested.

BELFAST — SHAPED BY VIOLENCE?

Winston Churchill observed: 'We shape our buildings; thereafter they shape us.' The social geography of Belfast – especially of its working-class neighbourhoods – cannot be understood without the role of communal violence. Nor can the patterns of that violence be understood without the context provided by the social geography. In any form of social violence, from rioting to international war, the control of space is of crucial importance. Territory offers security from attack and an opportunity to launch attacks. In our research on the social ecology of urban violence, Fred Boal and I found that 'where social conflict is endemic, it is often misleading to regard social violence as either a cause or an effect of social geography. It is both simultaneously, an inseparable component of the urban system.'[28]

Belfast today is a city whose very fabric bears the imprint of a violent past – but its history also shows that it can overcome those patterns.

A BELFAST BLITZ ADDENDUM

Frederick W. Boal

While the Troubles were of intermittent occurrence through much of the twentieth century, the German air raids of 1941 – the 'blitz' – were short, sharp and of savage intensity. We do not need to rehearse here the details of these raids. This has already been done by Brian Barton in his excellent book: *The Blitz: Belfast in the War Years*.[29] However, it still

FIGURE 13.17
Deaths, Easter Tuesday air raid, 15–16 April 1941 (residential addresses of victims)

(SOURCE LISTS HELD IN PRONI, LA65/3AG/2)

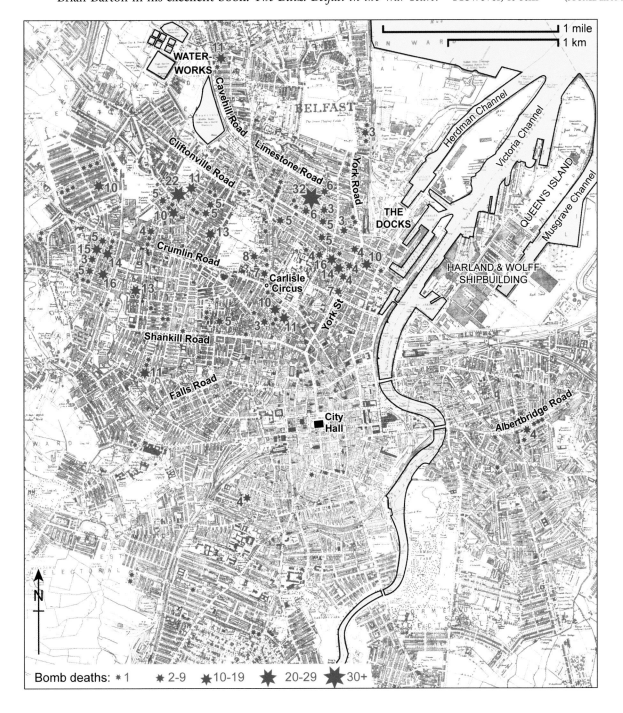

Bomb deaths: ✳ 1   ✴ 2-9   ✦ 10-19   ✯ 20-29   ★ 30+

233

FIGURE 13.18
Salvage crews in Westbourne
Street off the Newtownards
Road after the air raid of
4–5 May 1941

PRONI

is important for us to attempt to record within the covers of *Enduring City* the main dimensions of the Belfast blitz. Most strikingly, this 'event' was compressed into a period of only one month – from the 'Dockside Raid' of 7–8 April 1941 to what one might call the mild aftershock attack of the night of 5–6 May. In the Public Record Office of Northern Ireland there is to be found a street map of the city, with four areas pencil-shaded in different colours: green for the area impacted by the Dockside Raid, red for the 'Easter Tuesday Raid' of 15–16 April, blue for the 'Fire Raid' of 4–5 May, and black for the unnamed raid of 5–6 May. Concentrating on the first three (and, by far, the most significant) raids, we see that all left their own distinctive brutal footprints, each overlapping but not fully corresponding with the other.

The Dockside Raid, as its name suggests, particularly impacted on the docks and shipyard, with what one might now call collateral damage to residential areas in the inner east and inner north parts of the city. Thirteen people were killed.

The Easter Tuesday Raid caused some damage to the shipyard. However, it was the inner north residential side of the city that took the full brunt of the attack. In all, almost 900 people were killed (Figure 13.17) and 3,500 houses destroyed. It is likely that the port area with its shipbuilding and aircraft industries was the intended target, but errors on the part of the Luftwaffe led to many bomb loads being shed a few hundred metres astray. A description of the aftermath of this attack, as penned by J.B. Meehan for the Ministry of Public Security, provides us with the following:

> At daybreak the County Antrim side of the city presented a gruesome picture. The ruin fringed roads were blocked with great heaps of smoking debris and pocked with acrid smelling craters. Water ran through the rubble in rivulets, gas mains still spouted fountains of flame and walls crashed everywhere now and then where the firefighters still fought the flames.
>
> Mud and water, and everywhere the smell of wet, charred wood. Through this desolate scene, clambering over the rubble and picking their way over the maze of hose, an unending trek of civilians made their way to Rest and Feeding centres in the unblitzed area of the city. Many were carrying all their worldly belongings in small attaché cases or in knotted pillow slips. Others returned from their 'hideouts' to stand silent and benumbed before the wreckage of what once were their homes, or to search forlornly in the wreckage for belongings.[30]

The Fire Raid seems likely to have had the objective of destroying that part of the shipyard and aircraft industries that had escaped destruction three weeks earlier. This objective was largely achieved, but it would appear that, unlike the earlier raids, the city centre was also on the target list, where the tactical use of a mix of incendiaries and high explosives had a devastating effect. Residential Belfast was less severely affected than on Easter Tuesday, but considerable death and destruction was caused by high explosives in the area of the Newtownards Road in the east of the city (Figure 13.18) and also in the inner north. German records disclose that 95,992 incendiaries were used, together with 237 tons (240.8 tonnes) of high explosive. The death toll this time was much lower than in the Easter Tuesday Raid, with 191 deaths recorded. This reduction was due in large measure to the more effective targeting of the harbour industrial area, together with the fact that many people had fled the city to spend the night in the surrounding countryside (the so-called 'ditchers').

The raid of the following night, 5–6 May, was a mere pinprick, though not for the people of Ravenscroft Avenue, where a parachute mine exploded, killing 14. It is thought that this raid was carried out by a few aircraft that had diverted from a major attack on Clydeside.

One cannot help placing the death and destruction of the blitz alongside the death toll in the most recent Troubles or that of the first few days of the Battle of the Somme in 1916 (see chapter 12). About 1,000 people were killed in Belfast within one month in the blitz; more than 1,500 were killed in Belfast over a period of thirty years in the Troubles (though almost 1,000 of these occurred between 1971 and 1979), while 5,500 soldiers in the 36th (Ulster) Division became casualties (killed, missing or wounded) during the first two days of the Battle of the Somme (a large, but unknown, number of these being from Belfast). Generated internally or externally as they may have been, all of these events were severely traumatic experiences for Belfast.

NOTES

1   Boyd, Andrew (1969) *Holy war in Belfast,* Grove Press: Tralee.

2   Bardon, Jonathan (1992) *A history of Ulster,* Blackstaff Press: Belfast, p. 466.

3   The data for this chapter are based mainly on my own research in the Belfast newspapers for the two periods. However, other publications give different figures for the number of deaths in 1920–22. Budge and O'Leary (see note 10) give a higher total of 544 deaths, but do not give a source. The *Belfast Telegraph* for 18 September 1922 stated that in the period 1 July 1920 to 18 September 1922 there had been 436 deaths in Belfast, comprising 189 Protestants and 247 Catholics; my data give 489 deaths (including 35 members of the security forces). The most quoted statistics are those given by Farrell, p. 62 (see note 8): 'Between July 1920 and July 1922, 453 people had been killed in Belfast, 37 members of the Crown forces and 416 civilians; 257 Catholics, 157 Protestants and two of unknown religion.' These seem to be taken from Kenna, G.B. (1922) *Facts and figures of the Belfast pogrom 1920–1922,* O'Connell Publishing Company: Dublin. Some of the discrepancy may arise from my inclusion of all accidental deaths; see note 14.

4   Off-duty part-time members of the Crown forces who died in circumstances where their official role was irrelevant (e.g. shot at random during widespread disturbances) were classified as civilians.

5   Parkinson, Alan F. (2004) *Belfast's unholy war,* Four Courts Press: Dublin, p. 181.

6   *Ministry of Home Affairs, Divisional Commissioners Bi-monthly Reports,* 16 January 1922, Public Record Office of Northern Ireland (PRONI), HA5/312.

7   Compton, Paul A. (1978) *Northern Ireland: a census atlas,* Gill and Macmillan: Dublin, p. 8.

8   Farrell, Michael (1976) *Northern Ireland: the Orange state,* Pluto Press: London.

9   Bardon (1992) *A history of Ulster.*

10 Budge, Ian, and O'Leary, Cornelius (1973) *Belfast: approach to crisis, a study of Belfast politics, 1613–1970,* Macmillan: London, p. 143.

11 Bardon (1992) *A history of Ulster,* p. 473.

12 Hepburn, Anthony C. (1990) 'The Belfast riots of 1935', *Social History,* 15.1, pp. 75–96.

13 Hepburn (1990) 'The Belfast riots', p. 96.

14 As for the 1920–22 period, the main source of data for this section has been newspaper reports. These have been complemented by the invaluable work of David McKittrick, Seamus Kelters, Brian Feeney and Chris Thornton in their 1999 book *Lost Lives,* Mainstream Publishing: Edinburgh. In common with their approach, I have included deaths arising from accidents with security forces' weapons. Official tabulations normally exclude these, while including accidental deaths from paramilitary weapons.

15 The difference also reflects the different degree of forensic input to inquests. In the 1920s inquests were held much sooner after deaths than in the later period with little or no evidence other than from eyewitnesses. (In one case, a man was shot in the morning and the inquest was held in the afternoon in a building opposite the murder site.)

16 Moloney, Ed (2002) *A secret history of the IRA,* Allen Lane: London.

17 Bruce, Steve (1992) *The Red Hand: Protestant paramilitaries in Northern Ireland,* Oxford University Press: Oxford.

18 Fay, Marie-Thérèse, Morrissey, Mike, and Smyth, Marie (1997) *Mapping Troubles-related deaths in Northern Ireland, 1969–1994,* INCORE: Londonderry.

19 St Anne's ward, used in the 1981 census, comprises the former Court ward and most of the former Central ward.

20 These two figures slightly oversimplify the sectarian conflict, as both sides have killed their co-religionists accidentally or by mistake while intending to kill members of the other group.

21 Murray, Russell, and Boal, Frederick W. (1980) 'Forced residential mobility in Belfast 1969–1972', in Harbison, Jeremy, and Harbison, Joan (eds) *A society under stress,* Open Books: Shepton Mallet, pp. 25–30.

22 Sluka, J.A. (1989) *Hearts and minds, water and fish: support for the IRA and INLA in a Northern Irish ghetto,* JAI Press: Greenwich, CT.

23 Darby, John (1990) 'Intimidation and interaction in a small Belfast community: the water and the fish', in John Darby, Nicholas Dodge and Anthony C. Hepburn (eds) *Political violence: Ireland in a comparative perspective,* Appletree Press: Belfast.

24 Murray, Russell C., and Osborne, Robert (1977) 'Segregation on Horn Drive – a cautionary tale', *New Society,* 21 April.

25 Darby, John, and Morris, Geoffrey (1974) *Intimidation in housing,* Northern Ireland Community Relations Commission: Belfast.

26 Poole, Michael A., and Boal, Frederick W. (1973) 'Religious residential segregation in Belfast in mid-1969: a multi-level analysis', in Brian D. Clark and Michael B. Gleave (eds) *Social patterns in cities,* Institute of British Geographers, Special Publication No. 5, pp. 1–40.

27 Doherty, Paul, and Poole, Michael (1997) 'Ethnic residential segregation in Belfast, Northern Ireland', *Geographical Review,* 87.4, pp. 520–36.

28 Murray, Russell C., and Boal, Frederick W. (1979) 'The social ecology of urban violence', in David T. Herbert and David M. Smith (eds) *Social problems and the city: new perspectives,* Oxford University Press, Oxford.

29 Barton, Brian (1989) *The Blitz: Belfast in the war years,* Blackstaff Press: Belfast.

30 Ministry of Public Security (1941) *Report on air raids,* PRONI, CAB/3A/68/B.

Mind and Body

14

Health in Belfast

The Vital Statistics
of Poverty

Alun Evans

Writing in 1898, Frank McGibben made predictions about the state of things in Belfast a century later in *Belfast in the Year 2000 AD*[1] Frank, a blind baker, had undoubtedly got the idea from Edward Bellamy's *Looking Backward*, which was published in 1887. Bellamy had predicted state medicine and credit cards in Boston by the year 2000. McGibben does not do as well in his predictions but, in fairness, he does hint at some form of social welfare, for women at least.

FIGURE 14.1
Carrick Hill Place, off Peter's Hill, in the 1960s

KEN MCNALLY

Although the beginning of the twentieth century was a time of relative economic prosperity in Belfast,[2] based on linen, shipbuilding, rope-making and tobacco, there was still considerable destitution, much unrelieved, as the social security safety net had a very wide mesh. A link between poverty and ill health was well recognised in the eighteenth century in the concept of 'Medical Police' (in the sense of public administration). The French/Bavarian physician Johann Peter Frank saw 'the extreme poverty of the people' as 'the richest source of disease'.[3] In England, Thomas Percival, Edwin Chadwick and Benjamin Guy Babington, among others, investigated these issues. It was not until around the end of the nineteenth century, however, that studies carried out by Charles Booth in London and Seebohm Rowntree in York incontrovertibly established the link between poverty and disease.[4]

In Belfast a stark example of a link between poverty and mortality was the phenomenon of the 'Co. quarter'. The Belfast Co-operative Society paid its customers a quarterly dividend but the poor and the improvident often ran up a slate, which also had to be cleared on a quarterly basis. Even into the late 1960s (Figure 14.1), a peak in housewives attempting suicide could reputedly be anticipated in hospital casualties on the Co. quarter; some, inevitably, were successful.

A rudimentary dispensary system had been established in Dublin in 1782,[5] and this was extended widely across Ireland by the Medical Charities Act 1851, largely in response to the Great Famine of 1845–9.[6] This divided the island into 723 dispensary districts. A black ticket entitled patients to a visit to a dispensary; a red ticket denoted a domiciliary visit (known in the trade as a 'scarlet runner'). This system persisted in what was to become the Republic of Ireland until after the passing of the Irish Health Act 1970, which introduced the General Medical Services; in Northern Ireland the system operated until the inception of the National Health Service in 1948.

FIGURE 14.2
Paupers outside the Union
Workhouse on the Lisburn Road
in 1903, awaiting the royal visit

ULSTER MUSEUM

In the eighteenth century the Irish parliament had established infirmaries, which were supported by public and philanthropic sources. By 1841 there were thirty-nine of these, and after 1898 they came under the control of the newly created county councils. There were also mental asylums and purely charitable hospitals. In 1838 the English Poor Law Amendment Act, with some modifications, was extended to Ireland and over the next thirteen years 119 workhouses were built. The system evolved, particularly in 1847 with the Poor Law Extension Act, which introduced Outdoor Relief, and in 1862 the non-destitute sick were admitted. Subsequently the Local Government (Ireland) Act 1898 gave the Poor Law Guardians greater scope for providing relief. This could take two forms: indoor (that is, within the workhouse; see Figure 14.2), or outdoor (that is, outside the workhouse). It should be remembered that workhouses were made as unpleasant for the inmates as possible to deter people from entering them. As we shall see, the Belfast Poor Law Guardians, based on the site of what is now Belfast City Hospital, were particularly miserly and discriminatory in operating the system.[7] The Republic abolished the Poor Law, which it had inherited in 1924, while in England and Wales the powers were transferred to local authorities in 1928. In Northern Ireland, however, the Poor Law continued until 1948.

THE LIBERAL REFORMS

The discovery, around the time of the Boer War (1900–02), that 40 per cent of the potential army recruits were medically unfit to serve had a galvanising effect on public health concerns in Britain and Ireland. Indeed, a much higher proportion of men from 'classic' slum areas such as Salford and south Wales were rejected.[8] This led to the setting up of the Inter-Departmental Committee on Physical Deterioration. There were other reports around that time and, in 1903, a Viceregal Commission on the Poor Laws was established to try to find 'a more economical system for the relief of the sick, and all classes of destitute poor in Ireland'. The commission's report expressed greatest concern about tuberculosis.[9] It recommended the preservation of the dispensary system in Ireland.

Despite the deliberations of both these bodies, the government adopted an entirely different approach after the Liberal landslide of 1906: the Liberal reforms. It had been recognised that the poor had had a raw deal. These reforms are usually associated with David Lloyd George, but Winston Churchill, then a Liberal, had a considerable hand in their drafting. The Non-contributory Pensions Act 1908 established the right to a pension at the age of seventy years. It used a person's childhood entries in the manuscript enumerators' returns of the 1841 and/or 1851 censuses as proof of age or, failing this, it is reported, a subject's recall of the Big Wind of 1839 was accepted as evidence in Ireland. The National Health Insurance Act 1911 applied to Ireland but there were important differences.[10] In England it was financed by employer and employee on the insurance premium principle, as there was a long tradition of friendly societies. It was applied compulsorily to a restricted class of employees, but not their dependants. It covered limited medical benefits from a general practitioner and was administered by insurance committees, which were quite separate from local authorities. In Ireland, on the other hand, clauses were inserted that denied medical benefit to those insured (but did provide maternity benefit). This came about because of opposition from the more affluent of the medical profession and the Catholic hierarchy, and bungling by the Irish Medical Association, which represented the dispensary doctors.

Ireland had thus failed to establish an important element of a welfare state, but at least there still remained the dispensary system. From Ireland's point of view, the most crucial of these reforms was the Maternity and Child Welfare Act 1918. Fifty-four thousand Irish soldiers were to die in the Great War and the birth rate had fallen considerably. Allied to this were the high infant mortality rates, which, although slightly lower than in England and Scotland, showed no sign of falling. Around this time it was pointed out that the infant mortality of 90 per 1,000 births in Ireland was higher than the mortality rate for soldiers at the front – 'a baby had a greater chance of dying than its father in France'.[11] Until then, apathy surrounded infant and maternal mortality and, according to Ruth Barrington, this was due to 'the invidious assumption that infant mortality was nature's way of weeding out the unfit early in life'.[12] The Maternity and Child Welfare Act was long overdue.

SOCIAL DEPRIVATION

FIGURE 14.3
Socialist *Health in Belfast* pamphlet, 1944; cover illustration by Marjorie Olley, who studied at the Belfast Art College.

BELFAST CENTRAL LIBRARY

One of the Liberal reforms that Ireland missed out on was the 1907 Education Act, which had introduced a school health service. The Belfast Health Commission of 1908 had highlighted the unsatisfactory state of schools in so wealthy a city and after Northern Ireland was created in 1921, and the Education Act of 1923 was passed, things generally improved in the North. School meals for needy children were provided by 1926 (see chapter 15). Belfast's economy, however, was not faring so well by this time: by 1932 unemployment had risen to 32 per cent (twice that of Great Britain) and it was to peak in 1938.[13] Protestant workers tended to be skilled and the Catholics unskilled, and therefore poorer. The Orange Order had Lodges for various trades – for example Frank McGibben was a member of the Bakers' Lodge – which helped to ensure steady employment.[14] Lily Coleman, chairman of the Belfast Board of Guardians in 1928–29, liked to remark to Catholic claimants with large families, 'there's no poverty under the blankets'.[15] The Guardians were so obsessed with saving money that it was like the old joke about the farmer who wanted to see how little he could feed his horse, but unfortunately the horse died before he could finish the experiment. The link between poverty and sickness has already been noted. By 1932 the Guardians were saving so much money that a mere 5 per cent of approximately 100,000 unemployed in Belfast were receiving relief. In protest the unemployed of both religions united in demonstrations. An Unemployment Act was passed in 1934 and the next year Outdoor Relief was being provided. In 1938 the Guardians were replaced by two commissioners: it was found that the Guardians had been rewarding themselves with free groceries and coal and there was an unexplained purchase of 546 yards of corduroy. Moreover, the workhouse master was creaming off four-fifths of the inmates' pensions for his personal use.

There were more scandals to come: in 1941 malpractice at Whiteabbey Sanatorium was investigated.[16] The medical superintendent and the matron were rumoured to be having an affair – she went to the extraordinary lengths of reading a letter to the inquiry, written by a leading gynaecologist, to confirm that she was a virgin. The Corporation Tuberculosis Committee was also involved in malpractice at the sanatorium, having purchased highly unsuitable blackout material and tried to force the purchase of an unfavourable site for a new sanatorium at an exorbitant price. The committee was stood down. The Republic had its own scandal: the Irish Hospital Sweepstakes had operated from 1930, but, although the Sweepstakes had funded the construction of the Irish health system, questions were asked in the 1970s as to whether some funds might have found their way into the coffers of the IRA, the pockets of mailmen in Canada or have been made available to certain politicians in Dublin.[17]

Thomas Carnwath, an Ulsterman from Strabane and an ex-deputy chief medical officer in England, reported on Belfast's health services late in 1941.[18] In terms of several health indicators Belfast was doing pretty badly. Moreover, the administration of services was haphazard, being split between the Poor Law, the government and Belfast Corporation. To make matters worse, the Corporation had woefully failed to provide housing and adequate air-raid shelters and this was to be pitifully exposed by the German air raids of April and May 1941. The moderator of the Presbyterian Church was shocked by the appearance of those who had been left homeless by the blitz: 'wretched people, very undersized and underfed down-and-out-looking men and women ... Is it creditable to us that there should be such people in a Christian country?'[19] If he had read the report by his own Church's Social Service Committee published two years earlier, he would not have been so surprised.[20] Carnwath was responsible for the establishment, in 1941, of the Northern Ireland Tuberculosis Authority (it was in operation until 1959) and, in 1942, the introduction of free school milk.

THE NATIONAL HEALTH SERVICE

British economist William Beveridge's *Report on Social Insurance and Allied Services*, published in 1942, led to the establishment of the National Health Service (NHS) in 1948. The Socialist Medical Association, founded in 1930 to replace an earlier body, did much to influence the Labour Party to set up state medicine, but it was appalled when its recommendations were watered down. Writing about the association in 1971, Stark Murray stated: 'The Belfast Branch produced its own pamphlet [in 1944] which set the ball rolling on the form of an organized service for Northern Ireland'[21] (Figure 14.3). The pamphlet quoted from the Carnwath report and included data demonstrating how badly Belfast was doing in terms of health in comparison to other United Kingdom cities: in 1941 the infant mortality rates in Leeds, Hull, Newcastle on Tyne, Middlesbrough and Belfast were 61, 76, 76, 76 and 91 per 1,000 registered births, respectively. The Belfast Branch of the Socialist Medical Association, comprising young doctors and other health-care workers, was very active. Its initial meetings were held under the auspices of the Northern Ireland Labour Party and subsequently at the Grand Central Hotel in Royal Avenue, thanks to swollen attendances. According to Dr William Calwell,[22] the only member to stand as a Labour candidate (twice unsuccessfully), the branch had been spurred into action by the health and welfare scandals and the severity of the depression in Belfast during the 1930s (Figure 14.4).

In 1944 a Ministry of Health and Local Government was launched and on 30 October 1948 Northern Ireland joined the NHS. This was established by just one of a cluster of Acts, which formed the welfare state. The northern state would enjoy full parity with the rest of the UK, provided there was parity in

FIGURE 14.4
During the depression years, from December 1931 to May 1934, slips at Harland and Wolff lay idle.

ULSTER FOLK & TRANSPORT MUSEUM

taxation.[23] The extension of the NHS to Northern Ireland improved medical care dramatically, and many saw it as a just reward for the considerable war effort that had been made. A General Health Services Board provided medical services for the entire region and a Hospitals Authority supervised all the hospitals, with the sole exception of Belfast's Mater Infirmorum Hospital (which was run by the Sisters of Mercy for the Catholic Church and did not join until 1971).[24] It was observed that the provision of free spectacles and false teeth made the biggest difference of all, as previously they had been beyond the means of almost everyone, with the exception of the very wealthy.

October 1973 saw a major overhaul of the NHS in Northern Ireland.[25] The objective was to remove the dichotomies between the hospital and community sectors, and between treatment and prevention. The existing structures were merged into four Health and Social Services Boards to run services on behalf of the Department of Health and Social Services. Belfast became a part of the Eastern Board Area. Six months later a similar system was introduced in Britain; however, there the social services remained a separate body. Almost immediately the Organization of Petroleum-Exporting Countries (OPEC) crisis occurred and rising fuel prices meant that the NHS across the UK became increasingly underfunded. In Northern Ireland throughout the 1980s and 1990s further administrative changes were tried and the wisdom of retaining four Health and Social Services Boards for such a small region was increasingly brought into question.

PUBLIC HEALTH

Public health covers a wide range of issues such as the control of infectious disease, sewage disposal and water supplies, the inspection of meat, and the control of offensive trades.

In England and Wales the initial major pieces of legislation were the Public Health Acts of 1848 and 1870; in Ireland the most significant Act dates from 1878.[26] One of the few differences between the measures introduced in England and Wales and those in Ireland was the requirement in the latter for an 'intervening ventilated space' between the two entrance doors to lavatories in public buildings, which, whatever their sanitary benefits, still provide greater privacy. The Irish Act, bolstered by the Local Government Order of 1900, established the provision for environmental health officers, who reported to a medical officer of health.

Water Pollution

A clean water supply is of foremost concern – indeed, it is more valuable than all the drugs in the pharmacy. Therefore, it is vital that the water supply and sewage are rigorously separated. Whenever humankind settles to initiate agriculture, it has always been, where possible, close to water. Very soon the water becomes polluted by human and animal faeces and urine. That is why beer became such a valuable commodity, as it provided something safe to drink.[27] The major waterborne bacterial diseases are cholera and typhoid, and the major viral diseases are hepatitis A and poliomyelitis.

At the end of the nineteenth century Belfast got its water from a number of small local reservoirs. From 1901 it began a supply by gravity feed from reservoirs in the Mourne

Mountains, 40 miles (64.4 km) south of the city.[28] This is very soft upland water, which throughout the second half of the last century was repeatedly shown in cross-sectional ('snapshot') studies to be associated with coronary heart disease. However, after adjusting for confounding factors, such as socio-economic status and smoking, such associations have tended to disappear. More recently, additional water has been piped to the city from Dunore Point, Lough Neagh, which has the advantage of being an inexhaustible supply of relatively hard water. However, in severe westerly storms the water becomes muddy, and hot weather causes algal bloom, which has worsened with an increased use of agricultural fertiliser. At such times, extra chlorine is added to bleach the water, to the detriment of its taste. Nitrosamines, generated by nitrate use, may constitute another hazard. Finally, it may be noted that Belfast's water supply is non-fluoridated. Fluoridation does reduce dental decay somewhat but its introduction can be politically sensitive, owing to ill-founded rumours of deleterious health effects.

FIGURE 14.5
Early nineteenth-century houses in Millfield, Belfast: the houses had no yards and all used the common privy at the end of the street.

ULSTER MUSEUM

In the late nineteenth century there were upwards of 20,000 houses (out of a total of 50,000) with dry or outdoor ash closets in Belfast.[29] These had to be emptied manually and, in many cases, because some of the dwellings were back to back (Figure 14.5), the ordure had to be carried through the houses for disposal. A bye-law later required that houses should have a common entry at the back. By this time Dublin had largely moved over to water closets, and Belfast was to follow. Unlike the Continent, the British Isles adopted a dual system of sewage and storm water sharing the same pipes, the idea being that rainfall would flush the sewage along. However, as brick sewers subsided over the years solid matter became trapped in low-lying parts. Torrential rain then flushed this solid matter into the River Lagan through relief culverts. Happily this pollution has been largely remedied, and with the recent clean up of the river, salmon are reported to have returned.

At the start of the twentieth century, when horses were used for haulage and transport, another health problem was the large number of dunghills polluting the city. Other livestock exacerbated the problem – pigs, for example, were fattened on family leftovers and the owners were reluctant to have the dunghills cleared away because they represented a financial asset.

Throughout the 1890s, typhoid fever was endemic in Belfast and the intermediate source of infection was probably shellfish. Concern over pollution in Belfast Lough, where 'sea-lettuce' was proliferating, led in 1898 to a Royal Commission, which was asked to advise about sewage disposal in the city. In 1907 the Belfast Health Commission was set up to examine the issue further. Thomas Carnwath was involved in these investigations.[30] The solution was to construct a culvert that would discharge effluent from holding tanks at Duncrue Street beyond the mouth of the lough during the first half of the ebb tide. This replaced an earlier, leaky wooden chute. Despite this improvement, sewage disposal continued to pose problems throughout the century

FIGURE 14.6
A young woman weaving
Jacquard at Brookfield Linen
Company, *c.* 1900

ULSTER MUSEUM

and, until recently, a large boat discharged an additional several hundred tons of solid matter each day off the Copeland Islands. Today these 'solids' are incinerated.

Air Pollution

Air pollution predisposes to bronchitis and emphysema, and small, inhaled particles may raise serum fibrinogen, which is a risk factor for coronary heart disease.

Originally Belfast's linen mills (Figure 14.6) relied on water power, which gave way to steam power fuelled by coal, with the result that the environs of mills were smoky. Such conditions had health implications for those working in the mills and living nearby. As mill-owners wanted their staff to live close at hand to minimise absenteeism, a great many households were affected. By the middle of the twentieth century air pollution in Belfast remained comparable to that in Sheffield, a notorious 'black spot' in terms of air pollution. However, with the demise of the mills, and heavy industry generally, in the second half of the century air quality steadily improved. The Clean Air Act (Northern Ireland) 1964 cut down sulphur dioxide emissions considerably,[31] although it was impossible to enforce a smoke-free zone in all parts of the city, as the Troubles recurred around the same time. This was particularly true in west Belfast, where civil disobedience became *de rigueur*. However, as motor cars have increased in number, so have emissions of nitrogen oxides, which may predispose to asthma.

HEALTH INDICATORS

FIGURE 14.7
Life expectancy at birth in the six
counties that came to constitute
Northern Ireland, 1895–1997

SOURCE: GOVERNMENT
ACTUARY'S DEPARTMENT

A number of health indicators are conventionally employed to assess the health status of a population and to draw comparisons with others. However, as they tend to include only readily accessible data, they have their limitations. Life expectancy is a useful indicator. Figure 14.7 presents life expectancy at birth throughout the twentieth century for the six counties that came to constitute Northern Ireland. The data have been constructed from life tables; however, separate data are not available for Belfast. Over the period 1895–1997, life expectancy in males increased by 27 years, and in females by 33 years. By far the biggest contribution to these gains has come from a huge decrease in infant mortality: obviously if you die in the first year of life you stand to lose more potential years of life than if you die aged fifty. Another important contribution has come from the decline in infectious

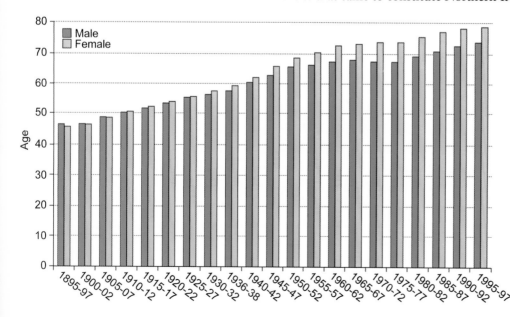

disease mortality, which particularly afflicted the young. In Belfast, from 1936–40 tuberculosis was responsible for half the deaths in the 15–24 age group.[32]

The reversal in the life expectancy in males and females over the century merits some comment: males could expect to live about six months longer than females at the start of the century, whereas at century end females could expect to live five years longer. Several factors are responsible for this pattern: at the start of the century women were dying in childbirth (5 per 1,000 births, with half these deaths due to puerperal fever) and death from tuberculosis was particularly common in female linen workers aged 25–44. Later in the century coronary heart disease had started to cut into life expectancy, particularly in males.

The crude death rate is a readily accessible statistic, and although 'crude' in the sense that it is unadjusted for age and therefore strongly affected by population structure, it is robust because total mortality can be assessed fairly accurately. As has been remarked by actuaries, 'Where there's death there's hope' – meaning, at least the data are more reliable than for specific causes of death, as diagnoses and classification may drift over time. Figure 14.8 shows the death rates in Belfast over the century, dropping from 22 per 1,000 population to around 12 per 1,000, with slight fluctuations over the period. Another way to look at this is to examine the pattern of death (not shown in the Figures): from 1899–1901, 21 per cent of deaths occurred in infancy and 20 per cent in people aged over 60 years; the corresponding percentages for 1997–99 were 2 and 85.

How did Belfast fare in terms of infant mortality throughout the twentieth century? These are robust data and provide a good indicator: the number of live births and deaths can be assembled fairly easily, and because the age band is so narrow, comparisons over time are valid. The data are presented in Figure 14.9. At the beginning of the century infant mortality stood at just over 150 per 1,000 live births, and at century end it was just 6 per 1,000. Almost three-quarters of this decrease occurred in the first half of the century and over the second half of the century Belfast badly lagged behind the rest of the UK, but lately has caught up.

Top
FIGURE 14.8
Death rate per 1,000 of the population, Belfast, 1901–99

Bottom
FIGURE 14.9
Infant mortality rate per 1,000 live births, Belfast, 1901–99

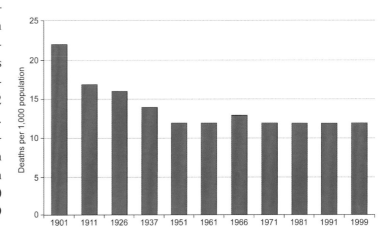

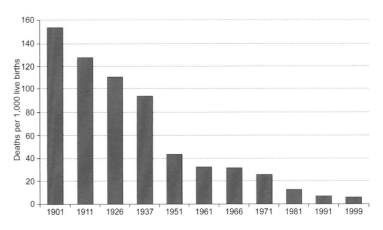

In Dublin in 1915 the rate was 160 per 1,000 births and the rate for the Republic of Ireland in 1995 stood at 6.4 per 1,000 births, compared to the UK at 6.2, Finland at 3.9, with the European Union average at 5.6. Maternity grants and superior antenatal, obstetric and postnatal care all played their part, but better nutrition and improved socio-economic wellbeing undoubtedly exerted their effect too. Because of concern over the high infant mortality at the beginning of the twentieth century, Lady Aberdeen's Women's National Health Association set up its first Baby Club in Belfast in 1908 (Figure 14.10). The 1907 Notification of Births Act was non-mandatory in Ireland and by 1915 only Belfast and Dublin had adopted it. Significantly, the Act facilitated the introduction of domiciliary health visiting.

FIGURE 14.10
The Women's National Health Association of Ireland held its first Baby Club in Ballymacarrett in 1908.

ANNA DAY

Around this time, Coey Bigger, medical commissioner to the Local Government Board, highlighted the social class gradients which were present in infant mortality.[33] It was a Strabane man, Thomas Henry Craig Stevenson, who introduced the system of socio-economic grading, which has proved so informative, into the 1911 British census. He published his paper *The Vital Statistics of Wealth and Poverty* in 1928.[34] There sadly remain social class gradients in infant mortality today. In the 1980s Belfast rates of breast feeding were amongst the lowest in the world, and this too showed a social gradient.

Although medical advances played their part in the lowering of infant mortality, better nutrition and improvements in economic circumstances were probably as important. The live birth rate has also declined from 31 to 13 per 1,000, with a slight upturn in the 1950s and 1960s, but the caveats about interpreting crude death rates also apply here. The more widespread use of effective contraception undoubtedly played a part. Maternal mortality is another success story: around 1900 it stood at about 5 per 1,000 births, by the start of the NHS it stood at around 2 per 1,000 and by the start of the second millennium it had virtually disappeared.[35] Antibiotics and blood transfusion contributed to this.

INFECTIOUS DISEASES

There was also a transformation in mortality from infectious diseases over the course of the twentieth century. In the first decade of the century these diseases (including tuberculosis but excluding pneumonia) accounted for 30.5 per cent of all deaths in Belfast, as opposed to 28.5 per cent and 22.5 per cent in Dublin and the rest of Ireland, respectively. During this period deaths from the principal epidemic diseases (smallpox, measles, scarlet fever, typhus, typhoid, diphtheria, whooping cough and diarrhoea) in Ireland accounted for 1.5 per 1,000 population, compared to 0.9 for England. The big killers in Belfast were tuberculosis, followed by diarrhoea, measles, whooping cough, typhoid, influenza, diphtheria and scarlet fever. Deaths from smallpox were already rare thanks to vaccination, and typhus only claimed a few lives a year, and then petered out. Diphtheria clung on as a cause of death until 1951.[36] In fact, all these diseases were controlled by the 1960s. By the second millennium, deaths from infectious disease were rare, accounting for less than 0.3 per cent of all deaths. We tend to think that this advance is all thanks to the introduction of immunisation and antibiotics, but scrutiny of the trends confirms that infectious diseases were all starting to fall well before their introduction,[37] albeit at a slower rate in Belfast than elsewhere in the UK. The fall was linked to better nutrition and the application of good public health practice such as sanitation (Figure 14.11) and quarantine. It should be recognised, of course, that for vaccines to be effective a good uptake to produce 'herd immunity' is highly important to prevent serial transmission through a population: in the 1980s the level of measles immunisation in Belfast fell to below 6 per cent, but with the recrudescence of the disease, uptake improved dramatically.

Tuberculosis was a truly enormous problem, dominating all the other infectious diseases put together and in some ways behaving like a chronic disease (similar to AIDS). From 1894 to 1905 the tuberculosis death rates in the cities of Dublin, Belfast and Cork were 3.6, 3.3 and 3.9 per 1,000 of the population, respectively; in Glasgow in

1904 it was 1.76, in Manchester in 1905 it was 1.67, and in Blackburn in 1905 it was 0.94. Stubbornly, these rates showed no sign of decreasing.[38] In 1907 Lady Aberdeen launched her crusade against tuberculosis through the Women's National Health Association. Her favourite dictum was 'Public Health is purchasable', a phrase she had borrowed from Hermann M. Biggs of New York.[39] The association placed particular emphasis on fresh air: at one meeting an enthusiastic convert was heard to call out, 'I'll get the windows open tonight if it kills him!' A particularly ingenious idea was turf spittoons, which were burned when full. To its credit the association was instrumental in pushing the 1908 Tuberculosis Bill (Ireland) through parliament,[40] although compulsory notification of infection was vetoed by the Irish Parliamentary Party.[41] Further provision for treating tuberculosis was made under the Irish Health Insurance Act. In his report of 1941, Carnwath compared death rates from tuberculosis in Belfast with those of English county boroughs outside London, showing 'that Belfast still lags a long way behind', but he failed to quote the actual data his comment was based upon.[42] His report led to the establishment of the Northern Ireland Tuberculosis Authority and by 1954 the rates had subsided to the levels of England and Wales.[43]

SEXUALLY TRANSMITTED DISEASE

Tuberculosis often comes in association with sexually transmitted disease, particularly today, as AIDS depresses the immune system. Such was the case after the Great War when the soldiers returned; the Royal Army Medical Corps had standing orders for 'mercurial rubbers' – a Queen's University Medical School *aide-mémoire* of the time went: 'Hydrarg. Cum Creta. and Pot. Iod. for them that don't believe in God.'

Drug addiction in many ways behaves like an infectious disease, in that it manifests 'serial transmission' through a population. After the fall of the Shah of Iran in 1979 when the Shiite fundamentalists took over, many rich Iranians bought heroin in order to export their wealth. A lot of this heroin ended up in Dublin, where security was not very tight, and which until then did not suffer a drug problem. Intravenous administration with dirty syringes meant that very soon Dublin had an HIV problem too, which predisposes to our old friend tuberculosis. Tight security and moralistic paramilitaries kept hard drugs out of Belfast for a long time but that has now changed. Belfast may appear to have less AIDS than elsewhere, perhaps because a harsh moral climate causes sufferers to migrate. The 'Special' (venereal disease) clinic at the Royal Victoria Hospital up until the mid-1960s could be approached through a discreet door opening directly from the Grosvenor Road. On Sunday mornings in the 1930s a urethral dilatation clinic was held for male patients with chronic gonorrhoea: it was known as 'The Bible Class'.

CHRONIC DISEASES

It is not feasible to look at chronic diseases meaningfully over the twentieth century because of diagnostic changes and the totally different age structure at the beginning of the century and the end of it. Cancer and cardiovascular disease are diseases of ageing. Cancer Registry data from the mid-1990s do not suggest any glaring differences between Belfast and Dublin, although colorectal and oesophageal cancer may be more common in Northern Ireland.[44] In the second half of the century Belfast suffered an epidemic of coronary heart disease (heart attacks), which has been declining since the early 1980s. Figure 14.12 shows how in the mid-1980s incidence rates for myocardial infarction varied with the socio-economic status of the electoral ward in which the victims resided: the rates were particularly high in the working-class areas of north and west Belfast and low in affluent south Belfast.[45] Delay times to initiation of intensive care also tended to be shorter in the more affluent areas. Diet and smoking status have strong social class determinants. Figure 14.13 shows unpublished cross-sectional data from the World Health Organisation Belfast MONICA Project's 1983–84 population survey: smoking prevalence (a strong risk factor for heart attacks, strokes and several types of cancer) was correlated with social class and deprivation but generally higher in those who did not participate in the survey (that is, non-response is a risk factor in itself).[46] This information was assembled by means of postal questionnaires and telephone interviews. Paradoxically, car ownership was associated with higher levels of leisure-time physical activity, reflecting socio-economic wellbeing and, probably, better access to nicer places to exercise.

In PRIME, a prospective follow-up study of 10,600 middle-aged men recruited in the early 1990s in Northern Ireland and France, high levels of 'hostility', which are supposed to predispose to heart attacks, were more common in France where heart disease is rare; conversely, high levels of 'social support', which are said to be protective for heart disease, were more

FIGURE 14.12
Map of standardised myocardial infarction ratios in the 107 wards of the Belfast MONICA Project area, 1983–85

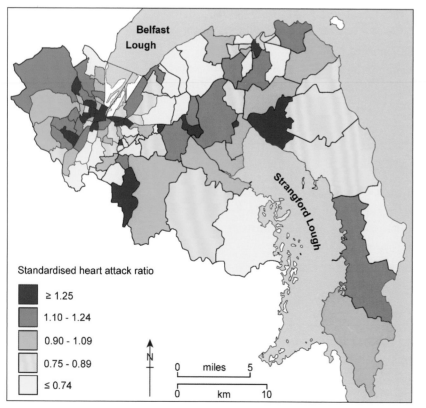

Standardised heart attack ratio

■	≥ 1.25
▨	1.10 - 1.24
▦	0.90 - 1.09
░	0.75 - 0.89
□	≤ 0.74

common in Belfast, where heart disease is common.[47] (Despite their moderately high levels of risk factors for heart disease, the French enjoy relatively low heart attack rates.[48] This phenomenon, which was originally recognised by the great Newry physician, Samuel Black, in 1819, has become known as the French Paradox.[49]) In addition, men screened in Northern Ireland had higher blood pressure on Mondays and Tuesdays than men in France on the same days,[50] presumably due to a pressor effect[51] from either drinking or stopping drinking. This was almost certainly due to differences in the pattern of alcohol consumption between the two countries. In Northern Ireland PRIME, men are weekend drinkers (61 per cent drank alcohol, but two-thirds of consumption took place on Friday and Saturday nights), whereas in French PRIME, nine-tenths of men drank alcohol, with consumption spread evenly throughout the week.[52] Moreover, over five years of follow-up, a greater alcohol consumption was associated with a lower amount of heart disease in France – an effect that was conspicuously absent in Belfast.

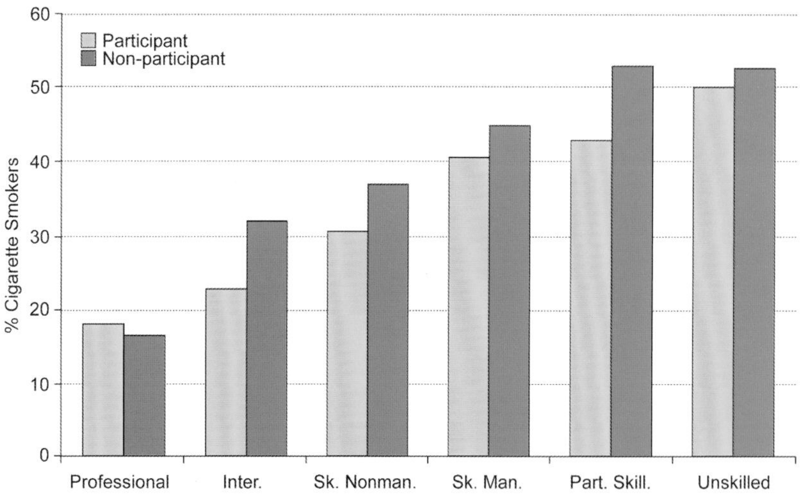

FIGURE 14.13
Social class and cigarette smoking, Belfast MONICA Project First Population Survey, 1983–84

INDUSTRIAL DISEASE

The linen industry was noted for high mortality from tuberculosis particularly in female workers of susceptible age (25–34 years), who made up the majority of the workforce. They shared poor nutrition and socio-economic circumstances, and worked in close proximity, in humid conditions, for long hours (see Figure 14.14). Death in this age group was predominately from haemoptysis – haemorrhage from the lungs. Figure 14.15 shows typical kitchen houses for accommodating linen workers. A wheeze from the

Below left
FIGURE 14.14
York Street Weavers, 1936. The York Street Spinning Mill, the largest in Europe, was badly damaged in the blitz and closed in 1951.

ALUN EVANS

Below right
FIGURE 14.15
Linen workers' kitchen houses at Economy Place, off York Street, 1971

ALUN EVANS

effects of inhaling flax-dust, known locally as 'pousy' (from French *poussif*, meaning 'wheezy, short-winded'), was experienced by some; it deteriorated during the working week, suggesting an allergic cause. Flax byssinosis became a prescribed (eligible for compensation) industrial disease, but later evidence linked it with cigarette smoking. Linen workers also often went barefoot and so were liable to infections of the toenails.[53] In the shipyards, riveters' chests became pock-marked from the red hot rivets they had failed to catch, and 'red leaders' – workers who applied protective lead paint – were at risk in this sinister trade. Asbestos laggers, known as 'white men' because they were festooned with the lethal fibres and never wore face masks,[54] developed mesotheliomata (a tumour of the lining of the lungs), yet kept their trade within the family because the pay was so good. In the early 1960s about one-fifth of the male population of Belfast had asbestos bodies in their lungs at autopsy.[55] Accidents were also very common.

THE TROUBLES

The worst of Belfast's Troubles broke out in August 1969. In March 1972, after the bombing of the Abercorn restaurant, in which 2 were killed and over 70 injured, John Robb, the surgeon, then based in the Royal Victoria Hospital, described on radio the amputations, sometimes multiple, it had been necessary to perform on some of the victims. He observed, 'You cannot create a healthy society from one which has been dismembered.'[56] At that time a 'disaster' was defined as fifteen or more people arriving simultaneously at an Accident & Emergency department. By the time John Robb gave a lecture in Edinburgh in 1973 (Figure 14.16) the Royal Victoria Hospital had dealt with 46 such disasters; by comparison, William Rutherford found 42 for the rest of the UK between 1951 and 1971.[57] Characteristically, the suicide rate almost halved[58] – you are not going to kill yourself if someone wants to do it for you – and depressive illness also declined. However, in the long term, studies have suggested that mental health has deteriorated in Belfast and Northern Ireland as a whole.[59]

HOSPITAL ARCHITECTURE

In 1966 the old workhouse at Belfast City Hospital was demolished to make way for a new tower block, which opened in the mid 1980s, vastly over budget. (The blind baker got this wrong: he had predicted the workhouse would be owned by a firm of grocers in the year 2000.[60]) The Royal Victoria, the other main teaching hospital in Belfast, was opened in 1903. It had a Plenum ventilation system, in which huge Sirocco fans sucked in ten million cubic feet of air per hour through sisal ropes down which water dripped. Very soon, by making adjustments, it was found possible to control the relative humidity in the wards, so the Royal can fairly claim to be the first air-conditioned building in the world (see chapter 3).[61] The old building was demolished in 2003 to make way for a new hospital, but happily the main corridor, under

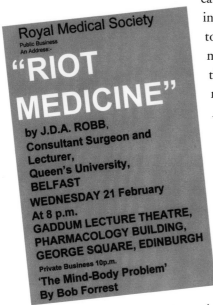

FIGURE 14.16
Poster for John Robb's
'Riot Medicine' lecture,
Edinburgh, 1973

ALUN EVANS

which the main ventilation duct ran, and the fans, will be preserved (Figure 14.17).

One more interesting architectural detail deserves to be recorded. The streets adjoining the Durham Street Tuberculosis Institute, which opened in 1918, were surfaced in Australian eucalyptus blocks embedded in tar to deaden the noise of passing drays and the Clydesdales' shoes. It was rumoured that it would float away in a flood, but it never did.

MEDICAL EDUCATION

Like nearly everything else in Belfast, medical education was segregated: all Catholic students went to the Mater Infirmorum Hospital until it joined the NHS in 1971, but all newly qualified doctors had to sign an oath of allegiance to the Crown. Although the non-medical hospital staff tended to reflect the religious denomination of the local population, in the Royal Victoria and the Mater the consultant staff very definitely did not, although recently things have become more equitable.

Queen's University Medical School has a proud tradition of high quality teaching and turning out capable, caring doctors. Its research record, however, over more recent years has not been as good. There are several possible reasons for this. In the past some of the best Catholic graduates have had to leave, usually for North America, because they could not get the jobs they wanted in the Belfast Medical School, and one observer saw this as 'the unacceptable face of Ulster medicine'.[62] In the 1970s some actually emigrated for fear of attack by loyalist sectarian murder squads. On the other hand, there is a tendency for the very best Protestant school-leavers to go to medical schools in Britain and not to return on qualifying. Moreover, the Troubles have made it very difficult to attract good

FIGURE 14.17
The main corridor at the Royal Victoria Hospital in 1903
ROYAL VICTORIA HOSPITAL

FIGURE 14.18
'The father of emergency medicine': Frank Pantridge, who introduced mobile coronary care and developed the portable defibrillator.

ALUN EVANS

graduates from outside Northern Ireland to take their place. For those who choose to work in Belfast, the demanding joint appointment system means that consultants employed jointly by the hospital and the university frequently find that each institution tries to claim 100 per cent of their time. And lastly, a failure to invest in the training of biostatisticians has resulted in a lack of essential staff to undertake some of the complex analyses demanded by modern medical research.

A few Queen's University graduates have made truly innovative contributions to the world of medicine. Sir Robert McCarrison, who qualified with first class honours in 1900, subsequently worked in India, where he became director of nutritional research, making significant contributions to the study of deficiency diseases and nutritional epidemiology by comparing the diets of different tribes.[63] However, although 'he was honoured for his discoveries', he was 'completely ignored by government and the medical profession at a time when medical thought was absorbed in the study of disease rather than on prevention and the promotion of health'.[64]

Sir Ivan Magill invented the endotracheal tube, which is the standard anaesthetic equipment used worldwide. He presented a description of it for an MD in 1920 but his thesis was turned down.[65] After the Troubles recurred in 1969 it became standard procedure to intubate all seriously injured patients as they arrived at the Royal Victoria's Accident & Emergency Department.

In the 1940s, in the field of obstetrics, C.H.G. Macafee introduced his 'conservative treatment', which he dubbed 'masterly inactivity'. This involved observing, and intervening as little as possible in cases of placenta praevia (when the placenta encroaches over the mouth of the womb, resulting in bleeding and occasionally more serious consequences). Up until Macafee's contribution, the baby was sometimes sacrificed to save the mother.[66]

In 1966 physician and cardiologist Frank Pantridge, in order to counter the high early mortality from heart attacks in Belfast, introduced the cardiac ambulance, or mobile intensive care unit, and subsequently developed the world's first portable defibrillator. He also conceptualised the automatic defibrillator. When you fly anywhere in the world today, it is highly probable that your plane will have a defibrillator on board. Known as 'the father of emergency medicine', his concepts have been applied all over the world (Figure 14.18).[67]

The Queen's Medical School has also produced one or two more controversial figures. In the early 1990s, James Wisheart, cardiac surgeon at Bristol Royal Infirmary, and former chief executive Dr John Roylance were struck off by the General Medical Council after it was revealed that 29 of the 53 children operated on in Bristol between 1988 and 1995 had died – a much higher figure than the national average.[68] It was largely as a result of that case that clinical governance, with its provisions for recertification and revalidation, was imposed upon the UK's medical profession in 1997.

CONCLUSION

There is an old Dublin saying: 'In the North they care too much about the Crown and the half-crown.' The monetary allusion would reflect Belfast's glorious industrial past rather well, albeit that it was built on a large, highly skilled, badly paid and poorly unionised labour force. Moreover, working environments were often damaging to health. After the boom of the early twentieth century, unemployment grew, and given the inextricable links between poverty and health, inequalities in the health of Belfast's citizens increased. Nevertheless, the city's population enjoyed huge improvements in health during the twentieth century, especially after the introduction of the NHS, although inequalities have stubbornly persisted.

NOTES

1 Evans, A. (2000) Epilogue, in F. McGibben, *Belfast in the year 2000 A.D.*, Donaldson Archives: Belfast, pp. 93–103. This is one of the very few Utopian novels written by a working-class author (Geoghegan, V. (2003) Personal communication).

2 Bardon, J. (1982) *Belfast: an illustrated history*, Blackstaff Press: Belfast, pp. 156–91.

3 Quoted in Crew, F.A.E. (1949) 'Social science as an academic discipline', in A. Massey (ed.) *Modern trends in public health*, Butterworth: London, pp. 46–79.

4 McKeown, T., and Lowe, C.R. (1974) *An introduction to social medicine*, Blackwell Scientific Publications: Oxford, pp. 132–53.

5 Geary, L. (2004) personal communication.

6 Barrington, R. (1987) *Health, medicine & politics in Ireland 1900–1970*, Institute of Public Administration: Dublin, pp. 1–112.

7 Devlin, P. (1981) *Yes we have no bananas: outdoor relief in Belfast, 1920–39*, Blackstaff Press: Belfast, pp. 63–173.

8 McKeown and Lowe (1974) *Social medicine.*

9 Barrington (1987) *Health, medicine.*

10 Barrington (1987) *Health, medicine.*

11 Barrington (1987) *Health, medicine.*

12 Barrington (1987) *Health, medicine.*

13 Bardon (1982) *Belfast.*

14 Evans (2000) 'Epilogue'.

15 Devlin (1981) *Outdoor relief.*

16 Maguire, W.A. (1993) *Belfast*, Ryburn Publishing: Keele, pp. 158–59.

17 Hegarty, S. (2003) 'The bleeding heart racket', *Irish Times*, 6 December, p. 18.

18 Carnwath, T. (1941) 'Report to the special committee of Belfast Corporation on the municipal health services of the city', 24 December.

19 Maguire (1993) *Belfast*, pp. 158–59.

20 Beacham, A. (1939) *Report of a survey of living conditions made in a representative working-class area in Belfast November 1938–February 1939*, Presbyterian Church in Ireland Social Service Committee: Belfast.

21 Stark Murray, D. (1971) *Why a National Health Service?* Pemberton Books: London, p. 65.

22 Calwell, W. (1999) personal communication.

23 Bardon (1982) *Belfast*, pp. 246–76.

24 Anon. (*c.* 2000) *A short history of the Mater Infirmorum Hospital, Belfast*, [n.p.], p. 34.

25 Ministry of Health and Social Services (1972) *Guide to the new structure for health and personal services*, HMSO: Belfast.

26 Blaney, R. (1988) *Belfast: 100 years of public health*, Belfast City Council and the Eastern Health and Social Services Board: Belfast, pp. 3–62.

27 Vallee, L.V. (1998) 'Alcohol in the western world', *Scientific American*, June, pp. 62–68.

28 Loudan, J. (1940) *In search of water, being a history of the Belfast water supply*, Mullan: Belfast.

29 Blaney (1988) *Belfast.*

30 Elwood, J.H. (1982) 'Thomas Carnwath', *Ulster Medical Journal*, 51, pp. 98–109.

31 Lynas, K.H. (1970) 'Air quality in Belfast since 1955', *Proceedings of Seminar: Air pollution – impacts and control*, National Board for Science and Technology, pp. 30–36.

32 Carnwath (1941) 'Municipal health services'.

33 McKeown and Lowe (1974) *Social medicine.*

34 Stevenson, T.H.C. (1928) 'The vital statistics of wealth and poverty', *Journal of the Royal Statistical Society*, 91, pp. 207–30.

35 Evans, A. (1998) 'When health went public', *Journal of Health Promotion for Northern Ireland*, 2, pp. 2–7.

36 Blaney (1988) *Belfast.*

37 McKeown and Lowe (1974) *Social medicine.*

38 Byers, J.W. (1906) *Public health problems*, Mullan and Carswell: Belfast.

39 Dormandy, T. (1999) *The white death: a history of tuberculosis*, Hambledon Press: London, p. 183.

40 Evans, A. (1995) 'The Countess of Aberdeen's health promotion caravans', *Journal of the Irish College of Physicians and Surgeons*, 24, pp. 211–18.

41 Barrington (1987) *Health, medicine.*

42 Carnwath (1941) 'Municipal health services'.

43 Bardon (1982) *Belfast*, pp. 246–76.

44 Walsh, P.M., Comber, H. and Gavin, A.T. (2001) *All-Ireland cancer statistics 1994–1996: a joint report on incidence and mortality for the island of Ireland*, National Cancer Registry (Ireland): Cork, and Northern Ireland Cancer Registry: Belfast. For those who did not participate in the survey, data were collected by means of follow-up questionnaires, telephone calls and in some cases by visiting.

45 Patterson, C.C. (1989) 'Survivorship models applied to the study of coronary heart disease', unpublished PhD thesis, Faculty of Medicine, Queen's University Belfast.

46 Belfast MONICA Project (unpublished data).

47 Sykes, D.H., Arveiler, D., Salters C.P., et al. (2002) 'Psychological risk factors for heart disease in France and Northern Ireland: the prospective epidemiological study of myocardial infarction (PRIME)', *International Journal of Epidemiology*, 31, pp. 1227–34.

48 Evans A., Ruidavets, J-B., McCrum E.E., et al. (1995) '*Autres pays, autres coeurs?* Dietary patterns, risk factors and ischaemic heart disease in Belfast and Toulouse', *QJM*, 88, 469–77.

49 Evans, A. (1995) 'Dr Black's favourite disease', *British Heart Journal*, 74, pp. 696–97.

50 Marques-Vidal, P., Arveiler, D., Evans, A., et al. (2001) 'Different alcohol drinking and blood pressure relationships in France and Northern Ireland: the PRIME study', *Hypertension*, 38, pp. 1361–66.

51 A pressor effect is one which increases the level of blood pressure.

52 Marques-Vidal, P., Montaye, M., Arveiler, D., et al. (2004) 'Alcohol consumption and cardiovascular disease: differential effects in France and Northern Ireland, the PRIME Study', *European Journal of Cardiovascular Prevention and Rehabilitation*, 11, pp. 336–43.

53 Maguire (1993) *Belfast*, pp. 158–59.

54 Piper, R. (2005) personal communication.

55 Elmes, P.C., and Wade, O.L. (1965) 'Relationship between exposure to asbestos and pleural malignancy in Belfast', *Annals of the New York Academy of Sciences*, 132, pp. 549–57.

56 *Irish News* (1972) 6 March, p. 1.

57 Rutherford, W.H. (1972) 'Experience in the Accident and Emergency Department of the Royal Victoria Hospital with patients from civil disturbances in Belfast 1969–1972, with a review of disasters in the United Kingdom 1951–1971', *INJURY, British Journal of Accident Surgery*, 4, pp. 189–99.

58 Lyons, H.A. (1972) 'Depressive illness and aggression in Belfast', *British Medical Journal*, 1, pp. 342–44.

59 O'Reilly, D., and Stevenson, M. (2003) 'Mental health in Northern Ireland: have "the Troubles" made it worse?', *Journal of Epidemiology and Community Health*, 57, pp. 488–92.

60 Evans (2000) 'Epilogue'.

61 Banham, R. (1967) 'The architecture below', *The Listener*, pp. 196–97.

62 Pantridge, F. (1991) *An unquiet life*, 4th edn., Pantridge Foundation NI: Belfast, p. 81.

63 Sinclair, H.M. (ed.) (1953) *The work of Sir Robert McCarrison*, Faber and Faber: London.

64 http://www.mccarrisonsociety.org.uk/his.htm, accessed 23 February 2006.

65 Clarke, R. (2000) 'Giants of Ulster medicine', *Northern Ireland Medicine Today: Millennium Supplement*, pp. 2–3.

66 Macafee, C.H.G. (1945) 'Placenta praevia – a study of 74 cases', *Journal of Obstetrics and Gynaecology of the British Empire*, 52, pp. 313–24.

67 Arnold, P. (2001) 'A paper that saved my life', *British Medical Journal*, 322, p. 1570.

68 http://www.studentbmj.com/back_issues/0299/data/0299mm.htm, accessed 23 February 2006.

At the beginning of the twentieth century Belfast was a city divided in both religion and class. In schools the religious division came about as a result of the pressure the Churches had put on the National Schools system over the previous seventy years to ensure that most children were educated in schools of their own denomination (Figure 15.1). The class division had been emphasised by industrialisation and the associated influx of workers and their families to the city. By the end of the century these divisions in schooling had reduced and the number of children being educated in integrated schools, although small, was growing. And a changing society had increased the proportion of the population that could be described as middle class.

15
Educating the City

E.J. Creighton

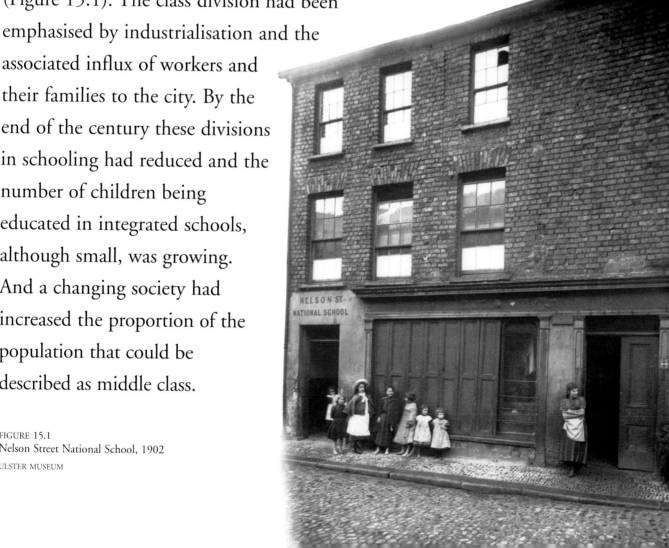

FIGURE 15.1
Nelson Street National School, 1902

In 1900 Belfast was the major industrial city in Ireland and when the 1901 census was taken it had a population that had trebled in the previous forty years and stood at almost 350,000. This rapid rise in population meant increasing numbers of children had to be educated, but there was serious neglect in primary school accommodation, as education in Belfast, as throughout Ireland, had been underfunded for years. There was also the problem of denominationalism, which had existed for centuries.

EARLY TWENTIETH-CENTURY SCHOOLS

At the start of the century elementary schools in Belfast were National Schools under the control of the Board of Commissioners for National Education in Dublin, which kept a very tight control on all aspects of education and did not allow any initiative, or rate support, from local government. The original idea for National Schools when they were set up in 1832 was for the introduction of a non-denominational system, with priests and ministers being excluded from teaching posts. This was attacked by the various religious denominations in Ireland and at first the Churches opposed the national system, but modifications to the rules allowed them more control and over the years the majority of children were taught the religious doctrine of their own faith in denominational National Schools. These changes particularly satisfied Catholic clerics, who could now exert influence on the schools they managed.

FIGURE 15.2
Malone National School, *c.* 1905–10

ULSTER MUSEUM

There was concern about the physical conditions and overcrowding in many of the National Schools in Belfast by the beginning of the century (Figure 15.2). The Belfast Corporation appointed a special committee of representatives of school managers in March 1907 to investigate the extent of the problem. Their highly critical report was presented to the Corporation at a meeting that was summarised in the next day's *Belfast Evening Telegraph*. Some schools were described 'as not capable of being properly ventilated and so cold in winter that children could not work, while sanitary arrangements were a disgrace to civilisation, and undoubtedly the origin of many epidemics and maladies, which caused not a few early deaths'.[1] The report concluded that additional accommodation was needed for some 7,000 children, and to provide this, a sum of over £40,000 was required. Representatives of the Belfast Corporation approached the Commissioners for National Education in Dublin for a liberal grant towards the improvement of primary school accommodation in the city. They were informed by the commissioners that ample grant provision was already in place for the building of new schools and that loans for a period of thirty-five years were available to schools not owned by the commissioners. So the grant application was turned down and few school managers were prepared to go into debt in order to repair their school premises.

Further concern about primary school accommodation was expressed at the quarterly meeting of the Belfast Corporation in May 1913, when a deputation from the United Committee of the Church of Ireland, Presbyterian and Methodist Churches presented a memorial highlighting the pressing need for additional primary schools in the city. The United Committee noted that in 1908 accommodation had been required for 7,000 children, but now, according to information from the 1911 census, this figure had risen to 15,000. It also noted that the National Board of Education had increased the standard space required by each pupil from 9 to 10 square feet (2.7 to 3.0 square metres). The committee argued that £100,000 was needed to meet this requirement. A Catholic member of the Corporation, Councillor Patrick Dempsey, defended the condition of schools in the city managed by the Catholic Church. He noted that inspections by the National Commissioners had not found Catholic National Schools overcrowded or unhygienic and new schools had been built and paid for by the Church. He suggested that Protestant Churches should follow suit. Although the Corporation discussed the problem, it was prevented by National Board of Education regulations from using rates revenue to pay for schools.

A last attempt to improve Belfast primary school accommodation, before the formation of a separate Northern Ireland government, was made with the introduction of the Primary Education (Belfast) Bill 1919. This called for rate aid for Belfast schools and local government involvement in the control of schools. Ulster Unionist Party MPs were strongly in favour, but fearing that the reforms would let local government, and thus the Unionists, have a say in controlling Catholic schools, the Catholic hierarchy opposed the measure and Irish Parliamentary Party MPs blocked the passing of the Bill in parliament.

THE EDUCATION ACT 1923

The establishment of the Northern Ireland state in 1921 led to the expectation that the newly formed Ministry of Education would reform the way schools in the North were funded and repair the damage caused by the years of neglect. In June 1921 Lord Londonderry was appointed by Prime Minister Sir James Craig as the first Minister of Education in the Unionist-dominated government. He undertook to reform the severely underfunded education service and started by establishing a committee of inquiry in September 1921. Chaired by Robert Lynn – UUP MP for West Belfast and editor of the *Northern Whig* – the Lynn Committee, as it came to be called, consisted of thirty-two members representing both primary and secondary education, though none represented the Catholic Church. Cardinal Michael Logue, Catholic archbishop of Armagh, had declined Lord Londonderry's invitation to nominate four representatives. However, such was the depth of ill-feeling against Catholics in the new Northern Ireland parliament, that it is doubtful that the presence of Catholic nominees would have influenced the committee's report.[2] The only Catholic member of the Lynn Committee was Andrew Napoleon Bonaparte Wyse, an Irish civil servant who had transferred from the Dublin government and was vastly experienced in education matters. After serving on the committee, he was put in charge of all public elementary schools and became permanent secretary in the Ministry of Education from 1927 to 1939.

In June 1922 the Lynn Committee presented its interim report to the Northern Ireland parliament, which served as the basis for the Education Act of 1923, and three classes of primary schools were formed in that year.

Class I

Class I schools were those built with finance from the local rates and Ministry of Education grants, and schools that were successfully transferred to the local education committee by their previous managers. All costs of furnishing, heating, maintenance and repair were paid from local rates. The capital expenses for the new schools and the renovations to the old were to have one-third raised from the local rates and two-thirds from central government.

Class II

Managers of Class II schools accepted the establishment of special school management committees consisting of four representatives appointed by the manager or trustees of the school and two representatives of the local education committee; they became known as 'Four and Two Committees'. Half the costs of furnishing, heating, maintenance and repair were paid from local rates. The capital expenses for new buildings and the expansion of the old were to have two-thirds provided from central government, one-sixth from local rates and the remainder from school patrons. These schools maintained local management control, while receiving some financial support from the rates.

Class III

Class III schools were those whose managers had decided to remain entirely independent of the local education committee. They received no support from the local rates, but grants towards the costs of heating and cleaning were paid directly by the Ministry of Education. The Ministry of Education could make discretionary loans towards capital expenditure but the entire amount had to be repaid.

Schools managed by the Catholic Church elected to remain outside the control of the local education committee and so opted for Class III status (with the exception of the Christian Brothers' elementary schools, which opted for Class II status). The remaining school management committees had to decide whether to transfer their schools or remain partially or totally separate from the local education committee.

In all three classes, the Ministry of Education paid teachers' salaries in full. Elementary education was to be both literary and moral, and based on instruction in reading and writing of the English language, and in arithmetic, but there were serious problems regarding religious instruction. For children attending the Class II and Class III schools, decisions regarding the provision of religious education could be made by school managers. For children attending Class I schools, however, the 1923 Education Act was controversial. The Government of Ireland Act 1920 prevented the Northern Ireland parliament making laws that established or endowed any particular religion. The doctrine of individual denominations or, indeed, any doctrines agreed by the Protestant Churches could not be taught during compulsory school hours or paid for by public money.

It was soon clear that the secularisation of Class I schools was politically unacceptable. Protestant Church leaders were immediately opposed to the Act and most school managers were not prepared to transfer schools to the local education committee as Class I schools. The Orange Order joined the Protestant Churches in protest at the potential lack of religious instruction in schools. Lord Londonderry steadfastly refused to modify his Education Act, but in 1925 Craig backed down in face of fierce opposition and an Education Amendment Act was quickly passed in that year. In 1926 Lord Londonderry resigned over the affair and returned to England.

The offending clause in the Education Act prohibiting local education authorities from providing religious instruction in Class I schools was now removed. The Protestant Church leaders were satisfied with the amendment and the transfer of schools to the local education committees began.

BELFAST EDUCATION COMMITTEE

After partition, Belfast Corporation became a local education authority and the first meeting of the Education Committee took place on 14 December 1923.[3] It inherited approximately 200 National Schools with their foundations in various beliefs and educational ideologies. The majority were Church schools under clerical management, but there were a few endowed schools, including two originating in the Sunday school movement. Other schools had been founded by charitable organisations or were privately owned. From the start, the Education Committee set out to improve the conditions in schools for as many children residing in the borough as possible and to do it efficiently. They appointed Major Rupert Stanley, the principal of the Municipal College of Technology, as the director of education on 1 January 1924. Stanley developed a deep understanding of the workings of the Belfast Education Department, which ensured the smooth running of the department until his retirement in 1941.

The Education Committee decided that it was essential to obtain the fullest possible information on the number of children of, and approaching, school age and so a census was taken of children in the city between the ages of three and fourteen years. The police carried out the distribution and collection of the census papers and the staff of the Corporation's School Attendance Department undertook the enumeration and classification. The resulting analysis indicated that there was insufficient accommodation available (Table 15.1).

One way to reduce the overcrowding would have been to remove the several thousand children under six years of age who attended school without the right to do so, being outside the statutory ages of attendance, six to fourteen years. However, to take this action would have been socially undesirable as their mothers were working, usually in the linen mills, and those under six were allowed to remain. Further, the education authorities were keen to encourage children over fourteen to remain at school.[4]

Plans were made to build new schools and close the most dilapidated buildings. The Education Committee from the start took great care in the planning, building and furnishing of these new schools and a Sites and Buildings Sub-Committee was set up in January 1924 with responsibility for recommending new sites and the alteration, enlargement or renovation of existing buildings when a school transferred. It was also responsible for the control of the Education Architect's Department and the submission of plans and estimates to the main Education Committee. William George Davies from Chelmsford, Essex, was appointed as education architect in April 1924, and he planned Euston Street and Templemore Avenue Public Elementary Schools, the first new schools to be built in Belfast by the Education Committee, each with accommodation for 1,000 pupils. Loans of £30,000 for Euston Street and £26,000 for Templemore Avenue were raised and sanctioned by the Ministry of Education and the schools were opened in July 1926 (Figure 15.3). They were bright and airy with central heating, electric lighting and large playgrounds, and new facilities, like a chemical laboratory and rooms for house-wifery and handicrafts, were provided. (Templemore Avenue school has been commemorated in one of the new 'cultural murals' which are a recent addition to the gable walls of east Belfast, see Figure 15.4).

As a result of the controversy regarding religious instruction, only five schools in Belfast transferred to the management of the Education Committee to become Class I schools in the school year 1924–25. Once transferred, the education architect planned the improvements necessary to meet the requirements of the committee, which usually included a new central heating system, electric lighting and proper sanitary arrangements.

TABLE 15.1
Education Census, School Enrolment and Accommodation in Belfast, 1924

Education census	
Children 3–14 years	83,563
Deduct those born between 1 March 1914 and 28 January 1921	-24,193
Total children aged between 6 and 14 years	59,370
Ministry of Education returns of children on school rolls	
Total number of children attending school	64,064
Deduct children below school age*	-8,555
Add children attending private schools	+2,750
Add children of school age not attending school	+900
Total demand from school-age children	59,159
School accommodation available (from School Attendance Department)	
Number of pupils for which accommodation is available	55,876
Add Christian Brothers schools	+969
Total accommodation available	56,845

SOURCE: Education Committee Minutes, 28 March 1924, PRONI, LA/7/7AB/1

*Statutory age of attendance in 1924 was 6–14 years; however, younger children with working mothers were allowed to attend school.

Many schools did not have a playground and land was acquired where possible to provide an area outside the school buildings where pupils could play. One of the first schools to apply for transfer was Strand National School in Connsbrook Avenue in east Belfast, which had been built in 1913 from capital raised by the Duffin family and friends and managed by distinguished residents of the neighbourhood. A loan of £10,000 for the extension and refurbishment of the school was raised by the Education Committee and sanctioned by the Ministry of Education. Land adjoining the school was rented at £39 per annum and the extension built. Additional playgrounds were laid out – some tarred and some grassed. The school was redecorated and the railings and wall, which were in poor condition, were replaced with new ones to match the railings and wall round the new extension (Figure 15.5).

When the Education Amendment Act was passed in 1925 many more schools were transferred and put in good order. A Transfer of Schools Sub-Committee had been appointed in 1924 and was responsible for the administration of these transfers. The degree of reconditioning depended on the proposed life of each school, as many were intended to be used only for a short time until new or enlarged buildings were ready for occupation. This allowed the Education Committee to close schools that were in poor condition, while others were amalgamated.

FIGURE 15.3
Official opening of Templemore Avenue Public Elementary School, 1926; *front row, left to right*: William Robertson, Councillor Donald Cheyne, vice-chairman of the Education Committee, Sir Thomas Dixon, Alderman Duff, and Lord Mayor Sir William Turner (who opened the school); *background, left to right*: Major Rupert Stanley, director of education, Councillor Major Hall Thompson, chairman of the Sites and Building Committee, and Sir Frederick Moneypenny, city chamberlain.

BELFAST NEWS LETTER

FIGURE 15.4
Mural on a gable in Major Street, commemorating Templemore Avenue School

STEPHEN A. ROYLE

CATHOLIC SCHOOLS

As noted earlier, Catholic schools in Northern Ireland opted for Class III status and from 1923 received no support from local rates, with the exception of Christian Brothers' elementary schools, which accepted Class II status and were managed by Four and Two committees from April 1927.[5] For the rest, the Ministry of Education gave discretionary grants towards capital expenditure but the entire amount had to be repaid. Children attending Catholic schools had not been educated in poor accommodation, however, as the Catholic Church continued to raise money for their schools after partition. The finances of Class III schools improved with the passing of the 1930 Education Act, when grants of 50 per cent of the cost of approved capital works were awarded. The education architect drew the plans for St Comgall's Boys' and Girls' Public Elementary Schools, which were built on the site of the old Model School in Divis Street and opened in 1932, and St Patrick's Public Elementary School in Lancaster Street. He also conferred with the architect who designed St Kevin's Boys' and Girls' Public Elementary Schools on the Falls Road, which opened the same year.

TEMPLEMORE AVENUE PRIMARY SCHOOL OPENED 2ᵈ JULY 1926

Grants for capital works continued to increase over the years, albeit slowly, rising to 65 per cent with the passing of the 1947 Education Act. Then, after much debate, maintained status was granted in 1968, when all voluntary primary, secondary and special schools accepting one-third representation from the local education authority received in return 100 per cent maintenance and equipment costs from that authority and 80 per cent capital costs from the Ministry of Education, rising to 85 per cent in 1975. The Council for Catholic Maintained Schools, set up in 1987, played a part in influencing the Department of Education for Northern Ireland to increase expenditure on Catholic schools, and today 100 per cent funding is in place.

SCHOOLS MEDICAL SERVICE

The Education Committee, working through the Schools Medical Service Sub-Committee and the Recreation Sub-Committee, looked after the health, welfare and physical activities of all Belfast school children. The Schools Medical Service Sub-Committee was set up to fulfil Part 8, Health and Well-Being of Scholars, of the 1923 Education Act, and was responsible for all school children in Belfast. It began by sending a delegation to Glasgow, Edinburgh, Leicester and London to investigate the schemes for the medical inspection and feeding of pupils in those areas. From the beginning, the Education Committee considered it important to look after necessitous children, as they could not get the best out of their schooling if they were hungry, and very poor families could not afford school textbooks or stationery. In Belfast, provision of free meals for necessitous children in 1925 was granted when the total weekly income of the family, after rent and taxes had been deducted, was less than five shillings (25p) per head. Premises for a central kitchen were found in Tamar Street and the first free meals were provided for 132 children in Canton Street Hall on 10 February 1926. Further centres were set up throughout the city for all necessitous children who were entitled to free meals. In June 1927 the decision was also made to provide free meals during school holidays; however, the uptake was less than expected, with only half the children who had promised to attend actually doing so. During the depression years there was an increase in the number of children entitled to free meals, and in November 1932, 4,800 children were receiving a hot meal each day. Necessitous children also received free textbooks.

The Schools Medical Service had been set up by the Public Health Department of the Corporation before the 1923 Education Act was passed and subsequently transferred to the Education Committee. Dr T.F.S. Fulton, the chief of the service, was later remembered in the naming of Fleming Fulton Special School. His annual reports to the committee were realistic and direct. In one of his first reports he classified 51 of the 197 school buildings as totally unsuitable for school purposes. He had a staff of doctors, dentists, nurses and head-cleansers, many working part-time. Doctors and dentists visited all schools in Belfast and examined every child but only with parental permission, with the result that some children did not benefit from this crucial service. The children were examined on entry to school and on leaving, and any pupils with health problems were

TABLE 15.2
Scale of Charges for Various Treatments at School Clinics in Belfast, 1925

Dental treatment	1 shilling (5p) per head per annum
Minor ailments	free treatment for two weeks, then 1 shilling (5p) for next three months and 2 shillings (10p) for following six months
Provision of spectacles	7s. 6d. (37.5p) per pair prescribed
X-ray treatment for ringworm	full cost to be paid by parents
Tonsil and adenoid treatment	7s. 6d. (37.5p) for the operation and 1 shilling (5p) per day in clinic

SOURCE: Education Committee Minutes, 1925, PRONI, LA/7/7AB/1

re-examined as often as was thought necessary. A report to the Education Committee on 11 April 1924 on the school inspections carried out in eight schools during the two weeks ending 29 March 1924, for example, recorded that 487 children had been examined. Among the problems found were 107 children with defective vision, of whom only 7 wore glasses; 87 with enlarged tonsils, of whom 31 required immediate treatment; 102 with 5 or more decayed teeth; 18 with heart conditions; and 10 having or suspected to have tuberculosis. In the same period, nurses examined 3,275 children and found 11 per cent had nits and 1 per cent had lice. These children were referred to the school clinic for head cleansing. Dentists treated 256 children in the clinic and 21 were given a general anaesthetic for extractions. Parents paid for treatments carried out in the school clinics according to a fixed scale (Table 15.2).

The original Central Clinic for school children at 122 Great Victoria Street was closed in 1927 when the new Central Clinic, along with the Education Committee offices, was opened in the old Town Hall premises in Victoria Street. Twelve beds were provided for children requiring operations to remove tonsils and adenoids, but the parents of a number of children refused the operation claiming that they could not afford to pay the charge. Six boys and six girls were admitted twice a week for this treatment, and operations were carried out forty weeks a year. One lady, aged eighty-one when I interviewed her, remembers having her tonsils removed in the Central Clinic. She came from a large family living in a kitchen house, and sleeping on her own for two nights at the clinic was a treasured memory of childhood. Two branch clinics were already in operation. The first, at 28 The Mount, was opened in October 1925. The second, at 4 Carlisle Terrace, was opened in February 1926. It was reported to the Education Committee that 181 children had attended the Carlisle Terrace clinic on 10 February that year. A sun lamp was installed in Carlisle Terrace for the treatment of debilitated children, bought with £50 donated anonymously in 1926 (see, for example, Figure 15.6). Some treatments were not provided through the Schools Medical Service and operations for the correction of squints were not considered necessary.

FIGURE 15.6
An undernourished boy receiving UV treatment for rickets at the North Belfast Mission

NEWTOWNABBEY METHODIST MISSION

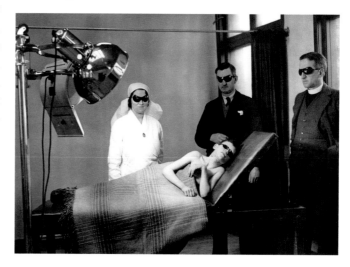

RECREATION FOR SCHOOL CHILDREN

FIGURE 15.7
Pavilion and caretaker's house,
North Road playing fields, 2005

E.J. CREIGHTON

The Recreation Sub-Committee was established in November 1925 and set out to make arrangements for organised games for public elementary school children. It secured the co-operation of sports bodies in the city such as the Irish Football Association and the Irish Hockey Union and used them to help locate suitable grounds. The Irish Life Saving Association helped establish swimming and life saving for school children in the public baths. There were competitions in various sports, and trophies and medals were provided from funds raised by a series of dances. The first dance was held in the Municipal College of Technology on 23 January 1926 and raised £17, a not inconsiderable sum at the time.

The Education Committee was not only concerned with providing new schools and reconditioning old ones: it also provided playing fields for elementary school children. The first was in east Belfast at North Road, where land was acquired for playing fields and a new public elementary school. The Ministry of Labour approved the scheme for the laying-out of these playing fields as an Unemployment Relief scheme and granted 75 per cent to go towards wages and expenditure. The playing fields were opened in May 1928 with a display of games and sports put on by the children. A combined pavilion and caretaker's house was erected in 1930 (Figure 15.7). In June 1935 the Education Committee gave elementary school children permission to use the playing fields in the afternoons and evenings, and cards were issued to identify children and permit entry. This plan was not successful, as few children availed themselves of the opportunity.

TABLE 15.3
Class I Schools Built by
Belfast Education Authority, 1926–39

Public elementary school	Year opened
Euston Street Senior	July 1926
Templemore Avenue	July 1926
Everton	January 1927
Park Parade	November 1927
Mersey Street	April 1929
Fane Street	April 1929
Glenwood	August 1930
Mountcollyer	October 1930
Strandtown	February 1931
Linfield Senior	October 1931
Hemsworth Square Senior	March 1932
Elmgrove	January 1933
Grosvenor	September 1933
Seaview	May 1934
Avoniel	September 1935
Nettlefield Junior	September 1936
Argyle Senior	March 1937
Edenderry	November 1937
Beechfield	April 1938
Botanic	June 1939
Grove Junior	November 1939
Orangefield	December 1946*

SOURCE: Education Committee Minutes, 1926–39,
PRONI, LA/7/7AB/1–7

*Orangefield was built before the outbreak of the
Second World War but was not officially opened until
December 1946.

SCHOOL BUILDING

The school built at the North Road playing fields was Strandtown Public Elementary School, which was the ninth school built by the Education Committee (Figure 15.8). It was designed by Reginald S. Wilshere, formerly chief assistant architect at Essex County Council. Wilshere, who had taken over from William Davies when he returned to England in April 1926, planned most other schools built in Belfast before the Second World War. Strandtown opened in February 1931, providing accommodation for over 1,000 children. That the appearance of the school has hardly changed since it was built is due to the advanced approach of the architect. Awarded the gold medal of the Royal Institute of British Architects (RIBA) for his work on Strandtown school, he was the first to receive the Ulster Medal for architecture awarded triennially by the institute; the medal can still be seen at the main entrance to the school.

The Education Committee prioritised the building and improvement of public elementary schools and no secondary or nursery schools were built using local authority money between the wars, although some grants were given towards the maintenance costs of existing schools. By the start of the Second

World War twenty-two new public elementary schools had been built (Table 15.3). Figure 15.9 shows that these schools were distributed across the Protestant areas of the city.

SCHOLARSHIPS

The school leaving age before the Second World War for most children was fourteen, so few had the opportunity to make the transition from elementary to secondary education, and even fewer to reach higher education. Higher education was limited to those who could afford to pay for it; the city funded an average of only five university scholarships per year. Secondary education was provided in grammar and non-denominational technical schools. Where parents could fund their children there was no problem, but for children from poor families the city provided only 50 scholarships for secondary schools a year – 30 for boys and 20 for girls. Applicants were examined in 'English, English Composition, Geography, Drawing, Arithmetic, Algebra and Geometry' and the top 100

FIGURE 15.8
Strandtown Primary School, North Road

STEPHEN A. ROYLE

FIGURE 15.9
Location of public elementary schools built in Belfast, 1926–39

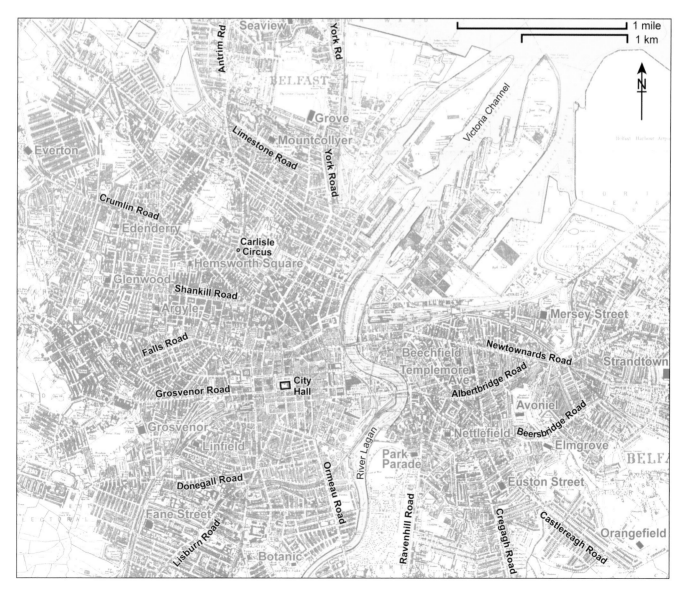

children were interviewed by a Board of Examiners before the scholarships were awarded. Each year the progress of the scholarship holders was assessed before they were supported for another year. Scholarships to commercial junior school were also offered to 4 girls and 2 boys a year.

With the limited number of scholarships available, not all schools prepared children for these examinations and not all children were given the opportunity to sit them. One lady, aged eighty-two when I interviewed her, clearly remembers that although her headmaster spoke to her mother about continuing her education, her mother felt unable to agree, as she was required to work to contribute to the household income like her brother and five sisters. The Education Committee assessed the means of the parents or guardians of all who were awarded a scholarship and if they were considered capable of paying the fees, the scholarship place was withdrawn.

SECOND WORLD WAR

The Second World War saw 18 schools in Belfast destroyed and 34 damaged by enemy bombing, mostly around the docks area of the city. The central kitchen in Tamar Street was also destroyed. No construction work on schools took place during the war years and the last school to be built before the war, Orangefield Public Elementary School, was not opened but used for wartime activities and, for a time, as a prisoner-of-war camp. One former pupil recalled seeing a German notice still displayed on a wall when the school finally opened in 1946.

From 1942 an improvement in services saw the provision of free milk to necessitous children and a more general school meals service was made available. Scholarships to grammar schools were increased from 50 to 200. The Edenderry Nursery School was placed under the control of the Education Committee, and the first grammar school under the control of the Education Committee was opened in January 1945. This was Grosvenor High School, which at that time occupied part of the existing Grosvenor Public Elementary School in Roden Street.[6]

POSTWAR — A NEW START

The 1947 Education Act, based on the 1944 Butler Act in Britain, changed the education system in Northern Ireland. The school leaving age was raised from fourteen to fifteen (a measure that was not fully implemented until 1957 due to insufficient school accommodation).[7] Secondary education was provided for all children. Pupils were to leave elementary schools at eleven, with a selection of the top 20 per cent destined for grammar schools. Local authorities paid the scholarships for the children in their areas who qualified for grammar schools, which were obliged to reserve places for successful candidates. The majority of children went to secondary intermediate schools, and to meet the initial demand in Belfast five of the new primary schools – Edenderry, Glenwood, Linfield, Mountcollyer and Park Parade – were changed to intermediate schools.[8] A programme of building began, and before his retirement in 1954 Wilshere was responsible for five new intermediate schools and two more primary schools. Catholic schools remained in the voluntary sector but now received 65 per cent capital grants, as well as being funded for the full cost of lighting and heating. Since the remainder of the money required for new Catholic schools still had to be raised, few voluntary secondary schools were built during the 1950s. The Ministry of Education attempted to introduce a third type of school in Belfast – the technical intermediate school – but the Education Committee rejected this move and avoided its implementation; as a result, technical subjects continued to be taught in secondary intermediate schools.[9]

A serious lack of facilities for physical activities benighted Belfast schools during and after the war. Figure 15.10 shows a physical education class exercising out of doors at Fane Street School on a rainy day in 1944. Many schools did not have halls and some playgrounds had been commandeered for air-raid shelters. The Education Committee quickly began to improve the situation by renting nearby premises for schools without halls, which were often used by more than one school. The new secondary intermediate schools and the grammar schools managed by the committee were provided with fully equipped gymnasiums and teachers were trained in physical education. The new intermediate schools were built mainly on the outskirts of the city, where land was available and playing fields could be included in the complex. Other purpose-built playing fields were provided throughout the city and in 1959–60 the Schools Capital Investment Programme showed an estimated expenditure of £252,000 on these facilities.

The Education Committee continued to build and look after educational affairs in Belfast until its responsibilities were transferred to the Belfast Education and Library Board on 1 October 1973, fifty years after the Belfast Education Authority had come into existence.

FIGURE 15.11
Queen's University Belfast
SCENIC IRELAND

Tertiary Education

The postwar era saw an increase in the number of scholarships to university awarded by the Education Committee. Scholarships were now awarded to all suitable candidates on a means-tested sliding scale, where the poorest received a full scholarship and better-off candidates received less, until eventually there was no value to the scholarship. In 1949, 38 scholarships were awarded, rising to 90 by 1952, with numbers increasing thereafter,[10] but by the beginning of the 1950s more than 60 per cent of all students at Queen's University Belfast (Figure 15.11) did not qualify for a scholarship and had to rely solely on family financial support.[11] By 1960, however, all students who gained admission to Queen's University were entitled to a scholarship. Despite this advance, university entrants did not represent an equal distribution across all socio-economic classes, and as late as 1973 only a quarter of undergraduates came from 'manual' working-class backgrounds.[12] These schemes continued to be revised over the years, and in 2000, 651 new undergraduate students entered Queen's University from the city of Belfast. All this took place in a context that saw the number of full-time students at Queen's rise from 2,276 in 1952 to 12,838 in 2000.[13]

As for further education, since the first decade of the twentieth century the Municipal College of Technology had been the sole provider for those who could afford it and the few who obtained scholarships. The 1947 Act initiated the development of further education, and on 1 December 1948 the Whitla Building in Stanhope Street was the first further education centre opened by the Education Committee; it was used by day-release students employed by the Post Office. The College of Technology increased its range of subjects and new buildings were opened at Millfield in 1962. In east Belfast, Rupert Stanley College, officially opened on 27 May 1965 by the then eighty-eight-year-old former director of education after whom it had been named, continued the work of providing further education in the city.[14]

Although the segregation of Protestant and Catholic children in primary and secondary education continued, the rapid expansion of colleges of further education provided non-denominational education for many over the age of sixteen. Several specialist colleges were opened to replace the unsuitable premises they occupied. The College of Domestic Science opened in Garnerville in 1962, the College of Art and Design in

York Street in 1968, and the College of Business Studies in Brunswick Street in 1971. In November 1963 the Lockwood Commission, set up to review higher education in Northern Ireland, recommended the establishment of a new university and an Ulster college to provide non-degree courses, which resulted in the opening of the New University in Coleraine in 1968 and the Ulster College at Jordanstown in 1971. The Ulster College became a polytechnic (Figure 15.12), expanding rapidly, and following a government review, the New University and the Ulster Polytechnic were amalgamated to form the University of Ulster in 1984. The University of Ulster at Jordanstown, just north of the city limits, serves the Belfast area and beyond.

TABLE 15.4
Integrated Schools in and around Belfast, 2000

Integrated school	Opened
Lagan College	1981
Forge Controlled Integrated Primary	1985
Hazelwood College	1985
Hazelwood Integrated Primary	1985
Cranmore Integrated Primary	1993
Lough View Integrated Primary	1993
Malone Integrated College	1997

SOURCE: Northern Ireland Council for Integrated Education, Annual Report 2002–03

Non-Denominational Education

The last three decades of the twentieth century saw the establishment of non-denominational primary and secondary education in Northern Ireland. In a challenge to segregation in schools, the All Children Together movement was set up in 1972 in north Down by a group of Catholic parents whose children were attending Catholic-controlled schools. Over the next few years the General Assembly of the Presbyterian Church and the Church of Ireland Synod agreed to support the principle of integrated education, but the Catholic Church continued to argue for Catholic children to be educated in Catholic schools. Despite this opposition, a poll conducted for *Fortnight* magazine in May 1973 showed substantial support for integrated education among parents from both religious communities: 64 per cent of Catholics and 59 per cent of Protestants.[15] Five years later, the 1978 Education (Northern Ireland) Act allowed a school to be treated as integrated if a ballot set up by the school committee showed that 75 per cent of parents approved the change.

FIGURE 15.13
Lagan College at its second location, 1982

LAGAN COLLEGE

It was clear that integration would work only if there was a mix of children from all denominations at the schools. Schools and parents campaigning for integration faced an uphill battle on two fronts. As well as the continued resistance of the Catholic authorities, Protestant clergy proved slow to acknowledge change, although their Churches supported the principle of integration. And since the Department of Education would not agree to fund a school until it proved its viability, parents had to support the school financially in the interim. The first integrated school in and around Belfast (and indeed in Northern Ireland), Lagan College, opened its doors in 1981 (Figure 15.13), and six more had been opened in and around Belfast by the end of the century (Table 15.4).

CONCLUSION

The integrated sector is growing but it is only a very small part of education provision in Belfast today, as shown in Table 15.5. There are resources such as the Workers' Educational Association (Figure 15.14), and others shown on the Belfast Education and Library Board's website[16] include the Belfast Institute of Further and Higher Education, the School of Music, a Hospital School, as well as special schools (Figure 15.15), resource centres, assessment centres and reading recovery units. The Irish language is used as a medium of instruction in several schools retaining a link to the ancient ethnic variety of Belfast (Figure 15.16), and the changing ethnic variety in the twenty-first century is shown by the need for a unit to teach English as a foreign language.

TABLE 15.5
Schools in the city of Belfast* 2004–5

Primary schools		Post Primary schools	
Controlled	45	Controlled secondary	8
Catholic maintained	35	Catholic maintained secondary	12
Irish medium maintained	7	Irish medium maintained secondary	1
Integrated	3	Integrated secondary	2
Grammar school preps	8	Controlled grammar	2
		Voluntary Catholic grammar	6
		Voluntary other grammar	8

*schools within the Belfast Education and Library Board area
SOURCE: Department of Education for Northern Ireland (www.deni.gov.uk)

Below left
FIGURE 15.14
Since 1910, the Workers' Educational Association has assisted communities to organise education that responds to their particular needs.

WEA NI

Below right
FIGURE 15.15
Fleming Fulton Special School, Upper Malone Road, Belfast

FLEMING FULTON SCHOOL

Over the twentieth century Belfast changed greatly. One aspect of change was the fall in the numbers of children in the city since 1901, as demonstrated in Table 15.6. Families are now smaller and many couples moved out of the city, especially during the recent Troubles. Smaller numbers have undoubtedly lessened the pressures on accommodation. Education for many children was once provided in crowded classrooms, which were, as we have heard, a 'disgrace to civilisation'. Today smaller numbers of children attend good quality, well-equipped schools with playgrounds, and playing fields are available. There is secondary education for all to sixteen years, although the controversial selection procedure for grammar school places has continued into the new century. Post-secondary education is provided by further education colleges, where a wide range of courses, both academic and vocational, are open to all, and limited family income does not preclude attendance. As for higher education, eighteen-year-olds and older have two local universities, as well as those 'across the water' and across the border, and changes in funding mean that family income no longer needs to prevent able students from gaining a degree as long as they are willing to take out student loans.

The Belfast Education and Library Board motto – 'Towards a learning city' – provides an inspiring catchphrase for the new millennium, and the people of Belfast can be justly proud of the wide range of educational facilities now available for their edification and enjoyment.

TABLE 15.6

Number of Children of Aged 5, 9, 14 and 16 Years in Belfast, 1901, 1951 and 2001

Number of children	1901	1951	2001
Age 5	7,926	7,891	3,576
Age 9	6,945	7,532	4,016
Age 14	6,993	7,087	4,124
Age 16	7,161	6,991	4,155

SOURCE: complied from census records

FIGURE 15.16
Meanscoil Feirste, an Irish language school on the Falls Road

BRIAN HUGHES

NOTES

1   *Belfast Evening Telegraph* (1908) 3 January.
2   McGrath, M. (2000) *The Catholic Church and Catholic Schools*, Irish Academic Press: Dublin.
3   The discussion in this and other sections of the chapter is based on material held in the Education Committee Minutes, Public Record Office of Northern Ireland (PRONI), LA/7/7AB/1.
4   Akenson, D.K. (1973) *Education and enmity: the control of schooling in Northern Ireland 1920–1950,* David and Charles: Newton Abbot.
5   McGrath (2000) *Catholic schools.*
6   Bardon, J. (1982) *Belfast: an illustrated history*, Blackstaff Press: Belfast.
7   McNeilly, N. (1973) *Exactly fifty years: the Belfast Education Authority and its work, 1923–1973,* Blackstaff Press: Belfast.

8   Bardon (1982) *Belfast.*
9   McNeilly (1973) *Exactly fifty years.*
10 McNeilly (1973) *Exactly fifty years.*
11 Clarkson, L.A. (2004) *A university in troubled times, Queen's Belfast 1945–2000,* Four Courts Press: Dublin.
12 Clarkson (2004) *Queen's.*
13 Clarkson (2004) *Queen's.*
14 McNeilly (1973) *Exactly fifty years.*
15 McGrath (2000) *Catholic schools.*
16 http://www.belb.org.uk, accessed on 20 February 2006.

The chasms that separated the classes at the beginning of the twentieth century in Belfast ensured striking differences in the amount of leisure time available and how it could be used. Atop the social pile there were around 300 wealthy families, nearly all Protestant, living at Strandtown or on the higher ground on the Malone Road and the Antrim Road. To a remarkable degree these families were interrelated. The men met in boardrooms, at the Harbour Office and the Chamber of Commerce, and dined with each other at the Ulster Club or the Reform Club. At the weekends they sailed on Belfast Lough and played golf. Their wives rarely moved out of their social circle but were deeply involved in charitable and Church work. Then, perhaps 6,000 families could afford to employ a maid and be considered members of the middle classes. Some could also afford to play golf and most could save enough to take the family on an annual holiday to the seaside. Church organisations depended heavily on their support and leadership.

16
Popular Culture

Jonathan Bardon

FIGURE 16.1
Children from the inner city on Belfast Central Mission's annual excursion to Bangor in the early 1900s

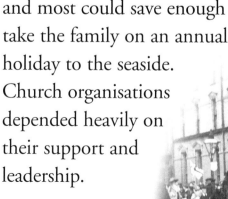

THE CHARITABLE AND THE DEPENDENT

A remarkable range of charities provided a crucial service to citizens and absorbed the energies of those with leisure, education and means (Figure 16.1). Smaller hospitals, such as the Samaritan, 'exclusively devoted to the treatment of diseases peculiar to women', depended entirely on benefactors and on voluntary subscriptions. Inevitably, most of the organisations which absorbed the charitable energies of the middle class were either Catholic or Protestant. They included: the Shankill Road Mission; the Discharged (Protestant Male) Prisoners' Aid Society; Nazareth House; the Ulster Magdalene Society, Donegall Pass; the Presbyterian Orphan Society; the Roman Catholic Ladies' Clothing Society; the Elim Home for Destitute Boys and Girls, 'to rescue orphans, homeless and destitute street arabs'; the Provident Home for Friendless Females of Good Character, 'who would otherwise be exposed to temptation'; and the Methodists' Belfast Central Mission which fed 3,500 every Christmas Day. City fathers and their wives were expected to give their time to be trustees of such funds as Lady Johnson's Bounty (which gave £12 per annum to 'unmarried females, being Protestants, of sober, honest life, above fifty years of age'); the Ulster Children's Aid Society (set up in 1910 'to rescue children from destitution and vagrancy, and from immoral and criminal surroundings'); and Mrs Wilson's Bequest 'to widows of sober, honest life'.

Just over a quarter of male manual workers were skilled artisans (the great majority of them Protestants) earning between 35 shillings and 45 shillings (£1.75 and £2.25) a week (after seven years of apprenticeship) and renting parlour terraced houses at 5 shillings or 6 shillings (25p or 30p) a week. They were acutely aware of their privileged position in the working class, which they strove to protect through their trade unions – indeed, around half of all trade unionists in Ireland were from Belfast. They worked a fifty-four-hour week but their work was precarious in times of trade recession and often dangerous (it was reckoned that every ship completed at Queen's Island cost a baker's dozen of lives).

GOD AND MAMMON

The unskilled – roughly equal numbers of Protestants and Catholics – could expect wages of no more than half those paid to the skilled, and a working week of between sixty-four and sixty-eight hours. Few were in trade unions until the protracted Dock Strike of 1907 when they largely went down to defeat. Their kitchen houses were rented at between 3s. 6d. and 4s. 6d. (17.5 p and 22.5p) a week, sometimes accommodating two families each. There was no expectation of holidays and even a tram ride was a luxury.[1] The continuing vigour of the Catholic renewal ensured high attendance at Mass. The evangelical revival, for all its successes in the countryside and with other classes, had difficulty in reaching the poorest of the Protestant working class – in 1908 only one in fifteen in Ballymacarrett were thought to attend church. However, only 797 citizens in the 1911 census refused to record their religious affiliation. After attending church, artisans and their families in their Sunday best could go to the Custom House steps to listen to the Methodist choir, speeches by socialist propagandists and anti-Catholic sermons given by preachers of the Belfast Protestant Association. In the evenings they might sample sermons from other Protestant churches, after which the unattached would walk up and down the Cregagh Road for a discreet viewing of the opposite sex. Privacy was a rare privilege in even the most respectable parlour houses until the 1960s – the sending of children to afternoon Sunday school provided a precious opportunity for an hour or so of undisturbed physical intimacy.

There was much comment on the 'immoral' behaviour of the unskilled working classes. Certainly Saturday nights were characterised by heavy drinking. Though public houses were overwhelmingly male establishments, women could patronise the extraordinary number of spirit grocers in the city. Edwardian Belfast had a licensed public house or shop for every 328 inhabitants. Apart from passing legislation that effectively closed down spirit groceries, the Northern Ireland government resisted the strident demands of prohibitionists. Temperance crusaders caused the Licensed Vintners Association to make an official complaint about 'so-called religious gatherings' outside bars in York Street and on the Crumlin Road every Saturday night. 'The noise and din created when they commence to sing is terrific,' the vintners explained. 'Meetings are invariably held at a corner where there is a public house. The members concerned do not mind a meeting being held there at intervals, but do object to one every Saturday night.'[2]

FIGURE 16.2
Dancers on the Bangor Boat celebrating the opening of the United Co-operative Bakery on Ormeau Road, 1906

ULSTER MUSEUM

Betting shops were illegal, but with the aid of newspaper sellers and bookmakers' touts, gambling flourished in the narrow streets. Many kept greyhounds and whippets, though it was not until 1927 that a dog-racing track – the first in Ireland – opened in Celtic Park. Later another track was set up at Dunmore. Dozens of men could be seen walking greyhounds before breakfast in the Woodvale and Falls parks and on race days trams were lined up to take devotees to and from the meetings. The outbreak of the Troubles in 1969 dealt dog-racing a mortal blow and the Park shopping centre supplanted the Celtic Park track. This pursuit, like horse- and pigeon-racing, cut across sectarian barriers. Horse-racing drew punters to venues such as the National Club in Berry Street, where legendary bookmakers Danny McGarry and Tim O'Connor took bets and paid out on Monday mornings. Later, keen followers of form would meet in the Morning Star in Pottingers Entry to gather intelligence for the Maze, Downpatrick and Comber race meetings.

For much of the century, save for spells of unemployment, time for recreation was severely limited. For many, female linen employees in particular, the working day – apart from breaks for breakfast and lunch – was so long that there was precious little time remaining for looking after the children, tending the fire, visiting the corner shop, and dealing with the laundry and cooking. The highlight of the year would be a works charabanc outing or a trip on the Bangor Boat (Figure 16.2). Domestic servants were lucky to snatch any free time at all. For most, the working week ended early on Saturday afternoon – much had to be packed into the remainder of that day, especially for Protestants intent on keeping the Sabbath holy.

Young working-class children had far more leisure time than their parents. During playtime at school and after school they could play handball, football and 'chaseys'; tussle; skip to rhymes only slightly varied from those in other major cities in the United Kingdom; and devise pranks such as pulling at a door knocker unseen, using a thread.

John Boyd remembered: 'We youngsters kept a sharp look-out for vans that we could "hop" – that is, we'd let them pass without taking any apparent notice of them, then we'd crouch double, race after them, and hop on the back without being noticed.'[3] From just after Easter to well into May, children singing 'Our Queen up the river with your yah-yah-yah' danced along the streets in high-heeled shoes and old lace curtains, accompanying their queen and collecting money for sweets, cakes and oranges (Figure 16.3). Games such as rally-o, cribby, kick-the-tin and mossycock, the racing of home-made guiders, and the marbles and hook-and-cleek seasons thrived in the narrow streets not yet clogged by parked cars.

The hectic boom immediately after the First World War was followed by a slump, which extended into a protracted depression. Men had leisure thrust upon them without the means to do very much with it. They gathered at street corners to play cards, push-halfpenny, toss-penny or marbles (known as 'bulking'). Recalling the 1930s, Hugh Shearman observed that 'Belfast has surely been unusual in having had so many grown men playing marbles … and at least one of the public parks had a special piece of tarmacadam laid down for them.'[4] No doubt brought to the city from its County Armagh home, bullet throwing had its keen adherents, though the throwing of solid iron balls nearly as large as a cricket ball in the streets was understandably illegal.

STAGE AND SCREEN

Throughout the nineteenth century the theatre in Belfast – notably the Alhambra in North Street (Figure 16.4), the Empire in Victoria Square and the Royal in Arthur Square – struggled to win respectability. The genteel were offended by violent pushing at entrance doors, drunken rowdyism, amateurs refusing to get off stage after intervals and the reek of urine flowing down channels in the aisles. This changed with the opening of the Grand Opera House in Glengall Place in 1895 – capable of seating 3,500, this sumptuous and extravagantly decorated theatre was a further demonstration that Belfast had become Ireland's largest and most prosperous city. Only the élite could afford seats in the dress circle at 4 shillings (20p) and boxes between £1 and £2. The proprietor, Fred Warden, could not rely on middle-class custom to fill the seats. For this reason the bulk of the fare offered consisted of melodramas, musical comedies, farces and variety acts that would appeal to those paying sixpence (2.5p) for gallery seats. However, the existence of such an appropriate venue attracted prestigious touring companies from Britain, including the Carl Rosa Opera Company, D'Oyly Carte, and Frank Benson and his Shakespearean Company. Humbler citizens were quite prepared to give Shakespeare a try; though when Benson was performing, one correspondent writing to the *Northern*

Whig deplored 'the scandalous conduct of the denizens of the gallery during the entire intervals between the acts, keeping up continually great disorder, and for a time turning the gallery into a pandemonium deafening and ear-splitting, with every description of noise'.[5]

The diet offered by theatres in Belfast was generally indistinguishable from that available in cities across the Irish Sea. The Ulster Literary Theatre, impressed by the success of the Irish Literary Theatre, sought to remedy this and put on its first production in St Mary's Hall in Bank Street in 1902. Protestants though these activists mostly were, they were separatists swimming against the strong unionist tide, then rousing itself to oppose Home Rule. Only when the Ulster Literary Theatre shook itself free of attempts to ape the stylised verse plays on heroic Ireland by Yeats did it begin to attract respectable audiences. Some of these northern playwrights tackled sensitive problems of intercommunal division and clashing political aspirations. Lewis Purcell dealt with mixed marriage in *The Pagan* and Gerald McNamara (Harry Morrow), deftly mixing the past and present, captivated audiences with *Thompson in Tír na nÓg*, *No Surrender* and *Suzanne and the Sovereigns*. The *Northern Whig* observed of the last play: 'Neither Orangeman nor Nationalist with a spark of humour could help laughing consumedly as absurdity was heaped upon absurdity.'[6] These plays gave pleasure, however, partly because they did not make audiences uncomfortable – sectarianism was reduced to being a colourful provincial phenomenon.

Belfast was the most literate corner of Ireland and the very divisions in the community ensured a wide choice of daily newspapers and weekly journals. The unionist *Belfast Evening Telegraph*, *Belfast News Letter* and *Northern Whig*, and the nationalist *Irish News* had little to fear from cross-channel dailies until the 1960s. The most politically independent was the *Nomad's Weekly*, a lively paper that did much to expose corruption in Belfast Corporation. The Presbyterian *Witness* and the Methodist *Christian Advocate* covered a wide range of subjects and were not afraid to challenge the establishment; they frequently concerned themselves with social issues, such as the problem of deprivation.

The launch of the *Oceanic*, the largest man-made moving object constructed up to that time, was celebrated on that evening, 14 January 1899, by the projection of footage of the ceremony at Queen's Island onto the outside walls of the *Belfast Evening Telegraph* building in Royal Avenue. Soon after, the city's variety theatres slowly began to include short film screenings in their programmes, but Belfast still had only one purpose-built cinema, the Electric, until 1 August 1910. Thereafter, growth was remarkably rapid. By the beginning of 1914 the city had twelve picture houses to meet the demand for longer films, such as D.W. Griffith's

FIGURE 16.4
The Alhambra theatre,
North Street

ULSTER MUSEUM

FIGURE 16.5
Stanley Wylie at the organ in
the Ritz cinema, Fisherwick
Place, 1940s

BELFAST CENTRAL LIBRARY

FIGURE 16.6
The Ritz, the largest cinema in
Northern Ireland, opened in
Fisherwick Place in 1936.

ULSTER MUSEUM

Birth of a Nation and those featuring Charlie Chaplin. By the end of the First World War around one-quarter of the population was going to the cinema at least once a week. The large city centre houses showed the latest films and provided organs (Figure 16.5) or orchestras – the one at the Picture House in Royal Avenue had forty instrumentalists – which played in accompaniment to silent films from specially provided scores. The much cheaper suburban cinemas screened films (usually worn and scratched) often years after their first release in central Belfast, generally with a lone pianist in accompaniment.

Entertainments advertised in the *Belfast Evening Telegraph* on Tuesday 2 April 1912 – the day the *Titanic* sailed out of Belfast Lough – included: The Four Cheres, supported by a 'strong vaudeville company', at the Empire; *The Knave of Spades*, a detective drama, at St George's Hall; the Belfast Postal Band in the Ulster Hall; *The Corsican Brothers*, a thrilling drama, in the Theatre Royal; and Lady Little in the Hippodrome, nineteen years old, only twenty-three inches high and weighing a mere ten and a quarter pounds. The Grand Opera House was showing 'The Wonderful Kinemacolor Pictures', including: 'With our King and Queen in India; Calcutta Races; Winter Scenes in Sweden; Marvellous Egyptian Sunsets; Run with the Exmoor Staghounds; review of Troops by King and Kaiser &, &'.

Most of the larger cinemas had installed sound equipment by 1931 but some, unwilling to face the cost, closed down instead. Fears that unemployment and deprivation in the wake of the depression would reduce audiences proved unfounded. Between 1935 and 1937 Belfast acquired an additional twelve cinemas, several of them luxurious suburban houses designed by McBride, McNeill and Thomas. The Ritz, the Curzon, the Park and the Broadway all opened on one day, 12 December 1936 (Figure 16.6).[7] By the end of the decade cinemas were to be found in the city centre, all the main suburbs, and on the main roads leading into Belfast. The theatre held its own, however, and Belfast shared in the interwar popularity of musicals such as *The Student Prince*, *Rose Marie* and *The Desert Song*. Live variety was the staple fare; Harry Lauder and Gracie Fields were sure of capacity audiences; and Jack Payne, Henry Hall and Mrs Jack Hylton brought their big bands to the stage.

FROM 2BE TO BBC

Those who peruse the back issues of Belfast newspapers up to the beginning of the Second World War will be struck by the high quality of writing and by the extensive coverage given to local events. The violence of 1920–22, for example, was chronicled day after day in extraordinary detail by reporters who clearly put their own lives in danger each night – editorial interpretations sharply differed but accounts of events coincided to a remarkable degree. Certainly citizens did not turn to the radio for local news.

From a studio on the first floor of a disused linen warehouse at 31 Linenhall Street, 2BE, the Belfast station of the British Broadcasting Company, made its first broadcast on 15 September 1924. Newspaper proprietors succeeded in imposing severe restrictions reducing the latest news to terse bulletins. In addition, the director of programmes insisted that bulletins 'give but the barest publicity to tragedies and other sordid happenings'. This state of affairs continued and, although the 1935 York Street riots had led to the deaths of fifteen people, the BBC provided no details or comment – listeners were simply told that 'a riot had arisen'.

FIGURE 16.7
Thompson's Quartette, Thompson's Café, 1930
ULSTER MUSEUM

By the time of the formal opening of the station on 25 October 1924, over 5,000 licences had been issued in Belfast. A wireless set could be bought for 7s. 6d. (37.5p), but most citizens (many without licences) were listening in on crystal sets. Music was the main offering during the first years. Local musicians must have been run ragged because the lines from Britain were so uncertain that most of the overwhelmingly classical musical output had to be produced in the Belfast studio. The *Belfast Evening Telegraph*'s music critic haughtily denounced the popularisation of classical music: 'Music is no longer the cherished mistress of the connoisseur … Music is being degraded by its widespreading.' Even some cafés had live musicians (Figure 16.7). It does seem that the appeal of classical music was being extended by the BBC. Support for live broadcasts of orchestral concerts, with such distinguished conductors as Sir Henry Wood and Adrian Boult, was so great that often hundreds were turned away. In 1932, for example, there were 24 public broadcast concerts, 14 in the Ulster Hall and 10 in the YMCA's Wellington Hall (Figure 16.8). By that time much of the output came directly from London but the Linenhall studios offered a regular diet of talks and plays.

FIGURE 16.8
BBC orchestra at the YMCA's Wellington Hall, Wellington Place, 1931
ULSTER MUSEUM

WARTIME

In the autumn of 1939 the great majority of people in Northern Ireland, including the prime minister, Lord Craigavon, assumed that the battle lines would be safely confined to the European mainland. It was not until 1940, as German tank units struck through the Ardennes, that it slowly became apparent that Belfast might be vulnerable. In that year restrictions were placed on the travel of touring companies and, in response, the Grand Opera House formed its own repertory company, the Savoy Players. No doubt because Éire remained neutral,

the only Irish dramatist to meet the approval of the producer, Frederick Tripp, was George Bernard Shaw. Tripp was rewarded by capacity audiences for performances every weeknight and twice on Saturdays. Jimmy Dugan, the commissionaire at the gallery door of the theatre, recalled that nearly 1,700 squeezed into the 'gods': 'They all came in with a rush. Many's a time I was put on my back when I opened the door down below.'[8]

During the air raids of the spring of 1941, Dugan was one of thousands whose homes were destroyed. Audiences shrank as tens of thousands evacuated to the countryside, and more thousands tramped to the outskirts of the city to sleep in the open for fear the Luftwaffe would return. The Queen's, Midland and Lyric cinemas were almost destroyed in the blitz and others were damaged. Audiences soon recovered, however – the cinemas providing warmth, comfort and welcome distraction for those with blitzed homes who were being put up in spartan conditions in church halls and rest centres. The sound newsreel had first covered Belfast in a major feature on the Outdoor Relief riots in 1932; now it was a vital source of information for citizens on the progress of the war.

In the summer of 1941 Hitler turned his attention to the Soviet Union, and the following year the first American troops to land in Europe stepped ashore at Dufferin Quay on 26 January. Their arrival coincided with the return of evacuated citizens to Belfast, which was rapidly becoming an arsenal of victory. After two decades of economic decline and deprivation, workers and their families had full employment and money to spare in their pockets. The city now enjoyed one of the liveliest and most varied periods of public entertainment.

In the 1930s the Empire theatre had been the centre of home-produced drama (Figure 16.9). Then, in the winter of 1939–40, three companies joined forces to set up the Ulster Group Theatre. It had no theatre of its own and it therefore leased the Ulster Minor Hall, opening in March 1940 with four plays over twelve weeks. It emerged with a small profit, but it was the extended run of St John Ervine's *Boyd's Shop* that ensured viability. 'Some quality in St John Ervine's play reminded men and women of homely virtues reported missing if not already dead in those sombre early days and black nights of the War,' Sam Hanna Bell observed.[9] American servicemen helped to swell the audiences. On one occasion, after a production of *The Drone* was preceded by a Chekhov curtain-raiser, an American said to Tomelty: 'Look, I don't understand this. This thing starts off in Russia and lands in Co Down.'[10] For three weeks in 1944 the US Army presented *This is the Army* at the Grand Opera House and the author, Irving Berlin, made an appearance. By the end of the war the cultural life of Belfast seemed to thrive in an atmosphere of euphoria and self-congratulation.

FIGURE 16.9
Ali Baba at the Empire, Victoria Square, 1936
ULSTER MUSEUM

POSTWAR CINEMA, THEATRE AND LOCAL BROADCASTING

To prevent enemy aircraft from using regional frequencies to help them find their targets, the BBC in Belfast had closed down. The people of Belfast, of course, listened avidly to the Home Service and the Forces Programme both for news of the war and for entertainment. A few months after the end of the war the Linenhall studios began to make programmes for both network services. *Irish Rhythms*, created by David Curry, became one of the most listened to series of programmes ever broadcast by BBC radio. Local opinion was divided, however: traditional musicians questioned whether it was Irish music at all, while unionists were displeased because they believed that Ulster culture was being supplanted by Irish culture.

The period immediately after the war is considered to be the golden era of radio and this was particularly so for audiences in Northern Ireland. News output remained paltry, but producers such as Denis Johnston, Sam Hanna Bell and John Boyd ensured that programmes were more inclusive, more informative, more entertaining and much better crafted than before, in a wide range of outside broadcasts, documentaries and talks. *The McCooeys*, written by actor-playwright Joseph Tomelty, was first broadcast on 13 May 1949 and rapidly became the most popular and discussed programme ever broadcast in Northern Ireland (Figure 16.10). Henry McMullan, the programme director, once got a telephone call from Lord Brookeborough:

> On one occasion the Prime Minister of the day rang me up, on a personal basis, saying could I put *The McCooeys* on at half past seven because they were having frightful trouble, because they all said firmly 'No dinner until *The McCooeys* is over' and this was Saturday night? 'And as well as that you do it on a Monday,' he said. I said very firmly: 'It's got its placing, and that's where it's going to stay.'[11]

The McCooeys ran for seven years until in 1957 Tomelty was injured in a serious motor-car accident and was unable to continue the series. By then television's challenge to radio's domination was well under way.

Local theatres faced changes as actors pursued their careers in broadcasting and in London, notably Joseph Tomelty, who had partially recovered from his accident, Harry Towb, James Ellis and Denys Hawthorne, while Colin Blakely, Stephen Boyd and Harold Goldblatt became Hollywood stars. Jack Hudson and James Young, the great comic actor, assumed management of the Group Theatre, which was justifiably subtitled the 'Home of Ulster Comedy'. Between 1940 and 1955 the theatre was responsible for giving fifty plays their first performances. The first new theatre to be built in Belfast for fifty years was the Belfast Arts Theatre, opened in Botanic Avenue on 17 April 1961. This was the creation of Dorothy and Hubert Wilmot, who had formed a drama group in 1944. In the end it proved financially impossible for such a theatre, without Arts Council

FIGURE 16.10
One of the most popular radio serials ever broadcast from Belfast, *The McCooeys* ran for seven years, until 1957.

BBC NI

FIGURE 16.11
A production of *Romeo and Juliet* at the Lyric Theatre, Derryvolgie Avenue

LYRIC THEATRE

FIGURE 16.12
James Green at the UTV *Early Bird* link-up

ULSTER FOLK & TRANSPORT MUSEUM

subsidies, to survive by offering an unrelieved diet of serious contemporary plays. Hubert Wilmot explained that 'only by presenting *entertainment* can the living theatre survive the intense competition brought about by TV and the rapidly-changing pattern of living in the last few years'.[12] In a questionnaire the audience voted overwhelmingly for musicals and comedies and Wilmot gave in to them. The most reliable audience-pullers were farces by Sam Cree.

Cinema audiences were at their greatest in 1946 when people would regularly go out twice a week for a show, which included the 'big picture', a support feature (the 'B' movie), cartoons, a newsreel and a trailer. Children needed only three pence (under 2p) or two empty 2 lb jam jars to get in to matinées. Frank Murray vividly recalls the long dark tunnel leading down to the front seats in the Broadway on the Falls Road: at the end of the last film many tried to stay on for the next show but they were diligently hunted down and expelled by usherettes probing the rows with their torch beams. The future seemed so secure that the Rank Organisation in the mid-1950s found it worthwhile to acquire the lion's share of the city's leading cinemas. This proved a bad investment: the fast-growing popularity of television kept people in their homes, which were rapidly gaining in comfort. Thirteen picture houses closed down in the 1960s and the only gain was the opening of the Queen's Film Theatre in 1968, which brought to enthusiasts foreign language and art-house films not shown in other Belfast cinemas.

The demolition of the Empire theatre in 1961 demonstrated that by now managing live theatre required a special kind of commitment. Mary O'Malley certainly possessed this dedication and she and her husband, Pearse, formed the Lyric Players Theatre in 1951, creating a theatre seating fifty people at the back of their Derryvolgie Avenue house (Figure 16.11). Around half the plays were Irish, but American, Russian, Spanish, Italian and Chinese plays were also performed. Another remarkable addition to Belfast's cultural life was the Festival at Queen's University. This was largely the creation of a dynamic Englishman, Michael Emmerson, who, after making a successful start in 1963, was appointed professional director by the Students Representative Council the following year. He organised recitals by such stars as Russian pianist Sviatoslav Richter and Indian sitar virtuoso Ravi Shankar, but it was the great variety of events ranging from late night review to jazz, folk, modern dance, poetry readings and stand-up comedy that gave the festival such a wide appeal.

An agreement to provide a Northern Ireland television service was made in 1949 but it was not until 1952, as Queen Elizabeth II's accession to the throne approached, that a rather unseemly rush was made to put up a temporary transmitter. Only a tiny proportion of the BBC's output received in Belfast was locally produced. It included *Today in Northern Ireland*, a weekday evening programme of news and features lasting a mere five minutes; *Studio Eight*, a weekly magazine;

and a total of six half-hour documentaries a year. The arrival of Ulster Television in October 1959 at last offered viewers a choice (Figure 16.12). Partly because of the competition, the hands of those who were calling for more adventurous programming in the BBC were strengthened.

It was only from the early 1960s that broadcasters were able to cast aside the extreme timidity of previous decades to provide listeners and viewers with a meaty diet of news and investigative journalism. Coverage of the 1964 Divis Street riots and later housing protests, and the provision of adequate air time to critics of the government certainly made the people of Belfast more politically aware. Television news film of demonstrations against the Vietnam War, the black civil rights movement in America, the brutal ending of the Prague Spring in 1968 and the student riots in Paris the same year did more than local reports, however, to make street protest respectable. By then television had become such a powerful medium that it was sapping the vigour of more traditional sources of news and entertainment.

There had been forty-two picture houses in Belfast in 1957. By 1969 there were only twenty. The onset of protracted political and sectarian violence further hastened this decline. The Broadway was set on fire and for several years the city centre all but closed down each night from 7 p.m. onwards. On 23 September 1977 fire bomb attacks severely damaged the ABC, the New Vic and the Curzon and, by the end of the 1970s, only six cinemas remained. A reduction in street violence and the changing character of the campaigns conducted by the paramilitaries in the 1980s helped nightlife to revive in Belfast, and the release of immensely popular blockbusters such as *Star Wars* began to bring back cinema audiences.[13] Along with other cities in the UK, multiplex screens ushered in a new era of cinema-going, most notably at Yorkgate, the Dublin Road and the Odyssey.

FIGURE 16.13
Come Dancing from the Plaza Ballroom in Chichester Street in the 1960s

BBC NI

THE SHOWBAND YEARS

Belfast had good claim to be Ireland's dancing capital. During the 1950s, 1960s and early 1970s the dance halls tended to cluster in a remarkably small area. The pleasing spring of the upper mezzanine floor of Leisureworld in Queen Street is a reminder that it was once the hugely popular Romano's Ballroom. Close by, in Fountain Street, was Maxim's. The Maritime Club in College Square North became the famous venue for Van Morrison's group Them. Perhaps the grandest ballroom of all was the Plaza on Chichester Street (Figure 16.13). It hosted heats of the BBC's *Come Dancing* and boasted a revolving stage and luxurious rest rooms with mirrors, even for the men. It acquired a reputation for attracting teddy boys and was slowly shunned by the more respectable patrons, who preferred the Saturday night dances in the Technical College's Central Hall. The Celebrity Club, later taken over by the shop chain C&A, in Donegall Place, flourished in the 1960s, as did the Starlight, which later became the Boom Boom Room, at the corner of Arthur Square and Castle Lane on the site of the Theatre Royal. Bouncers at the Astor in College Court knew that demand always exceeded supply and would simply refuse entry if they did not like the look of the faces of aspiring patrons. Many found it worthwhile ascending four floors to the Orpheus in the Belfast Co-operative building in York Street. And on Saturday nights the driveway to the Floral Hall at Hazelwood (Figure 16.14) was crammed with cars right down to the Antrim Road. Close at hand, on the corner of Donegall Park Avenue and the Shore Road, was the Satellite Ballroom.

Mastering the foxtrot, the quickstep and the tango often called for tuition in studios such as Betty Staff's in Great Victoria Street, John Dosser's in Ann Street, or Clarke's Dance Studio, which was still thriving in Donegall Street in 2005. Right up to the start of civil unrest in 1969 all the city dance halls were freely patronised by a mixed clientele of Catholics and Protestants. A particularly busy time was during 'dinner hour' – especially in the Plaza, whose lunch-hour sessions were hugely popular with city centre workers. Afternoon 'tea dances' could attract bored housewives seeking the opportunity to flirt with younger men who were branded, generally with some exaggeration, as 'gigolos'. Many parish churches organised dances and some in the lower Falls attracted Protestants from the neighbouring Shankill on Sunday afternoons. Dance halls did not serve alcohol but a few gave out cigarettes at the door for later in the evening when, at a prearranged point, all lights were turned off for the cigarette dance – 'I used to hold the fag because I couldn't smoke,' Kathleen Mack remembered of dances in St Comgall's. The most popular dance halls in the Shankill were the Rialto on Peter's Hill and the Beresford at the bottom of Brown Square. These smaller venues were called jigs and the live music was often supplied solely by an accordion player and a drummer.[14]

Top right
FIGURE 16.14
Floral Hall, 1936: this popular Art Deco ballroom in Hazelwood closed in the early 1970s with the onslaught of the Troubles.

ULSTER MUSEUM

Below
FIGURE 16.15
The McPeake Family in their house on Springfield Street, 1983

BILL KIRK

The Embassy Club in Fountain Street, however, allowed patrons to bring in alcohol; it soon acquired a reputation as a 'dive', attracting ladies of low repute.

Belfast citizens took enormous pride in the success of home-produced stars such as Ruby Murray from Benburb Street, who began her career as a member of the Richview Presbyterian church choir, made her first public appearance in ankle socks in St Mary's Hall, shot to fame after appearing in a *Quite Contrary* show on BBC television, reached number 1 in the hit parade with 'Softly, Softly', and had a record five hits in the Top 20 simultaneously. Moreover, during this period, Ronnie Cleghorn from Cregagh, who adopted the name Ronnie Carroll, achieved international fame as a crooner with 'Roses are Red'. The folk music revival was quickly embraced in Belfast at the beginning of the 1960s. However, traditional music, in particular the playing of uileann pipes, for long had its dedicated devotees in Catholic districts. Now groups such as the McPeake Family (Figures 16.15) began to enjoy a much wider cross-community following and just before the onset of the Troubles it was not uncommon in bars with singing licences to hear young middle-class Protestants joining in choruses of republican ballads such as 'The Foggy Dew' and 'Sean South of Garryowen'.

The larger city centre ballrooms needed to attract big names to sustain their reputations. A particularly Irish phenomenon – thriving in the 1950s, 1960s and early 1970s – was the touring showbands. At one time there were around 3,000 musicians, wearing black winklepickers and with hair slicked down with Brylcreem, in some 500 bands on the road. All the most prestigious showbands played in Belfast. They included: the Freshmen from Ballymena; the Plattermen from Omagh with its splendid brass section; the Royal Showband with Brendan Bowyer as the lead; Joe Dolan; Dickie Rock; George Jones of Clubsound (Belfast's most popular band); the Capitol Showband; and Teddie Palmer and the Rumble Band (Figure 16.16). In the early 1970s the showband scene

FIGURE 16.16
Teddie Palmer and the Rumble Band in High Street, 1970. Teddie is in the middle.
WWW.IRISH-SHOWBANDS.COM/
TEDDIE PALMER

began to lose its appeal. Competition from pubs and discos, which served alcohol, was largely responsible but in Belfast intense rioting swiftly caused nightlife in the city centre to atrophy. Finally, the Miami Showband massacre, as it came to be known, brought the showband scene to a tragic and grisly conclusion in July 1975; three band members were shot dead and another was seriously injured in an Ulster Volunteer Force (UVF) gun attack, and two UVF men were killed when their bomb exploded prematurely.

High profile performers needed the largest venue, the King's Hall at Balmoral. Louis Armstrong played there on 25 April 1962 before 3,000 people, stepping on stage as the Jimmy Compton band was playing a jazz version of 'When Irish Eyes are Smiling'.[15] The Ritz was also a capacious venue for such visitors as the Beach Boys (though local opinion was that the warm-up band, Derek Dean and the Freshmen, stole the show). The Beatles made their appearance at the Ritz in November 1963, and at the King's Hall the following year, while the Rolling Stones chose the Ulster Hall as their venue in July 1964 and the ABC in September 1965. The Jimi Hendrix Experience played the Whitla Hall on 27 November 1967, Hendrix's birthday, and a cake was presented to him on stage.

Jazz enjoyed a dedicated following in Belfast, particularly during the 1960s. Performances were best suited to smaller venues such as Sammy Houston's Jazz Club in Great Victoria Street, the Salisbury Avenue Bowling Club and the Cavehill Lawn Tennis Club. Rugby clubs, tennis clubs such as the Fruithill Tennis Club in Andersonstown, the Bankers' Club above Queen's Arcade, the Christian Brothers Club in Cornmarket and the Drill Hall in Queen's University provided favoured venues for young members of the middle class.

THE YEARS OF VIOLENCE

In retrospect it is remarkable that so much public entertainment survived the violence in the city from the spring of 1969 onwards. However, during the bloodiest years, from 1971 to 1976, the city centre became deserted in the evenings as public houses closed early, cinemas closed down altogether and public transport all but ceased after dark. Out-of-town venues picked up the trade lost from the centre, although they, too, were vulnerable to the bomber. In the enclaves, shebeens – illegal drinking clubs – sprang into existence side by side with legitimate clubs which attracted an exclusively Catholic or Protestant clientele. In such dens dark deeds were plotted and on occasion perpetrated. Parts of the city less affected by the violence continued to attract 'mixed' (largely middle-class) custom; they included the Queen's University area, the Upper Newtownards Road and the Stormont area. The jazz scene remained remarkably vibrant: mainstream jazz was centred in the Glenmachan Hotel in east Belfast; the Jubilee bar in Cromac Square specialised in rhythm and blues; and full modern jazz orchestras of up to fifteen players drew large west Belfast audiences to the Friar's Bush in Dunmurry. The Festival at Queen's continued to flourish: Emmerson left in 1971 and the successor who organised the festival in its most dynamic years was another Englishman, the history lecturer Michael Barnes. Michael Palin, who made a regular appearance at the annual event, observed: 'I find in the city and people of Belfast an energy potential, a reserve of wit and intelligence and unaffected enthusiasm which I haven't found on the same scale anywhere else.'[16]

During the worst years of the Troubles the people of Belfast ventured out of their homes – particularly during the long winter nights – only when they had to. The broadcast media became not only the prime source of entertainment but also of news, often of crucial local relevance. Downtown Radio was the first station to provide news at hourly intervals throughout the day. It was the Ulster Workers' Council strike in May 1974 that demonstrated the need for a round-the-clock local news service. The BBC's response was to launch Radio Ulster as a separate station in 1975.

Early in 1983 Padraig O'Malley, an American political scientist, described Belfast as 'ugly and sore to the eye, the will to go on gone … a modern wasteland … Only the ghettoes have their own vitality. By early evening Belfast is abandoned.'[17] Patrick Bishop, who covered Ireland for the *Observer* between 1979 and 1982, went so far as to compare the provincial capital to 'Berlin after a thousand bomber raid'. He continued:

> The poverty is ancient and ingrained. The buildings seem to be suffering from a contagion that has covered them with boils and scabs. Single terraces stand in isolation in rubble lakes where bonfires perpetually burn, watched by tough, ragged little boys and skinny dogs. Every surface is etched minutely and obsessively with graffiti.[18]

FIGURE 16.17
The start of the Belfast Marathon at the Albert Bridge, May 1986
BELFAST TELEGRAPH

RECOVERY AND RIVERSIDE REVIVAL

Yet even as these impressions were being written, the transformation of Belfast had begun. In part this was due to changes in tactics by the paramilitaries, particularly the Provisional IRA. No longer subjected to body searches, citizens were able to pour in and out of the security gates at will. As the city centre was coming back to life, punk rockers could be seen meeting in Cornmarket on Saturday afternoons. Bright shops and boutiques blossomed, and flower tubs, thousands of trees, new paving and modern lamp standards adorned the main streets. An ambitious scheme to provide floodlighting for large buildings helped to create an atmosphere of greater safety at night. High profile events began to be staged, such as the annual Belfast Marathon (Figure 16.17), which started in 1982. For years the sole city centre venue for *haute cuisine* of assured quality was Restaurant 44 in Bedford Street. Then, between 1982 and 1985, 41 restaurants, 38 cafés and 55 hot-food bars opened in downtown Belfast. 'The spirit of the Blitz has been institutionalised so that people preserve and protect what bits of normality remain to them,' Patrick Bishop wrote in 1984. 'There is something brave and encouraging about the indefatigable diners and the denizens of the discos.'[19]

FIGURE 16.18
The Hole in the Wall Gang
BBC NI

Around £86 million was invested in commercial development in the inner city between 1982 and 1985, and it was estimated that in 1984 alone day-trippers from the Republic spent £120 million in the region, much of it in Belfast. Following the massive protest on Saturday 23 November 1985 against the Anglo-Irish Agreement signed at Hillsborough, the urban myth circulated that a Dublin day-tripper, seeing a dense crowd just ahead, asked whether or not it was the queue for Argos.

The Grand Opera House had been forced to close its doors in 1972 and, unused, the fabric of the building decayed rapidly. Primarily with the support of the Northern Ireland Arts Council, the decision was made to carry out a restoration, and on 15 September 1980 the theatre reopened with a gala performance. An imaginative and varied programme attracted capacity audiences for *Tosca*, Brian Friel's *Translations* and other shows including the pantomime *Cinderella*, with Frank Carson as Buttons, which attracted 97 per cent audiences.

Despite an intensification of violence during the first four years of the decade, the 1990s demonstrated that young people were more determined than ever to go out and socialise in public places. Popular 'clubbing' venues included: the Limelight in Ormeau Avenue; the Beaten Docket in Amelia Street; Ziggy's in Blackstaff Square; the Botanic Inn and the Wellington Park Hotel on the Malone Road; the Manhattan and Lavery's in Bradbury Place; and Renshaw's in University Street. The Empire, a converted church in Botanic Avenue, attracted enthusiastic support for its comedy club and it was here that the Hole in the Wall Gang first established its reputation (Figure 16.18). Ice skating had been established as a popular recreation as early as the 1930s in the King's Hall; from the 1980s it enjoyed renewed popularity, particularly for those too young to go clubbing, at the Dundonald International Ice Bowl.

The showpiece of the 1989 Belfast Urban Area Plan had been the Laganside scheme to transform around 300 acres (121 ha) of the port's waterfront into a tourist and leisure complex. The Lagan Bridge opened in 1994, immediately easing the flow of traffic and assisting access as the paramilitary ceasefires began to bring a quickening to the city's social life. Once the Waterfront Hall opened its doors in 1997, the riverside began to thrive as a centre for opera, ballet, conferences, nightclubs and performances by popular stars and groups. As the final weeks of the second millennium approached, the people of Belfast could see the £91 million Odyssey complex begin to take shape to provide a 10,000-seat arena, with an ice rink for ice hockey (Figure 16.19) and ice shows, a science centre, an IMAX theatre and a pavilion on a 23 acre (9.3 ha) site.

FIGURE 16.19
The Belfast Giants playing at home in the Odyssey arena.
MICHAEL COOPER

NOTES

1   Gribbon, Sybil (1982) *Edwardian Belfast: a social profile*, Appletree Press: Belfast, pp. 13–20.

2   Law, Gary (2002) *Historic pubs of Belfast*, Appletree Press: Belfast, p. 10.

3   Boyd, John (1985), *Out of My Class*, anthologised in Patricia Craig (1999) *The Belfast anthology*, Blackstaff Press: Belfast, p. 194.

4   Shearman, Hugh (1949) *Ulster*, anthologised in Craig (1999) *Belfast anthology*, p. 361.

5   Gallagher, Lyn (1995) *The Grand Opera House, Belfast*, Blackstaff Press: Belfast, p. 31.

6   Bell, Sam Hanna (1972) *The theatre in Ulster*, Gill and Macmillan: Dublin, p. 30.

7   Open, Michael (1985) *Fading lights, silver screens: a history of Belfast cinemas*, Greystone Books: Antrim, pp. 1–8.

8   Gallagher (1995) *Grand Opera House*, p. 59.

9   Bell (1972) *Theatre in Ulster*, pp. 70–72.

10 Bell (1972) *Theatre in Ulster*, p. 73.

11 Bardon, Jonathan (2000), *Beyond the studio: a history of BBC Northern Ireland*, Blackstaff Press: Belfast, p. 84.

12 Bell (1972) *Theatre in Ulster*, p. 112.

13 Open (1985) *Fading lights*, pp. 12–17.

14 Lavine, Kirsten (2002) *Twin spire life: a social history of St Peter's*, Cathedral Community Services: Belfast, p. 93; Haslett, Albert (1999) *Albert Haslett's memories of the Shankill*, privately published: Belfast, p. 39.

15 *Belfast Telegraph* (1999) 'That's entertainment', 10 April.

16 Walker, Brian, and McCreary, Alf (eds) (1994) *Degrees of excellence: the story of Queen's Belfast 1845–1995*, Institute of Irish Studies, Queen's University Belfast: Belfast, p. 142.

17 O'Malley, Padraig (1983) *The uncivil wars: Ireland today*, Blackstaff Press: Belfast, p. 15.

18 *Observer* (1984) 19 February.

19 *Observer* (1984) 19 February.

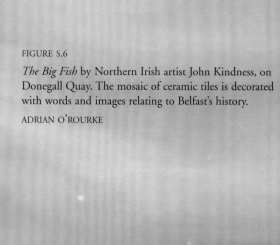

FIGURE S.6

The Big Fish by Northern Irish artist John Kindness, on Donegall Quay. The mosaic of ceramic tiles is decorated with words and images relating to Belfast's history.

ADRIAN O'ROURKE

The Belfast Mosaic

17
'The Place Had Character'

Patricia Craig

'IS THEM 'UNS BATE?'

Belfast at the start of the twentieth century seems both strange and familiar, like a childhood friend resurfaced after many years. It was a different place in those days, its grandeur more apparent, its privations more extreme.

FIGURE 17.1
View of Belfast, looking from Alexandra Park towards the shipyard, 1935

NATIONAL GEOGRAPHIC, BERNARD F. ROGERS, JR.

Like virtually every town and city in existence, Belfast may be seen as a palimpsest of obliteration and renewal – and, as you strip back each successive layer, over the last hundred years or so, an image emerges of an increasingly mysterious and archaic Belfast, with wide, sparsely populated streets in its centre, horse-drawn traffic, terraces of fine, plain buildings interspersed with ebullient oddities such as the Grand Opera House (1895) and its neighbour after 1907, the Royal Hippodrome.

In 1907, city-centre traffic was electrified, so the poet John Hewitt, born in that year, could later recall:

> I heard about but truly never knew
> The old horse-trams with trace-boys for the hills ...

Hewitt's childhood trams, on the other hand, were 'trolley-roped, electrical / Sparking at corner-points, and double-ended', and seemed specially designed to enable a spirited boy to sprint upstairs, change the seat-backs round, 'and watch the whole town pass below you there'.

FIGURE 17.2
Ligoniel tram, *c.* 1947

COLOUR RAIL

The town, indeed, could nearly be taken in in one go, with nothing much in the way of urban development beyond Tate's Avenue on the Lisburn Road, and 'the Plains' – an area of grassland – stretching all the way from Botanic Avenue to Rugby Avenue. Stockman's Lane was right out in the country; in various other directions, the Waterworks, the Holywood Arches and the City Cemetery marked the outskirts of Belfast.

Kites in Spring (subtitled *A Belfast Boyhood*) enshrines some aspects of Hewitt's early years in a thoughtful and illuminating sonnet sequence.[1] You have the older generation, unadorned Ulster men and women, schoolteachers, Methodists, socialists or Orangemen, sober or extroverted; the great events and issues of the day – the sinking of the *Titanic*, Home Rule, the Ulster Division marching towards the Somme, the Troubles of 1922. At one point, the infant Hewitt is lifted in someone's arms above a crowd assembled to hear the great Sir Edward Carson characteristically denouncing something or other – his 'right fist thrust in challenge or rebuke' – an experience not destined to deflect that independence of outlook for which the poet will become renowned. Ancestral promptings, his friendship with a Catholic neighbour's son –

> Just my own age. His Christian Brothers' school
> to me seemed cruel. As an altar boy
> he served with dread. His magazines were full
> of faces, places, names unknown to me.
> Benburb, Wolfe Tone, Cuchullain, Fontenoy.
> I still am grateful, Willie Morrisey ...

– and his own level-headedness combined to make him a passionate advocate of tolerance, tolerance extended even to ideologies he found alien and agitating, such as Catholicism, which seemed to him then 'a dark mythology'.

He wasn't alone in this. 'No pope, no priest, no surrender, Hurrah!' This bracing refrain, back in the 1860s, was dinned into the ears of another Belfast infant, James Owen Hannay, who continued to relish the spirit of defiance it encapsulated, while repudiating Orange bigotry, which was raging through the North (alongside its Catholic counterpart). In 1912 – under his penname of George A. Birmingham – Hannay wrote his classic novel, *The Red Hand of Ulster*, about the current Home Rule crisis.[2] This novel reviews, in ironic mode, the absurdities arising from hot-headed political activity. Working to an impeccable logic, the author turns every ideological orientation on its head. For example, an ardent Sinn Féiner, having looked around for the most potent source of rebellion against Britain and locating it amongst the unionists of the North, finds himself accepting the editorship of a loyalist newspaper – and loyalists tie themselves in knots asserting their allegiance to Britain, whilst fomenting resistance to Britain's proposed settlement of the Irish Question. 'Ulster will fight' is their watchword; and an ultimate state of deadlock is reached when the refusal of Home Rule is backed by a demand for a complete British withdrawal from Ireland. Birmingham has tremendous fun with this and all the other colourful contradictions which make up his theme, but his purpose is serious enough: to bring a touch of sanity and enlightenment to a world dominated by anger, fanaticism and deep-rooted sectarian prejudice.

It has been argued that Birmingham's loyalists are exhibiting a debased variety of that 1790s radicalism which culminated in the United Irish uprising, before engendering offshoots attuned to more than one shade of political belief.[3] The radical standpoint became an attribute of both separatism and unionism, as the whole vexed question of religious, political and cultural allegiance intensified and diversified during the nineteenth century. For example, professing political unionism didn't rule out the deepest commitment to

FIGURE 17.3
Thousands of men assemble at Belfast City Hall to sign the Solemn League and Covenant, opposing Home Rule, September 1912.

FIGURE 17.4
Belfast Street scene, drawing
by J. Humbert Craig, 1938

ELIZABETH C.B. FOYE

FIGURE 17.5
Louis MacNeice, drawing by
Jeffrey Morgan, 1995

JEFFREY MORGAN

cultural nationalism, as the case of Sir Samuel Ferguson illustrates. And the linking of free thought and Protestantism was at odds with the growing tradition of *Catholic* republicanism which came to prevail in the twentieth century, once the 'Irish-Ireland' movement had got under way. George A. Birmingham brings the deepest understanding to bear on these and other complexities of the day, and presents his findings with a kind of Alice-in-Wonderland alacrity.

At street level, things were simpler. The whole farrago resolved itself into 'them' and 'us'. 'Is them 'uns bate?' was a question directed at the journalist and author F. Frankfort Moore as he made his way home on foot in the early hours of the morning following the defeat of Gladstone's first Home Rule Bill. 'Them 'uns' – Irish nationalists – were indeed 'bate', and the news raised a cheer from Sandy Row Orangemen and others waiting to hear of their rivals' humiliation. The outcome caused processions, noise and excitement to fill the streets on the following evening; and it wasn't long before a clash of factions supervened. F. Frankfort Moore's *The Truth about Ulster* (1914) treats endemic unrest (of which this was just one manifestation) in a jocular, tongue-in-cheek spirit which produces a distancing effect.[4] His lively account of riots and ructions imposes a sportive overtone on Belfast bigotries.

Other ways of dealing with the subject included partisan outrage: only Catholics (or Protestants) suffered during an eruption of violence; and only Protestants (or Catholics) were going peaceably about their business when an attack occurred. In one work of fiction, the sight of a band of men in the distance causes consternation in a couple of Shankill Road girls: '"Look!" cried Maggie Reilly, "It's the Catholics coming to wreck the Shankill ..."'. It's a time of riots, when 'Islandmen' – shipyard workers – meet at five in the morning and march 'in a solemn phalanx down the big road and on into the city and over the Queen's Bridge to their work'. They are armed with 'deadly-looking weapons' – crowbars, clubs, picks, steel rivets and anything else they can lay their hands on: armed and banded together for protection against the onslaught of pokers, delph and kitchen stools which people fling at their heads as they pass through Catholic quarters. And that's not all: it is known that men caught on their own have been 'dragged down some of the bad lanes off North Street and half killed'.[5] On the other hand – according to T.J. Campbell, an *Irish News* journalist from 1891, the Protestant shipyard workers were constant aggressors at North Street and Carrick Hill, with their iron bolts and rivets.[6] 'And one read black where the other read white', as Louis MacNeice has it, wearily, 'his hope / The other man's damnation. Up the Rebels, to hell with the Pope ...'. MacNeice (born in 1907), remembers his Northern childhood and a few of its aggravations:

> ... The noise of shooting
> Starting in the evening at eight
> In Belfast in the York Street district;
> And the voodoo of the Orange bands
> Drawing an iron net through darkest Ulster,
> Flailing the limbo lands –
> The linen mills, the long wet grass, the ragged hawthorne ...[7]

Though he was born in Belfast ('... between the mountain and the gantries, / To the hooting of lost sirens and the clang of trams'), it wasn't long before MacNeice was taken to Carrickfergus with his family, when his father became rector of St Nicholas's church there. Belfast stayed in his mind, a mite unfairly, as a hideous and hidebound city, a place of smoke and dust and repellent creeds. And yet: MacNeice's urbane exasperation with its egregious goings-on was only a part of his ambivalent attitude to the place. It doesn't, indeed, diminish the force with which he enumerates its demerits: the unending 'morose vendettas', industrial grime, the tawdry image of Cathleen Ni Houlihan, the thousands of Williams, 'waving thousands of swords and ready to fight, / Till the blue sea turns to Orange'. And revisiting Belfast in the 1930s,[8] he allows himself for a moment to relish its views of mountains and lough, the swans on the Lagan, even its distinctive personality – harsh but full-blooded. 'The place had character', as MacNeice's friend and fellow BBC man, W.R. Rodgers, acknowledged:

> Nothing was ever the same in Belfast, for the place had character. The very stones in the street rose up and exerted themselves in cobbles – 'pavers' we called them – and the great roads grumbled along on granite setts. Many's a time my knees would be dangling with blood-and-iodine ribbons, for I was born very close to the ground and I knew the flagstones like the palm of my hand. You had to know what crack in the pavement not to walk on, for this one was lucky and that one unlucky, this stone was good for spinning tops and that one for skipping games.[9]

W.R. Rodgers's pre-First World War Belfast, as delineated in his radio broadcast of 1955, *The Return Room*, is a place of fun and games despite its Presbyterian ambience, rich in urchin antics and all sorts of local wonders – the squalling crowd of youngsters at a dusty terminus after a day's outing; Mary Marley the rag woman with her resonant street cry, 'New delph! New delph! Any ould regs! Any ould regs!'; eggs coloured yellow from a whin-blossom dye and rolled down a slope at Dundonald Cemetery in an Easter ritual; wee barefoot fellows from low-down streets. Belfast is the 'city with the brick-red face and the

FIGURE 17.6
Roundabout, east Belfast, 1935

NATIONAL GEOGRAPHIC,
BERNARD F. ROGERS, JR.

bowler hat of smoke', the 'city of ships and shawlies, doles and doyleys', as exuberantly astir as Dylan Thomas's Llareggub. Rodgers's astonishing buoyancy and word-intoxication – Orange bands are part of the 'humdrummery of history', 'all that "Adamnation"' he himself is heir to – are allied to a feeling for biblical imagery which he uses to striking effect:

> The apple blushed for me below Bellevue,
> Lagan was my Jordan, Connswater
> My washpot, and over Belfast
> I cast out my shoe.[10]

THE FAUBOURG MALONE

Rodgers, MacNeice and Hewitt, all born in the early years of the century, were middle-class boys, all shielded, to varying degrees, from the uproars of the slums. During the greater part of the century, indeed, the impulse to write fiction or poetry in Belfast was largely a prerogative of the middle classes, largely – but not exclusively – the Protestant middle classes (there were exceptions, of course, most notably Michael McLaverty and then Brian Moore, but change in this area was slow to come about). A variety of social, economic and psychological impediments was responsible for excluding most others from the field of literary activity. By the 1960s, however, writers from diverse backgrounds were poised to infiltrate what was previously cut-off terrain (as we shall see) … Firmly within the middle-class tradition – as well as those mentioned above – are Forrest Reid (1875–1947), C.S. Lewis (1888–1963) and the eagle-eyed essayist and commentator Denis Ireland (1894–1974), who described his birthplace as 'a strange, tough, hybrid town, with a forest of factory chimneys on both banks of the Lagan'. Born into a linen manufacturing family, Denis Ireland inhabited a world of 'Edwardian young gentlemen from the *faubourg* Malone':

> The drawing-room, with its grand piano in a corner and its palm tree in a pot, was on the first floor of a high red-brick house in a high red-brick terrace … At one end of the street was a Presbyterian church and a prospect of green hills; at the other an Episcopal church and a vista of dark mountain. At both ends gaily-painted horse-trams ran from the city to the suburbs and the open country, then not so far away.[11]

In those days, Denis Ireland tells us, 'linen merchants and their progeny scraped in along with the lower ranks of the gentry':[12] hence his presence at a skating party held at Ballydrain, *c.* 1910, on a frozen lake surrounded by dark woods, an occasion adorned by footmen in top boots and white breeches carrying rugs and hampers, bonfires, and a pair of expert skaters exciting envy in everyone else. The woods turning purple in the frosty dusk, the glow from the fires reflected in the ice, the furs and shooting-brakes and ancient landaus, lend a Muscovite glamour to the scene.

Only a few years later, skating on the lake at Ballydrain had become an amusement of the hoi polloi. Forrest Reid, in his novel of 1915, *At the Door of the Gate*, has his sensitive young lower-class hero, Richard Seawright, take a girl to Ballydrain and impress her with his beauty and grace as he executes some ice-skating movements.[13] (Reid's own fascination with the charms of boyhood is well documented. In his work, it gets its most engaging expression in the *Young Tom* trilogy of 1931–44.) The scene, the author informs us, is 'bright, gay, animated', with the hats and dresses of skating girls taking on 'a strange brilliance against the background of dark trees and frost-bound woodland'.[14] This is an aspect of Belfast not often highlighted.

Richard, like Forrest Reid himself, is inappropriately apprenticed to a tea merchant, though his life thereafter takes several melodramatic turns unexperienced by his creator. Reid, as is well known, embraced in his youth a kind of classical Greek paganism very much at odds with the spirit of workaday, church-going Belfast. It included a deep susceptibility to the beauty of the natural world and this inclines him to take a hostile view of the industrial city. We remember Peter Waring, in the novel of that title (1937), succumbing to affront as the seediness of his new lodgings in the Markets area is disclosed to him: 'The gas works and a public lavatory hardly ten yards away.'[15] But even for Forrest Reid, the city is not all dirt and squalor. In a moment of reverie, he salutes

> ... the beauty of an autumn afternoon in the Ormeau Park at dusk, when, with the dead leaves thick on the deserted paths, I had sat listening to a German band playing somewhere out of sight beyond the railings. Through the twilight, with its yellow twinkling of street lamps, the music floated ... The beauty of the Lagan Valley ... while the grey light gradually faded from the marsh-lands beyond the tow-path, and the trees stooped down over their own dark images ...[16]

FIGURE 17.7
A Reynolds Stone engraving from the 1957 edition of Forrest Reid's *Apostate*
FABER AND FABER

Born in 1875 at Mount Charles in the university district, Forrest Reid grew up at a time when a pair of stone lions graced University Square, and a poultry woman's cart coming up Botanic Avenue was a common sight. These details, and others, are recounted in *Apostate* (1926), Reid's first volume of reminiscences. The backward look enables him to deprecate some brash new features of Belfast: the grandiose City Hall on the site of the graceful old White Linen Hall, with its sparrows flying in and out of the ivy on the walls; a vulcanite factory replacing Molly Ward's old cottage-cum-teashop on a bank of the Lagan.

Belfast's saving grace, for Forrest Reid and many others, was its setting. Stand on the Holywood Hills – as C.S. Lewis recommends in *Surprised by Joy* (1955) – look across the lough to the mountains of Antrim, greyish-blue in the distance, and you can nearly ignore the noisy, busy city disfiguring the valley in between. Nearly, but not completely: the 'forest of factory chimneys, gantries and giant cranes ... whining and screeching of trams ...' and shipyard clamour insinuate themselves unpleasantly into C.S. Lewis's consciousness, even while he savours the contrast between nature and manufacture. But a further resource is available to him: '... Step a little way – only two fields and across a lane and up to the top of the bank on the far side – and you will see, looking south with a little east in it, a different world'. The peace and enchantment of County Down, 'the land of longing, the way to the world's end'. With this vista in front of him, the germ of the land of Narnia was implanted in C.S. Lewis's mind.[17]

BIGOTSBOROUGH

Narnia, dreamland: these are unexpected products to come out of utilitarian Belfast. Forrest Reid's 'platonic eroticism', his pursuit of a perpetual alluring adolescence, led him into some literary byways and resulted in an evocation of boyhood 'dream days' more vividly realised than Kenneth Grahame's.[18] V.S. Pritchett, in a 1981 review of *The Green*

301

Avenue[19] (Brian Taylor's biography of Forrest Reid), remembered visiting the author at his Ormiston Crescent home in 1923, and being surprised at Belfast's indifference to one of its most distinguished literary offspring. On reflection, he *wasn't* surprised, Belfast being what it was: a 'depressing and bigoted city of linen mills and shipyards'. This, indeed, was, and to some extent remains, the standard perception of the place, its drollery, its spectacular surroundings and its democratic heritage notwithstanding. One minor Edwardian novelist, James Douglas – author of a mightily peculiar work of fiction called *The Unpardonable Sin* (1907) – went so far as to rename Belfast *Bigotsborough*: 'The clash of broken glass was a familiar sound in the streets of Bigotsborough.'[20]

Whatever the unrestrained Douglas thought he was doing, with his tale of a young Methodist minister from the Shankill Road (he calls it the Shankhill) and a red-haired woman named Fionula Shane who first appears riding a black horse up the Falls Road, à la Maud Gonne – whatever Douglas's reformist intention may have been, it's unlikely that his preposterous novel would have found a receptive audience among a plain Belfast readership, or tempered its pig-headedness one whit. There were other, more felicitous, attempts to suggest a way out of the sectarian impasse. John Hewitt's concept of civil amelioration – his 'tolerant and just society', which seemed to be for ever in the offing – grew out of that political optimism which arose at times in the North, only to be over-whelmed by atavistic alignments. At one moment, an enlightened social policy was the goal; then tribal loyalty supervened. The old conflict and its eruptions were 'all very wearisome and very perplexing', Benedict Kiely wrote in 1945; and certainly, as he stated, no citizens of Belfast 'could congratulate themselves on the uncouth, vicious thing that comes to life at intervals to burn and kill and destroy'. Nevertheless – in that immediate post-Second World War era, with regeneration very much in the air – Kiely sensed the presence of 'new ideas, generous ideas ... ideas as energetic as the inspiration that built the factories, deepened the river, marked the black water with the shadows of tall cranes and leaning gantries'.[21] The novelist Brian Moore was another who, at that moment, believed the global conflict had put Belfast's squabbles into perspective, that the Orange-and-Green past would – finally – stop exerting its baleful influence, and a more even-handed society come into being.

AGGRAVATIONS

Tackling the theme of sectarian antagonism was an inescapable obligation as far as most Belfast writers were concerned, whether they went about it in a spirit of derision or denunciation. It was something to be deplored to the fullest extent; however, a funda-mental difficulty facing liberalism in Belfast was the fact that much of the city's fiction and poetry was written, willy-nilly, from a Protestant or a Catholic point of view. (It is true that a distinction was made between a sectarian standpoint and political idealism, whether of a romantic republican or a liberal unionist variety.) So, the Ballymacarrett hero of St John Ervine's *The Wayward Man* (1927) strays into the Catholic Short Strand area and is promptly set upon by 'a gang of rough youths';[22] while in Michael McLaverty's *Call My Brother Back* (1939) a mob of Orangemen armed with bludgeons swarms into the shipyards to batter the heads of Catholic workers. In the same disturbance, a Brother is shot dead standing at the window of Clonard Monastery.[23]

Actually, this novel – McLaverty's first and most persuasive – with its down-to-earth lucidity and artistic cohesiveness, provides one of the most compelling accounts we have of that disordered period just before and after partition. After its Rathlin Island opening, *Call My Brother Back* takes shape in the Beechmount district of west Belfast, with its rows of red-brick houses, pigeon sheds, hens scratching in the dust, brickyards and brickfields, all presided over by the homely bulk of the Black Mountain. The child's-eye-view (McLaverty's hero, Colm MacNeill, is a young pupil at St Malachy's College) lends a special poignancy to the author's descriptions of a rough-and-ready street and family life, a life about to be overtaken by harrowing events. The descriptions are meticulous and vivid:

> Sitting up in their beds the MacNeills heard the volleys of shots crackling like breaking sticks. Colm was the only one who knew that Alec was out with the Republicans, for that evening he had told him as he gave him his pocket-book and asked him to pray. Now as he listened with cold fear to the air alive with shots he couldn't pray; he thought of Alec with a light rifle at his shoulder firing from the cover of an entry or from behind a lamp-post.

Throughout his narrative, McLaverty is acting on the principle he later recommended to Seamus Heaney (recounted in the Heaney poem 'Fosterage'[24]): '... to hell with overstating it: / Don't have the veins bulging in your biro'. Economy and verisimilitude are qualities which distinguish *Call My Brother Back*, along with its disabused approach to the disruptions of the day. There is no attempt to glorify militant republicanism, even though the author remains deeply aware of the cobbled-together basis of the Northern state, and all its implications for harmony in the city.

Much Belfast literature has been aggravated into existence by violence and injustice – especially, perhaps, in the last thirty years of the century (though the tradition goes back much further, back, indeed, to the songs and ballads of 1798 and beyond). At its simplest, dramatic disaffection lends itself to the type of thriller exemplified in F.L. Green's *Odd Man Out* of 1945. The impact of this novel was greatly enhanced by Carol Reed's film version (1947) with James Mason as the wounded gunman staggering in a state of semi-hallucination from one emblematic quarter of the city to another:

> He loitered near the empty ruins of houses, wondering if within those sockets there was a corner sheltered from the icy wind ... But children were playing amidst the stark shapes of those shattered walls. He gathered his strength and went on, trying to avoid the dim pools of light below some of the lamp standards, moving out of sight of men and women returning from the day-shifts in factories and shipyards, until opposite him he saw on the far side of the road a wide gate leading to a contractor's yard.[25]

The film, even more than the novel (which goes in for the kind of overwriting decried by McLaverty), encapsulates the glamour of the clandestine commitment. That, however, was not the only resource of the social rectifier. As a counterpart to the romantic-republican ideology in literature, you have the plague-on-both-their-houses school of writing which found an outlet, during the 1940s, in the work of poets such as Roy McFadden and Robert Greacen ('... Scatter sad smoke into their eyes / That the stung

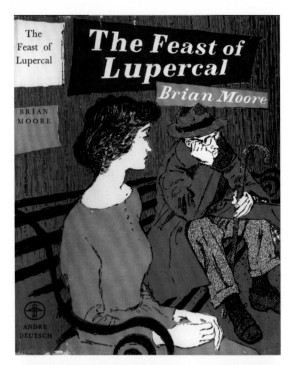

FIGURE 17.8
Dust jacket for Brian Moore's
The Feast of Lupercal, 1958

STEPHEN RUSS AND ANDRÉ DEUTSCH

FIGURE 17.9
Dust jacket for M.F. Caulfield's
The Black City, 1952

RANDOM HOUSE

tears may wash the scales / Clean from their vision ...').[26] Some years later, Belfast's best-known expatriate novelist, Brian Moore, born in Clifton Street in 1921, counted a powerful exasperation among his literary assets: exasperation with every facet of Belfast life, from its Catholic/Protestant divide to its backwardness and bad weather. His attitude to his birthplace was productively ambivalent, however, taking account of its pungency as well as its imperfections: 'the place had character' (*pace* W.R. Rodgers). *The Emperor of Ice-Cream* (1966), Moore's belated *Bildungsroman*, achieves an upbeat authenticity in its depictions of wartime Belfast; *Fergus* (1970) gets to grips with portions of a fraught adolescence, as part of a surreal comedy which is also a telling piece of social indictment. Even *The Feast of Lupercal* (1958), in which a virgin Catholic schoolmaster is put through a course of sexual mortification, and *The Lonely Passion of Judith Hearne* (1955), with its ageing spinster heroine succumbing to drink – even these are invigorating rather than dispiriting, because of the energy and confidence the author brings to his elaborations of social shortcomings in the Catholic North. *Judith Hearne*, indeed, has come to be regarded as a quintessential Belfast novel, with its loss of faith/face theme and rainy Camden Street location.[27]

In 1952 came a brave attempt (if less ambitious and forceful than Moore's) to sum up the atmosphere and exacerbations of mid-century Belfast. This was M.F. Caulfield's *The Black City*,[28] the events of which take place against a background familiar to detractors of the city: the mean streets seething with narrow hatred and bigotry, the cloth-capped men, shawlie women and tattered children forming a kind of stylised backdrop to the story, the rain forever soaking the slated rooftops and gurgling in the clogged gutters of worn-down footpaths. *The Black City* (Belfast is not named in the book though many of its landmarks are: the Albert Clock, Mooney's Irish House in Arthur Square, the York Street Flax Spinning Mill, the Imperial Cinema) has no unifying centre of consciousness but proceeds by way of paradigmatic set-pieces: the Twelfth of July with its inflammatory outpourings at the Field and consequent street violence, the raggedy IRA unit assembling halfway up the Cave Hill to practise freeing Ireland.

There were times when Belfast seemed benighted in ways unconnected with its exorbitant faction-fighting motif. Industrial oppression, for example, is the burden of Richard Rowley's[29] workers' monologues (for example, 'The Stitcher' of 1918: 'The needles go leapin' along the hem, / And my eyes is dizzy wi' watchin' them. / My back aches cruel, as I lean / An' feed the cloth to the machine ...').[30] The concern with working conditions, and working-class hardship, leads on to 1930s socialism and trade unionism, both of which are at the core of Sam Hanna Bell's *The Hollow Ball* (1961).[31] This novel conveys the strongest possible flavour of Belfast's red-brick streets, with the dismal prospect of unemployment looming even more insistently than usual, in the prevailing bleak conditions. It was a time when the street corner vied with the betting shop and the pub as a centre of social activity.

Moving further up the social scale, into faded local magnate territory, a sense of provincial deadliness gets into Janet McNeill's examinations of missed opportunities and lives of genteel desperation, as in the case of unmarried Laura Percival in *Tea at Four O'Clock* (1956), who sits observing enervating rituals in her large house up the Holywood Road, and looking out at more lively activity going on elsewhere:

> A couple of aeroplanes rose briskly from Sydenham airport behind the house; children from the tiny gardens of the housing estate which had crept to the high garden walls of Marathon called and cried as they threw balls to each other; from the Queen's Island across the river came the noisy fever of the shipyards. Time was moving again. The twenty years were indeed over, but there might still be twenty more. Tiredness came on Laura like a blow.[32]

FIGURE 17.10
Smithfield, by Tom Carr
ANN MCKEOWN

A DEMOCRATIC SPIRIT

Before the 1960s, Belfast writing – for all its low-toned sagacity or flashes of illumination – was largely a local affair, and ill-equipped as such to engage the world's attention. But things were about to change. Seamus Heaney's 'From the Canton of Expectation' sets the scene:

> And the next thing, suddenly, this change of mood.
> Books open in the newly-wired kitchens.
> Young heads that might have dozed a life away
> against the flanks of milking cows were busy
> paving and pencilling their first causeways
> across the prescribed texts. The paving stones
> of quadrangles came next and a grammar
> of imperatives, the new age of demands.
> They would banish the conditional for ever,
> this generation born impervious to
> the triumph in our cries of de profundis.
> Our faith in winning by enduring most
> they made anathema, intelligences
> brightened and unmannerly as crowbars.[33]

Suddenly, political and intellectual energies were conscripted in the service of civil rights, as a democratic spirit surged over the hidebound North. It was a time of buoyancy, before it all fell apart. Two lasting legacies from these heady days, however, were the ruling out of a return to the full sectarian state, and the opening up of literary possibilities. Within ten years or so, the city (and the province) once famous for philistinism had become famous for poetry, as Belfast found itself nurturing an outbreak of talent which coincided – piquantly – with the onset of murderousness and destruction. The story is well known: how the Heaney–Mahon–Longley–Simmons quartet burst full-fledged on the literary scene, chock-full of cogency and assurance, to be joined in due course by others including Frank Ormsby, Ciaran Carson, Tom Paulin and Paul Muldoon; how Medbh McGuckian, Robert Johnstone, Gerald Dawe,[34] and others of comparable gifts then came to the fore, so that people began to talk about a Troubles literature, as though the mess the North had got itself into was the dominating factor, and not these writers' cryptic, compassionate or civilised responses to it. Indeed, the cataclysm and its accompanying pressures made themselves felt in literature in oblique and enlightening ways, from Michael Longley's electrifying poem 'The Butchers'[35] (a free translation of an episode from Homer's *Odyssey*, whose title also carries a suggestion of Belfast's most notorious murder gang of the 1970s, the Shankill Butchers) to Paul Muldoon's 'For history's a twisted root / with art its small translucent fruit / and never the other way round'.[36]

FIGURE 17.11
Northern poets: (*left to right*)
Michael Longley, Derek
Mahon, John Hewitt and
Seamus Heaney, *c.* 1966

Belfast, while it 'tore itself apart and patched things up again' (in the words of Ciaran Carson),[37] gained an intensified sense of its fragility and its singularity, as poet after poet salvaged something significant from the self-destructing city. 'I grew up among washing-lines and grey skies', Derek Mahon writes,

> pictures of Brookborough on the gable ends,
> revolvers, RUC, B-Specials, law-'n-order,
> a hum of drums above the summer glens
> echoing like Gotterdammerung over lough water
> in a violent post-industrial sunset blaze ...[38]

And Tom Paulin:

> I make that crossing again
> And catch the salt freshness
> Of early light on Queen's Island.
>
> I lay claim to those marshes,
> The Lagan, the shipyards,
> The Ormeau Road in winter.[39]

FROM TEDIUM TO TERRORISM

Not far behind the poets came the prose writers, Maurice Leitch, for example, with his explorations of psychic disorder afflicting whole communities (in *Silver's City*, 1981, Belfast has become 'the true terrain of nightmare');[40] John Morrow making rugged black comedies out of disruptive goings-on in the backstreets; or Bernard MacLaverty displaying a humorous-Catholic angle on growing up in the city (in the best of his short stories and in his novel *The Anatomy School* of 2001) – 'The next day Martin and another boy, Maguire, had been asked to give out the Holy Water.'[41]

Holy water went to some people's heads. From the mid-1970s on, 'Troubles' fiction began to run riot all over the more or less decorous blueprint of Belfast prose. Much of it was, indeed, of a quality to be deplored (trite or overblown), as the dangerous example of certain assured authors suggested the construction of narratives was easy, when it was nothing of the sort. ('Troubles trash' is the label attached to the worst of these Belfast would-be thrillers – hundreds and hundreds of them.) But some clear-headed, truthful and enterprising works emerged out of the meretricious mishmash. You can point to Glenn Patterson's novels, for instance, with their unostentatious evocations of postwar housing estates, the refurbished (post-Troubles) city centre – 'restaurants, bars and takeaways proliferated along the lately coined Golden Mile'[42] – and violence off-stage. Or the exuberant Robert McLiam Wilson might spring to mind, writing wryly or ironically about Belfast's 'troublespot' status: 'Belfast was only big because Belfast was bad' – and never mind its allure, 'the city … ringed with mountains and nudged by the sea'.[43] David Park has a good collection of stories, *Oranges from Spain* (1990);[44] and Deirdre Madden (b. 1960) is another sophisticated author (though not at her best with the Belfast of *Hidden Symptoms* [1988], which treats a case of sectarian murder and its effect on the sister of the victim).[45]

FIGURE 17.12
Shaw's Bridge, by John Luke, 1939
NEVILLE MCKEE

Belfast has always provided its writers with something to take a stand against, whether it's tedium or terrorism. Right from the years before the First World War, dominated by shipyard gantries, grimy faces under shawls and caps, and dramas in cobbled back streets, through the hungry twenties and down-at-heel thirties, and through the boredom of mid-century Sundays with chained-up swings bespeaking Sabbath inviolacy, to the years of carnage and chaos – through all this, images of Belfast in literature have testified to the city's distinctiveness and resilience. It makes an impact, for reasons both good and bad.

Mad, bad Belfast gets a showing in one recent – 2001 – episodic work of fiction, *No Bones* by Anna Burns, which posits a world of burnt-out houses, bomb-toting schoolgirls and playground shootings, fast sex as a prelude to committing an atrocity, and delinquents ordered to turn up sharp at seven o'clock to be kneecapped: 'I did warn youse, youse pack of eejits.'[46] Here we find a type of republican involvement (the setting is Ardoyne) entirely divested of the stirring or idealistic overlay which characterised old-fashioned nationalism. Equally, the cosiness of questions like 'Is them 'uns bate?' denotes a mode no longer available to writers intent on tackling contemporary issues in all their variety, and bringing into existence something that might have seemed unthinkable in the mid-century and earlier: a modern, complex, endlessly inventive and forward-looking Belfast literature.

NOTES

1 Hewitt, John (1980) *Kites in Spring: a Belfast boyhood*, Blackstaff Press: Belfast.

2 Birmingham, George A. (1912) *The Red Hand of Ulster*, Smith, Elder: London.

3 See, for example, Tom Paulin (1984) 'Nineteen Twelve', in *Ireland and the English crisis*, Bloodaxe: Newcastle upon Tyne.

4 Moore, F. Frankfort (1914) *The truth about Ulster*, Everleigh Nash: London.

5 Boles, Agnes (1912) *The Belfast boy*, David Nutt: London.

6 Campbell, Thomas Joseph (1941) *Fifty years of Ulster*, Irish News: Belfast.

7 MacNeice, Louis (1938) *Autumn journal*, section XVI, Faber and Faber: London.

8 MacNeice, Louis (1938) *Zoo*, Michael Joseph: London.

9 Rodgers, W.R. (1955) *The return room*, BBC Radio broadcast.

10 Rodgers, W.R. (1971) from 'Epilogue to the character of Ireland', *Collected poems*, Oxford University Press: Oxford.

11 Ireland, Denis (1939) *Statues round the City Hall*, Cresset Press: London.

12 Ireland, Denis (1973) 'Victorian ice ballet', in *From the jungle of Belfast: footnotes to history, 1904 to 1972*, Blackstaff Press: Belfast.

13 Reid, Forrest (1915) *At the door of the gate*, Edward Arnold: London.

14 Reid (1915) *At the door of the gate*.

15 Reid, Forrest (1937) *Peter Waring*, Penguin: Harmondsworth.

16 Reid, Forrest (1926) *Apostate*, Constable: London.

17 Lewis, C.S. (1955) *Surprised by joy: the shape of my early life*, Geoffrey Bles: London.

18 Grahame, Kenneth (1895), *Dream days*, John Lane: London; Grahame, Kenneth (1895) *The golden age*, John Lane: London.

19 Pritchett, V.S. (1981) 'Escaping from Belfast', *London Review of Books*, 5–18 February (review of Brian Taylor [1980] *The green avenue: the life and writings of Forrest Reid, 1875–1947*, Cambridge University Press: Cambridge).

20 Douglas, James (1907) *The unpardonable sin*, E. Grant Richards: London.

21 Kiely, Benedict (1945) *Counties of contention*, Mercier Press: Cork.

22 Ervine, St John (1927) *The wayward man*, W. Collins: London.

23 McLaverty, Michael (1939) *Call my brother back*, Longmans, Green: London.

24 Heaney, Seamus (1975) 'Fosterage', in *North*, Faber and Faber: London.

25 Green, F.L. (1945) *Odd man out*, Michael Joseph: London.

26 McFadden, Roy (1943) 'Train at midnight', in *Swords and ploughshares*, Routledge: London.

27 Moore, Brian (1966) *The emperor of ice-cream*, André Deutsch: London; Moore, Brian (1970) *Fergus*, Holt, Rinehart and Winston: New York; Moore, Brian (1958) *The feast of Lupercal*, André Deutsch: London; Moore, Brian (1955) *The Lonely Passion of Judith Hearne*, André Deutsch: London.

28 Caulfield, M.F. (1952) *The black city*, Jonathan Cape: London.

29 Richard Rowley was the penname of the Belfast businessman Richard Valentine Williams (1877–1947).

30 Rowley, Richard (1918) 'The stitcher', in *City songs and others*, Maunsell: Dublin.

31 Bell, Sam Hanna (1961) *The hollow ball*, Cassell: London.

32 McNeill, Janet (1956) *Tea at four o'clock*, Hodder and Stoughton: London.

33 Heaney, Seamus (1987) 'From the canton of expectation', in *The haw lantern*, Faber and Faber: London.

34 Some of these poets are not native to Belfast, though all have lived there and all are well placed to probe beneath its surface.

35 Longley, Michael (1991) 'The butchers', in *Gorse fires*, Secker and Warburg: London.

36 Muldoon, Paul (1987) '7, Middagh Street', in *Meeting the British*, Faber and Faber: London.

37 Carson, Ciaran (1987) 'Travellers', in *The Irish for no*, Gallery Press, Oldcastle.

38 Mahon, Derek (1997) 'Death in Bangor', in *The yellow book*, Gallery Press: Oldcastle.

39 Paulin, Tom (1980) 'The other voice', in *The strange museum*, Faber and Faber: London.

40 Leitch, Maurice (1981) *Silver's city*, Secker and Warburg: London.

41 MacLaverty, Bernard (2001) *The Anatomy School*, Jonathan Cape: London.

42 Patterson, Glenn, (1992) *Fat lad*, Hamish Hamilton: London.

43 Wilson, Robert McLiam (1996) *Eureka Street*, Secker and Warburg: London.

44 Park, David (1993) *Oranges from Spain*, Phoenix: London.

45 Madden, Deirdre (1988) *Hidden symptoms*, Faber and Faber: London.

46 Burns, Anna (2001) *No bones*, Flamingo: London.

'LIKE THE PAST ITSELF'

18
Village Voices

Patricia Craig

'I was born in a village in the city of Belfast, and I grew up in that village,' writes the novelist and social commentator Hugh Shearman. He goes on:

> I believe that nearly everybody who has lived in Belfast, or in any other large city, will discover that the city is really divided internally into a number of little village communities, distinct areas inside the city which come to have a separate, self-contained life of their own, through the common interests, activities and institutions of the people who live there.[1]

FIGURE 18.1
Chichester Park,
Antrim Road, *c.* 1907

Shearman's particular 'village' (he was born *c.* 1915) is the Cliftonville suburb on the north side of Belfast, a place decked out with 'grave and formal old houses' whose gardens run down behind them to stables opening on to a lane at the back. This decorous district can also claim John Hewitt, born in 1907, whose childhood home was at 96 Clifton Park Avenue:

> Our avenue was long, a thoroughfare
> for carts with coals, bread, milk, or passing through;
> you'd risk no sprint across it, or but few
> so frequently those cartwheels trundled there.
> Houses with tiny gardens set before
> some peopled with schoolteachers, ministers,
> with civil servants, factory managers –
> the largest with steep steps up to the door.[2]

The unalarming streets made an appropriate background to the doings of 'a happy boy' (as Hewitt described himself), with their atmosphere of reassurance and 'village' amenities far removed from the exigencies of the slums. Cliftonville, Belmont, Balmoral, Cherryvalley: these districts, and others like them, disdained the kinds of notoriety attaching to other, more colourful areas of Belfast, such as Millfield or Sandy Row. Consequently, they are not so conspicuous in the city's iconography. However, writers brought up in such localities, and looking back, have a knack of endowing them with a plangent notability. Roy McFadden's 'Ballyhackamore',[3] for instance:

> Only a step from childhood –
> My mother crippled with baskets
> Myself leafing The Magnet
> Only a stoned crow's
> Flight from the trees in Stringer's Field
> Alight with the flash of trams
> On the Upper Newtownards Road –
>
> For Ballyhackamore
> And the cottages
> Still a townland
> Went on regarding
>
> Paddy Lambe's and its sawdust
> Smart's Butchery with its sawdust
> And the church with the iron bell …

'Ballyhackamore' embodies a complicated *Weltschmerz,* while the emotion suggested by Derek Mahon's 'Glengormley',[4] for example, has more to do with a sardonic distancing from the accoutrements of suburban nicety:

> Wonders are many, and none is more wonderful than man,
> Who has tamed the terrier, trimmed the hedge
> And grasped the principle of the watering-can.
> Clothes pegs litter the window ledge
> And the long ships lie in clover. Washing lines
> Shake out white linen over the chalk thanes.

But then Mahon's luminous and multilayered poem 'Courtyards in Delft',[5] with its starting point in a painting by Pieter de Hooch, homes in on an intensely envisaged local tableau:

> I lived there as a boy and know the coal
> Glittering in its shed, late-afternoon
> Lambency informing the deal table,
> The ceiling cradled in a radiant spoon.
> I must be lying low in a room there,
> A strange child with a taste for verse,
> While my hard-nosed companions dream of war
> On parched veldt and fields of rain-swept gorse ...

The phrase 'fields of rain-swept gorse' returns us to the slopes of the Cave Hill, eternally visible from Glengormley, no less than other vantage points. Just as 'local village feeling constantly merges into the larger city outlook' (as Hugh Shearman puts it), so you have certain landmarks available to all the city's inhabitants, whatever their home territories.

The Cave Hill is one of these, with its summit known as McArt's Fort (romantically) or Napoleon's Nose (colloquially). Praised by Alice Milligan in an early poem[6] – 'Look up from the streets of the city, / Look high beyond tower and mast, / What hand of what Titan sculptor / Smote the crags on the mountain vast?' – the Cave Hill is a major presence, with its outline suggesting 'a vast and very realistic profile of a recumbent man's face'. So it looked to the naturalist Edward Allworthy Armstrong, whose *Birds of the Grey Wind* (1940) begins with a remembrance of this marvellous mountain:

FIGURE 18.2
The Cave Hill, *c.* 1901

There were several ways to the summit and I knew them all. There was the winding 'Sheep's Path' which led through shrubberies beloved of thrushes ... higher up beyond the beechwoods was a rugged scree where scrumptious raspberries could be picked at the cost of scratches on hands and knees. A little further a vast amphitheatre came into view; we called it 'the Devil's Punchbowl'. Rising sheer from it were magnificent black cliffs ...[7]

The poet Gerald Dawe, reflecting on the mood of the late 1950s/early 1960s – 'post-war, Protestant' – is conscious of another way of reading the Cave Hill: 'always there, like the past itself, high above us'.[8] There it stands, a readymade symbol, abundant in historical reverberations (Wolfe Tone, Henry Joy McCracken), suggesting loftiness of outlook as opposed to a low-down one-sidedness. For the plain people of Belfast, though, it was just a local curiosity, albeit one to be cherished. It is often referred to in evocations of the city. Sometimes it makes an unexpected appearance. The final chapter of Freeman Wills Crofts's 1930 detective novel *Sir John Magill's Last Journey* is called 'The Cave Hill', and, indeed, the denouement of the story takes place on a wild night up the Sheep's Path, with a powerful wind blowing the rain in solid sheets into Inspector French's homely face. A 'big hill with a flat top and a precipitous front' is the author's less than enticing description of this significant section of Belfast's mountain range.[9]

The Cave Hill acquired other associations, though, especially after the opening of the Floral Hall at Hazelwood (in 1936), with its scope for dance-hall laxity. Gavin Burke, the young ARP[10] protagonist of Brian Moore's *The Emperor of Ice-Cream* (1966) is careful to carry a raincoat – on a sunny afternoon – when he walks with a girl along the edge of the old quarry and up a mountain path. His lecherous purpose – 'He ... spread his raincoat on the rough grass' – comes to nothing, since he's up against cast-iron Catholic chastity.[11] Others, especially foolhardy young women, have a different story to tell, like the heroine of Joan Lingard's *Sisters by Rite*, who allows a strange man to escort her up the Cave Hill and afterwards can never look that fraught landmark in the face.[12]

It's useful to keep an eye on it, however, if you want a forewarning of any change in weather. 'Napoleon's Nose was clearly profiled against a brilliant blue sky. Any bad weather on the way would first have to swathe Napoleon's Nose in clouds before descending on us a few minutes later'.[13] The action of Margery Alyn's sprightly novel *The Sound of Anthems* (1983) takes place in one of Belfast's villages – Whitewell/Greencastle, between the Antrim Road and the lough shore with the Cave Hill rising steeply up behind it like the wrath of God (the wrath of a Protestant God, if your family can count itself among the exiguous Catholic minority of Serpentine Parade). It's 1945, and on the flat lands on the lough side of the Shore Road stand rows of tiny white-washed dwellings whose occupants await rehousing at the whim of the Belfast Corporation. For Alyn's eleven-year-old heroine, Jennifer Marshall, the ordinary furores of pre-adolescence are complicated by questions of caste and class. Why is her grandmother (halfway to the

Cave Hill) raised above her co-religionists in the row houses? And – a crucial matter – can a Catholic legitimately take part in Victory celebrations?

Jennifer's grandmother, we soon learn, was burned out of her house during the Troubles of the early 1920s; however, this and other enormities of the past have undergone a more-or-less benign transformation. They've been re-created as the stuff of yarns to entertain the neighbours round the fire on a winter's evening. In this buoyant novel, the sectarian instinct is treated as an adult's quirk, or at worst a routine response to some automatic taunt ('She's mad because she can't join the Girls' Brigade'). The rancour is taken out of it. When it does erupt in a menacing fashion, it's a cause of puzzlement to the alert young heroine: 'I put my head in my hands. I didn't understand anything any more.'

Jennifer is not the only one who fails to understand why some amicable form of co-existence can't be worked out; or – since such a thing does prevail at times of abated tribalism – why it can't be enshrined in some impartial legislation. Nevertheless, in Greencastle, Castlereagh, Springfield and other localities all over Belfast, it's the area's sectarian colouring that determines its character. Each district's sense of itself is tied up most strongly with the trappings of a divisive heritage. You've only to cite the Falls Road, or Sandy Row, as your place of origin (to take those extreme examples) to provoke a tacit assumption about your angle on the North.

A HAPPY LAND?

Coming along the Shore Road towards the city centre, you reach York Road and then York Street, at one time a place of conspicuous and rumbustious 'character'. 'Saturday night in York Street' was something of a byword for ebullience. Around the time of anti-Home Rule agitation, the noise of shooting, recalled by Louis MacNeice, was a regular occurrence: 'Starting in the evening at eight, / In Belfast in the York Street district'. With its warren of red-brick streets, its looming mills and factories (including the York Street Flax Spinning Mill), its 'Orange' atmosphere, its corner shops serving local needs, like John McCollum's long-defunct bakery, its high unemployment and consequent kicking of heels at innumerable grimy corners ... with all these ingredients, the York Street district embodies hardship and gusto, with a Protestant Belfast slant. As a literary entity, though, it has achieved less prominence than certain other parts of the city. However – in recent years – its bygone ambience has attained a permanent shape at the hands of a resourceful storyteller. Sam McAughtry's *The Sinking of the Kenbane Head* (1977)[14] may be read as a testimonial to the author's beloved elder brother, a casualty of wartime naval action in the North Atlantic. But at the same

FIGURE 18.4
Belfast street scene, *c.* 1912

ALEXANDER HOGG

time, the narrative accommodates many robust vignettes of life in the York Street hinterland between the 1920s and the war years: a life of pawn shops, the ubiquitous garb of shawls and caps, fecundity balanced by infant mortality, greyhound racing, the Church Lads' Brigade, the importance of degrees of respectability along an unexalted social scale.

Typical in its sidelights on sectarian ritual, as in much else, the book contains a 'burning-out' episode, albeit a half-hearted one, in which the author's Catholic uncle is driven out of his Collyer Street home. He's known in the street, and no one dislikes him – but, in accordance with a deadly pattern, these bitter rituals demand a periodic enactment. His neighbours set fire to his kitchen table – not to do him harm, just to make a denominational point. Multiply this chilling rite a hundredfold, and you end with the kind of whipped-up rampage that destroyed Bombay Street in 1969.

The central motif of *The Kenbane Head*, the loss of a brother in horrific circumstances, makes it a kind of mirror image of Michael McLaverty's *Call My Brother Back* of 1939, with its tragedy rooted in an earlier, local conflict, and its setting in the small streets of Beechmount, with their back yards and pigeon sheds, and clothes lines with flapping linen on waste ground strewn with cinders and pieces of corrugated tin.[15]

Of course, the Protestant backstreet house was famous for its neatness – 'a big stone step, and a clean-swept floor'[16] – just as its Catholic counterpart had a throughother aspect (according to the stereotypes, at any rate). Gerald Dawe's wry poem 'Little Palaces'[17] – 'Everything is right with the world. / Even the kerbstones are painted'– gets the picture. Dawe, from north Belfast, recalls 'parlours coming down with knick-knacks', footsteps echoing down an entry, late-opening corner shops, 'lower-middle-class, three-storied houses with little gardens, fronting the main road', with small back-to-backs tucked in behind them. The main road was the Antrim Road, still in the late 1950s/early 1960s a place of 'mixed' allegiances (to the Pope or the Queen); it was also, a decade or so earlier, home to the journalist and author Cal McCrystal,[18] whose family moved into the area when he was four. Previously, the Catholic McCrystals had lived a bit shakily in Protestant east Belfast, following an integrationist impulse on the part of the journalist father; but by 1939 the family was ensconced in Baltic Avenue (and later in Ponsonby Avenue), in the parish of Newington, and young Cal was enrolled at the local Holy Family primary school, like Brian Moore (before him) and Bernard MacLaverty (after him).

It was a fairly secure environment, but a frisson of danger came from the nearness of impoverished, Protestant, Tiger Bay. Whenever the inevitable juvenile hostilities were in progress, one set of boys armed with washing-line poles might be seen tilting at another brandishing home-made catapults, with shouts of 'Proddie pigs' and 'Dirty Fenians' proclaiming each side's affiliation. Some young Catholics, though, evaded even this degree of contact with their ideological counterparts. The Moore children, for instance, were taught to give the same wide berth to Protestants as they might to the bearers of an infectious disease such as measles or leprosy. It made for an even more than usually enclosed upbringing.

In his early story 'A Vocation', Brian Moore (uncharacteristically) evokes the atmosphere of his part of Belfast, and a childhood overshadowed by elementary church teaching: 'Q. *Who made the world?* A. *God*. The world was sweetie shops, Alexandra Park, the Antrim Road, Newington School, Miss Carey's garden, and the big pond in the Waterworks ...'[19] This restricted world has other incarnations. 'We lived in a terrace of dilapidated Victorian houses whose front gardens measured two feet by the breadth of the house. The scullery, separated from the kitchen by a wall, was the same size as the garden,' writes Bernard MacLaverty, in 'A Rat and Some Renovations' from his first collection of stories,[20] economically re-creating a low-toned, rather shabby, common-or-garden neighbourhood. In another story, 'Across the Street',[21] a retired policeman heads each day with his walking stick to sit impassively on a bench in Alexandra Park regarding its mild activities – 'Judith Hearne' territory (though the actual site of Miss Hearne's miseries is Camden Street in the university district), with its quintessential exudations of dampness and drabness. Moore, as is well known, believed the proper response to such an environment was to take oneself out of it at the earliest opportunity. For all the energy and good humour of its depiction, the Moore version of mid-century Belfast, awash in the accoutrements of provincial stagnation, is a place of murk and backwardness, and stuck in that mode for ever.

It's a far cry from Joseph Campbell's hymn to an old-world Newtownbreda:

> 'Tis pretty tae be in Baile-Liosan;
> 'Tis pretty tae be in green Magh-luan;
> 'Tis prettier tae be in Newtownbreda,
> Beeking under the eaves in June.
> The cummers are out wi' their knitting and spinning,
> The thrush sings frae his crib by the wa',
> And o'er the white road the clachan caddies
> Play at their marlies and goaling-ba.[22]

Or from Denis Ireland's thickly wooded Lagan Valley, only a mile or two upriver from the city centre, with 'an old red-brick Georgian mansion' standing derelict in the sunlight (one might hope that it has since been renovated). The same author has faintly ironic praise for Wellington Park, 'a leafy suburb' lined with twinkling gas-lamps,[23] with its interminable high teas taking place in substantial villas, and featuring silver muffin dishes and silver kettles. Prosperous south Belfast, home to the city's manufacturing élite. Indeed, the Malone Road, with its posh accent, was, and to some extent remains, a target for local debunkers.

Swanky and secluded, but not exactly cultivated in a literary sense, this part of the city was apt to breed a critical attitude in those among its offspring who went on to find cultural fulfilment elsewhere – the poet and architectural historian Maurice Craig, for instance, whose boyhood in South Belfast (according to an essay in his 1990 collection, *The Elephant and the Polish Question*) was 'circumscribed, cloistered and colourless'.[24] It's an unrelenting indictment. Nevertheless, that the district was affluent and comfortable,

FIGURE 18.5
Adelaide Park, South Belfast, by David Evans, 1993
DAVID EVANS

315

and retained these characteristics throughout the century, surprised some 1990s visitors to the city – such as the poet Carol Rumens, who came anticipating blight, a landscape filled with '... bleachworks and burnt-out cars'; and got instead fuchsias, larch and cedar trees, tranquil and alluring avenues, places where 'peace, and love, and money, are made'.[25]

Even here, however, reverberations from the late-century Troubles were felt. A car bomb exploding in the early 1970s obliterated one house and damaged others, and for a long time afterwards in the neighbourhood, bits of metal and shattered glass were swept up along with autumn leaves, or caught in lawn-mowers, causing showers of sparks (as recounted in C.E.B. Brett's *Long Shadows Cast Before*, 1978). It seemed that no area, however 'residential', could count itself invulnerable to terrorist attack.[26] This was a new departure. Previously, the flourishing middle classes had achieved considerable success in the effort to keep themselves apart from the sites of potential social breakdown. A re assuring distance existed between 'the sloblands and the snoblands' (Denis Ireland's phrase) – though as Michael Longley remarks in his fragment of autobiography, *Tuppenny Stung* (1994), an odd exception to the usual class-sequestration was south Belfast's Lisburn Road: '... on the right, as you drive towards Lisburn, gardenless shadowy streets; on the left, rhododendrons and rose bushes'.[27] A product of one side, though educated (to primary level) on the other, Longley was in a good position to observe the gulf between his neighbours at home, with their drawing-rooms and vestibules, and his schoolfriends inhabiting tiny terraced houses lacking indoor lavatories. A continuous adjustment of behaviour and, especially, accent, was necessary to get him inconspicuously from one environment to the other. Now, however, things have evened out. Since those days of the 1940s and 1950s, a certain shabbiness has overtaken the posh side of the road and a certain gentrification the other. 'On this stretch alone there was a patisserie, a couple of smart, discreetly fronted clothes shops that were more like art galleries, their windows almost bare, and a florist of exotic appearance selling voracious-looking plants of bizarre shape'. These post-cease-fire perceptions of the Lisburn Road occur in Keith Baker's engrossing thriller *Engram* (1999), in which a young woman regains her wits after four years in a coma resulting from a car crash and walks, a mite unsteadily, out through the doors of Musgrave Park Hospital and 'into the June sunshine'.[28] In this novel – unlike its predecessor *Inheritance* (1996)[29] – the Troubles get a look-in only as a peripheral spectre.

However, it's true to say that the sad catalogue of atrocities has left no part of the city unscathed, and virtually no stretch of pavement without its bloody associations. You can't help being conscious of a bitter irony when you read something like Michael Longley's sombre poem 'The Ice Cream Man' (addressed to his younger daughter):

> Rum and raisin, vanilla, butter-scotch, walnut, peach:
> You would rhyme off the flavours. That was before
> They murdered the ice-cream man on the Lisburn Road
> And you bought carnations to lay outside his shop ...[30]

– when you read this in conjunction with Joseph Campbell's 'The Kendy Man' – 'Rosy's Lumps, Peggy's Leg, / Taffy Lick an' Yellow Man –' with its buoyant refrain, 'Oh, what a happy land is Ireland!'[31]

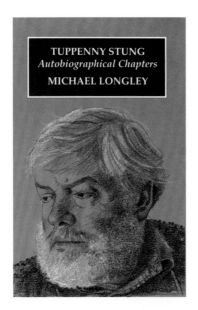

FIGURE 18.6
Portrait of Michael Longley by Jeffrey Morgan featured on the front cover of Longley's *Tuppenny Stung* (1994)

JEFFREY MORGAN

A few Belfast writers, particularly in the earlier part of the century, made themselves into exemplars of a humorous local aggrandisement:

> Belfast could think itself lucky to be part of Ballymacarrett, we thought. We had all we needed within our boundaries. ... We were industrialised, yet we had the countryside practically on our doorsteps. I remember fields and hedges along almost the whole length of the Albertbridge Road from the Methodist Church at Templemore Avenue to the Newtownards Road ... I remember when you could smell the country in Castlereagh Street, by the Beersbridge Road, smell the mingled odours of whin blossoms and crops and cattle and seaweed, the lovely smells of Down, full of turf smoke.

FIGURE 18.7
Glenard by John Middleton
JANE MIDDLETON GIDDENS

Here St John Ervine, in his amiable reminiscences for the *Belfast Telegraph* (1944–45), cries up the felicities of his boyhood, of which the most felicitous is an accident of geography: 'I was a Ballymacarrett boy'. (The tone here is in contrast to his novels' Edwardian stolidity, with their mainspring in a thoroughly quotidian wanderlust, not regional enthusiasm.)

Another Ballymacarrett boy looks back from a rather more alienated perspective. 'I cannot now admit to a feeling of nostalgia [for the place],' writes John Boyd in the second volume of his autobiography, *The Middle of My Journey* (1990), 'even though when I was growing up it satisfied all my needs. For then I was hardly aware of its ... air of squalor and staleness, the sour stench from the River Lagan at low tide in summer, the acrid stench from the fertiliser factory on the Mountpottinger Road ...'[32] Indeed, volume one, *Out of My Class* (1985), harks back to a time when the sights and sounds of a vigorous street life took precedence over the taint of industrial detritus. This is the Lord Street end – the rowdy end – of Templemore Avenue, *c.* 1922:

> ... there was never any peace and quiet. Always neighbours gossiping, shouting and laughing; coal carts, milk carts, bread carts, carts of all kinds passing up and down; then, all day long, the out-of-work corner boys ... playing football with a hanky ball, or playing a noisy game of marbles, or getting drunk on a Friday or Saturday night. Father said they were good for nothing, would neither work nor want, and were always causing trouble.[33]

After closing time, the Saturday-night drunks would often lie stretched on the pavement bawling out party songs such as 'The Boyne Water'. This was conspicuously loyalist territory, and defined by that circumstance. '[T]o find an "Irish" or "British" identity is seen as embodying the quintessence of being at home,' writes Gerald Dawe in his Introduction to *Styles of Belonging* (1992), a polemical collection of essays dealing with cultural consciousness.[34]

This is true, but – as with any contemplation of Belfast, or Ulster, allegiances – complications enter in. One Belfast writer, Thomas Carnduff, possessed a strong identity along these lines but nevertheless deplored 'the inevitable demarcation line between a Catholic and a Protestant quarter of the city'. Describing himself as a Sandy Row

Protestant, Carnduff at the same time claimed the title of Irishman, insisting that 'Belfast is an Irish city', and that 'the Protestants of Belfast are as Irish as the Catholics'.[35] Of course they are, just as all the people of the North have their baleful history and intractable present in common; but that doesn't stop them carrying on like a bunch of ferrets in a sack. And Sandy Row, Belfast's Orange quarter *par excellence*, normally flaunts its opposition to any form of Irishness, and even more to the (concomitant) snares of Rome. 'What pride we enjoyed for living so near to Sandy Row – the Boys of Sandy Row, stalwarts of our Orange Order.'

Thoughtful adults such as Robert Harbinson (b. 1928), deeply aware of the implications of what they relished without question during their Sandy Row (or similar) childhoods, may go on to question the impulse behind the pageantry of the whole Orange occasion, but something of that pristine exhilaration stays with them: 'Such sights! Such music, churning the Protestant blood in our veins! ... As expression of loyalty to a Protestant throne it would have been hard to find anything finer ... Unsurpassable day!' he goes on, applauding the formidable Sandy Row Lodges, including the 'Loyal Sons of William' in their glittering regalia, and the carnival atmosphere at Finaghy Field, where (of course) a kind of cartoon anti-popery prevails. In *No Surrender* (1960), however, the main narrative drift is to underline the everyday deprivations afflicting Sandy

FIGURE 18.8
Dust jacket for *No Surrender* by Robert Harbinson (1960)

Row (a one-time weavers' quarter), deprivations barely alleviated by the ritual flamboyance of 'the Twelfth': 'Mill chimneys, caked under their black lichen of smoke ... row upon wretched stillborn row ... Misery and darkness.'[36] Add the narrow entries backing on to the coalyards of the Great Northern Railway, churches and mission halls by the score and the ubiquitous corner shop, and you get the shabby surroundings of a decent enough, but inescapably unkempt upbringing.

The jammed-together houses and grimy pavements could hem you in. However, 'the rows of houses did not go on for ever', and beyond them lay a natural playground, the Bog Meadows, complete with abundant wildlife and tinker caravans, an enterprising child's paradise. For Robert Harbinson and his friends, though, the tantalising mountain at the far side of the Bog Meadows was out of bounds, as one of Thomas Carnduff's 'demarcation lines' came into play. Dubbed 'the Mickeys' Mountain' by Sandy Row boys, this hill stood guarding the 'Fenian' territories of Whiterock, Ballymurphy, the Falls Road and the St James's district – whose inhabitants experienced a similar trepidation about venturing beyond their stretch of the Bog Meadows, towards Sandy Row. These lines were etched deep in the fabric of Belfast social life.

Take Finaghy, where the poet Robert Johnstone was growing up in the late 1950s and 1960s:

> Finaghy is a junction on the Lisburn Road, between Upper Malone and Andersonstown. When I was born it was an outpost of the suburbs ... Walking south-east you were quickly into the gentle landscape of the Lagan Valley. The cars along the Malone Road provided a diversion rather than an irritant, and you could measure your walk by turning at the cottage on the corner of Dunmurry Lane. Its garden always seemed to be overflowing with the colours of flowers. Walking north-west towards the mountains ... you crossed over a rustic railway bridge which the trains would blast black on both sides, leaving a smoke-ring enveloping the road. There was a little station, complete with ticket office and waiting room. The houses grew more sparse from there, until you got into the more severe upland scenery, where there were the wilds of Collin Glen and all the promise of what lay over the other side. In the third direction, down the Lisburn Road towards Dunmurry and Lambeg, there were thick woods and low marshy fields.[37]

Johnstone's *Images of Belfast* (1983), from which this passage is taken, pinpoints the area beyond the railway bridge as alien territory, and the whole of west Belfast as 'somewhere I could not get to past the concrete blocks'. It wasn't only concrete blocks, but 'a different mental universe' that formed the barrier. And yet: reading *Falls Memories* (1982) by Gerry Adams,[38] Robert Johnstone is conscious for a moment of a shared inheritance of expectations and escapades. It is all the same city, whether it's the Tivoli or the Clonard Picture House you funk 'bunking' into; or whether the prewar ceremony of the May Queen is enacted in the streets around Sandy Row ('Gorgeously apparelled ... the Queen paraded in clothes of vivid crepe paper': Robert Harbinson) or in the Falls ('... the Queen was crowned at a window-sill; a green paper apron was pinned on to her, a veil, the remnants of a window curtain adorned her head, and yellow crepe paper was fastened to her wrists and ankles': Michael McLaverty[39]). The pawn shop was as familiar a resort to the people of the Pound Loney as it was to those of York Street. Sam McAughtry's '... having to pawn things occasionally' is matched by Paddy Devlin's 'my mother's wedding ring and my father's Sunday suit were regularly in and out of the pawnbroker's ...'.[40] It's the same city, as Denis Ireland has it:

> ... the floodlit walls and illuminated signs of new cinemas de luxe blaze in stentorian reds and greens amongst the quiet gardens and avenues of suburbs north, south, east and west. In red-brick villas sheltered by shady trees little men in shirt-sleeves are reading the *Evening Telegraph* under the light of electric chandeliers; others who wouldn't be seen dead in shirt-sleeves are flocking to the Little Theatre to see Hay Fever by Mr Noel Coward; at dark street corners still others are posting up green placards commemorating the death of Wolfe Tone. But it is all the same city.[41]

VERSIONS OF THE FALLS

However, for Denis Ireland, some parts of the city are more impenetrable than others. 'The house ... stood in a leafy suburb of Belfast, overlooking open country and the blue curve of Colin mountain. From one bedroom there was a view at night of a string of streetlamps strung along the blackness of the Black Mountain; the Falls Road, that was; a place full of foreigners and Catholics, from which there sometimes came the sound of shots.'[42] This tongue-in-cheek comment, perhaps, has a core of unambiguous apprehension.

Possibly, it is only when you know a district from the inside out that you're qualified to define its quirks. Gerry Adams's, Michael McLaverty's or Paddy Devlin's Falls, for example, has its own idiosyncrasies and its own momentum. The now-vanished streets of the Pound, Divis, Grosvenor Road and Dunville Park districts, and so on, once resounded to the bells of nearby St Peter's, summoning people to one religious carry-on after another (as Paddy Devlin recalls). Catholicism was engrained in the ethos of the area (though the Falls produced the odd freethinker over the decades, autodidacts whose spiritual home was the Carnegie Library on the corner of Sevastopol Street).

By the mid-century, Falls Road Catholicism was allied to a powerful republican tradition, a tradition fuelled by memories of injustice and atrocities going back to the 1920s and beyond, men shot dead in their own back yards, bullet holes disfiguring bedroom walls, attempts to break up republican funeral cortèges. Some atrocities were products of more recent turbulence: 'There was another crowd at the junction of Ashmore Street ... they were setting fire to a bar at the corner and looting it. Then some of the men began running down the street and breaking windows of the houses in Conway Street. The crowd were throwing petrol bombs in after they broke the windows ...' 'Naming the Names' (from which this description is taken) is a very bitter story by Paddy Devlin's daughter, Anne Devlin, about the making of a terrorist.[43]

The 'names' of Anne Devlin's title refer to the lost streets of the Falls – 'Osman, Serbia, Sultan, Raglan, Bosnia, Belgrade ...' – streets that harboured a community of exceptional vitality and robustness, if local lore and literature are anything to go by. From 'the little whitewashed public house' on the corner of the Grosvenor Road (mentioned by Cathal O'Byrne in his 1946 collection of 'historical sketches', *As I Roved Out*[44]) – from the quaintness of that, to the desolations and desecrations of the 1970s, barricades thrown together out of building materials filched from nearby sites, graffiti and paint-patched walls (described by Mary Costello in *Titanic Town*, 1992[45]), the Falls has distilled a strongly individual flavour.

You find certain constants in literary embodiments of the Falls – the miserable terraces housing vibrant people, children's street games and excursions up the Black Mountain, police raids, the flamboyant old biddy adept at repartee ('I cudn't like ye even if I rared yeh ... You cudn't fight your way out of a wet paper bag ...'[46]), the justifiability of its disaffection. But it's not all hardship and outrage. A novel like Danny Morrison's *West Belfast* (1989)[47] – to take that example – with its opening scene featuring elderly people chatting happily to one another as they sit in the sun outside their front doors, sparrows taking a dust-bath and youngsters carrying on, pinpoints the innocence of a time before distorting pressures and events came into play. It's the summer of 1963: the M1 motorway on the drained Bog Meadows has just been opened; Bombay Street is still intact. Divis Flats is an abomination of the future.

The entire Falls complex came into being in the nineteenth century partly to accommodate workers in the various mills and factories scattered about the area – Grieve's, the Blackstaff, Durham Street Flax Spinning Company – and indeed the linen industry – like shipbuilding – generated a culture of its own. 'You'll easy know a doffer', the famous song goes. 'Years ago [Ross Street] had echoed to the clatter of millworkers crowding the pavement as they linked their way to and from work'[48] – perhaps the same barefoot mill girls 'linked together, swinging their tea cans and laughing', who merrily taunted the embarrassed young protagonist of Michael McLaverty's *Call My Brother Back*: 'Aw, Lizzie, luck at Lord Alphonsus!'[49] 'Happy days, my mother claims, the mill girls chattering, linking arms,' says a voice in Ciaran Carson's poem, 'August 1969' (which opens with the burning of Grieve's Mill).[50]

Carson's is, indeed, the most intensive appraisal to date of the striking Falls Road locality (more striking than ever in his ingenious hands). Both in poetry and prose, he juxtaposes myth, locale, reality, recollection and creative speculation, to bedazzling effect. If he starts with reminiscence, it isn't too long before things get wrapped in murk and mystery:

> ... Back in the fifties, I'd look forward to October or November, when, every other day, smog would penetrate and cloak the still-dark morning streets with various murks of yellow ... muffled in my overcoat and balaclava, I would step into the incandescent wall of coalsmoke smog. I'd inhale its acid aura through my woollen mouthpiece. Launching tentatively into it, I'd feel my way with fingertips: doors and hyphenated window-sills; verticals and horizontals; the untouchable gloom at the end of a gable wall.[51]

Next, a thoroughfare presiding over the narrow streets, comes the Falls Road itself and its 'shop-front sequence: Angelone's Ice Saloon; Muldoon's the Barber's; McPeake's "Wallpaper, Radio and Drugs"; Kavanagh's the Butcher's and so on. Such details are – of course – extremely evocative, but their purpose here is not exactly nostalgic or therapeutic (though it has elements of both). Carson's literary impulse is more akin to an explosive device poised to deconstruct 'the dark city of Belfast'[52] – and in particular his version of the Falls – while at the same time raising it to an astral level. It's partly a matter of imbuing the commonplace with a kind of haphazard allusiveness and illumination:

> Tobacco-scent and snuff breathed out in gouts of factory smoke like
>   aromatic camomile;
> Sheaves of brick-built mill-stacks glowered in the sulphur-mustard fog
>   like campaniles.[53]

Nevertheless, Carson as retrospective map-maker is deeply aware of the actual layout of Belfast and all its enclaves – 'proper nouns with lineages of real names and topography behind them – Shankill, Falls, Ardoyne, Rosetta ...'.[54] And Smithfield, of course, fire-bombed out of existence on a dolorous night in 1974. 'Since everything went up in smoke, no entrances, no exits.'[55]

'All the strange little shops that you saw nowhere else', admired by Robert Johnstone,[56] selling all manner of second-hand goods; described by Herbert Moore Pim in 1917 as 'a storehouse of treasures',[57] and more recently by Robert Harbinson as a place of pilgrimage – 'Arabian Nights Smithfield'[58] – this covered market made a tangible link with Belfast's irretrievable past, and intangibly enriched the lives of its many devotees. 'Belfast would be nothing without a visit to Smithfield,' says a character in one of Bernard MacLaverty's stories.[59] The whole eccentric and enticing area is now as much a fragment of the past as 'the snug little village of Ligoniel' or 'the old, old, stone-built hamlet of Springfield',[60] its ambience to be savoured only in the imagination. 'You walk around Smithfield in my dream', is the opening line of Michael Longley's poem 'The Rag Trade'.[61] The loss of Smithfield has diminished the city.

TITANIC TOWN

The title of Mary Costello's memoir-cum-novel, *Titanic Town*, carries a number of astringent implications. It suggests a place with a terrifically inflated view of its own importance, heading towards disaster (for *iceberg*, read implacable attitudes). Belfast is also, of course, literally the home of the *Titanic*, and the ill-starred ship has loomed inescapably among the city's icons ever since the news of its destruction reached its birth – or berth – place, on 15 April 1912. Its importance as a symbol has to do with the sheer exorbitance of its conception, and its ending; but the *Titanic* is also tied up with Belfast pride in the splendid feats of shipbuilding for which the industrial city was once revered.

> ... shipyard hymns
> Then echoed from the East: gantry-clank and rivet-ranks,
> Six-county hexametric
> Brackets, bulkheads, girders, beams, and stanchions;
> convocated and Titanic,

writes Ciaran Carson in 'Second Language';[62] as an Irish-speaker born off the Falls Road, the language of the shipyards, of the scientific, mainly *Protestant* culture of Belfast is as alien to him as Angelus bells and church litanies are to a writer like Sam McAughtry (say). There were certain parts of the city – York Street and east Belfast – which nurtured an industrial expertise and concomitant self-esteem, and recent years have seen a drive to reinstate the regard for technology – 'Harland & Wolff, Short Bros. & Harland, Musgrave's, Sirocco Works, Mackie's, Workman Clark – names that once filled me with effete dread now ... ring with the sound of Larkin's metallic and rough-tongued bell', admits the critic John Wilson Foster (from east Belfast), in his book *The Titanic Complex* (1997).[63]

Belfast's shipyards were once notorious for the kind of rampant sectarianism that

FIGURE 18.10
Black Mountain, Lenadoon, by Catherine McWilliams, 2000

CATHERINE McWILLIAMS

galvanised the playwright (and ex-shipyard worker) Sam Thompson, back in the 1950s, into pillorying those involved, in *Over the Bridge* (first performed in 1960), which treats an extreme instance of anti-Catholic bigotry.[64] But since the whole shipyard culture has become redundant, things are perceived differently, or at least a shift of emphasis has taken place. The tendency at present is to cry up the hardihood and professionalism of the 'Islandmen', as well as those employed in related industries, and the areas they once inhabited take due credit today for the dynamism of their industrial past.

The Andersonstown of Mary Costello's book is not one of these areas. Once – between the wars – right out in the country, then a loose collection of new estates, still half-rural, and now an immensely built-up, populous suburb, Andersonstown has come through the Troubles with its republicanism intact. *Titanic Town*, subtitled *Memoirs of a Belfast Girlhood*, and written with verve and humour, assesses the early years of the conflict in this part of west Belfast in terms of wrecked nerves and restricted social activities ('violence alone enlivened my girlhood, for I was allowed out only to go to school and mass'[65]). It's a plastic-bullet-and-valium existence that Mary Costello is describing; but her – mainly – zestful narrative proceeds by way of understatement and the comic contretemps: 'The sight of a stately middle-aged woman in a well-cut suit with matching bag, shoes and gloves, yelling abuse and obscenities was beginning to attract the attention of the street.' It's the 1970s, when everything was beginning to fall apart.

INTO THE MAW OF TIME

'Shankill, Falls, Ardoyne, Rosetta ...' Belfast's various villages, bastions of commotion or conservatism, have all contributed a pungent local colouring to the literary city. You've only to read an allusion to Ballymurphy in a poem by Seamus Heaney[66] to gain an immediate sense of that run-down, slogan-ridden quarter, with the wall of the City Cemetery hard by and the Black Mountain above. And so it goes, ad nauseam. Each district has donated something of its special quality to one literary undertaking after another; and literature, reciprocally, has fixed the image of these places in the public mind, and rescued them for posterity, as change and decay take their toll, and the whole city suffers accelerated erasure and renewal, erasure and renewal: 'two-up-one-down terraced houses, shipyards, spinning mills, tobacco manufactories, tram depots, pubs, chapels, churches, ropeworks, barracks, corner shops, arcaded markets, railway stations, graving-docks, cinemas, post offices and photographic studios ...'[67] all vanished, like snow off the roofs of the Georgian terraces round the College of Technology – and like the terraces themselves – into the maw of time.

NOTES

1   Shearman, Hugh (1949) *Ulster*, Robert Hale: London.
2   Hewitt, John (1980) *Kites in Spring*, Blackstaff Press: Belfast.
3   McFadden, Roy (1977) 'Ballyhackamore', in *Verifications*, Blackstaff Press: Belfast.
4   Mahon, Derek (1968) 'Glengormley', in *Night crossing*, Oxford University Press: Oxford.
5   Mahon, Derek (1982) 'Courtyards in Delft', in *The hunt by night* (1982) Oxford University Press: Oxford.
6   Milligan, Alice (1954) 'Mountain shapes', in *Collected poems*, Gill and Macmillan: Dublin.
7   Armstrong, Edward Allworthy (1940) *Birds of the grey wind*, Oxford University Press: Oxford.
8   Dawe, Gerald (2003) 'Belfast and the poetics of space', in Nicholas Allen and Aaron Kelly (eds), *The cities of Belfast*, Four Courts Press: Dublin.
9   Crofts, Freeman Wills (1930) *Sir John Magill's last journey*, Collins: London.
10 Air Raid Precautions: civilian body formed to help combat the effects of bombing during the Second World War.
11 Moore, Brian (1966) *The emperor of ice-cream*, André Deutsch: London.
12 Lingard, Joan (1984) *Sisters by rite*, Hamish Hamilton: London.
13 Alyn, Margery (1983) *The sound of anthems*, St Martin's Press: New York.
14 McAughtry, Sam (1977) *The sinking of the Kenbane Head*, Blackstaff Press: Belfast.
15 McLaverty, Michael (1939) *Call my brother back*, Longmans, Green: London.
16 This line comes from the famous Belfast children's song 'My Aunt Jane'.
17 Dawe, Gerald (1991) 'Little palaces', in *Sunday school*, Gallery Press: Oldcastle.
18 McCrystal, Cal (1997) *Reflections on a quiet rebel*, Michael Joseph: London.
19 Moore, Brian (1956) 'A vocation', *Tamarack Review*, Autumn.
20 MacLaverty, Bernard (1977) 'A rat and some renovations', in *Secrets and other stories*, Blackstaff Press: Belfast.
21 MacLaverty, Bernard (1987) 'Across the street', in *The Great Profundo and other stories*, Jonathan Cape: London.
22 Campbell, Joseph (1909) ''Tis pretty tae be in Baile-Liosan', in *The mountainy singer*, Maunsel: Dublin.
23 Ireland, Denis (1973) *From the jungle of Belfast*, Blackstaff Press: Belfast.
24 Craig, Maurice (1990) *The elephant and the Polish question*, Lilliput: Dublin.
25 Rumens, Carol (1993) 'Variant readings', in *Thinking of skins*, Bloodaxe: Newcastle upon Tyne.
26 Brett, C.E.B. (1978) *Long shadows cast before: nine lives in Ulster, 1625–1977*, J. Bartholomew: Edinburgh.
27 Longley, Michael (1994) *Tuppenny stung*, Lagan Press: Belfast.
28 Baker, Keith (1999), *Engram*, Headline Feature: London.
29 Baker, Keith (1996) *Inheritance*, Headline Feature: London.
30 Longley, Michael (1991) 'The ice cream man', in *Gorse fires*, Secker and Warburg: London.
31 Campbell, Joseph (1963) 'The kendy man', in *Poems of Joseph Campbell*, Allen Figgis: Dublin.
32 Boyd, John (1990) *The middle of my journey*, Blackstaff Press: Belfast.
33 Boyd, John (1985) *Out of my class*, Blackstaff Press: Belfast.
34 Dawe, Gerald (1992) Introduction, in Jean Lundy and Aodán Mac Póilín (eds) *Styles of belonging, the cultural identities of Ulster*, Lagan Press: Belfast.
35 Carnduff, Thomas (1954 and 1994) *Life and writings*, Lagan Press: Belfast.
36 Harbinson, Robert (1960) *No surrender*, Faber and Faber: London.
37 Johnstone, Robert, and Kirk, Bill (1983) *Images of Belfast*, Blackstaff Press: Belfast.
38 Adams, Gerry (1982) *Falls memories*, Brandon: Dingle.
39 McLaverty, Michael (1942) *Lost fields*, Jonathan Cape: London.
40 Devlin, Paddy (1993) *Straight left*, Blackstaff Press: Belfast.
41 Ireland, Denis (1939) *Statues round the City Hall*, Cresset Press: London. Press.
42 Ireland (1939) *Statues round the City Hall*.
43 Devlin, Anne (1986) 'Naming the names', in *The way-paver*, Faber and Faber: London.
44 O'Byrne, Cathal (1946) *As I roved out*, Irish News Publications: Belfast.
45 Costello, Mary (1992) *Titanic town: memoirs of a Belfast girlhood*, Methuen: London.
46 Adams (1982) *Falls memories*.
47 Morrison, Danny (1989) *West Belfast*, Mercier Press: Cork.
48 Morrison (1989) *West Belfast*.
49 McLaverty (1939) *Call my brother back*.
50 Carson, Ciaran (1987) 'August 1969', in *The Irish for no*, Gallery Press: Oldcastle.
51 Carson, Ciaran (1997) *The star factory*, Granta: London.
52 Carson (1997) *The star factory*.
53 Carson, Ciaran (1993) 'Second language', in *First language*, Gallery Press: Oldcastle.
54 Carson (1997) *The star factory*.
55 Carson, Ciaran, (1987) 'Smithfield Market', in *The Irish for no*.
56 Johnstone and Kirk (1983) *Images*.
57 Pim, Herbert Moore (1917) *Unknown immortals*, Talbot Press: Dublin.
58 Harbinson (1960) *No surrender*.
59 MacLaverty (1977) 'St Paul could hit the nail on the head', in *Secrets*.
60 Boles, Agnes (1912) *The Belfast boy*, David Nutt: London.
61 Longley, Michael (1979) 'The rag trade', in *The echo gate*, Secker and Warburg: London.
62 Carson (1993) 'Second language'.
63 Foster, John Wilson (1997) *The Titanic complex: a cultural manifest*, Belcouver Press: Vancouver.
64 Thompson, Sam (1960) *Over the bridge* (play first performed at the Empire theatre, Belfast, published 1970, Gill and Macmillan: Dublin.
65 Costello (1992) *Titanic town*.
66 Heaney, Seamus (1975) 'Whatever you say, say nothing', in *North*, Faber and Faber: London.
67 Carson (1997) *The star factory*.

FIGURE S.7
The Lagan Weir at Night

SCENIC IRELAND

Into the Twenty-First Century

For many years the economic and social history of our city has, unfortunately, been a lesson in the inevitability of decline. To the weary citizen it has often seemed that so much of what made Belfast a great city lay not in our future, but in our past.[1]

So comments Councillor Ian Crozier in his Foreword to *Belfast: The Masterplan 2004–2020*. It is a bleak assessment of a city that 100 years ago could pride itself on having the vision to create an energy and water infrastructure in imaginative and entrepreneurial ways, and that boasted innovative and cutting-edge technological expertise in textiles, shipbuilding, engineering and more.

19
Belfast
The Way Ahead

Marie-Thérèse McGivern

Opposite
FIGURE 19.1
The Albert Memorial clock, recently restored by Belfast City Council
BELFAST CITY COUNCIL

Below
FIGURE 19.2
Belfast City Hall looking north to Cave Hill behind
BELFAST CITY COUNCIL

It seems as if the city has spent the last century slowing down at an increasingly rapid rate. While Belfast shared the fate of many old industrial centres in the 1970s and 1980s that failed to recognise the global changes occurring around them, this impact was further compounded by thirty years of sectarian and political strife that left the city with a legacy of dereliction, devastation and largely impotent governance structures.

THE RE-EMERGENCE OF BELFAST

The peace process and the Good Friday Agreement of 1998 were turning points in this cycle of decline. The impact of this process, with a general worldwide economic upturn, created a sustained period of growth and investment in the city. New buildings rose from derelict sites, cranes dominated the horizon, new jobs were created, and unemployment fell from over 14 per cent to its present level in 2006 of 4.6 per cent. The waterfront was transformed and the old Gas Works site in Cromac Street was rejuvenated. And the unimaginable occurred – Belfast became a tourist destination (Figures 19.1 and 19.2), pushing visitor figures from 1.3 million in 1998 to 5.3 million in 2003[2] and, in the process, created a new service infrastructure of hotels, restaurants and attractions (Figure 19.3).

The city has witnessed strong regeneration (Figures 19.4), but while this commercial activity has been read as a new dawn, the belief that it marks a return to the ebullient and thrusting city of 1900 may be premature. The success of the years 1998–2005 cannot mask the difficulties of a city with serious underlying social, economic and structural problems. Peace may have brought an end to most violence, but Belfast now contends with a marked sectarian geography and physical divisions – the peace walls – separate communities. Population levels continue to fall as the attractions of the surrounding suburbs and dormitory towns supersede those of the city. And, economically, a weak and still dependent private sector is swamped by an oversized public sector, and innovation remains at one of the lowest levels in the United Kingdom.

Still, it is clear that the city has recently made significant gains and these continue. Belfast has potential and now faces choices about its future and the best way forward. To be totally successful, it will require the ability to deal with its structural problems and create a developmental pathway to the future.

THE BARCELONA BLUEPRINT

The period of the recent Troubles gave Belfast a unique combination of problems, but apart from the impact of violence the city shared the same fate of many cities across the developed world. It was not only the decline of an old industrial structure that gave these cities their negative image, it was also the rise of globalisation and the movement of jobs to the new economies of Asia. By the early 1990s cities were seen as the repositories of crime, social deprivation, stress, alienation and other problems. They suffered huge population losses, as citizens who could afford to move from the centres departed in search of the peace and prosperity of the suburbs, leaving behind many increasingly concentrated areas of poverty and its allied predicaments.

The abandonment of cities finally began to be questioned with the dawning realisation that neglected, rundown, urban centres had the potential to hold back broader national economic visions and strategies. In the 1990s the development of new urban policy imperatives were evident in the Clinton administration in the United States and, around the same time, in the European Union. The resurgence of the near-bankrupt city of New York proved a powerful symbol in the US, and in Europe the growth and development of Barcelona demonstrated that cities were capable of change and recovery (Figure 19.5). The pronouncement of the death of cities now seemed premature; despite all the problems to be found in modern urban settings, people still lived there and businesses still located there. And cultural/knowledge development, for the most part, remained focused on urban areas.

The EU, long dominated by an agricultural bias, began to develop an urban agenda as the economic contribution cities could make to European competitiveness became clear, allied with the fact that around 70 per cent of the population of Europe lived in urban areas. In the UK a new Labour government also began to put in place a policy infrastructure and implementation process for urban development. And by the year 2000 the US Department of Housing and Urban Development had produced its fourth annual *State of the Cities Report*,[3] which commented on the sustained growth and progress American cities had made in the face of the challenges of the new economy, diversity and the need to promote balanced growth. Thus, by the beginning of the twenty-first century, cities were once again high on the political agenda.

Lessons of city revival are clearly emerging. It is now indisputable that there are many opportunities to develop cities as exciting, attractive,

FIGURE 19.5
Peix by Frank Gehry in the Vila Olimpica, Barcelona
SCENIC IRELAND

FIGURE 19.6
The Lagan Weir floodlit at night
BELFAST CITY COUNCIL

prosperous and equitable places to live. The European examples of Barcelona, Madrid and Helsinki indicate the potential to drive change as the way forward. Buoyed by these examples, UK cities such as Newcastle upon Tyne, Liverpool and Manchester have also sought to change their futures with a certain degree of success. The current issue for Belfast is whether it has the ability, and some may argue, the will and the commitment, to follow the example of these cities and bring about changes that can create a successful city for the twenty-first century (Figure 19.6).

WHAT MAKES A SUCCESSFUL CITY?

There is now a large body of research dedicated to finding the magic formula that creates a successful city. While many theories have emerged, most studies point to three essential components: economic competitiveness, quality of life factors and strategic capacity.

The economic competitiveness of a city is dependent on a number of factors. Basic requirements include an economy that is diverse, not dependent on any one single sector or on one size of firm. Competitive cities also require skilled workforces as modern economies become more dependent on knowledge-intensive sectors; they should also be accessible and well connected both internally and externally. They will also display high levels of innovation and investment in Research and Development (R & D).

Quality of life factors, while not seen as the foundation elements of making a city successful, are increasingly seen as the 'soft' factors that give a city the edge as a location for living or doing business. Good quality natural environments with easy access, distinctive built environments, excellent cultural facilities, quality housing and a good public realm are some of the factors that create liveable attractive cities. The so-called 'urban renaissance agenda' is seen as the second leg of the stool of competitiveness and success for the modern city.

The third leg concerns the ability of a city to create a coherent and consensual vision for the future, with the capacity to deliver it. In this, the significance of networks and relationships between key players and institutions, the political capability to deliver, and the influence at regional and national levels are all fundamentally important. Competitiveness strategies have to be crafted; they do not just emerge. Consequently leadership, partnership and politics are powerful contributors to long-term development and success.

HOW COMPETITIVE IS BELFAST?

How does Belfast measure up to these three key elements for urban competitiveness and success, and does it have the potential to become a truly successful city of the twenty-first century?

In 2003 Belfast City Council invited Michael Parkinson of Liverpool's John Moores University to undertake research to establish the competitiveness of the city.[4] At the time the council made its approach, Parkinson, an expert on European urban regeneration, was working on a comparative study of core cities in the EU. His report, published in January 2004,[5] indicated that 8 English core cities – Birmingham, Bristol, Leeds, Liverpool, Manchester, Newcastle upon Tyne, Nottingham and Sheffield – while having embarked on an urban and economic renaissance in recent years, still did not make as great a contribution to national economic welfare as 15 comparable cities in continental Europe. According to Parkinson, they were failing to punch at their weight and were falling behind London. His report concluded that although the picture was not good, it was not entirely bleak, as it was clear that cities could change and catch up if the right ingredients could be brought together and blended effectively.

In April 2004 Parkinson presented the findings of his Belfast study at the State of the City conference, organised by Belfast City Council. His conclusions indicated that Belfast was doing some things well and others very badly and it needed to sharpen its act if it wanted to compete with the best European cities. In particular, innovation, connectivity and the quality of the workforce required serious action for improvement. However, the report also showed, despite perceptions to the contrary, that Belfast's performance was better than that of many large English cities. For example, Belfast had performed well over the previous seven years, with Gross Value Added (GVA) up 47.3 per cent between 1995 and 2001, from £3,862 million to £5,688 million, which was well ahead of both regional and national levels. And because Belfast is the hub of the region in terms of productivity, employment and population, Parkinson claimed that its role in the regional economy required greater policy recognition.

Indeed, the role and function of cities in regional economies are being increasingly recognised in national and European policy development. While the link between the two is complex and causation is still not precisely understood, there are no examples of successful regions in Europe with failing cities at their core. Core regional cities are now seen as a key element in providing regional competitiveness, as they are generally the regional location for the most intensive development. Belfast is the centre and hub of the metropolitan area and, in turn, the Belfast Metropolitan Area is the hub of the region. Over 300,000 are employed there, 47.3 per cent of all jobs in Northern Ireland are located there and 38 per cent of the population reside there. Nearly half of inward investment is secured in this area.

Productivity measures in Belfast place it above all the English core cities and a number of European cities. Although this Gross Domestic Product (GDP) figure is boosted by public sector employment, it remains a good indication of competitiveness and offers potential for further development. Employment figures, while small by relative standards, still establish Belfast as the regional employment centre; and although unemployment levels in Belfast are high by continental standards, many English cities have higher scores. Belfast also has a well-qualified workforce, with 24 per cent of its working-age population qualified to degree level – a real potential source of strength that can be utilised. The problem, however, is that at the other end of the educational spectrum 26.9 per cent of Belfast's working population has no qualifications at all – higher than any of the English core cities and presenting a very serious challenge if real competitiveness

is to be developed. The city also falls behind in terms of transport connectivity. While the connections to the rest of the UK have increased, those to Europe remain low, in comparison with other cities. This situation is now changing rapidly with an ever-increasing number of European destinations and the launch of a direct North American route in 2005. These are positive signs but continued growth is needed.

Perhaps most critical of all is Belfast's record on innovation (Figure 19.7). British cities perform poorly on this score in comparison to their European counterparts and Belfast scores lower still. Indicators such as employment in high technology sectors, R & D spend, and lifelong learning are all low for Belfast. As innovative capacity is seen as an absolute prerequisite to ongoing sustainable success, these scores underline a need for serious focus on this issue.

Parkinson's report also comments on the population figures for Belfast. In competitiveness terms, larger cities generally do better, and Belfast at 277,000 is a relatively small European city. Moreover, the population continues to fall, although the decline is slowing down considerably from the rapid loss the city experienced in the last decades of the twentieth century. This trend needs to be reversed if Belfast is to become a successful city.

Governance difficulties faced by Belfast are highlighted in the report, with Parkinson arguing that successful cities exhibit the capacity to create a common vision and consensus around action. In his view, Belfast lacks a champion, a single body, normally a municipality in Europe, that can create a coherent and consensual vision and implementation path for the city.

Top right
FIGURE 19.7
The new Northern Ireland Innovation Centre in Belfast's Science Park, Titanic Quarter

BELFAST CITY COUNCIL

Below
FIGURE 19.8
Sirocco wasteland

ROBERT SCOTT

While it would be comforting to dwell on what to many may be the surprise good news on employment, productivity and skilled workforce, overall Parkinson paints a stark picture of a city facing deep structural problems and large scale challenges, which need to be fundamentally addressed and for which solutions must be found (Figure 19.8). Otherwise the economic outlook for the city seems poor. Coupled with this bleak economic picture is the reality of issues related to the continuing sectarian geography of the city, which has resulted in the frequent inclusion of non-economic factors in decisions relating to economic development. Furthermore, despite ongoing public intervention strategies since the 1970s, the city continues to have significant concentrations of poverty.

HOW ATTRACTIVE IS BELFAST?

If economic competitiveness is the first leg of the stool of success for cities, we have seen that quality of life factors are undoubtedly the second (Figure 19.9). If Belfast is to become a sustainable successful city it will not be enough to have a strong economy; the city must have the ability to attract and retain key workers, residents and visitors. For some cities a focus on this aspect has been their starting point for revival. The so-called 'Bilbao effect' is seen as a blueprint in this regard (Figure 19.10). A city in the Basque region of Spain suffering the problems of a failing shipbuilding industry, Bilbao entered into a partnership with the Guggenheim Foundation to build a cultural space by the river, undertook a massive programme of regeneration around the river and city centre, including a new underground designed by Norman Foster, and created a new airport designed by Calatrava. The rest, as they say, is history. This successful process has been copied by cities across the world.

Above
FIGURE 19.9
Signs of a burgeoning café culture on Botanic Avenue near Queen's University
BELFAST CITY COUNCIL

How cities look and feel, then, is important to their success. While Belfast City Council has no statutory responsibility for planning in the city, as part of its contribution to the Belfast Metropolitan Plan process undertaken by the Department of the Environment for Northern Ireland, the council consulted widely among the citizens and stakeholders in the city, which resulted in the publication *Becoming a Better Place*.[6] The council broadly endorsed the role and function created for Belfast by the Regional Development Strategy and was keen to carry the spirit of a city at the heart of the region down into a detailed plan for the city. *Becoming a Better Place* summarised the views expressed across the city on the things people wished to see in Belfast – quality design, better public transport, excellent public spaces, good parks and green land; the list was long but the process demonstrated that people were interested in and concerned about their environment and wanted to see it improved. Many suggested the need for a masterplanning process for the city, and in 2003 a masterplan was published. Commissioned by the Council, Colin Buchanan and Partners, which won the tender, was asked to analyse the social, economic and physical needs of the city and to propose a framework for its revival in the timeframe of 2004–2020. The resulting masterplan pulled no punches in its assessment: 'The city is congested and fragmented with a fragile core, resulting from years of instability, unfocused planning and divergent promotional approaches …'. Its conclusion placed much of the blame on public agencies: 'For half a century, public policy in Belfast, whether formed by central or local government, has been largely concerned with managing the decline of the city.'[7]

Below
FIGURE 19.10
The Guggenheim Museum in Bilbao, designed by Frank Gehry
THE ART ARCHIVE/NEIL SETCHFIELD

The report went on to catalogue a range of problems revealed by an audit of the physical environment: Belfast was dominated by roads and traffic, it was a poor retail product, low-quality public realm, with inadequate and outdated transport connections and poor linkage between parts of the city. The absence of a targeted regeneration strategy had led, in the consultants' view, to piecemeal developments that worked in pockets of the city but not as a whole. For example, the recent riverside developments (Figure 19.11) were cut off from other parts of the city and their benefits were not fully utilised. The city's assets – the River Lagan, the city parks and the surrounding mountains – required animation and better accessibility. The arterial routes required major upgrading and public art needed to be boosted and developed. Presentation of the city was poor with uninspiring gateways, clear sectarian signage, safety issues and, of course, peace walls dominating. Neighbourhoods had suffered from under-investment, especially in the disadvantaged areas of the city.

For those concerned with the transformation of Belfast, this presented a daunting list of problems. The masterplan suggested five areas that required sustained and major attention:

1 the need for an energised core with a new centre city area proposed
2 a revived middle city with enhanced linkages to the centre and out to the suburbs
3 a sustained and integrated neighbourhood renewal
4 a new approach to releasing and enhancing the environmental assets of the city, including the river and the parks
5 a complete makeover in the presentation of the city

To achieve this, a number of key priorities for change were suggested. The first target for renewal was the current structures of governance in the city. It was argued that Belfast was over-administered, over-institutionalised and over-governed. Echoing Parkinson, the view of Buchanan and Partners was that effective city governance and leadership were required to make a city successful. The fragmentation of public sector management worked against quick decision-making and had 'retarded Belfast's development'. Without rationalisation and simplification, Belfast would continue to be seriously hampered in building long-term sustainable success.

The consultants further argued that the population size of the city also negated long-term success. A growing population is a sign of health – it signals a city where people want to work and live. While Northern Ireland's population is growing and the region now receives a net inflow of immigrants after a sustained period of net emigration, this trend is not mirrored in Belfast, which, as we have seen, has shown a continuing population decline over the last decade. If Belfast is to become a vibrant and prosperous city, a reversal is needed. The consultants proposed a population increase from the current 277,000 to 400,000 by 2025 – an increase of 1.8 per cent per year – to achieve this goal. While this may seem a challenging target, the masterplan states that it is realisable and that other UK cities have achieved similar objectives.

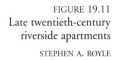

FIGURE 19.11
Late twentieth-century
riverside apartments

STEPHEN A. ROYLE

336

Of course, such an increase would also require major changes in residential patterns and housing density – issues that are highly controversial in Belfast.

A re-energised core is an essential prerequisite in this plan. This new centre, larger than the currently defined city centre, would run from the docklands and Titanic Quarter (Figure 19.12), east and north of the city, through the retail centre (Figure 19.13) to Queen's University and the Belfast City Hospital in the south. This area includes most of Belfast's core economic drivers and also much of its cultural infrastructure. Consideration should be given to creating an integrated plan for sustained renewal, the consultants argue, rendering this area the most dynamic economic space in the region and a window on the global economy. Such proposals in relation to Belfast may appear to stretch credibility and yet other cities have achieved this kind of change. An energised core needs effective linkage to a series of dynamic neighbourhoods. This requires two elements – an enhanced public transport system and an integrated neighbourhood renewal process. In all the proposals outlined, the need to link land-use planning with economic development was underlined as seminal to progress.

The *Masterplan* document presents a picture of a city in need of major work. While it does have some positive things to say about Belfast, especially the speed with which it has used the period of peace to begin rebuilding, its overarching message is a tale of missed opportunities, and fragmented and piecemeal development. In other words, Belfast has a mountain to climb if it is to envisage, undertake and achieve the kind of physical revival that cities like Manchester and Newcastle upon Tyne have witnessed.

FIGURE 19.12
The lead architect's vision for the Titanic Quarter, showing visitor attractions on the very slipways from which the *Olympic* and *Titanic* were launched

TITANIC QUARTER

FIGURE 19.13
An artist's impression of the £320 million retail centre at Victoria Square
MULTI DEVELOPMENT UK LIMITED

FIGURE 19.14
New construction under way at
the Gasworks Business Park

BELFAST CITY COUNCIL

FIGURE 19.15
An audience enjoys an
outdoor performance during
the Festival of Fools in the
Cathedral Quarter, 2004.

BELFAST CITY COUNCIL

In finally creating a plan for the city, the Department of the Environment's Belfast Metropolitan Area Plan was welcomed by the council. Nevertheless, the council expressed its disappointment in the plan's failure to set out a clear long-term vision for development in the urban area and described it as ultimately lacking in imagination and ambition for the city. Taken together, however, the Parkinson report and the masterplan provide Belfast with an energising way forward.

In summary, Parkinson presented a challenging 'to do' list for the city. In essence, he suggested major structural action to increase the asset base of the city and to build on strengths. Crucial elements included the need to increase significantly the percentage of those of working age with formal qualifications and such a process would immediately have repercussions for education supply in the city. Work to increase significantly the connectedness of Belfast was recommended, building new direct routes to a much larger range of destinations and ensuring that digital technology was enhanced to improve networking and access in the city. Fundamental action is also required to increase innovation in the city, building stronger links between the universities and the private sector, increasing R & D budgets in both the private and public sectors and creating more spin-off companies. The whole role and function of the private sector (Figure 19.14), in Parkinson's view, requires major strengthening to allow the economy to become less reliant on the public sector. The population also needs to increase. A formidable list, but the evidence indicates that cities can do this – the economies of Helsinki and Madrid, for example, have been transformed over the last decade, and cities such as Lille, Rotterdam and Turin are also experiencing rapid positive growth.

Population was again a starting point for the masterplanning exercise, which also provided a substantial 'to do' list for Belfast if recovery and growth are to become real and sustainable. A population increase to 400,000 over the succeeding twenty years was recommended. Action is required to reinvigorate the centre city and create a new economic and cultural hub in the core of the city, with an increase in residential accommodation, and the city's heritage is to be protected. The drawing up of a 'quarters' plan was proposed, with linkages from one to the other. The car should be relegated and the dominance of roads challenged by the provision of good walking and cycling paths, and facilities. The quality of the public realm is to be vastly improved and infrastructure for tourism development enhanced (Figure 19.15). This centre core needs quick and easy access to renewed neighbourhoods, with issues of multiple deprivation and social exclusion targeted rigorously and in an integrated way. Land-use planning and economic development needs to be pulled together and integrated into one system, and brownfield and derelict sites require major and high-quality development. Finally, a major overhaul of the presentation of the city was proposed: gateways upgraded; signage improved; and the issue of sectarian territorial marking and peace walls faced squarely and resolved.

QUESTIONS OF LEADERSHIP

The economic, social and physical conditions of Belfast, while showing signs of positive health, are still in a fragile state and require concerted effort and effective action if they are to become the assets of success and the foundation for building a new city. If we look back to the beginning of the twentieth century, we see a city facing equally big challenges – the successful provision of a clean water supply and sewage disposal, the lighting of streets and homes, the location of industry and the increase of prosperity through commerce. Actively pursuing a vision of a world-class city, these issues were tackled by a confident Belfast Corporation, whose motto, 'Pro tanto quid retribuamus' (What shall we give in return for so much?),[8] indicates a strong sense of place and duty.

One hundred years on, the question must be asked – has Belfast the ability to create the kind of leadership required to take the city forward? Such leadership is not just about the formal political organisation of the city, it is also about the quality of networks and relationships, the degree of partnership and collaboration and the speed with which alliances emerge and decisions are made. It is the third leg of the stool of success and is ultimately an equally crucial factor.

What, then, are Belfast's chances of moving forward, of creating actions to meet the challenges and finding solutions for success? The picture is not a good one. The fragmentation of decision-making in Belfast is a recurring problem. The city, governed by eleven government departments and numerous quangos, has a council with few powers. Over the last few decades there has been a further proliferation of 'partnerships' to do everything and anything. This process was fuelled by a European funding imperative, the absence of political stability and the democratic deficit of a non-functioning political system. While partnerships can be very positive for development, it is clear that Belfast has become encumbered by the sheer number and volume of such arrangements, so much so they are now an impediment rather than a help.

The numerical range of 'actors' in the city would, of course, not necessarily be problematic if in some way they were 'joined up', had a common vision and worked to a similar framework. Analysis of the current situation, however, reveals that this is not the case. A recent study carried out by the Development Department of Belfast City Council indicated that there are currently fifty-five separate strategies operating in Belfast covering the area of 'development'. Not surprisingly, a significant overlap and duplication between organisations has occurred, while, conversely, problems and issues are being lost through 'gaps'. The architecture of governance is dominated by a single-focus mentality, a lack of cohesion and consensus, which has led to empire-building and lack of trust. While individually each of these actors is committed and often working to the best of their ability, there is no common will and commitment to the advancement of Belfast as a whole. In Parkinson's words, Belfast has no champion.

Elsewhere, responsibility for 'championing' a city is generally centred on an active municipality with strong links to other sectors – public, private and voluntary. In the current situation, while Belfast City Council may have ambitions to become a champion for the city, it will still be a significant period of time before changes foreseen by the Review of Public Administration (RPA)[9] will give it the powers to take on the role. The RPA has the potential to address a number of issues raised by both Parkinson and Buchanan and Partners. A larger council with significantly more responsibilities and powers working collectively with a vastly reduced number of other councils for the region could create successful blueprints and actions for Belfast and for Northern Ireland. Estimates for change, however, talk of three to four years, which does not bode well for a city in need of urgent change. By that time Belfast will have been bypassed by many other cities.

Is it possible in the interim to create other ways to achieve common commitment and action for the development of Belfast? In relation to the wider UK, the development of urban development corporations and urban regeneration companies (models developed to create quicker reacting alliances for development in cities) may offer some potential to Belfast. These models, however, also require common commitment to the principle of single cohesive action and, inevitably, in a Belfast scenario, this means that all existing agencies must be willing to sacrifice and negotiate position for the greater good of the city, which requires a maturity of purpose that some would argue is still not widely evident in Belfast.

A great prize could be won for citizens today and for future generations if the governing bodies could come together to present Belfast as a city with a single vision. As we have seen, such bodies in other cities have managed to find a way to work together – some galvanised by a major shock, such as the bombing of the centre of Manchester or, in the case of Newcastle/Gateshead, facing the abyss of permanent large scale unemployment as the local shipbuilding industry died (Figure 19.16). The peace process offered that opportunity to Belfast, but the city has not fully capitalised on all its potential. Perhaps the city just relaxed once major violence ceased – but peace is not just the absence of war.

FIGURE 19.16
Gateshead Millennium Bridge
AD INFINITUM

Belfast faces the future with many assets and with the possibility of becoming a successful modern European city (Figure 19.17). That prize is within its reach but until a single unifying vision can be found and a powerful leadership is in place to drive it forward, the city runs the risk of stagnating and becoming a provincial backwater and, by extension, of hampering fundamentally the future of Northern Ireland. The challenge is a big one, but the history of Belfast is a story of practicality, straight talking, courage and tenacity. Whether it succeeds in the twenty-first century will depend on its ability to harness these same qualities for the future. Belfast has the ability; it only requires a committed and visionary leadership – a champion – to become truly enduring.

FIGURE 19.17
Belfast City Council's
Waterfront Hall at the
heart of the Laganside
redevelopment

BELFAST CITY COUNCIL

NOTES

1   Councillor Ian Crozier, chair of Development Committee, Belfast City Council, quotation from his Foreword in Colin Buchanan and Partners (2003) *Belfast: the Masterplan 2004–2020: an executive summary*, Belfast City Council: Belfast.

2   Belfast City Council (2003), *Belfast tourism monitor,* Belfast City Council: Belfast.

3   United States Department of Housing and Urban Development (2000) *State of the Cities Report,* United States Department of Housing and Urban Development: Washington.

4   Parkinson, M. (April 2004) *Belfast: state of the city?*, Belfast City Council: Belfast.

5   Parkinson, Michael, et al. (2004) *Competitive European cities: where do Core Cities stand?*, Office of the Deputy Prime Minister: London.

6   Belfast City Council (2001) *Becoming a better place*, Belfast City Council: Belfast.

7   Colin Buchanan and Partners (2003) *Belfast: the Masterplan.*

8   Belfast City Council's website, http://www.belfastcity.gov.uk/armsins.asp (accessed 19 July 2005).

9   Northern Ireland Executive Review of Public Administration, http://www.rpani.gov.uk (accessed 2 July 2005).

FIGURE SOURCES AND ATTRIBUTIONS

p. i WAG 3822 © National Museums and Galleries of Northern Ireland, Ulster Folk & Transport Museum

p. ii © Chris Hill, www.scenicireland.com

p. v © Robert Scott

p. vi Photograph reproduced with the kind permission of Alun Evans

FOREWORD

F.1 10/21/18 History Collection, photograph © National Museums Northern Ireland 2006. Collection Ulster Museum, Belfast. Photograph reproduced with the kind permission of the Trustees of the National Museums Northern Ireland.

F.2 Dust jacket for *A Social Geography of Belfast* by Emrys Jones (1960), by permission of Oxford University Press.

SECTION 1

S.1 © National Library of Ireland

CHAPTER 1

1.1 Supplied by ERA Maptec 2006. Original imagery USGS.

1.2 Frederick W. Boal

1.3 Stephen A. Royle

1.4 Stephen A. Royle

1.5 Stephen A. Royle

1.6 Stephen A. Royle

CHAPTER 2

2.1 *The Long Bridge, Belfast,* Andrew Nicholl (1804–86), photograph © National Museums Northern Ireland 2006. Collection Ulster Museum, Belfast. Photograph reproduced with the kind permission of the Trustees of the National Museums Northern Ireland.

2.2 Belfast City Council

2.3 With permission of D.E.M. Macafee (now held by the National Library of Ireland)

2.4 W10/21/58 Welch Collection, photograph © National Museums Northern Ireland 2006. Collection Ulster Museum, Belfast. Photograph reproduced with the kind permission of the Trustees of the National Museums Northern Ireland.

2.5 1C/High St/780 History Collection, photograph © National Museums Northern Ireland 2006. Collection Ulster Museum, Belfast. Photograph reproduced with the kind permission of the Trustees of the National Museums Northern Ireland.

2.6 Linen Hall Library

2.7 3493 © National Museums and Galleries of Northern Ireland, Ulster Folk & Transport Museum

2.8 W10/21/171 Welch Collection, photograph © National Museums Northern Ireland 2006. Collection Ulster Museum, Belfast. Photograph reproduced with the kind permission of the Trustees of the National Museums Northern Ireland.

2.9 Belfast City Council

2.10 Stephen A. Royle

2.11 Stephen A. Royle

2.12 10/21/263 History Collection, photograph © National Museums Northern Ireland 2006. Collection Ulster Museum, Belfast. Photograph reproduced with the kind permission of the Trustees of the National Museums Northern Ireland.

2.13 Public domain

2.14 W10/21/53 Welch Collection, photograph © National Museums Northern Ireland 2006. Collection Ulster Museum, Belfast. Photograph reproduced with the kind permission of the Trustees of the National Museums Northern Ireland.

SECTION 2

S.2 H1712 © National Museums and Galleries of Northern Ireland, Ulster Folk & Transport Museum

CHAPTER 3

3.1 Paul Larmour

3.2 © Chris Hill, www.scenicireland.com

3.3 © Chris Hill, www.scenicireland.com

3.4 © Chris Hill, www.scenicireland.com

3.5 Paul Larmour

3.6 Paul Larmour

3.7 © Chris Hill, www.scenicireland.com

3.8 © Paul Lindsay, www.scenicireland.com

3.9 © Chris Hill, www.scenicireland.com

3.10 © Chris Hill, www.scenicireland.com

3.11 © Chris Hill, www.scenicireland.com

3.12 © Chris Hill, www.scenicireland.com

3.13 Paul Larmour

3.14 © Paul Lindsay, www.scenicireland.com

3.15 © Paul Lindsay, www.scenicireland.com

3.16 Paul Larmour

3.17 © Chris Hill, www.scenicireland.com

3.18 © Chris Hill, www.scenicireland.com

3.19 © Chris Hill, www.scenicireland.com

3.20 © Chris Hill, www.scenicireland.com

CHAPTER 4

4.1 © Esler Crawford

4.2 New map drawn by Maura E. Pringle; data courtesy of Frederick W. Boal

4.3 New diagram drawn by Maura E. Pringle; data courtesy of Frederick W. Boal

4.4 New map drawn by Maura E. Pringle; data courtesy of Frederick W. Boal

4.5 New diagram drawn by Maura E. Pringle; data courtesy of Frederick W. Boal

4.6 New diagram drawn by Maura E. Pringle; data courtesy of Frederick W. Boal

4.7a Public domain. Reproduced from the 1900 Ordnance Survey of Ireland diagram.

4.7b Public domain. Reproduced from the 1937 Ordnance Survey of Northern Ireland map.

4.7c © Crown Copyright 2006. Ordnance Survey of Northern Ireland. Permit number 60132. Reproduced from the 1961 Ordnance Survey of Northern Ireland one-inch map with the permission of the Controller of Her Majesty's Stationery Office.

4.7d © Crown Copyright 2006. Ordnance Survey of Northern Ireland. Permit number 60132. Reproduced from the 2003 Ordnance Survey of Northern Ireland 1:50,000 map with the permission of the Controller of Her Majesty's Stationery Office.

4.8 © Paul Lindsay, www.scenicireland.com

4.9 New diagram drawn by Maura E. Pringle; data courtesy of Frederick W. Boal

4.10 New diagram drawn by Maura E. Pringle; data courtesy of Frederick W. Boal

4.11 WAG 1038 © National Museums and Galleries of Northern Ireland, Ulster Folk & Transport Museum

4.12 New diagrams drawn by Maura E. Pringle; data courtesy of Frederick W. Boal

4.13 New diagram drawn by Maura E. Pringle; data courtesy of Frederick W. Boal

4.14 Frederick W. Boal

4.15 New map drawn by Maura E. Pringle; data courtesy of Frederick W. Boal

4.16 New map redrawn by Maura E. Pringle from original by Emrys Jones (1960)

4.17 New map drawn by Maura E. Pringle; data courtesy of Frederick W. Boal

4.18 Stephen A. Royle

4.19 © Irish News

4.20 a, b, c, d: Frederick W. Boal

4.21 New diagram drawn by Maura E. Pringle; data courtesy of Frederick W. Boal

CHAPTER 5

5.1 With the kind permission of Mollie Newman

5.2 W10/46/44 Welch Collection, photograph © National Museums Northern Ireland 2006. Collection Ulster Museum, Belfast. Photograph reproduced with the kind permission of the Trustees of the National Museums Northern Ireland.

5.3 BT1151 © National Museums and Galleries of Northern Ireland, Ulster Folk & Transport Museum

5.4 Amended from M.D. Thomas (1956) 'Manufacturing industry in Belfast, Northern Ireland' *Annals of the Association of American Geographers,* 76, pp. 175–96, Blackwell Journals

5.5 Copyright holder not traced

5.6 New diagram by Maura E. Pringle; data courtesy of Mark Hart

5.7 New diagram by Maura E. Pringle; data courtesy of Mark Hart

5.8 New diagram by Maura E. Pringle; data courtesy of Mark Hart

5.9 Belfast City Council

5.10 © Chris Hill, www.scenicireland.com

5.11 New diagram by Maura E. Pringle; data courtesy of Mark Hart

5.12 New diagram by Maura E. Pringle; data courtesy of Mark Hart

5.13 New map by Maura E. Pringle; data courtesy of Mark Hart

CHAPTER 6

6.1 W.A. Camwell, reproduced with the kind permission of The National Tramway Museum, Crich Tramway Village, Derbyshire

6.2 WAG 3822 © National Museums and Galleries of Northern Ireland, Ulster Folk & Transport Museum

6.3 INF/7A/7/3 © Public Record Office of Northern Ireland. Photograph reproduced with the kind permission of the Deputy Keeper of the Records, Public Record Office of Northern Ireland.

6.4 W10/21/18 Welch Collection, photograph © National Museums Northern Ireland 2006. Collection Ulster Museum, Belfast. Photograph reproduced with the kind permission of the Trustees of the National Museums Northern Ireland.

6.5 INF/7A/12/9 © Public Record Office of Northern Ireland. Photograph reproduced with the kind permission of the Deputy Keeper of the Records, Public Record Office of Northern Ireland.

6.6 HL/BEL/160 Hogg Collection, photograph © National Museums Northern Ireland 2006. Collection Ulster Museum, Belfast. Photograph reproduced with the kind permission of the Trustees of the National Museums Northern Ireland.

6.7 New diagram by Maura E. Pringle; data courtesy of Austin Smyth

6.8 Redrawn by Maura E. Pringle from original by Stan Letts

6.9 New diagram by Maura E. Pringle; data courtesy of Austin Smyth

6.10 Belfast City Council

6.11 New diagram by Maura E. Pringle; data courtesy of Austin Smyth

6.12 New diagram by Maura E. Pringle; data courtesy of Austin Smyth

6.13 New diagram by Maura E. Pringle; data courtesy of Austin Smyth

6.14 New map by Maura E. Pringle; data courtesy of Austin Smyth

6.15 New diagram by Maura E. Pringle; data courtesy of Austin Smyth

6.16 New diagram by Maura E. Pringle; data courtesy of Austin Smyth

6.17 Redrawn by Maura E. Pringle; original courtesy of Austin Smyth

6.18 Stephen A. Royle

6.19 © Esler Crawford

6.20 Stephen A. Royle

6.21 © Paul Lindsay, www.scenicireland.com

6.22 Austin Smyth

SECTION 3

S.3 © Esler Crawford

CHAPTER 7

7.1 H10/21/304 Hogg Collection, photograph © National Museums Northern Ireland 2006. Collection Ulster Museum, Belfast. Photograph reproduced with the kind permission of the Trustees of the National Museums Northern Ireland.

7.2 WAG3169 © National Museums and Galleries of Northern Ireland, Ulster Folk & Transport Museum

7.3 W10/21/127 Welch Collection, photograph © National Museums Northern Ireland 2006. Collection Ulster Museum, Belfast. Photograph reproduced with the kind permission of the Trustees of the National Museums Northern Ireland.

7.4 10/21/62 History Collection, photograph © National Museums Northern Ireland 2006. Collection Ulster Museum, Belfast. Photograph reproduced with the kind permission of the Trustees of the National Museums Northern Ireland.

7.5 Y8596 History Collection, photograph © National Museums Northern Ireland 2006. Collection Ulster Museum, Belfast. Photograph reproduced with the kind permission of the Trustees of the National Museums Northern Ireland.

7.6 H47/01/98 Hogg Collection, photograph © National Museums Northern Ireland 2006. Collection Ulster Museum, Belfast. Photograph reproduced with the kind permission of the Trustees of the National Museums Northern Ireland.

7.7 HL Belfast 50 History Collection, photograph © National Museums Northern Ireland 2006. Collection Ulster Museum, Belfast. Photograph reproduced with the kind permission of the Trustees of the National Museums Northern Ireland.

7.8 W10/21/238 Welch Collection, photograph © National Museums Northern Ireland 2006. Collection Ulster Museum, Belfast. Photograph reproduced with the kind permission of the Trustees of the National Museums Northern Ireland.

7.9 © Margaret Campbell 2005

7.10 L4476/10 © National Museums and Galleries of Northern Ireland, Ulster Folk & Transport Museum

7.11 © Robert Scott

7.12 2052 Belfast, Ulster and Irish Studies, Belfast Central Library

7.13 © Chris Hill, www.scenicireland.com

CHAPTER 8

8.1 © Patrick Dalton, with the kind permission of the Rector of St Columba's Church, Belfast

8.2 Public domain

8.3 10/21/266 Hist & Top Collection, photograph © National Museums Northern Ireland 2006. Collection Ulster Museum, Belfast. Photograph reproduced with the kind permission of the Trustees of the National Museums Northern Ireland.

8.4 New map by Maura E. Pringle; data in public domain

8.5 Photograph courtesy of Northern Ireland Housing Executive

8.6 © Crown Copyright 2006. Ordnance Survey of Northern Ireland. Permit number 60132. Based upon the 1938 Ordnance Survey of Northern Ireland one-inch map with the permission of the Controller of Her Majesty's Stationery Office.

8.7 Picture reproduced with kind permission of Belfast Telegraph Newspapers Ltd.

8.8 With the kind permission of Mollie Newman

8.9 Building Design Partnership

8.10 Building Design Partnership

8.11 Photograph courtesy of Northern Ireland Housing Executive

8.12 Photograph courtesy of Northern Ireland Housing Executive

8.13 Frederick W. Boal

8.14 Ulster Architectural Heritage Society

8.15 © Chris Hill, www.scenicireland.com

CHAPTER 9

9.1 10/81/37 Hist & Top Collection, photograph © National Museums Northern Ireland 2006. Collection Ulster Museum, Belfast. Photograph reproduced with the kind permission of the Trustees of the National Museums Northern Ireland.

9.2 LA7/3G/1 © Public Record Office of Northern Ireland. Photograph reproduced with the kind permission of the Deputy Keeper of the Records, Public Record Office of Northern Ireland. Inset: as Figure 9.7

9.3 W10/29/13 Welch Collection, photograph © National Museums Northern Ireland 2006. Collection Ulster Museum, Belfast. Photograph reproduced with the kind permission of the Trustees of the National Museums Northern Ireland.

9.4 Frederick W. Boal

9.5 Linen Hall Library

9.6 New map by Maura E. Pringle; data courtesy of Frederick W. Boal

9.7 © Crown Copyright 2006. Permit number 60132. Reproduced from the 2003 Ordnance Survey of Northern Ireland 1:5000 map with the permission of the Controller of Her Majesty's Stationery Office. Inset: as Figure 9.2

9.8 © Robert Scott

9.9a H10/29/210 Hogg Collection, photograph © National Museums Northern Ireland 2006. Collection Ulster Museum, Belfast. Photograph reproduced with the kind permission of the Trustees of the National Museums Northern Ireland.

9.9b: Laganside Corporation

9.9c Stephen A. Royle (thanks to the GMB for permitting access to its first floor window)

9.10 Frederick W. Boal

9.11a LA7/8HF/1 © Public Record Office of Northern Ireland. Photograph reproduced with the kind permission of the Deputy Keeper of the Records, Public Record Office of Northern Ireland.

9.11b LA7/8HF/1 © Public Record Office of Northern Ireland. Photograph reproduced with the kind permission of the Deputy Keeper of the Records, Public Record Office of Northern Ireland.

9.12a Laganside Corporation

9.12b LA7/3A/46 © Public Record Office of Northern Ireland. Photograph reproduced with the kind permission of the Deputy Keeper of the Records, Public Record Office of Northern Ireland.

9.13a Department of the Environment (NI)

9.13b Frederick W. Boal

9.14 Shepheard, Epstein and Hunter (London) and Building Design Partnership (Belfast)

9.15 Jason Apsley

9.16 Simmons Aerofilms

9.17 © Esler Crawford

SECTION 4

S.4 © EMPICS

CHAPTER 10

10.1 © Bill Kirk

10.2 Stephen A. Royle

10.3 © Chris Hill, www.scenicireland.com

10.4 © Chris Hill, www.scenicireland.com

10.5 Stephen Gallagher

10.6 New map by Maura E. Pringle; data courtesy of Kathy Apsley

10.7 New map by Maura E. Pringle; data courtesy of Kathy Apsley

10.8 New map by Maura E. Pringle; data courtesy of Kathy Apsley

10.9 Stephen Gallagher

10.10 Stephen A. Royle

10.11 © Paul Lindsay, www.scenicireland.com

10.12 Stephen Gallagher

10.13 © Down and Connor Diocesan Archives. Reproduced with the kind permission of the Bishop of Down and Connor.

10.14 © Chris Hill, www.scenicireland.com

10.15 © Chris Hill, www.scenicireland.com

10.16 Redrawn by Maura E. Pringle; data in public domain.

CHAPTER 11

11.1 H10/21/312 History Collection, photograph © National Museums Northern Ireland 2006. Collection Ulster Museum, Belfast. Photograph reproduced with the kind permission of the Trustees of the National Museums Northern Ireland.

11.2 Belfast City Council

11.3 William J.V. Neill

11.4 © Belfast Central Mission

11.5 Picture reproduced with kind permission of Belfast Telegraph Newspapers Ltd.

11.6 10/21/160 History Collection, photograph © National Museums Northern Ireland 2006. Collection Ulster Museum, Belfast. Photograph reproduced with the kind permission of the Trustees of the National Museums Northern Ireland.

11.7 TB10/21/9 Tourist Board Collection © National Museums Northern Ireland 2006. Collection Ulster Museum, Belfast. Photograph reproduced with the kind permission of the Trustees of the National Museums Northern Ireland.

11.8 © Bill Kirk

11.9 Picture reproduced with kind permission of Belfast Telegraph Newspapers Ltd.

11.10 Stephen A. Royle

11.11 © EMPICS

CHAPTER 12

12.1 The Art Archive/Imperial War Museum

12.2 National Library of Ireland

12.3 10/21/17 Hist & Top Collection , photograph © National Museums Northern Ireland 2006. Collection Ulster Museum, Belfast. Photograph reproduced with the kind permission of the Trustees of the National Museums Northern Ireland.

12.4 Linen Hall Library

12.5 Stephen A. Royle

12.6 New map by Maura E. Pringle; data courtesy of Nuala C. Johnson

12.7 H10/21/742 Hogg Collection, photograph © National Museums Northern Ireland 2006. Collection Ulster Museum, Belfast. Photograph reproduced with the kind permission of the Trustees of the National Museums Northern Ireland.

12.8 Stephen A. Royle

12.9 INF/7A/3/13 © Public Record Office of Northern Ireland. Photograph reproduced with the kind permission of the Deputy Keeper of the Records, Public Record Office of Northern Ireland.

12.10 © Belfast News Letter

12.11 Nuala C. Johnson

12.12 Stephen A. Royle

12.13 © Belfast News Letter

12.14 Stephen A. Royle

12.15 Stephen A. Royle

CHAPTER 13

13.1 Picture reproduced with kind permission of Belfast Telegraph Newspapers Ltd.

13.2 New map by Maura E. Pringle; data courtesy of Russell C. Murray

13.3 New map by Maura E. Pringle; data courtesy of Russell C. Murray

345

13.4 © *Irish Times*

13.5 New diagram by Maura E. Pringle; data courtesy of Russell C. Murray

13.6 New map by Maura E. Pringle; data courtesy of Russell C. Murray

13.7 New map by Maura E. Pringle; data courtesy of Russell C. Murray

13.8 New map by Maura E. Pringle; data courtesy of Russell C. Murray

13.9 Stephen A. Royle

13.10 Stephen A. Royle

13.11 New map by Maura E. Pringle; data courtesy of Russell C. Murray

13.12 New map by Maura E. Pringle; data courtesy of Russell C. Murray

13.13 New map by Maura E. Pringle; data courtesy of Russell C. Murray

13.14 New map by Maura E. Pringle; data courtesy of Russell C. Murray

13.15 New map by Maura E. Pringle; data courtesy of Russell C. Murray

13.16 © www.mediaphotos.com

13.17 New map by Maura E. Pringle; data courtesy of Edel McClean

13.18 CAB/3A/68/B © Public Record Office of Northern Ireland. Photograph reproduced with the kind permission of the Deputy Keeper of the Records, Public Record Office of Northern Ireland.

SECTION 5
S.5 © Chris Hill, www.scenicireland.com

CHAPTER 14

14.1 © Ken McNally

14.2 HL/BEL/154 266 Hogg Lantern Slide, photograph © National Museums Northern Ireland 2006. Collection Ulster Museum, Belfast. Photograph reproduced with the kind permission of the Trustees of the National Museums Northern Ireland.

14.3 Belfast Central Library

14.4 7598 © National Museums and Galleries of Northern Ireland, Ulster Folk & Transport Museum

14.5 BEL 156 Y8541 Hogg Collection © National Museums Northern Ireland 2006. Collection Ulster Museum, Belfast. Photograph reproduced with the kind permission of the Trustees of the National Museums Northern Ireland.

14.6 H10/31/16 Hogg Collection © National Museums Northern Ireland 2006. Collection Ulster Museum, Belfast. Photograph reproduced with the kind permission of the Trustees of the National Museums Northern Ireland.

14.7 New diagram by Maura E. Pringle; data courtesy of Robert Beatty

14.8 New diagram by Maura E. Pringle; data courtesy of Alun Evans

14.9 New diagram by Maura E. Pringle; data courtesy of Alun Evans

14.10 Anna Day

14.11 H10/21/1048 Hogg Collection © National Museums Northern Ireland 2006. Collection Ulster Museum, Belfast. Photograph reproduced with the kind permission of the Trustees of the National Museums Northern Ireland.

14.12 New map by Maura E. Pringle; data courtesy of Alun Evans

14.13 New diagram by Maura E. Pringle; data courtesy of Alun Evans

14.14 © Alun Evans

14.15 © Alun Evans

14.16 © Alun Evans

14.17 © Royal Victoria Hospital, photograph by R.J. Welch

14.18 © Alun Evans

CHAPTER 15

15.1 HL Belfast 184 History Collection, photograph © National Museums Northern Ireland 2006. Collection Ulster Museum, Belfast. Photograph reproduced with the kind permission of the Trustees of the National Museums Northern Ireland.

15.2 10/52/47 History Collection, photograph © National Museums Northern Ireland 2006. Collection Ulster Museum, Belfast. Photograph reproduced with the kind permission of the Trustees of the National Museums Northern Ireland.

15.3 © Belfast News Letter

15.4 Stephen A. Royle

15.5 Stephen A. Royle

15.6 © Newtownabbey Methodist Mission

15.7 E.J. Creighton

15.8 Stephen A. Royle

15.9 New map by Maura E. Pringle; data courtesy of E.J. Creighton

15.10 L3344/8 © National Museums and Galleries of Northern Ireland, Ulster Folk & Transport Museum

15.11 © Chris Hill, www.scenicireland.com

15.12 With the kind permission of Mollie Newman

15.13 © Lagan College

15.14 © Workers' Educational Association, Northern Ireland

15.15 © Fleming Fulton Special School

15.16 © Brian Hughes

CHAPTER 16

16.1 © Belfast Central Mission

16.2 Y11759 History Collection, photograph © National Museums Northern Ireland 2006. Collection Ulster Museum, Belfast. Photograph reproduced with the kind permission of the Trustees of the National Museums Northern Ireland.

16.3 10/19/15 History Collection, photograph © National Museums Northern Ireland 2006. Collection Ulster Museum, Belfast. Photograph reproduced with the kind permission of the Trustees of the National Museums Northern Ireland.

16.4 W10/21/207 Welch Collection, photograph © National Museums Northern Ireland 2006. Collection Ulster Museum, Belfast. Photograph reproduced with the kind permission of the Trustees of the National Museums Northern Ireland.

16.5 1679 Belfast, Ulster and Irish Studies, Belfast Central Library.

16.6 H10/21/564 Hogg Collection, photograph © National Museums Northern Ireland 2006. Collection Ulster Museum, Belfast. Photograph reproduced with the kind permission of the Trustees of the National Museums Northern Ireland.

16.7 H10/21/298 Hogg Collection, photograph © National Museums Northern Ireland 2006. Collection Ulster Museum, Belfast. Photograph reproduced with the kind permission of the Trustees of the National Museums Northern Ireland.

16.8 H10/21/1160 Hogg Collection, photograph © National Museums Northern Ireland 2006. Collection Ulster Museum, Belfast. Photograph reproduced with the kind permission of the Trustees of the National Museums Northern Ireland.

16.9 H10/21/1075 Hogg Collection, photograph © National Museums Northern Ireland 2006. Collection Ulster Museum, Belfast. Photograph reproduced with the kind permission of the Trustees of the National Museums Northern Ireland.

16.10 © BBC Northern Ireland, BBC NI Community Archive

16.11 © Lyric Theatre

16.12 L4481/4 © National Museums and Galleries of Northern Ireland, Ulster Folk & Transport Museum

16.13 © BBC Northern Ireland, BBC NI Community Archive

16.14 H10/12/38 Hogg Collection, photograph © National Museums Northern Ireland 2006. Collection Ulster Museum, Belfast. Photograph reproduced with the kind permission of the Trustees of the National Museums Northern Ireland.

16.15 © Bill Kirk

16.16 © www.irish-showbands.com and Teddie Palmer

16.17 Picture reproduced with kind permission of Belfast Telegraph Newspapers Ltd.

16.18 © BBC Northern Ireland, BBC NI Community Archive

16.19 © Michael Cooper

SECTION 6

S.6 © Aidan O'Rourke

CHAPTER 17

17.1 © National Geographic, Bernard F. Rogers Jr.

17.2 With permission of Colour Rail

17.3 Public domain

17.4 With permission of Elizabeth C.B. Foye

17.5 With permission of Jeffrey Morgan

17.6 © National Geographic, Bernard F. Rogers Jr.

17.7 Faber and Faber

17.8 Stephen Russ, jacket designer, and André Deutsch

17.9 With permission of Random House

17.10 With permission of Ann McKeown

17.11 Copyright holder not traced

17.12 With permission of Neville McKee

CHAPTER 18

18.1 Public domain

18.2 Public domain

18.3 © Paul Henry Estate

18.4 Patricia Craig

18.5 With permission of David Evans

18.6 With permission of Jeffrey Morgan and Michael Longley

18.7 With permission of Jane Middleton Giddens

18.8 Copyright holder not traced

18.9 Andersonstown News

18.10 With permission of Catherine McWilliams

SECTION 7

S.7 © Chris Hill, www.scenicireland.com

CHAPTER 19

19.1 Belfast City Council

19.2 Belfast City Council

19.3 © Paul Lindsay, www.scenicireland.com

19.4 © Chris Hill, www.scenicireland.com

19.5 © Chris Hill, www.scenicireland.com

19.6 Belfast City Council

19.7 Belfast City Council

19.8 © Robert Scott

19.9 Belfast City Council

19.10 The Art Archive/Neil Setchfield

19.11 Stephen A. Royle

19.12 © Titanic Quarter

19.13 © Multi Development UK Ltd.

19.14 Belfast City Council

19.15 Belfast City Council

19.16 © Ad Infinitum

19.17 Belfast City Council

Every effort has been made to trace and contact copyright holders before publication. If notified, the publisher will rectify any errors or omissions at the earliest opportunity.

KEY READINGS

CHAPTER 2

Bardon, J. (1982) *Belfast: an illustrated history*, Blackstaff Press: Belfast

Beckett, J. C., and Glasscock, R.E. (eds) (1967) *Belfast: origin and growth of an industrial city*, BBC: London

Beckett, J. C., et al. (1983) *Belfast: the making of the city*, Appletree Press: Belfast

Benn, G. (1823) *The history of the town of Belfast*, A. Mackay: Belfast (reprinted, Davidson Books: Ballynahinch, 1979)

Brett, C.E.B. (1985) *Buildings of Belfast 1700–1914*, Friar's Bush Press: Belfast

Gillespie, R., and Royle, S.A. (2003) Irish Historic Towns Atlas, no. 12, *Belfast, part I, to 1840*, Royal Irish Academy: Dublin; in association with Belfast City Council

Moss, M.S., and Hume, J.R. (1986) *Shipbuilders to the world: 125 years of Harland and Wolff*, Blackstaff Press: Belfast

CHAPTER 3

Larmour, P. (1987) *Belfast, an illustrated architectural guide*, Friar's Bush Press: Belfast

Perspective (Journal of the Royal Society of Ulster Architects – 1992 onwards)

Sayers, R.M. (1934) *Belfast Telegraph guide to Belfast and surrounding districts*, Baird: Belfast

Ulster Architect (1984 onwards)

Young, R.M. (edited by W.T. Pike) (1909) *Belfast and the Province of Ulster in the 20th Century*, W.T. Pike: Brighton

CHAPTER 4

Boal. F.W. (1969) 'Territoriality on the Shankill-Falls divide, Belfast', *Irish Geography*, 6, pp. 30–50

Boal, F.W. (1995) *Shaping a city: Belfast in the late twentieth century*, Institute of Irish Studies, Queen's University Belfast: Belfast

Boal, F.W. (2002) 'Belfast: walls within', *Political Geography*, 21, pp. 687–94

Census of Ireland: Ulster 1901 (1902) HMSO: Dublin

Census of Ireland: Ulster 1911 (1912) HMSO: London

Census of Northern Ireland 1926 (1928) HMSO: Belfast

Census of Population Northern Ireland 1937 (1938) HMSO: Belfast

Census of Population Northern Ireland 1951 (1953) HMSO: Belfast

Census of Population Northern Ireland 1961 (1963 and 1964) HMSO: Belfast

Census of Population Northern Ireland 1971 (1973) HMSO: Belfast

Compton. Paul A. (1978) *Northern Ireland: a census atlas*, Gill & Macmillan: Dublin

Compton. Paul A. (1995) *Demographic review: Northern Ireland 1995*, Northern Ireland Economic Council: Belfast

Jones, Emrys (1960) *A social geography of Belfast*, Oxford University Press: Oxford

Northern Ireland Census 1991: Belfast Urban Area Report (1992) HMSO: Belfast

Northern Ireland Census 2001, www.nicensus2001.gov.uk/nica/public/index.html (accessed 8 July 2005) (2001 onwards)

CHAPTER 5

Bardon, J. (1982) *Belfast: an illustrated history*, Blackstaff Press: Belfast

Beckett, J.C., et al. (1983) *Belfast: the making of the city*, Appletree Press: Belfast

Boal, F.W. (1995) *Shaping a city: Belfast in the late twentieth century*, Institute of Irish Studies, Queen's University Belfast: Belfast

CHAPTER 6

Building Design Partnership (1969) *Belfast Urban Area Plan volume 1*, Building Design Partnership: London

Compton, P.A. (1990) 'Demographic trends in the Belfast region with particular emphasis on the changing distribution of the population', in P. Doherty (ed.) *Geographical perspectives on the Belfast region*, Geographical Society of Ireland: Newtownabbey, Special Publications No. 5, pp. 15–27

Forbes, J. (1970) 'Towns and planning in Ireland', in N. Stephens and R.E. Glasscock (eds) *Irish geographical studies in honour of E. Estyn Evans*, Department of Geography, Queen's University Belfast: Belfast, pp. 291–311

Hendry, J. (1984) 'The Development of Planning in Northern Ireland', in M. Bannon and J. Hendry (eds) *Occasional papers in planning No. 1 – planning in Ireland: an overview*, Department of Town and Country Planning, Queen's University Belfast: Belfast, pp. 21–42

Organisation for Economic Co-operation and Development (OECD) (2000): *Urban renaissance, Belfast's lessons for policy and partnership*, OECD: Paris

Schaeffer, K.H., and Sclar, E. (1975) *Access for all: transportation and urban growth*, Penguin Books: London

CHAPTER 7

Bardon, J. (1982) *Belfast: an illustrated history*, Blackstaff Press: Belfast

Blaney, R. (1988) *Belfast: 100 years of public health*, Belfast City Council and Eastern Health and Social Services Board: Belfast

Budge, I., and O'Leary, C. (1973) *Belfast: approach to crisis*, Macmillan: London

McNeilly, N. (1974) *Exactly fifty years: the Belfast Education Authority and its work, 1923–73*, Blackstaff Press: Belfast

Scott, R. (2000) *A breath of fresh air: the story of Belfast's parks*, Blackstaff Press: Belfast

CHAPTER 8

Aitken, J.M. (1967) 'Regional planning in Northern Ireland', paper published in the *Report of Proceedings of the Town and Country Planning Summer School*: London

Boal, F.W. (1995) *Shaping a city: Belfast in the late twentieth century*, Institute of Irish Studies, Queen's University Belfast: Belfast

Brett, C.E.B. (1986) *Housing a divided community*, Institute of Public Administration: Dublin; in association with the Institute of Irish Studies, Queen's University Belfast

Buchanan, R.H., and Walker, B.M. (eds) (1987) *Province, city and people: Belfast and its region*, Greystone Books: Antrim

Hendry, J. (1984) 'The Development of Planning in Northern Ireland', in M. Bannon and J. Hendry (eds) *Occasional papers in planning No. 1 – planning in Ireland: an overview*, Department of Town and Country Planning, Queen's University Belfast: Belfast

Morrison, J.W.O. (1990) 'Making Belfast work', paper published in the *Report of Proceedings of the Town and Country Planning Summer School*: London, pp. 32–5

Organisation for Economic Co-operation and Development (OECD) (2000) *Urban renaissance: Belfast's lessons for policy and partnership*, OECD: Paris

CHAPTER 9

Blair, May (1981) *Once upon the Lagan: the story of the Lagan Canal*, Blackstaff Press: Belfast

Cochrane, S.R., and Weir, D. (n.d.) *The development and operational control of the Lagan Weir and its impoundment, 1987–1997*, Laganside, School of Civil Engineering, Queen's University Belfast, and Construction Service, Department of the Environment (NI): Belfast

Department of the Environment (NI) (1978) *River Lagan: report of a working party*, HMSO: Belfast

Mitchell, Walter F. (1994) *Belfast Rowing Club 1880–1982*, Belfast Rowing Club: Belfast

Shepheard, Epstein and Hunter and Building Design Partnership (1987) *A concept plan for Laganside*, Shepheard, Epstein and Hunter and Building Design Partnership: London and Belfast

Sweetnam, Robin, and Nimmons, Cecil (1985) *Port of Belfast*, Belfast Harbour Commissioners: Belfast

CHAPTER 10

Boal, F.W., Keane, M.C., and Livingstone, D.N. (1997) *Them and us? Attitudinal variation among churchgoers in Belfast*, Institute of Irish Studies, Queen's University Belfast: Belfast

Brewer, John D. (2004) 'Continuity and change in contemporary Ulster Protestantism', *Sociological Review*, 52, pp. 264–82

Cassidy, E.G., McKeown, D., and Morrow, J. (2001) *Belfast: faith in the city*, Veritas: Dublin

Rafferty, Oliver P. (1994) *Catholicism in Ulster 1603–1983: an interpretative history*, Gill & Macmillan: Dublin

Richardson, Norman (ed.) (1998) *A tapestry of beliefs*, Blackstaff Press: Belfast

CHAPTER 11

Allen, Nicholas, and Kelly, Aaron (eds) (2003) *The cities of Belfast*, Four Courts Press: Dublin

Craig, Patricia (ed.) (1999) *The Belfast anthology*, Blackstaff Press: Belfast

Johnstone, Robert, and Kirk, Bill (1983) *Images of Belfast*, Blackstaff Press: Belfast

Neill, William J.V. (2006) *Urban planning and cultural identity*, Routledge: London

CHAPTER 12

Jarman, N. (1997) *Material conflicts: parades and visual displays in Northern Ireland*, Berg: Oxford

Jeffery, K. (2000) *Ireland and the Great War*, Cambridge University Press: Cambridge

Johnson, N.C. (2003) *Ireland, the Great War and the geography of remembrance*, Cambridge University Press: Cambridge

CHAPTER 13

Bardon, J. (1992) *A history of Ulster*, Blackstaff Press: Belfast

Boyd, Andrew (1969) *Holy war in Belfast*, Grove Press: Tralee

Fay, Marie-Thérèse, Morrissey, Mike, and Smyth, Marie (1997) *Mapping troubles-related deaths in Northern Ireland, 1969–1994*, Londonderry: INCORE

Hepburn, Anthony C. (1990) 'The Belfast riots of 1935', *Social History*, 15.1, pp. 75–96

McKittrick, David, et al. (1999) *Lost lives*, Mainstream Publishing: Edinburgh

Parkinson, Alan F. (2004) *Belfast's unholy war*, Four Courts Press: Dublin

Chapter 13 Addendum

Barton, Brian (1989) *The Blitz: Belfast in the war years*, Blackstaff Press: Belfast

CHAPTER 14

Bardon, J. (1982) *Belfast, an illustrated history*, Blackstaff Press: Belfast

Barrington, R. (1987) *Health, medicine and politics in Ireland 1900–1970*, Institute of Public Administration: Dublin

Barton, Brian (1989) *The Blitz: Belfast in the war years*, Blackstaff Press: Belfast

Blaney, R. (1988) *Belfast: 100 years of public health*, Belfast City Council and the Eastern Health and Social Services Board: Belfast

Buchanan, R.H., and Walker, B.M. (eds) (1987) *Province, city and people: Belfast and its region*, Greystone Books: Antrim

Byers, J.W. (1906) *Public health problems*, Mullan and Carswell: Belfast

Devlin, P. (1981) *Yes we have no bananas: outdoor relief in Belfast, 1920–39*, Blackstaff Press: Belfast

McGibben, F. (2000) *Belfast in the year 2000 AD*, Donaldson Archives: Belfast

McKeown, T., and Lowe, C.R. (1974) *An introduction to social medicine*, Blackwell Scientific Publications: Oxford

Maguire, W.A. (1993) *Belfast*, Ryburn Publishing: Keele

Townsend, P., and Davidson, N. (eds) (1988) 'Inequalities in health: the Black Report', in M. Whitehead (ed.), *The health divide*, Penguin Books: London, pp. 31–220

Tunstall-Pedoe, H. (2003) *MONICA monograph and multimedia sourcebook: world's largest study of heart disease, stroke, risk factors and population trends, 1979–2002*, World Health Organisation: Geneva

CHAPTER 15

Akenson, D.K. (1973) *Education and enmity: the control of schooling in Northern Ireland 1920–1950*, David and Charles: Newton Abbot

Atkinson, N. (1963) *Irish education: a history of educational institutions*, Allen Figgis: Dublin

Clarkson, L.A. (2004) *A university in troubled times, Queen's Belfast 1945–2000*, Four Courts Press: Dublin

McCann, J. (ed.) (1995) *Education and Northern Ireland: Christian perspectives*, Institute of Education, University of Hull: Hull

McGrath, M. (2000) *The Catholic Church and Catholic schools*, Irish Academic Press: Dublin

McNeilly, N. (1974) *Exactly fifty years: the Belfast Education Authority and its work, 1923–1973*, Blackstaff Press: Belfast

Sunderland, M. (1973) 'Education in Northern Ireland', in R. Bell, G. Fowler and K. Little (eds) *Education in Great Britain and Ireland, a source book*, Open University Press, Routledge and Kegan Paul: London, pp. 19–25

CHAPTER 16

Bardon, J. (2000) *Beyond the studio: a history of BBC Northern Ireland*, Blackstaff Press: Belfast

Bell, Sam Hanna (1972) *The theatre in Ulster*, Gill & Macmillan: Dublin

Gallagher, Lyn (1995) *The Grand Opera House, Belfast*, Blackstaff Press: Belfast

Gribbon, Sybil (1982) *Edwardian Belfast: a social profile*, Appletree Press: Belfast

Open, Michael (1985) *Fading lights, silver screens: a history of Belfast cinemas*, Greystone Books: Antrim

CHAPTERS 17 AND 18

Birmingham, George A. (1912) *The Red Hand of Ulster*, Smith, Elder: London

Carson, Ciaran (1997) *The star factory*, Granta: London

Craig, Patricia (ed.) (1999) *The Belfast anthology*, Blackstaff Press: Belfast

Harbinson, Robert (1960) *No surrender*, Faber and Faber: London

Ireland, Denis (1939) *Statues round the City Hall*, Cresset Press: London

Johnstone, Robert, and Kirk, Bill (1983) *Images of Belfast*, Blackstaff Press: Blackstaff

McLaverty, Michael (1939) *Call my brother back*, Longmans, Green: London

Moore, Brian (1955) *The lonely passion of Judith Hearne*, André Deutsch: London

Moore, Brian (1958) *The feast of Lupercal*, André Deutsch: London

Moore, Brian (1966) *The emperor of ice-cream*, André Deutsch: London

O'Byrne, Cathal (1946) *As I roved out*, Irish News Publications: Belfast

Ormsby, Frank (ed.) (1979) *Poets from the North of Ireland*, Blackstaff Press: Belfast

Ormsby, Frank (ed.) (1992) *A rage for order: poetry of the Northern Ireland Troubles*, Blackstaff Press: Belfast

CHAPTER 19

Begg, I. (ed.) (2002) *Urban competitiveness: policies for dynamic cities*, Policy Press: Bristol

Belfast City Council (2003) *Belfast: capital city 2003–2006*, Belfast City Council: Belfast

Clulow, R., and Teague, P. (1993) 'Governance structures and economic performance', in P. Teague (ed.) *The economy of Northern Ireland: perspectives for structural change*, Lawrence and Wishart: London, pp. 60–120

Colin Buchanan and Partners (2003) *Belfast: the masterplan 2004–2020: an executive summary*, Belfast City Council: Belfast

Department for Regional Development Northern Ireland (DRDNI) (2001) *Shaping our future: regional development strategy for Northern Ireland 2025*, DRDNI: Belfast

Hutchinson, M., and Parkinson, M. (2004) *Belfast: benchmarking a competitive European city*, Belfast City Council: Belfast

Office of the Deputy Prime Minister (November 2002) *Interim Report: Cities, Regions and Competitiveness*, Office of the Deputy Prime Minister: London

Parkinson, Michael, et al. (January 2004) *Competitive European cities: where do core cities stand?* Office of the Deputy Prime Minister: London

Tyler, P., and Belfast City Council (April 2004) *Turning Belfast around*, Belfast City Council: Belfast

US Department of Housing and Urban Development (2000) *State of the cities report*, US Department of Housing and Urban Development: Washington

INDEX

Page numbers in italics refer to illustrations and captions.

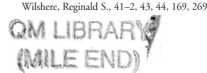